Identity Process Theory

Identity, Social Action and Social Change

Edited by

Rusi Jaspal

and

Glynis M. Breakwell

 **CAMBRIDGE**
UNIVERSITY PRESS

CAMBRIDGE
UNIVERSITY PRESS

University Printing House, Cambridge CB2 8BS, United Kingdom

Published in the United States of America by Cambridge University Press,
New York

Cambridge University Press is part of the University of Cambridge.

It furthers the University's mission by disseminating knowledge in the pursuit of
education, learning and research at the highest international levels of excellence.

www.cambridge.org
Information on this title: www.cambridge.org/9781107022706

© Cambridge University Press 2014

First published 2014

A catalogue record for this publication is available from the British Library

Library of Congress Cataloguing in Publication data
Identity process theory : identity, social action and social change / [edited by]
Rusi Jaspal, De Montfort University and Glynis M. Breakwell,
University of Bath.
    pages cm
Includes bibliographical references and index.
ISBN 978-1-107-02270-6 (hardback)
1. Group identity. 2. Social action. 3. Social change. I. Jaspal, Rusi,
1984– II. Breakwell, Glynis M. (Glynis Marie)
HM753.I3545 2014
305–dc23
2013036671

ISBN 978-1-107-02270-6 Hardback

For our parents
(RJ & GMB)

Contents

Figures

Tables

Contributors

CATHERINE E. AMIOT is Associate Professor at the Department of Psychology at UQAM. After completing her undergraduate and graduate studies at McGill University (BA, 1998), UQAM (M.Sc., 2001) and the University of Ottawa (Ph.D., 2004), she conducted postdoctoral research at the University of Queensland, Australia (2004–2006). Her research in social psychology focuses on social identity change and integration and the internalization of discriminatory social norms. Her work has been funded by Québécois, Canadian and Australian funding agencies.

ANAT BARDI is a senior lecturer in Psychology at Royal Holloway, University of London. Her research focuses on cultural and individual values and their effects on different personal outcomes. Recently her research has particularly focused on value change, including processes of change and conditions that facilitate or impede change in values.

JULIE BARNETT is currently Professor of Health Psychology at the University of Bath. She is a social psychologist with particular interests and expertise around public appreciations of risk, processes of public engagement and the policy-making process. She is currently working with the Multidisciplinary Assessment of Technology Centre for Healthcare, where she heads the group considering how best to incorporate user needs, practices and preferences in the development of medical devices. She has been involved in leading projects for Research Councils and Government Departments and Agencies.

DANIEL BAR-TAL is Branco Weiss Professor of Research in Child Development and Education at the School of Education, Tel Aviv University. His research interests are in political and social psychology, studying socio-psychological foundations of intractable conflicts and peace building, as well as development of political understanding among children and peace education. He has published twenty books and more than 200 articles and chapters in major social and political psychological journals, books and encyclopedias. Professor Bar-Tal served as President of the International Society of Political Psychology and has received various awards for his work.

DAME GLYNIS M. BREAKWELL has been a Professor of Psychology for over twenty years and is currently the Vice-Chancellor of the University of Bath, UK. She was the originator of Identity Process Theory and her research focuses upon identity processes, social representations, leadership in complex organizations and the psychology of risk management, perception and communication. She has published more than twenty books, several of which are on research methods.

XENIA CHRYSSOCHOOU (BA, Athens, Ph.D., Paris V) has worked in France and in Britain and is currently Professor of Social and Political Psychology at Panteion University, Greece. Her research concerns the social psychological processes involved in cohesion and conflict in contemporary societies, in particular, processes of identity and political participation, mobility and migration and justice issues. She has been an Expert for the Council of Europe and a member of the Executive Board of the European Association of Social Psychology (2008–2014).

MARCO CINNIRELLA obtained his Ph.D. in Social Psychology from the London School of Economics and is a senior lecturer in Psychology at Royal Holloway, University of London. His multi-methodological research explores varied aspects of identity and self, in particular: Islamophobic prejudice; the interplay between ethnic, national and religious identities; and the construction and expression of identity online. He is an associate fellow of the British Psychological Society and a member of the editorial board of the journal *Mental Health, Religion and Culture*.

ADRIAN COYLE is Senior Lecturer in the University of Surrey's School of Psychology where he is Course Director of the M.Sc. in Social Psychology. He has been working with Identity Process Theory for many years after first encountering it as a Ph.D. student under the supervision of Glynis Breakwell. His current research interests include the psychology of religion/spirituality, identity and the development of qualitative research methods. With Evanthia Lyons, he was editor of *Analysing Qualitative Data in Psychology* (2007).

JOHN DIXON is Professor of Social Psychology at the Open University, UK, and co-editor, with Jolanda Jetten, of the *British Journal of Social Psychology*. His publications include *Racial Encounter: the Social Psychology of Contact and Desegregation* (2005), co-authored with Kevin

Durrheim. He has also published numerous articles on the theme of place, space and political transformation.

KEVIN DURRHEIM is Professor of Psychology at the University of KwaZulu-Natal. He writes on topics related to racism, segregation and social change. His publications include *Race Trouble* (Durrheim, Mtose and Brown, 2011), *Racial Encounter* (Durrheim and Dixon, 2005) and *Research in Practice* (Terreblanche, Durrheim, Painter, 1999, 2006).

BIRGITTA GATERSLEBEN is Senior Lecturer in Environmental Psychology at the University of Surrey. Her work focuses on understanding sustainable consumer and mobility behavior and human experiences with the natural world. Recent work has explored the role of identity in understanding sustainable behaviors and the relationship between values and identity.

RUSI JASPAL holds degrees from the University of Cambridge, University of Surrey and Royal Holloway, University of London. He is currently Lecturer in Psychology at De Montfort University, Leicester, UK. Dr. Jaspal has published widely on Identity Process Theory, intergroup relations and the media, including recent articles on anti-Semitism, sexuality, ethnicity, national identity and climate change. He is the author of *Anti-Semitism and Anti-Zionism: Representation, Cognition and Everyday Talk* (forthcoming).

DANIELA S. JOPP is Assistant Professor of Applied Developmental Psychology. She received her Ph.D. from Freie Universität in Berlin, Germany. Her research focuses on the role of resources and psychological strengths (adaptive strategies such as coping and self-referent beliefs such as self-efficacy) for positive adaptation across the lifespan. In addition, she is examining factors contributing to successful ageing in very old age and is the Principal Investigator of the Fordham Centenarian Study and the Second Heidelberg Centenarian Study.

KATE MIRIAM LOEWENTHAL graduated and got her Ph.D. from University College London in the 1960s and has since taught in several universities, mainly Royal Holloway, University of London. Now retired, Kate M. Loewenthal is Professor Emeritus at Royal Holloway, visiting Professor at New York University in London, Heythrop College, University of London and Glyndwr University, Wales. Professor Loewenthal's teaching and research interests are in social and clinical psychology and the psychology of religion, particularly focused on mental health issues in different religious and cultural groups.

ANDRÉS DI MASSO is Lecturer in Social and Political Psychology at the University of Barcelona. His research focuses on public space, contested citizenship and the ideological construction of people–place relations. He is the author of several articles in the areas of political psychology, environmental psychology and applied social psychology.

NIAMH MURTAGH is a research fellow at the University of Surrey. Her interest in identity motivations emerged during her Ph.D. on voluntary career change and a common research interest through her subsequent work is that of the influence of identity processes on behavior change. She has gone on to explore this research interest in the domain of pro-environmental behaviors. Her current research is investigating identities, self-determined motivation and other factors influencing change to more environmentally responsible behavior.

NETA OREN is a visiting scholar at the Institute for Conflict Analysis and Resolution at George Mason University. She was awarded her Ph.D. in Political Science from Tel Aviv University and her Ph.D. dissertation was awarded the Israeli Political Science Association's best Ph.D. dissertation award for 2005. Her areas of research include conflict resolution, political psychology, political communication, public opinion and the Israeli-Palestinian conflict. She has presented her research at several international conferences and has published over twenty articles and book chapters.

SAMUEL PEHRSON is a lecturer at the Centre for Research in Political Psychology at Queen's University Belfast. His research centers on how social identities operate in civic and political life as people seek to understand, challenge, debate or deny unjust social relations and practices. This includes work on topics such as policing, immigration, racism and multiculturalism.

ELA POLEK received her Ph.D. in 2008 from the University of Groningen, the Netherlands and worked subsequently as a postdoctoral researcher in the Institute of Education and Royal Holloway, University of London. She is currently a lecturer in the School of Psychology, University College Dublin, Ireland.

STEPHEN REICHER is Professor of Psychology at the University of St Andrews. He is a past editor of the *British Journal of Social Psychology*, Scientific Consultant to *Scientific American Mind*, an Academician of the Social Sciences and a fellow of the Royal Society of Edinburgh. His work addresses the relationship between social identity and collective action. He has some 200 publications covering topics including crowd behavior, political rhetoric and leadership, national identity, intergroup hatred and, latterly, the psychology of domination and resistance.

ROXANE DE LA SABLONNIÈRE is an associate professor in psychology at the Université de Montréal, Canada. Her research focuses on the challenges people confront when they face dramatic social change, such as Aboriginal people in Canada and different groups in Mongolia, Russia, Kyrgyzstan and South Africa. Her theorizing involves reconceptualizing relative deprivation theory and understanding the processes associated with the integration of new cultural identities into the self-concept.

SHALOM H. SCHWARTZ is Emeritus Professor of Psychology at the Hebrew University of Jerusalem. He is a past president and honorary fellow of the International Association for Cross-Cultural Psychology. His recent research concerns (1) relations of basic individual values to socially significant attitudes and behavior and (2) antecedents and consequences of national and ethnic group differences in cultural value orientations. He has recently refined his theory of basic values that has been applied in studies around the world.

DARIO SPINI is a social psychologist and full Professor at the Faculty of Social and Political Sciences, Institute for Social Sciences, University of Lausanne, Switzerland. He is Director of the Swiss National Centre for Competence in Research LIVES: *Overcoming Vulnerabilities: Life Course perspectives.* His research interests include: frailty and health processes in very old age; identity, beliefs and well-being across the lifespan; war victimization and social representations of human rights; longitudinal and comparative methods and interdisciplinarity in life-course research.

ESTHER USBORNE conducts research into the role of cultural identity clarity for personal identity and psychological well-being. She has worked on projects that explore the importance of traditional language instruction for Inuit and First Nations children in Canada and community engagement in schools in Inuit communities. She holds a Ph.D. from McGill University and completed a post-doctoral fellowship at the Université de Montréal. She currently works for the Canadian Government on First Nations and Inuit health.

DAVID UZZELL is Professor of Environmental Psychology at the University of Surrey. He is particularly interested in the application of identity processes to understanding people's relationships to place, environmentally sustainable practices in the home and in the workplace and the role of heritage in the construction of national identity. He recently published (with Nora Räthzel) *Trade Unions in the Green Economy: Working for the Environment* (2013) reflecting his most recent research projects on the role of organized labor in sustainable production.

KONSTANTINA VASILEIOU is currently a Ph.D. student in the Department of Information Systems and Computing at Brunel University, UK. Her research focuses on socio-psychological approaches to understanding the use of medical technology. She completed her undergraduate studies in psychology and obtained an M.Sc. in Organisational and Economic Psychology at Panteion University of Social and Political Sciences, Greece. She also holds an M.Sc. in Research Methods in Psychology from the University of Surrey, UK. Other research interests include prejudice, intergroup relations and identity.

VIVIAN L. VIGNOLES obtained his Ph.D. from University of Surrey in 2000 and is now Reader in Social Psychology at University of Sussex. His main research interests are in self and identity processes and cross-cultural psychology. He has published over thirty journal articles and book chapters and he founded and directs the thirty-seven-nation *Culture and Identity Research Network*. He co-edited the *Handbook of Identity Theory and Research* (2011) and is an associate editor of *European Journal of Social Psychology*.

Foreword

Kay Deaux

My first encounter with Identity Process Theory came in the late 1980s, soon after the initial publication of Breakwell's (1986) *Coping with Threatened Identities*. Great Britain had proved to be the mother lode for my burgeoning interest in socially constructed identities: I first looked to the influential work of Henri Tajfel, then found Breakwell's work and soon after added Turner (1987) to my bookshelf of required readings (not coincidentally, both Breakwell and Turner were students of Tajfel). These works all resonated with me and with increasing frequency I began to use social identity rather than self as my concept of choice. Thinking in terms of group memberships and categories was not a wholly new endeavor, as I had long been interested in stereotypes that observers apply to recognizable groups of people. But in studying gender, for example, my comparisons of women and men aligned more with a traditional individual difference framework. While classic Social Identity Theory and the developing self-categorization work spoke to group-based definitions of self, Breakwell's work allowed me and many others, to keep the person more prominent in the story. Long a believer in the need to consider both personality process and situational influence (Deaux, 1992; Deaux and Snyder, 2012), I found in Breakwell's (1986) analysis a way to bring both elements into the explanatory frame.

In the nearly three decades since the publication of *Coping with Threatened Identities*, Identity Process Theory has grown in influence and expanded its theoretical network, as this volume created by Jaspal and Breakwell so richly demonstrates. This richness lies in wait for the reader to explore in the pages that follow. Here let me just highlight some key elements in the work emanating from Identity Process Theory that establish its distinctiveness and its contributions to the field of social and personality psychology.

The theory is, first and foremost, a dynamic model, concerned with the ways in which individuals define, construct and modify their identity. Originally introduced as a model of how people deal with threats to their identity, the work has expanded over the years to consider more general processes of identity construction and maintenance. As a pivotal concept in the introduction of Identity Process Theory, threat led some to think of the theory as primarily clinical in its goals, concerned with how people cope with unforeseen (and sometimes foreseen) events that can cause them to change their conceptions of self. Yet threat was from the beginning more fundamentally conceived by Breakwell as a window on, or crucible for testing, more general processes of change.

This emphasis on identity change was in itself somewhat revolutionary, given the state of the field at the time. Personality theorists such as Erikson had put forward the idea of a critical period for identity formation, with implications of stability thereafter. Social identity theorists had increasingly focused on the ad hoc construction of an identity group, despite Tajfel's initial grounding in long-standing intergroup relations. Into this landscape came a theory that talked about the motivations (identity principles) that lead people to absorb new information about themselves and to make changes that incorporate that information in their sense of self. As de la Sablonnière and Usborne assert in Chapter 10 of this volume, "IPT is one of the first and only theories to make change an essential, foundational component of one's psychology." Although those in the field of developmental psychology might justifiably dispute this assertion (and some personality psychologists as well), it is certainly true that social psychology as a field has only rarely incorporated change into its models and theories. A developmental theory of identity processes may remain the Holy Grail, as Breakwell says in Chapter 2, but the work presented in this volume surely shows us why that would be a relevant quest.

A focus on change inevitably requires us to consider just what is changing and the answers that Identity Process Theory provides – content and value – raise fundamental issues about the meaning of an identity. Meaning, within Identity Process Theory, is at once highly individual and inevitably social in its conception. Breakwell has always refused to maintain a sharp distinction between personal and social identity, a position that sets her theory apart from the traditional assumptions of Social Identity Theory (and a position that continues to generate theoretical debate, as exemplified by the Pehrson and Reicher chapter in this volume). In delving into the meanings that are associated with a person's identity, IPT investigators show how porous the line between personality and social can be. Identities signify distinctive content and value for the people that hold them; yet the source of these meanings must necessarily emerge from the social surroundings in which one exists. Symbolic interactionists such as George Herbert Mead and Sheldon Stryker laid

the foundation for a view of self as socially constructed and dependent on specific relationships with others; more recently, social representation theory expands the universe from which we as investigators can
seek to discover the meanings that people use to define and redefine
themselves.

A concern with meaning has led many identity process theorists to adopt
the framework of Social Representation Theory to develop further their
analysis of the relationship between the personal and the social. Personal
representations are assumed to be manifestations of more general societal
meaning systems, though it is psychological processes such as awareness
and acceptance that mediate individual incorporation of these meanings.
Here as elsewhere, Identity Process Theory accepts the possibility and
indeed the inevitability, of change, both in the personal endorsement of
meaning and in the available social repertoire. Further, change itself may
be initiated either at the level of the individual, whose identity is threatened in some way such that an adaptive response is required, or at the
level of society, where the consensual meaning of a particular concept
may shift with circumstances. Considerable explanatory mileage is gained
by the merger of Identity Process Theory and Social Representation
Theory, as the framework holds the promise of a full-spectrum theory of
person and context. Individuals operate not in a vacuum but in a world
of socially constructed and communicated meaning that inevitably shapes
their individual perspectives; at the same time, attention to individual psychological processes provides a workable account of how social meaning
is transmitted to and played out in the lives of individuals.

The theoretical tractility of Identity Process Theory is evident in its
engagement with multiple levels of analysis, as theorists move freely
between the personal and the social and between the individual and the
group. Methodological eclecticism, with a particular embrace of qualitative strategies, has also encouraged investigators to take the theory into
the field. Salient social issues, including migration, ongoing intergroup
conflicts and assessment of health risks, have been framed and explored
with the assumptions of Identity Process Theory. Here the pay-off of a
theoretical framework that includes both individual psychological process and contextual structures and forces becomes quite clear. In contrast to theories that focus on only one half of this conceptual territory
and that as a consequence inevitably come up short when attempting
to provide comprehensive analyses of complex social issues, the work
described in this volume has the conceptual range that is needed both to
improve our theories and to contribute to potential solutions.

Identity Process Theory is very much a theory in process. Yet the possibilities for change are not seen as threats to the theory's identity, either by

the editors or by the roster of authors included in this volume. One of the remarkable and refreshing aspects of this volume is the way in which it opens its pages to competing ideas and unresolved questions. Potentially competing theories are introduced as intellectual dilemmas that may be resolved; research programs are described in ways that encourage other investigators to become engaged in further work. Rusi Jaspal and Glynis Breakwell offer all readers of this volume both reason and opportunity for participation in these processes.

REFERENCES

Breakwell, G. M. (1986). *Coping with threatened identities*. London and New York: Methuen.

Deaux, K. (1992). Personalizing identity and socializing self. In G. M. Breakwell (ed.), *Social psychology of identity and the self-concept* (pp. 9–33). London: Academic Press.

Deaux, K., and Snyder, M. (2012). *The Oxford handbook of personality and social psychology*. New York: Oxford University Press.

Turner, J. C., Hogg, M. A., Oakes, P., Reicher, S. D., and Wetherell, M. S. (1987). *Rediscovering the social group: a self-categorization theory*. Oxford: Blackwell.

Acknowledgments

I would like to begin by thanking my friends and colleagues, Dr. Marco Cinnirella and Dr. Adrian Coyle, for introducing me to Identity Process Theory during my postgraduate years and for their support and encouragement ever since. I thank Professor Brigitte Nerlich for her friendship, advice and intellectual input during my work on this volume. I am immensely grateful to Professor Dame Glynis Breakwell for her support throughout my career, for broadening my knowledge of Identity Process Theory and for inspiring me to conduct research using the theory. It has been an absolute pleasure to co-edit this volume with Dame Glynis. Finally, I would like to thank my family for their patience with me as I was working on this and other books.

RJ

I would like to thank all my inspirational and challenging co-workers over the last 25 years, not least Rusi Jaspal, without whom this book would never have been written.

GMB

Part I

Introduction

1   Social psychological debates about identity

Rusi Jaspal

We live in an ever-changing social world, which constantly calls forth changes to our identities and actions. Advances in science, technology and medicine, political upheaval and economic development are just some examples of social change that can impact upon how we live our lives, how we view ourselves and each other and how we communicate. Social change can result in the salience and visibility of particular social categories, changes in the assimilation, accommodation and evaluation of these categories and new patterns of action. Similarly, individual psychological change – getting a new job, being diagnosed with a life-changing illness, growing old – can dramatically affect our sense of self, potentially forcing us to rethink who we are, our relationships with others and how we ought to behave in particular contexts. What social change and psychological change have in common is their power to affect radically our identities and actions.

This volume is about identity, change and action. The contributors to this volume address this tripartite relationship in diverse and complex social psychological contexts. The chapters endeavor to explore the antecedents of changes in identity and action, and their developmental trajectory. It is easy to see why the important task of examining the tripartite relationship between identity, change and action has generally been neglected by social psychologists. Core debates in the field have focused on questions about the "correct" unit of analysis (psychological or sociological); competition between the quantitative and qualitative paradigms; and epistemology. These divides have, to a large extent, impeded theoretical integration. Identity Process Theory (IPT) sits within this matrix of debate because of its integrative focus on the intrapsychic, interpersonal and intergroup levels, its methodological diversity and epistemological eclecticism. The theory constitutes a valuable explanatory tool for addressing pressing social psychological problems of the twenty-first century and aspires to acquire predictive power as it is refined and developed in empirical work. We decided to edit this volume amid a growing body of diverse empirical research based on the theory since the early 1980s. It has been used by social psychologists in particular but has broader appeal in the social sciences and among practitioners. Thus, Identity Process Theory has an important role to play in shaping the social psychology of identity, change and action.

As evidenced by the chapters in this volume, Identity Process Theory research has addressed a wide range of pressing real-world issues – national identity, post-conflict societies, sexual behavior, risk, place and environment and prejudice. Furthermore, unlike many Western social psychological theories, Identity Process Theory has been used as a heuristic tool in diverse geographical and cultural settings – the UK, Spain, Canada, India, Israel and others. Yet, the diversity that characterizes the theory can also make it difficult to delineate conceptually. This volume provides a summary of the development of Identity Process Theory and contextualizes the theory in the social psychology of identity, change and action.

Identity Process Theory

Identity Process Theory (Breakwell, 1986, 1988, 1992, 1993, 2001; Vignoles *et al.*, 2002a, 2002b) proposes that the structure of self-identity should be conceptualized in terms of its content and value/affect dimensions and that this structure is regulated by two universal processes, namely *assimilation–accommodation* and *evaluation*. The assimilation–accommodation process refers to the absorption of new information in the identity structure (e.g. coming out as gay) and the adjustment which takes place in order for it to become part of the structure (e.g. self-definition as gay and downplaying one's religion). The evaluation process confers meaning and value on the contents of identity (e.g. viewing one's sexual identity as a positive thing but one's religious identity negatively).

Breakwell (1986, 1992, 2001) originally identified four identity principles which guide these universal processes: (1) continuity across time and situation (*continuity*); (2) uniqueness or distinctiveness from others (*distinctiveness*); (3) feeling confident and in control of one's life (*self-efficacy*); and (4) feelings of personal worth (*self-esteem*). There has been some debate about the number of identity principles – some Identity Process Theory researchers have suggested additional principles although they have not met with universal approval (Breakwell, this volume; Vignoles, 2011). For instance, Vignoles *et al.* (2002a) proposed two additional identity "motives," namely *belonging*, which refers to the need to maintain feelings of closeness to and acceptance by other people and *meaning*, which refers to the need to find significance and purpose in one's life.

More recently, Jaspal and Cinnirella (2010) proposed the psychological coherence principle, which refers to the motivation to establish feelings of compatibility between (interconnected) identities.

A core prediction of Identity Process Theory is that if the universal processes cannot comply with the motivational principles of identity, for whatever reason, identity is threatened and the individual will engage in strategies for coping with the threat. A coping strategy is defined as "any activity, in thought or deed, which has as its goal the removal or modification of a threat to identity" (Breakwell, 1986, p. 78). Coping strategies can function at three levels: intrapsychic (e.g. denial, re-conceptualization), interpersonal (e.g. isolation), or intergroup (e.g. social mobilization). Some forms of threat may induce coping at multiple levels in order to optimize identity processes (Jaspal and Sitaridou, 2013).

Identity Process Theory provides a holistic model of (1) the structure of identity, namely its content and value dimensions and the centrality and salience of identity components; (2) the interaction of social and psychological factors in the production of identity content; (3) the inter-relations between identity and action. A key assumption of the theory is that, in order to understand the processes that drive identity construction, it is necessary to examine how individuals react when identity is threatened (Breakwell, 2010).

According to the theory, identity is the product of social and psychological processes. Breakwell (1986, 2001, 2004, 2010) has repeatedly acknowledged the role of social representations in determining the content of identity and the value of its components. Social representations determine how individuals assimilate, accommodate and evaluate identity components, what is threatening for identity and how individuals subsequently cope with threat. In formally allying Identity Process Theory with Social Representations Theory, Breakwell (1993, 2001, this volume) sought to provide greater insight into the *social* contexts in which individual identities are constructed and the social resources (images, notions, language) employed by individuals in constructing their identities. Crucially, the theory recognizes that individuals have agency in the construction and management of identity. In interaction with relevant social contexts, individuals construct systems of meaning for making sense of their lives, experiences and identities. To this extent, IPT can be described as a *social constructivist* model of identity processes (see von Glasersfeld, 1982).

Debates in the social psychology of identity

In order to understand the contribution of Identity Process Theory to the social psychology of identity, it is necessary to contextualize the theory historically. In many respects, the theory was ahead of its time – ambitiously seeking to articulate the intersections between the intrapsychic, interpersonal and societal levels of analysis and to provide a holistic framework within which identity, change and action could be collectively examined. With the exception of Tajfel's (1978, 1982) Social Identity Theory, social psychology seemed to have become more concerned with piecemeal theorizing, than with presenting integrative, holistic theoretical frameworks incorporating multiple layers of analysis. When Breakwell (1983, 1986, 1988) first began to articulate what subsequently became known as Identity Process Theory, there were already a number of social psychological models of identity. Yet, none seemed able to explain the micro- and macro-processes underlying the construction of identity, that is, the total identity of the individual. While it is necessary to be explicitly selective in discussing social psychological approaches to identity, some dominant approaches can be identified. In thinking about how these approaches relate to one another, a number of "divides" surface: US versus European; psychological social psychology versus sociological social psychology; realism versus social constructionism; qualitative versus quantitative.

Psychological social psychology

In general, US social psychological approaches to identity have consistently focused upon the individual level of cognition, viewing the individual as the primary unit of analysis. These approaches are positioned in what is often referred to as "psychological social psychology." Within this paradigm, Hazel Markus (1977) developed the concept of the "self-schema," which she described as a cognitive representation of the self used to organize information regarding the self and to guide the cognitive processing of self-relevant information. The concept of self-schema provided a purely cognitive account of selfhood, suggesting that cognitive abilities such as memory drove the construction of identity. Quite unlike Identity Process Theory, the self-schema model did not view selfhood as an agentive process on the part of the individual (as a social being) but rather as a process driven and constrained primarily by cognitive functioning.

The development of Identity Process Theory coincided with the publication of Markus and Nurius' (1986) paper "Possible Selves" in the *American Psychologist*. Prima facie, this concept seemed to begin to address the social dimension of selfhood. However, the primary concern lay in integrating cognitive (i.e. self-schemas) and emotional (i.e. fear) elements of the self by examining individuals' perceptions of (1) what they might become, (2) what they would like to become and (3) what they were afraid of becoming in the future. Crucially, these "possible selves" were regarded as noteworthy since they could motivate particular patterns of action. In their articulation of the concept of "possible selves," Markus and Nurius were now drawing attention to the agency of the current identity of the individual in shaping future identities. Moreover, the concept of possible selves initiated a debate on the link between identity and action (Oyserman and Markus, 1990; Riff, 1991). Yet, this line of research seemed to underestimate the importance of examining the social dimension of selfhood – that is, how social structure, the ideological milieu and, most importantly, social change could actively shape and constrain cognitive functioning in relation to the self. Moreover, the concept of possible selves did not fully articulate the social circumstances in which particular "selves" might be desired, resisted or adopted. Conversely, these were all concerns that underlay the development of Identity Process Theory and researchers who subsequently integrated the Possible Selves Concept and Identity Process Theory sought to address this very question (Vignoles *et al.*, 2008; see also Breakwell, 1986).

Identity Process Theory was clearly influenced by Bandura's (1977) Self-Efficacy Model. Bandura (1995, p. 2) defined self-efficacy as "the belief in one's capabilities to organize and execute the courses of action required to manage prospective situations." While dominant social psychological theories tended to view self-efficacy as a component of self-esteem, Bandura argued that they should be considered as two distinct facets of the self. Breakwell (1986) initially drew on Bandura's ideas concerning self-efficacy in describing self-protection at the intrapsychic level; that is, how individuals cope with threats to identity. More specifically, it was argued that "the individual may engage in the exercise of self-efficacy" in order to regain appropriate levels of the identity principles (Breakwell, 1986, p. 102). Although Bandura's Self-Efficacy Model suggested that self-efficacy was central to cognition, affect and behavior, its role in relation to identity construction remained underexplored. On the basis of extensive research into identity among young adults (Breakwell *et al.*, 1989; Fife-Schaw and Breakwell, 1990, 1991), self-efficacy was later incorporated into Identity Process Theory as a fourth principle of identity (Breakwell, 1992). This established greater linkage between identity and action partly by showing how the processes of identity could function to provide the individual with feelings of control and competence.

Identity Process Theory and the Self-Efficacy Model overlap in some of their core assumptions. Bandura was one of the first social psychologists to stress that one's sense of self-efficacy was dependent on one's *perceived* success in a given situation, rather than on one's actual success. Crucially, self-efficacy beliefs were dependent upon both social *and* psychological factors. Bandura stressed that self-efficacy should by no means be viewed as a personality trait but rather as "a differentiated set of self-beliefs linked to distinct realms of functioning" (Bandura, 2006, p. 307). Therefore, in his writings, Bandura consistently called for context-specific research that examined the specific situations and contexts in which self-efficacy beliefs might acquire salience. This ethos was echoed in Identity Process Theory. Bandura's (1977) Self-Efficacy Theory was concerned primarily with human agency in self-regulation – indeed, he argued that "[a]mong the mechanisms of agency, none is more central or pervasive than people's beliefs about their capabilities to exercise control over their own level of functioning and over events that affect their lives" (Bandura, 1993, p. 118). Similarly, the self-agency of the individual in constructing and regulating identity has always been a core assumption in Identity Process Theory.

Sociological social psychology

The 1980s also marked significant developments in the more sociologically oriented branch of social psychology. Drawing extensively on the Symbolic Interactionist Framework, Sheldon Stryker (1980; Stryker and Serpe, 1982, 1994) developed Identity Theory within this paradigm. The theory essentially argued that identities arose from role positions, that an individual could have many roles/identities, that these were arranged hierarchically in the self-concept and that they differed in salience. Unlike the mainstream approaches in US psychological social psychology, a key tenet of Stryker's Identity Theory was that social structure did indeed play an important role in dictating one's level of commitment to particular roles and, consequently, in rendering salient or latent particular identities in the self-concept. This partly laid the foundations for theory and research on the concept of "multiple identities," which was to become a buzzword in the social psychology of identity (Howard, 2000; Jaspal and Cinnirella, 2010; Roccas and Brewer, 2002). Furthermore, partly as a consequence of this debate, the *structure* of identity, which accommodated these identities, needed to be adequately theorized. In articulating the "black-box" of identity, Identity Process Theory was concerned partly with explaining the structure of identity – the value and content dimensions. Moreover, the model theorized the content of identity – its multiple elements, interactions between these elements and their relative salience and centrality (Breakwell, 1986).

Identity Theory and Identity Process Theory diverged in some of their assumptions regarding the social antecedents of identity development. While Identity Theory referred to "interactional possibilities," viewing symbolic interaction as the primary means of understanding identity development (Stryker and Burke, 2000), Identity Process Theory drew upon Moscovici's (1988, 2000) Social Representations Theory. The synthesis of these theories served to elucidate the *reciprocal* interrelations between the social and the individual – how social representations affected identity processes and how identity processes in turn shaped social representational processes. Indeed, Breakwell (this volume) argues that "individual identities are developed in the context of an abundance of social representations."

Since the mid 1970s, British social psychological theory and research on identity had come to be dominated by the Social Identity Approach, consisting initially of Social Identity Theory (Tajfel, 1974, 1978, 1981) and subsequently of Self-Categorization Theory (Turner *et al.*, 1987). Both theories have of course been elaborately discussed elsewhere (Brown, 2000; Hornsey, 2008; Reicher *et al.*, 2010). However, it is worth remembering and reiterating that Tajfel's Social Identity Theory was concerned primarily with explaining intergroup relations and therefore focused on that part of "an individual's self-concept which derives from his knowledge of his membership of a social group (or groups) together with the value and emotional significance attached to that membership" (Tajfel, 1978, p. 63). Tajfel never attempted to address individual identity in Social Identity Theory (Breakwell, this volume). Conversely, Identity Process Theory was designed to examine the "blackbox" of the total identity of the individual, that is, "the social, cognitive, conative and oretic processes that comprised identity" (Breakwell, 2010, p. 2). Although Identity Process Theory was, to some extent, inspired by the Social Identity Approach which argued that individuals sought self-esteem from their group memberships (Breakwell, 1978, 1979), it set out to explain and predict a distinct set of psychological phenomena.

Following Tajfel's death in 1982, John Turner and his colleagues (1987) developed Self-Categorization Theory, which was intended to complement, rather than replace or merge with, Social Identity Theory. Self-Categorization Theory set out to elaborate on Social Identity Theory, partly by addressing issues pertinent to individual identity, in addition to the intergroup level of human interdependence. The theory explicitly acknowledged the various levels of self-categorization: individual, group and superordinate/human. It proposed that these distinct levels of self-categorization could all shape intergroup behavior – thus, the focus of the theory remained on the intergroup level of analysis. Conversely,

Identity Process Theory deliberately abandoned the distinction between personal and social identity, because "seen across the biography, social identity is seen to become personal identity: the dichotomy is purely a temporal artefact" (Breakwell, 2001, p. 277). In Identity Process Theory, identity elements include traits, experiences and group memberships, all of which comprise the hierarchical structure of identity. This is not to suggest that Identity Process Theory cannot be used to shed light on intergroup issues – in fact, the theory has been used for this very purpose (Breakwell, 2004; Jaspal and Cinnirella, 2012; Jaspal and Yampolsky, 2011; Lyons, 1996; Oren and Bar-Tal, this volume). Despite the duality of both the Social Identity Approach and Identity Process Theory, both seeking to address the individual and social levels of analysis, their assumptions and foci are distinct – the models set out to explain quite different social psychological phenomena (Pehrson and Reicher, this volume).

Epistemological debates in identity research

Coping with Threatened Identities was published in an era of emerging debates around epistemology. Growing dissatisfaction with positivist, empiricist and laboratory-based approaches to social psychology led some social psychologists to advocate an alternative epistemological approach, namely social constructionism. Kenneth Gergen was possibly the most important intellectual leader in this movement. Gergen's ground-breaking article "Social Psychology as History" appeared in the *Journal of Personality and Social Psychology* in 1973. The article argued that, like all knowledge, psychological knowledge was culturally and historically specific and that psychological explanations therefore needed to incorporate the social, historical political and economic aspects of everyday life. In short, social constructionism problematized the "taken-for-grantedness" of social psychological knowledge (Gergen, 2001). Gergen was one of a growing number of social psychologists who were concerned about the potential ideological and oppressive uses of social psychology and who believed that the discipline was implicitly promoting the agenda and values of dominant and powerful groups in society to the disadvantage of marginalized groups. In the UK context, Harré and Secord (1972) voiced similar concerns and emphasized the agency of individuals as "conscious social actors" rather than as passive subjects. Like Gergen, they viewed language as a social resource for constructing particular versions of the world, events and other phenomena and, thus, as central to understanding human agency.

With the publication of *Discourse and Social Psychology: Beyond Attitudes and Behaviour* by Jonathan Potter and Margaret Wetherell in 1987, social constructionism re-emerged with a greater impact on British social psychology than ever before. Their critique of mainstream experimental and attitudinal research questioned the fundamental assumptions of "legitimate" psychological research and thereby initiated what is now referred to as the "turn to discourse" in British social psychology (Parker, 1989). Adopting a social constructionist epistemological position, some social psychologists began to refer to identity as a social discourse, itself constructed out of culturally available discourses (or linguistic resources), rather than as a sociocognitive phenomenon (Burr, 2003; Coyle, 2007). Suddenly, politics and ideology, rather than cognition and psychological processes, became driving forces in identity construction, since they governed the production of discourses in any given culture. In short, it became necessary to look at the sociopolitical contexts and ideological milieux of identity, rather than at the minds of individuals. Social constructionists dismissed personality traits as a meaningful way of conceptualizing identity and rejected sociocognitive approaches to examining identity construction. Rather, the new emphasis was on the social constructedness of identities (plural) in talk and text. Crucially, these identities were viewed as being "socially bestowed identities rather than essences of the person" (Burr, 2003, p. 106).

It is noteworthy that the "turn to discourse" engendered a deep suspicion of sociocognitive approaches to identity. It was assumed by some social constructionists that "there is nothing beyond the text" (e.g. Edwards *et al.*, 1995) and thus approaches that appeared to look "beyond the text" were often seen as misguided, fruitless attempts at understanding cognition. Identity Process Theory was itself developed in the era of the cognitive paradigm in social psychology and its partial focus on cognitive functioning, indicated by the theory's discussion of universal identity processes (i.e. assimilation–accommodation and evaluation) seemed to position it unequivocally within the cognitive psychological camp and outside of the social constructionist camp. However, as Coyle and Murtagh (this volume) show, branding Identity Process Theory a cognitive theory of identity constitutes an inaccurate simplification of the theory, which ignores its conceptual, methodological and epistemological breadth. Indeed, the allying of Identity Process Theory with Social Representations Theory meant that Identity Process Theory remained open to forms of social constructionism, albeit within a pluralist epistemological framework (Coyle, 2010; Jaspal and Coyle, 2010).

Methodological diversity in identity research

Contemporary social psychology is characterized by a methodological divide, which arose largely as a result of the growing acceptance of qualitative research methods in the 1980s (Harré and Moghaddam, 2012). As Coyle (2007) reflects, social psychologists viewed quantitative research methods as the only legitimate means of deriving social psychological knowledge, whereas qualitative methods were not viewed as sufficiently "rigorous" or "scientific" and were frequently regarded as the domain of sociologists. This methodological divide has had widespread implications for the social psychological research community – with some quantitative researchers refusing to take qualitative work seriously and some qualitative researchers defensively safeguarding a "pure" variant of their preferred methodological approach. This has been referred to as "methodolatry," that is "a slavish attachment and devotion to method" (Coyle, 2007, p. 26). This can have an analytically immobilizing effect for the research product since the analyst is discouraged from engaging in any methodological innovation and creativity. In these cases, there is little attention to what should in fact be a priority for the analyst, namely the research question.

Conversely, Identity Process Theory research has defied this methodological divide. Breakwell (1983, 1986, 1993, 2001) repeatedly asserted that a multi-methodological research program, comprising both quantitative and qualitative approaches, was necessary for understanding the complex processes that drive identity construction and development. Accordingly, Identity Process Theory researchers have employed a diverse range of quantitative methods, such as multi-level modeling (Vignoles *et al.*, 2002a, 2002b), multiple regression (Jaspal, 2011; Murtagh *et al.*, this volume) and path analysis (Breakwell *et al.*, 1991), as well as qualitative methods, such as interpretative phenomenological analysis (Timotijevic and Breakwell, 2000; Turner and Coyle, 2000; Vignoles *et al.*, 2004), thematic analysis (Jaspal and Cinnirella, 2010, 2012) and even discourse analysis (Coyle, this volume). More recently, Identity Process Theory research has cut across epistemological boundaries in pluralist research (Jaspal and Coyle, 2010). The contributions to this volume explicitly reiterate the need for methodologically and epistemologically pluralist approaches to the complex social psychological problems of today.

This concise overview of some of the dominant social psychological approaches to identity over the last three decades suggests that social psychology has become a somewhat fragmented discipline, fraught with disagreement and division. Yet, it is clear that, although many of the theoretical approaches described above have clearly made important contributions to understanding the social psychology of identity, both group and individual, they have said relatively little about the *processes* underlying the formation, development and maintenance of identity. In formulating the theoretical framework that subsequently became known as Identity Process Theory, Breakwell was attempting to understand these very processes – the "black box" of identity. Breakwell (2010) believed that one means of exploring the processes that drive identity construction, development and maintenance was to examine how individuals responded when identity was threatened. Moreover, in order to tap into complex social psychological processes concerning identity construction, threat and coping, it was always acknowledged that a diverse range of methodological approaches would be necessary. This volume provides a summary of the diverse research that has been conducted in this tradition over the last three decades.

Identity, social action and social change

There is a diverse range of theoretical approaches on either side of the "divides" in social psychology. In addition to summarizing the development of Identity Process Theory research, this volume focuses on two debates that have dominated contemporary social psychological approaches to identity. The chapters in this volume suggest that these debates feed back into our understanding of the interrelations between identity, social action and social change.

First of all, this volume acknowledges the distinction between individual and group-level theories of identity, which are associated with the US and European traditions of social psychology, respectively. Given that Identity Process Theory explicitly seeks to integrate these levels of analysis, contributors to this volume ask whether such integration is at all necessary and, if so, discuss the heuristic, theoretical and empirical advantages of a multi-level analysis.

Secondly, social psychology has typically concerned itself with the treatment of pressing societal issues, such as the following three examples: understanding the social and psychological circumstances that led to unthinkable atrocities, such as the Holocaust; explaining why people lay down their lives in the name of a nation or a religion; and predicting behavior change in the contexts of environmental and health issues. In many cases, social psychologists have developed convincing theories to account for these problems. Accordingly, the contributors to this volume ask how Identity Process Theory can provide unique and distinctive explanations and, in some cases, predictions for social psychological problems that have commonly been examined from other theoretical perspectives. As a holistic, integrative theory, Identity Process Theory can open novel avenues that allow researchers to explain and potentially predict relevant beliefs, attitudes and behaviors, shedding new light on key social psychological concerns.

Overview of the book

Over the last three decades, Identity Process Theory has been passionately debated by social psychologists. In Part I of the volume, Glynis M. Breakwell reflects on some of the major debates in Identity Process Theory research and clarifies and elaborates aspects of the theory.

Part II provides a detailed account of the various methodological approaches to Identity Process Theory research. Both chapters acknowledge the merits and limitations of quantitative and qualitative research methods. In Chapter 3, Adrian Coyle and Niamh Murtagh discuss qualitative methods in relation to Identity Process Theory and argue for a pluralist methodological and epistemological approach. In Chapter 4, Vivian L. Vignoles reviews the plethora of quantitative approaches employed in identity research and reflects upon the implications for Identity Process Theory. His chapter discusses the utility of particular quantitative methods at distinct levels of Identity Process Theory, with a particular focus on the value of multi-level modeling.

Part III of the volume is entitled "Integrating Theoretical Frameworks." Contributors to this section of the volume examine linkage between Identity Process Theory and their own theoretical frameworks. In Chapter 5, Samuel Pehrson and Stephen Reicher provide a Social Identity Approach perspective on Identity Process Theory, arguing in favor of a distinction between personal and social identity. In Chapter 6, Glynis M. Breakwell elaborates the interrelations between Identity Process Theory and Social Representations Theory. In her chapter on identity processes in culturally diverse societies, Xenia Chryssochoou bridges Identity Process Theory and models of acculturation, focusing upon how acculturation can be "customized" at a micro-individual level. In Chapter 8, Catherine E. Amiot and Rusi Jaspal compare and contrast their respective theoretical approaches to identity integration and use Identity Process Theory to explain how the self-concept may be potentially affected at various stages of identity integration. In the final chapter of this section, Anat Bardi, Rusi Jaspal, Ela Polek and Shalom Schwartz provide an individual differences perspective on Identity Process Theory in their theoretical and empirical integration of Identity Process Theory and the Schwartz Value Theory.

Part IV of the volume uses Identity Process Theory as a heuristic lens for examining identity processes and their relationship to social change in a variety of empirical, cultural and geographical contexts. The contributors to Part IV apply tenets of Identity Process Theory to pressing contemporary social psychological phenomena. In Chapter 10, Roxane de la Sablonnière and Esther Usborne highlight the important role of Identity Process Theory in developing a systematic social psychology of social change. Next, in their chapter on intractable conflict and collective identity, Neta Oren and Bar-Tal examine how the coping dimension of Identity Process Theory can provide important insights into our understanding of the eruption, persistence and potential changes in intractable conflicts. In Chapter 12, Marco Cinnirella discusses the social psychological antecedents of Islamophobia and thereby highlights the utility of Identity Process Theory in understanding and predicting prejudice toward outgroups. In Chapter 13, John Dixon, Kevin Durrheim and Andrés Di Masso examine prejudice in a distinct context. They explore the strengths and limitations of Identity Process Theory in addressing place identity, geopolitical change and "white" resistance to desegregation in South Africa. The next chapter by Dario Spini and Daniela S. Jopp examines the challenges to identity in old age and the contribution of Identity Process Theory to understanding these developmental challenges. In Chapter 15, Kate Loewenthal explores religion, identity and mental health from the perspective of Identity Process Theory. More specifically, it is argued that identity and identity-related processes may mediate and explain the relationship between religion and mental health outcomes. In their chapter on transport-related behavior, Niamh Murtagh, Birgitta Gatersleben and David Uzzell argue that identity threat can induce resistance to change in travel behavior and reflect upon the practical implications of an Identity Process Theory approach. In the final chapter of this section, Julie Barnett and Konstantina Vasileiou explore the applicability of Identity Process Theory and Social Representations Theory to understanding publics' appreciations of risk and reflect upon the implications of this for risk communication in a changing social world.

Our goal in producing this volume has been to summarize the development of Identity Process Theory over the last three decades and to demonstrate how the theory can provide unique explanations and predictions regarding beliefs, attitudes and behaviors that are crucially relevant to social psychological problems. The chapters in this volume provide resounding evidence that Identity Process Theory research is concerned primarily with the application of social psychology to real-world problems. This volume provides insightful responses to some of the core questions in the social psychology of identity, but there remain some unanswered questions. In editing this volume, we hope to initiate a debate about how Identity Process Theory can continue to shed light on some of these unanswered questions and thereby contribute to our understanding of important contemporary social and psychological issues.

REFERENCES

Bandura, A. (1977). Self efficacy: toward a unifying theory of behavioral change. *Psychological Review*, 84, 191–215.

Bandura A. (1993). Perceived self-efficacy in cognitive development and functioning. *Educational Psychologist*, 28, 117–148.

Bandura, A. (1995). *Self-efficacy in changing societies*. Cambridge University Press.

Bandura, A. (2006). Guide for constructing self-efficacy scales. In F. Pajares and T. Urdan (eds.), *Self-efficacy beliefs of adolescents* (pp. 307–337). Greenwich, CT: Information Age.

Breakwell, G. M. (1978). Some effects of marginal social identity. In H. Tajfel (ed.), *Differentiation between social groups* (pp. 301–336). London: Academic Press.

Breakwell, G. M. (1979). Illegitimate group membership and inter-group differentiation. *British Journal of Social and Clinical Psychology*, 18, 141–149.

Breakwell, G. M. (1983). Identities and conflicts. In G. M. Breakwell (ed.), *Threatened identities* (pp. 189–214). Chichester, UK: Wiley.

Breakwell, G. M. (1986). *Coping with threatened identities*. London: Methuen.

Breakwell, G. M. (1988). Strategies adopted when identity is threatened. *Revue Internationale de Psychologie Sociale*, 1, 189–204.

Breakwell, G. M. (1992). Processes of self-evaluation: efficacy and estrangement. In G. M. Breakwell (ed.), *Social psychology of identity and the self concept* (pp. 33–55). London: Academic Press/Surrey University Press.

Breakwell, G. M. (1993). Social representations and social identity. *Papers on Social Representations*, 2(3), 1–20.

Breakwell, G. M. (2001). Social representational constraints upon identity processes. In K. Deaux and G. Philogene (eds.), *Representations of the social: bridging theoretical traditions* (pp. 271–84). Oxford: Blackwell.

Breakwell, G. M. (2004). Identity change in the context of the growing influence of European Union institutions. In R. Hermann, T. Risse and M. B. Brewer (eds.), *Transnational identities: becoming European in the EU* (pp. 25–39). New York: Rowman & Littlefield.

Breakwell, G. M. (2010). Resisting representations and identity processes. *Papers on Social Representations*, 19, 6.1–6.11.

Breakwell, G. M., Fife-Schaw, C. R., and Devereux, J. (1989). Political activity and political attitudes in teenagers: is there any correspondence? *Political Psychology*, 10, 745–755.

Breakwell, G. M., Fife-Schaw, C. R., and Clayden, K. (1991). Risk-taking, control over partner choice and intended use of condoms by virgins. *Journal of Community and Applied Social Psychology*, 1, 173–187.

Brown, R. (2000). Social identity theory: past achievements, current problems and future challenges. *European Journal of Social Psychology*, 30, 745–778.

Burr, V. (2003). *An introduction to social constructionism*. London: Routledge.

Coyle, A. (2007). Introduction to qualitative psychological research. In E. Lyons and A. Coyle (eds.), *Analysing qualitative data in psychology* (pp. 9–30). London: Sage.

Coyle, A. (2010). Qualitative research and anomalous experience: a call for interpretative pluralism [Commentary]. *Qualitative Research in Psychology*, 7, 79–83.

Edwards, D., Ashmore, M., and Potter, J. (1995). Death and furniture: the rhetoric, politics and theology of bottom line arguments against relativism. *History of the Human Sciences*, 8, 25–49.

Fife-Schaw, C. R., and Breakwell, G. M. (1990) Predicting the intention not to vote in late teenage: a U.K. study of 17- and 18-year olds. *Political Psychology*, 11, 739–755.

Fife-Schaw, C. R., and Breakwell, G. M. (1991). The class basis of late teenage voting preferences. *European Sociological Review*, 7, 135–147.

Gergen, K. J. (1973). Social psychology as history. *Journal of Personality and Social Psychology*, 26(2), 309–320.

Gergen, K. J. (2001). *Social construction in context*. London: Sage.

Harré, R., and Moghaddam, F. M. (2012). *Psychology for the third millennium: integrating cultural and neuroscience perspectives*. London: Sage.

Harré, R., and Secord, P. F. (1972). *The explanation of social behaviour*. Oxford: Basil Blackwell.

Hornsey, M. J. (2008). Social identity theory and self-categorization theory: a historical review. *Social and Personality Psychology Compass*, 2(1), 204–222.

Howard, J. A. (2000). Social psychology of identities. *Annual Review of Sociology*, 26, 367–393.

Jaspal, R. (2011). *The construction and management of national and ethnic identities among British South Asians: an identity process theory approach*. Ph.D. dissertation, Royal Holloway, University of London, UK.

Jaspal, R., and Cinnirella, M. (2010). Coping with potentially incompatible identities: accounts of religious, ethnic and sexual identities from British Pakistani men who identify as Muslim and gay. *British Journal of Social Psychology*, 49(4), 849–870.

Jaspal, R., and Cinnirella, M. (2012). The construction of ethnic identity: insights from identity process theory. *Ethnicities*, 12(5), 503–530.

Jaspal, R., and Coyle, A. (2010). 'My language, my people': language and ethnic identity among British-born South Asians. *South Asian Diaspora*, 2, 201–218.

Jaspal, R., and Sitaridou, I. (2013). Coping with stigmatised linguistic identities: identity threat and ethnolinguistic vitality among Andalusians. *Identity: an International Journal of Theory and Research*, 13(2), 157–175.

Jaspal, R., and Yampolsky, M. (2011). Social representations of the Holocaust and Jewish Israeli identity construction: insights from identity process theory. *Social Identities: Journal for the Study of Race, Nation and Culture*, 17(2), 201–224.

Lyons, E. (1996). Coping with social change: processes of social memory in the reconstruction of identities. In G. M. Breakwell and E. Lyons (eds.), *Changing European identities: socio-psychological analyses of social change* (pp. 31–40). Oxford: Butterworth-Heinemann.

Markus, H. (1977). Self-schemata and processing information about the self. *Journal of Personality and Social Psychology*, 35, 63–78.

Markus, H., and Nurius, P. (1986). Possible selves. *American Psychologist*, 41, 954–969.

Moscovici, S. (1988). Notes towards a description of social representations. *European Journal of Social Psychology*, 18, 211–250.

Moscovici, S. (2000). *Social representations: explorations in social psychology.* Cambridge: Polity Press.

Oyserman, D., and Markus, H. R. (1990). Possible selves and delinquency. *Journal of Personality and Social Psychology*, 59(1), 112–125.

Parker, I. (1989). *The crisis in modern social psychology, and how to end it.* London and New York: Routledge.

Potter, J., and Wetherell, M. (1987). *Discourse and social psychology: beyond attitudes and behaviour.* London: Sage.

Reicher, S. D., Spears, R., and Haslam, S. A. (2010). The social identity approach in social psychology. In M. S. Wetherell and C. T. Mohanty (eds.), *Sage identities handbook* (pp. 45–62). London: Sage.

Riff, C. D. (1991). Possible selves in adulthood and old age: a tale of shifting horizons. *Psychology and Aging*, 6(2), 286–295.

Roccas, S., and Brewer, M. B. (2002). Social identity complexity. *Personality and Social Psychology Review*, 6, 88–106.

Stryker, S. (1980). *Symbolic interactionism: a social structural version.* Menlo Park, CA: Benjamin Cummings.

Stryker, S., and Burke P. J. (2000). The past, present and future of identity theory. *Social Psychology Quarterly*, 63, 284–297.

Stryker, S., and Serpe, R. T. (1982). Commitment, identity salience and role behavior: a theory and research example. In W. Ickes and Eric S. Knowles (eds.), *Personality, roles and social behavior* (pp. 199–218). New York: Springer-Verlag.

Stryker, S., and Serpe, R. T. (1994). Identity salience and psychological centrality: equivalent, overlapping, or complementary concepts? *Social Psychology Quarterly*, 57, 16–35.

Tajfel, H. (1974). Social identity and intergroup behaviour. *Social Science Information*, 13, 65–93.

Tajfel, H. (ed.) (1978). *Differentiation between social groups: studies in the social psychology of intergroup relations.* London: Academic Press.

Tajfel, H. (1981). *Human groups and social categories.* Cambridge University Press.

Tajfel, H. (1982). Social psychology of intergroup relations. *Annual Review of Psychology*, 33, 1–39.

Timotijevic, L., and Breakwell, G. M. (2000). Migration and threats to identity. *Journal of Community and Applied Social Psychology*, 10, 355–372.

Turner, A. J., and Coyle, A. (2000). What does it mean to be a donor offspring? The identity experiences of adults conceived by donor insemination and the implications for counselling and therapy. *Human Reproduction*, 15, 2,041–2,051.

Turner, J. C., Hogg, M. A., Oakes, P. J., Reicher, S. D., and Wetherell, M. S. (1987). *Rediscovering the social group: a self-categorization theory*. Oxford: Blackwell.

von Glasersfeld, E. (1982). An interpretation of Piaget's constructivism. *Revue Internationale de Philosophie*, 36(4), 612–635.

Vignoles, V. L. (2011). Identity motives. In S. J. Schwartz, K. Luyckx and V. L. Vignoles (eds.), *Handbook of identity theory and research* (pp. 403–432). New York: Springer.

Vignoles, V. L., Chryssochoou, X., and Breakwell, G. M. (2002a). Evaluating models of identity motivation: self-esteem is not the whole story. *Self and Identity*, 1(3), 201–218.

Vignoles, V. L., Chryssochoou, X., and Breakwell, G. M. (2002b). Sources of distinctiveness: position, difference and separateness in the identities of Anglican parish priests. *European Journal of Social Psychology*, 32(6), 761–780.

Vignoles, V. L., Chryssochoou, X., and Breakwell, G. M. (2004). Combining individuality and relatedness: representations of the person among the Anglican clergy. *British Journal of Social Psychology*, 43(1), 113–132.

Vignoles, V. L., Manzi, C., Regalia, C., Jemmolo, S., and Scabini, E. (2008). Identity motives underlying desired and feared possible future selves. *Journal of Personality*, 76(5), 1,165–1,200.

2   Identity Process Theory: clarifications and elaborations

Glynis M. Breakwell

IPT and the information age

It is 26 years (at the time of writing) since the first publication of *Coping with Threatened Identities* (Breakwell, 1986). Many changes have impacted upon psychology since then. These include:

- The channels of communicating – the digital revolution has freed research communities to speak to each other with an immediacy and on a scale (e.g. in numbers, geographical spread, or volume of transmission) inconceivable to most – even 20 or more years ago. It may be hard now to remember what it was like before Berners-Lee and Cailliau invented the World Wide Web in 1989, with the Internet being implemented in 1991. With the Internet we truly entered the Information Age. All academic disciplines have been changed as a consequence but perhaps none more so than psychology. Not only has its ways of working been changed but the very subject matter that it can research has been irrevocably altered. The quintessential concern of social psychology – interaction between people – has been transformed.
- Since the 1980s there has been a vast increase in the number of graduate psychologists – the massive expansion of the psychology-literate community has changed the everyday discourse about psychological questions and has accelerated the demand by policy-makers and practitioners for responsiveness in psychology to immediate societal problems.
- Agencies that fund research in psychology have increasingly demanded policy-relevance and, in many cases, an interdisciplinary approach (because societal problems are multifaceted and need analyses that span the social, political, economic and technological elements besides their psychological components).
- The tools available for capturing and recording information have radically changed – ranging from the complex and expensive (such as nuclear magnetic resonance imaging – NMRI) to the merely omnipresent (such as closed circuit television CCTV). These tools make the

data accessible to psychology possibly overwhelming in complexity and scale – unless carefully controlled and structured.

The methods for analyzing information – the computational power that is now available permits large data sets to be manipulated more effectively. The statistical techniques that have been developed and are now easily assimilated into psychological research designs allow much more complex multi-variate, multi-level relational models to be explored and tested. As a result of these changes, some areas within psychology have evolved rapidly in recent decades (notably neurocognitive psychology). Social psychology has changed, partly because it is affected by movements in other areas within the discipline (not least neurocognitive developments) but more because it has so many points of interface with other disciplines in the way in which it specifies its research questions. These contacts push social psychologists to absorb different methods and to understand additional theoretical frameworks.

In many ways, these changes of analytical capacity and research focus serve the interests of the development of IPT. The theory presented first in the 1986 book was an attempt to provide an integrative framework within which identity, threat to identity and strategies for coping with threat might be understood. The prime object was to achieve a better understanding of how people seek to cope with experiences that they find threatening to their identity. What has come to be labeled subsequently "Identity Process Theory" was essentially the central tenets of the model of identity, threat and coping proposed in that book. From the outset, the model recognized the complexities of the processes that it addressed. It sought to examine the dynamic between individual identity, interpersonal relationships and social structure. It attempted to describe, at a number of levels of analysis (the intrapsychic, interpersonal and intergroup), the processes whereby identity changes. IPT as a result is an enormously complex model, seeking to be comprehensive. Consequently, IPT should benefit from the developments that have been occurring in psychology: a move toward interdisciplinary approaches, from the availability of a variety of constellations of data over time, from the ability to explore multi-variate and multi-level relationships in those data and from a research focus upon societal changes that could be expected to create identity threats. The complexity and relevance of the empirical work informed by IPT that can be done now is much greater than anything possible at the time of IPT's inception.

However, it is not simply changes in empirical work that are driven by the macro-changes in the context of psychology. The digital tools now available permit the interaction, visualization and representation of the theoretical model itself. In 1986, to visually represent the dynamic relationship between the biological organism, the intrapsychic cognitive and conative processes, the social structure (including interpersonal networks, group memberships and intergroup relationships) and the social influence processes (establishing the ideological milieu) over time, I produced three two-dimensional figures. The third incorporated the other two in an attempt to indicate subtle interactions and changes over time. Those static figures could not capture the dynamism and multi-layered conceptualization that lay at the heart of IPT. In fact, they probably undermined an appreciation of the dynamism that is integral to the theory. Now, in stark contrast, it would be possible to generate a virtual reality, interactive representation of the theory. This would allow us to look at the knock-on effects within the theory when a specific proposition is modified or when new propositions are introduced (e.g. the introduction of additional identity principles).

Yet, in order to do this, it would require a detailed analysis of each component of the initial theory. Clear definitions of each element of the theory and the relationships between elements would be needed. These may be said to already exist in previous publications but fudges and omissions would soon become evident. Where clarifications and elaborations were necessary, it would become obvious. The point here is that the era in which we now work offers incredibly valuable tools for psychologists in their process of theoretical conceptualization but deploying those tools will make us much more rigorous in our theory formulation. The Information Age will promote theoretical development but it will be at the cost of theoretical ambiguity. Even fuzzy logic is couched in anything but fuzzy terms. It is evident that there are certainly clarifications and elaborations that are needed in IPT as a consequence of the challenges that have emerged from the empirical work that has been done since the original formulation. Some other changes are facilitated or potentiated by the new tools of the Information Age. This chapter examines some of the clarifications and elaborations that now seem necessary.

The anathema of orthodoxy

In talking about the evolution of IPT, I would like to reiterate something I have written elsewhere (Breakwell, 2010, 2011). I think that over the last three decades much of the activity and progress in Social Representations Theory (SRT) has been engendered because Serge Moscovici had the wisdom, foresight and courage needed to resist the temptation to impose an orthodoxy on the theory of social representations – despite suggestions from some that a definitive doctrine should be established (Breakwell and Lyons, 1996). In fact, Moscovici's stance has been quintessentially anti-orthodoxy. He has never drawn tight boundaries around the theory. He has never sought to eradicate divergent views. He has never silenced criticism. In fact, he has encouraged innovation in, and renovation of, the theory. This ensures that the theory continues to develop.

This willingness to encompass the novel also extends to methodological diversity. There is no "approved" method in social representations research (Duveen and Lloyd, 1993; Breakwell and Canter, 1993). Quantitative and qualitative approaches co-exist amicably within SRT's domain. This is enormously liberating for the researcher and theorist. It means that everyone has the scope to make a serious contribution to the evolution of the theory.

Of course, in any evolutionary process, not all new variants prove fit. Some will fail to reproduce – in the context of a theory, they will prove unproductive (false) and/or prove unattractive to the research community (dormant). They are false starts and dead ends. However, my point is that the inculcation of orthodoxy is not advantageous to the competitive process of theoretical evolution. I want to emulate Moscovici and, consequently, nothing that I say subsequently in this chapter should be taken to imply that I want to constrain the challenges to, or elaborations of, IPT. Of course, while orthodoxy may be anathema, it does not preclude me from having my own stance on a variety of issues where IPT has been challenged.

It may be worthwhile also to say something about methodological heterodoxy. I have never suggested that I favor particular methodological approaches when using IPT. My approach to research methods, as evidenced in many methods texts that I have written (e.g. Breakwell *et al.*, 2012), is omnivorous. Personally, I use whatever method is available to get the data that I need and to analyze it. I understand and acknowledge, the important epistemological debates that result in other researchers choosing not to do this. The import of those debates has allowed me to treat research information and conclusions derived from it with the utmost caution. Nevertheless, I believe that IPT benefits from being willing to implement a wide array of methodological tools.

Instead of debating whether qualitative or quantitative methods are optimal for IPT research, I would be keen now to focus upon trying to agree the meta-perspective that might be needed in identity research. The main targets for exploration in IPT work (such as the structure of identity, coping strategies or the manifestation of identity threat) seem to beg for longitudinal data collection strategies. The issues that concern us about the cultural or historical specificity of identity principles beg for cohort-sequential research designs. The concerns that we have about the value (i.e. the meaning) of self-report data when dealing with a dynamic response to identity threat call for the use of other types of information (e.g. archival or observational or physiological). These considerations point to the need for a diverse toolkit of data collection methods but more importantly suggest that the emphasis should be upon careful research study design. Design encompasses not just determining how and what data are collected and from whom but also how they are then analyzed and the findings represented. Before embarking on IPT research, it seems useful to apply a checklist of questions, such as the following: do I actually need longitudinal data to make the argument I need to make at the end of the study?; do I need greater diversity (age, culture, etc.) of participants to make my case?; am I over-reliant on self-report data?; and do I know how to analyze the relationships in the data collected comprehensively and can I adequately describe those relationships? I think that IPT will benefit from diversity in methodological approach as we go forward but I also think it will require methodological rigor.

Identity – personal, social, or just identity?

IPT is designed to be a comprehensive theory (rather than the sort of mid-range models that are so common in the history of social psychology, which are little more than single hypotheses). Its comprehensiveness is both a weakness and a strength. It is a weakness because it makes it complex, difficult to summarize, difficult to understand in its entirety, difficult to codify in a manner that makes it comprehensively falsifiable and so on. It is a strength because it offers a reasonably coherent explanation for a range of phenomena. Given its structure, IPT cries out for researchers to take parts of it and expand, reformulate or excise them through empirical and logical analysis. Hence there is a need for caution where the introduction of orthodoxies is concerned.

Indeed, there are a number of key components of IPT that cause controversy and have generated challenges and new ideas. In this chapter, I will offer my reflections on what has been argued about four of these challenges.

The first is fundamental to the theory. It concerns the basic conceptualization of identity that is used in IPT. IPT is a theory of identity – it is concerned with the holistic analysis of the *total identity* of the person. It proposes that this identity will encompass elements that are dynamically derived from every aspect of the person's experience – social category memberships, interpersonal relationships, social representational exposure, individual activity and observation and so on. IPT struggles to find a way of articulating the complex dynamic process of personhood that incorporates the personal and the social – the active, subjective conscious self and the objectified, known self. At the core of IPT is the assertion that the person seeks to construct and maintain an identity – and that this process is orderly (in the sense that there appear to be relatively predictable states of identity that are sought). It is clearly argued that this identity comprises many elements (some derived from social category membership; some derived from other aspects of experience within the social world). Identity is a multifaceted, complex phenomenon. It is both a dynamic process and a dynamic state of being. I will return to this subsequently.

The concern in IPT with the agentic role of the person has sometimes been taken to suggest that the theory is ignoring social identity. This is simply a misunderstanding of the theory. Social identities (derived from category memberships and representational processes) from an IPT perspective are elements in the total identity. To this extent, IPT complements and even incorporates, Social Identity Theory (Tajfel, 1978) – at least in SIT's original formulation. It was always meant to do so (I was, after all, Tajfel's Ph.D. student). I believe a comprehensive theory of identity should support models of intergroup relations and intra-group dynamics. Indeed, I am heartened to see how many theorists are now employing IPT and evolving it, in the context of the analysis of group conflict and societal change (many represented in this volume).

I think the personal identity–social identity dichotomy that has dominated discourse in social psychology is actually counterproductive when trying to understand the dynamism of identity development over the lifespan. In the original formulation of IPT the structure of identity is said to be described along two planes: the content dimension and the value dimension. The content dimension consists of the characteristics that define identity: the properties that, taken as a constellation, mark the individual as unique. It encompasses both those characteristics previously considered the domain of social identity (group memberships, roles, social category labels, etc.) and of personal identity (values, attitudes, cognitive style, etc.). The distinction between social and personal identity is not used in IPT because, seen across the biography, social identities are seen to become core components of personal identity: the dichotomy is purely a temporal artifact. In fact, the same logic can be used to argue that all identity is social since at some point in its development it will have relied upon social inputs. Whichever way you choose to look down the telescope, the end result is the same: there is an integrative identity – a dynamic entity that is continually responsive to the social context but not determined solely by the current social constraints.

Yet, I also believe that it is vital to be clear when the concept of identity is used whether one is talking about the integrative identity or some specific element therein. All too frequently we are imprecise in usage. I particularly dislike the idea that we should talk about individuals having "multiple identities." I realize that this is common parlance but I think this confuses matters. As soon as you talk about multiple identities it begs the question: how do they relate to each other? They cannot be realistically supposed to exist in a series of hermetically sealed units. Then you have the problem of theorizing the superordinate structure that accommodates these multiple identities. Faced with this conundrum, I prefer to think holistically about the identity and the elements that comprise it.

This does not avoid the need to talk about the structure of identity. In fact, it requires you do talk about the structure of identity. IPT originally offered a framework for thinking about the development of the structure of identity. It proposed that the development of identity structures has to be seen as a process occupying the person's whole lifespan. It suggested that the characteristics of the human biological organism (capacity for memory, sensory features, rate of growth, etc.) interact with the social context to provide the material for identity construction. It is argued that the neurocognitive capacities of the individual provide the ongoing core to identity processes. Essentially, the individual interprets experience and assimilates its implications into his or her identity. The relatively simple model offered by IPT originally for the identity structure was that this core would operate through the lifespan and the content and evaluation dimensions of identity would develop as the individual aged. The implication was that both content and evaluation would accumulate and be organized (largely in keeping with the principles of identity – of which, more later).

However, IPT does not say enough about the structure of identity. The theory was more focused on the processes of identity than upon structure. I want to offer a few thoughts that go some way to rectifying, or at least explaining, that omission in the original work. The early representation of the structure (the attempt at a three-dimensional movement through time, in a two-dimensional drawing that looked like a pyramid on its side with a rod through the middle) created an impression of static, if cumulative, development of the structure. It seemed to be a really simple structure – just two-dimensions plus time. Now – in a digital age – I would want a much more dynamic representation of structure. This would represent the universe of probabilistic possibilities as the individual moves through the lifespan. The analogy of the digital image – that can change in area of focus, can modify its pixel definition, can morph at changing speeds and in myriad directions and is subject to simultaneous multidimensional changes – is a better analogy for identity structure. Of course, this approach represents an enormous empirical challenge. How does the researcher actually capture data that describe this sort of structure adequately? You might try a thought experiment for yourself (rather like those Victorian scientists did) – how would you describe your own identity fully, not just now but over time? Try it. Whenever I try it, I come back to thinking about the schematics of the structure that underlie the rich descriptive content of my identity over time. There is the centrality of certain elements – by centrality I mean there are elements that seem to be the ones that other elements link to and depend upon (the socio-metric stars in the identity firmament). There is the salience of some elements. These are the elements that I consider very important and they appear readily when I think about myself. They are sometimes also central but not inevitably. A further structural feature is the transience/stability of elements. I am conscious that elements of identity do change their significance in the structure. Some that may have been very salient at an earlier age (though possibly they never disappear totally) to all intents and purposes are dormant. This phenomenon in the structure of the dormant elements is interesting because they can be activated (become relevant to action and decision-making). There is another property of the structure that may in part derive from the centrality dimension and might be called the looseness of the structure. For some individuals, the elements of identity seem to be a coherent densely meshed whole. But there seems to be a continuum that runs at the other extreme to a very loosely linked system of elements.

If you do the thought experiment on your own identity structure, I would expect that other characteristics of the structure will occur to you. As a consequence of my own considerations, I have concluded that it may be more appropriate to think of the biological (i.e. neurophysiological, etc.) processes as not being central to the structure of identity. They may be evident in the content of identity because some biological characteristics will have been represented in identity elements (e.g. sex represented in gender) but they are not per se part of the structure. However, they are fundamental to the functioning of the processes of identity and are core to them. This does represent a change to the original formulation of IPT.

The suggestion that the structure of identity should be more systematically studied within IPT might also be linked to possibilities now offered by computational mathematical models. In other disciplines (in chemistry, pharmacology, genomics and so on), where complex dynamic structures have to be described researchers are working with mathematicians to build computer models that allow them to test hypothetical changes in the interacting elements within the structures they describe. It may be worth considering doing this in IPT work. It is daunting, given the number of elements that would need to be considered, but it is a way to make systematic progress in this area – an area where cumulative developments have been difficult to establish.

The question of the cultural-specificity and lifespan variation in identity principles

The second challenge to IPT that I want to address comes from a concern about the possible assertion of cultural-specificity that may underlie the model. IPT proposes that the individual's identity is a dynamic social product of the interaction of the capacities for memory, consciousness and organized construal with the physical and societal structures and influence processes that constitute the social context. IPT proposes that identity resides in psychological processes but is manifested through thought, action and affect. Identity can be described in terms of both its structure and in terms of its processes. People are normally self-aware and actively monitor the status of their identity. The levels of self-monitoring and desired identity states may differ across the lifespan and it is considered possible that they may vary across different cultures.

The suggestion that there *may be* cultural-specificity in the identity principles (which are described further in the next section) that predict how people seek to manage their identity has led to some criticism of IPT. The criticism suggests that IPT is based on cultural relativism. I find this perplexing since, in the original statement of IPT and subsequently, I have simply argued that we do not know whether there are cultural differences that may be found in the emphasis given to different identity principles or indeed to the application of those principles in identity processes. I do not see this as an assertion of cultural relativism. I think what I would say is that I simply do not know. I have been very interested recently to see Vignoles' work (Vignoles *et al.*, 2011), which suggests universality in some identity principles. It is suggestive but it is not conclusive.

On the issue of variation across the lifespan, I think there is so much more still to do. A developmental theory of identity processes is in my opinion the Holy Grail. I am thinking here not just of the growth of identity during childhood or adolescence but also of the changes to identity during later years. Dario Spini and Daniela Jopp (in this volume) have argued that the role of memory depredation in aging (or more dramatically during dementia) must have a very significant role in the construction and maintenance of identity. Is identity memory-dependent? I recall the debates of the early 1980s when Ken Gergen and John Shotter were arguing there was no such thing as memory – that the self was not an entity that had any abiding existence. Instead, it was deemed to be socially constructed in each new exchange and context. I admit that I never understood their argument and I may be misrepresenting it. I certainly cannot conceive of an identity that is not memory dependent to some extent. This really does beg the question about identity in dementia and other conditions that affect memory systems. Nevertheless, this recognition of the changing capacities of memory over the lifespan does not in itself suggest that the identity principles that have been described in IPT are as a result to be considered less generic. Instead, it suggests that it is important to conduct research with populations that have different cognitive, or indeed conative, capacities to assess how identity process regulation has changed. It is possible, in fact likely, that a new variant of the model of the maintenance of identity structure will emerge. The identity principles that have been proposed in IPT up until now would need to be tested in the context of the new data.

What identity principles?

It has been indicated earlier that in IPT the structure of identity is said to be described along two planes: the content dimension and the value dimension. The content dimension of identity is organized. The organization can be characterized in terms of (1) the degree of centrality, (2) the hierarchical arrangements of elements and (3) the relative salience of components. And probably it has other organizing features as yet unspecified, as suggested by the thought experiment above. The organization is not, however, static and is responsive to changes in inputs and demands from the social context besides purposive reconstruction initiated by the individual. Each element in the content dimension is argued to have a positive or negative value/affect appended to it; taken together these values constitute the value/affective dimension of identity. The value/affective dimension of identity is constantly subject to revision: the value of each element is open to reappraisal as a consequence of changes in social value systems and modifications in the individual's position in relation to such social value systems.

In IPT, the structure of identity is postulated to be regulated by the dynamic processes of accommodation/assimilation and evaluation, which are deemed to be universal psychological processes. Assimilation and accommodation are two components of one process. Assimilation refers to the absorption of new components into the identity structure;

accommodation refers to the adjustment that occurs in the existing structure in order to find a place for new elements. The process of evaluation
entails the allocation of meaning and value/affect to identity contents,
new and old. The two processes interact to determine the changing content and value of identity over time; with changing patterns of assimilation requiring changes in evaluation and vice versa.

These two identity processes are guided in their operation by principles that define desirable states for the structure of identity. While the
actual states considered desirable and consequently the guidance principles, are *possibly* temporally and culturally specific, the original formulation of IPT claimed that currently in Western post-industrial cultures the
three discernible prime guidance principles were desire for continuity,
distinctiveness and self-esteem. Following a series of studies I directed,
sponsored by ESRC, some involving longitudinal cohort-sequential
designs (Banks *et al.*, 1992), a fourth guidance principle was added: efficacy (after the work of Bandura on self-efficacy, Bandura, 1997). These
four principles were said to vary in their relative and absolute salience
over time and across situations.

There has been considerable debate about the "principles." This has
centered on two issues:

1. Terminology – are they better thought of as "motives"?
2. Number – are there more than four?

In relation to the first issue, I can see that talking about "guiding principles" is clumsy – the label hardly trips off the tongue. More importantly, it is terminology that is not echoed elsewhere in the literature.
In contrast, talking about "motives" immediately links into a vast array
of psychological literature and suggests methods for empirical analysis.
My hesitancy in adopting the term "motive" originally emanated from
the history of the use of the concept. Too often in the past, "motive" has
been used in the same way that "need" was used in building theoretical
models. In seeking to explain an action, the psychologist invokes the idea
that the actor "needed" or "was motivated" to act in that way. When
asked how we know the actor "needed" to act in that way we are told
that he or she must have done so because he or she did act in that way.
It seems a circular argument: the existence of the need/motive is inferred
from the action it is assumed to explain. Now, I am convinced that when
"motive" is used as an alternate for "guiding principle" no circularity is
involved. On that basis, I would be happy to talk about the motives that
guide identity processes.

Nevertheless, a need or motive explanation can only ever be an interim
explanation (and this may not be a problem insofar as all theories are

interim approximations to explanation). It may be good enough for some purposes but in reality it represents a staging post en route to explaining also why the need/motive is present. In the current context, the superordinate explanation could include the operation of cognitive, conative, interpersonal or societal processes over significant time periods. Those processes might for instance be able to be described and to be modeled in the way they predispose, say, self-esteem to emerge as a fundamental guiding principle (or motive) for identity construction and maintenance. Capturing, or rather articulating, the variety of needs/motives that are at work is important but I think we should then ask whether we can explain why those needs/motives are present.

In fact, IPT goes on from describing a number of principles to talking about the routes whereby they come into existence. It describes the societal processes within which the identity processes are evolved. This is one of the ways in which IPT links into the notion of Willem Doise that social psychology needs to operate across a number of levels of analysis (see Breakwell, 1994). IPT is not only describing intrapsychic processes in talking about identity processes, it is attempting to explain their relationship with processes at other levels of analysis. This is one of the ways in which SRT becomes important for IPT (Breakwell, 1990, 1993, 2001a; and the later chapter in this volume by Breakwell). Social representations and the social influence processes that embody them certainly shape the identity principles at work – specifically when considered across long time periods. I will come back to this later.

In relation to the second issue, I should emphasize that I never thought four principles/motives was an exhaustive list (Breakwell, 1988). Various researchers have posited the existence of further identity principles. For example, Markowe (1996) argued for additional principles of *authenticity/integrity* and *affiliation* while studying the "coming out" process among lesbian women; Vignoles (2000) identified possible additional principles of *purpose* and *closeness to others* in interviews with Anglican parish priests; and Jaspal and Cinnirella (2010) suggested a *coherence* principle, based on their research into identity conflict among British Pakistani Muslim gay men. I suspect that each of these proposals has merit and a basis in data. The question that must be posed, however, before including any new guidance principle within the theory is the following: how far does it improve the explanatory power of the theory and does it offer additionality? The trick is to be inclusive without introducing redundancy. I have a feeling that some motives that have been proposed can be seen to be subsets of the four primes. Further empirical work is likely to establish yet more motives that fit into some hierarchy that all have a role to play in guiding identity processes. I would be keen to see that work done.

However, I think it would be useful to be vigilant in mapping the actual empirical relationships between these motives. I remember vividly when doing research with Chris Fife-Schaw on identity in 16–21-year-olds monitoring self-esteem and efficacy longitudinally and finding significant correlations between them over time. This introduces a challenge: how far are they just aspects of the same thing – the positive self-regard? Clearly, they are. Yet, they are not identical to each other. This we showed repeatedly since they varied in the extent to which they co-varied with important elements of identity (e.g. employment status, political affiliation – Breakwell et al., 1989; Fife-Schaw and Breakwell, 1991, 1992). The point here is that we were able to show that the two principles were doing different work in predicting responses to changes in elements of identity. I suppose that my underlying concern here is that in measuring the existence of a motive (i.e. a desired state for identity), we do not confuse the measurement of the desire to achieve a particular state for identity with the measurement of the state itself, and, in addition, we always compare the predictive power of any one motive with the predictive power of others (especially the four primes).

My conclusion in this area of debate, then, is that we should be establishing the range of identity principles/motives that are operating but that we should also be trying to explain why they are the principles that are at work (and this requires multiple levels of analysis). Furthermore, if pushed to decide, I would prefer to use the original nomenclature – identity principles – mainly for pragmatic reasons: consistency in applying a label for a theoretical construct reduces the likelihood of misunderstanding or misrepresentation and the opportunities for slippage in usage. Also, if a motive is just a principle by another name, why not stick with the original label.

The problem with threats

IPT grew from my analysis of the enormous body of literature from psychology but also from other disciplines that led me to conclude that a key to understanding the processes that drive identity development and expression lies in understanding how individuals respond when their identity is threatened (Breakwell, 1978, 1979, 1983). As a result of my own examinations of reactions to threat, with my collaborators over many years, I developed Identity Process Theory (Breakwell, 1986, 1988, 1992a, 1992b, 2001b; Breakwell and Lyons, 1996; Timotijevic and Breakwell, 2000; Vignoles et al., 2000, 2002a, 2002b, 2004).

IPT has, as a consequence, been seen as a theory about reactions to threats to identity. It is certainly that. In fact, a lot of the original book was devoted to describing the coping strategies that are employed when threat occurs. While some of the empirical work stimulated by IPT has examined coping processes (Mavridi and Breakwell, 2000; Hendy *et al.*, 2006; Breakwell *et al.*, 2003), the major emphasis has been upon describing the identity principles that are at work. This is possibly because it is recognized that IPT is not just a theory about reactions to threat to identity. It is a general theory of identity processes. The examination of reactions to threat is a means to exploring the way identity processes work to construct and maintain identity.

This is probably just as well since the way IPT defines threat to identity is open to much criticism and has been a source of debate among IPT researchers for as long as I can remember. According to the original formulation a threat exists when the identity processes (of assimilation–accommodation and evaluation) are not able to operate in accordance with the identity principles to construct and maintain identity. For a threat to evoke action, it must gain access to consciousness. It is therefore possible to distinguish between occupying a threatening position and experiencing threat. Some coping strategies will deny the existence of the threatening position and may mean that threat is not subjectively experienced. If in essence, coping strategies are effective, occupancy of a threatening position may lose its power to threaten.

Since the existence of a threat is quintessentially a subjective matter according to this definition, and, according to IPT, once recognized the individual will act to neutralize the threat using coping strategies, it becomes rather difficult to operationalize threat. Of course, the researcher can on an a-priori basis define situations in which threat is likely to occur – transitions in social status, for instance – but if IPT predictions are right, coping strategies will be engaged to deal with the consequent threat rapidly – so rapidly, indeed, that empirically on occasion it may be impossible to measure the subjective threat. The 1986 book acknowledges this dilemma.

Some researchers, including Vignoles (2011), have suggested the focus on the notion of threat is unnecessary. Identity is continually reconstructed in accordance with the motives that direct identity processes. I can take no issue with this assertion. I fully accept that identity is perpetually adjusting. The structure, the configuration of elements and the evaluations attached to them changes. IPT as a model of identity dynamics does not need to be singularly concerned with threat. It can be applied successfully to the general process of identity construction and maintenance.

This leads, however, to other considerations. What is the role of the identity principles in guiding identity processes when threat is not significant? The strangest thing for me from the longitudinal research that I have conducted (Banks *et al.*, 1992; Breakwell *et al.*, 1988; Breakwell, 1996a; Breakwell and Millward, 1997; Fife-Schaw and Breakwell, 1992) is the extent to which self-esteem and self-efficacy indices are constant in individuals over significant time periods. I take this to suggest that any changes that are wrought in identity are actually not effecting modifications in the overall subjective assessment of self-esteem or self-efficacy over time. People may be motivated to achieve greater self-esteem or self-efficacy but on the whole they are not shifting far from their baseline over time. Perhaps people are optimizing rather than maximizing compliance with identity principles.

It seems to me that there is a, perhaps routinized, battle going on to harvest optimal measures of distinctiveness, continuity, self-esteem and self-efficacy in the context of the changing social and emotional circumstances surrounding the individual. IPT researchers should focus more on the routine operation of the principles in achieving identity structure. This is just as interesting as examining their operation in high-profile "threat" situations.

Of course, I still think it is valuable to explore threats – clearly conceptualized as the obstacles to the principled operation of the identity processes. I would acknowledge that in the first instance it seems sensible empirically to work with situations of "potential threat" rather than focusing on subjectively perceived threat. The "potential threat" situation could be determined by asking a set of individuals from the same population as the target for analysis, but not in the same situation, whether they would expect the situation to be threatening. I rather like the idea of adopting a series of methods to operationalize threat. I agree with Vignoles that taking the simple way out and asking the individual if they feel threatened is not likely to yield anything valuable. Manipulation checks in this domain must be more sophisticated than that.

Elaboration and clarification concluded

This chapter has dealt with only four areas where elaboration and clarification of IPT need to be done. To summarize my clarifications:

IPT is a holistic theory of identity. It eschews the idea of multiple identities or the separation of personal and social identities.

IPT is not developmentally or culturally relativistic.

The original four identity principles may well need to be accompanied by others. They may need to be relabeled. The most important thing is to avoid introducing redundancy into the theory. Add new principles only if they offer additional predictive or explanatory power. When they are added, try to model their relationship to the others already posited. Moreover, try to explain why it is that these are the principles at work.

Finally, IPT explains change in identity. Threat should not be considered inevitably a momentous or traumatic occurrence (though, of course, sometimes it is). Threat at some level is continuous as social and personal circumstances change and consequently identity change is continuous. I would argue that it is nevertheless useful to study momentous threat and reactions to it and consequently methods for operationalizing threat need to be improved.

I would conclude by emphasizing that I do think IPT needs to evolve. I do find the contributions made recently very valuable. I am stimulated to do more myself as a result of this new work by others. As will be evident from other chapters in this volume, I regard the interface of IPT and SRT as a major arena for theoretical and empirical development.

REFERENCES

Bandura, A. (1997). *Self-efficacy: the exercise of control.* New York: Freeman.

Banks, M., Bates, I., Breakwell, G. M., Bynner, J., Emler, N., Jamieson, L., and Roberts, K. (1992). *Careers and identities.* Milton Keynes: Open University Press.

Breakwell, G. M. (1978). Some effects of marginal social identity. In H. Tajfel (ed.), *Differentiation between social groups.* (pp. 301–336). London: Academic Press.

Breakwell, G. M. (1979). Illegitimate group membership and inter-group differentiation. *British Journal of Social and Clinical Psychology*, 18, 141–149.

Breakwell, G. M. (ed.) (1983). *Threatened identities.* Chichester: Wiley.

Breakwell, G. M. (1986). *Coping with threatened identities.* London and New York: Methuen.

Breakwell, G. M. (1988). Strategies adopted when identity is threatened. *Revue Internationale de Psychologie Sociale*, 1(2), 189–204.

Breakwell, G. M. (1990). Social beliefs about gender differences. In C. Fraser and G. Gaskell (eds.), *The social psychological study of widespread beliefs* (pp. 210–225) Oxford University Press.

Breakwell, G. M. (1992a). Processes of self-evaluation: efficacy and estrangement. In G. M. Breakwell (ed.), *Social psychology of identity and the self concept* (pp. 35–55). London: Academic Press/Surrey University Press.

Breakwell, G. M. (1992b). L'Efficacité auto-imputée et l'éloignement: aspects de l'identité. *Cahiers Internationaux de Psychologie Sociale*, 15, 9–29.

Breakwell, G. M. (1993). Social representations and social identity. *Papers on Social Representations*, 2(3), 198–217.

Breakwell, G. M. (1994). The echo of power: a framework for social psychological research [The Myers Lecture]. *The Psychologist*, 7 (2), 65–72.

Breakwell, G. M. (1996a). Risk estimation and sexual behaviour: a longitudinal study of 16–21 year olds. *Journal of Health Psychology*, 1 (1), 79–91.

Breakwell, G. M. (1996b). Social representations of risk. *International Journal of Psychology*, 31 (3 and 4), 144.4.

Breakwell, G. M. (2001a). Social representational constraints upon identity processes. In K. Deaux and G. Philogene (eds.), *Representions of the social: bridging theoretical traditions*. Oxford: Blackwell.

Breakwell, G. M. (2001b). Promoting individual and social change. In F. Butera and G. Mugny (eds.), *Social influence in social reality*. Goettingen, Germany: Hogrefe & Huber.

Breakwell, G. M. (2004). Identity change in the context of the growing influence of European Union institutions. In R. Hermann, T. Risse and M. B. Brewer (eds.), *Transnational Identities: Becoming European in the EU* (pp. 25–39). New York: Rowman & Littlefield.

Breakwell, G. M. (2010). Resisting representations and identity processes. Special Issue: *Papers in Social Representations*, 19, 6.1–6.11 (in honour of Gerard Duveen: Social Representations and Social Identities: Inspirations from Gerard Duveen).

Breakwell, G. M. (2011). Empirical approaches to social representations and identity processes: 20 years on. Special issue of *Papers on Social Representations*, 20, 17.1–17.4; ISSN 1021–5573.

Breakwell, G. M., and Canter, D. V. (eds.) (1993). *Empirical approaches to social representations*. Oxford University Press.

Breakwell, G. M., Collie, A., Harrison, B., and Propper, C. (1984). Attitudes towards the unemployed: effects of threatened identity. *British Journal of Social Psychology*, 23, 87–88.

Breakwell, G. M., Fife-Schaw, C., and Devereux, J. (1988). The relationship of self-esteem and attributional style to young people's worries. *Journal of Psychology*, 122(3), 207–215.

Breakwell, G. M., Fife-Schaw, C., and Devereux, J. D. (1989). Political activity and political attitudes in teenagers: is there any correspondence? *Political Psychology*, 10 (4), 745–755.

Breakwell, G. M., and Lyons, E. (eds.) (1996). *Changing European identities: social psychological analyses of change*. Oxford: Butterworth-Heinemann.

Breakwell, G. M., and Millward, L. J. (1997). Sexual self-concept and sexual risk-taking. *Journal of Adolescence* 20, 29–41.

Breakwell, G. M., Pont-Boix, J., and Lyons, E. (2003). The study of collective action among older people: a social psychological perspective. *The Annals of the Marie Curie Fellowships*, Vol II. 50–159.

Breakwell, G. M., Smith, J., and Wright, D. (eds.) (2012). *Research methods in psychology*. London: Sage.

Duveen, G., and Lloyd, B. (1993). An ethnographic approach to social representations. In Breakwell, G. M. and Canter, D. V. (eds.), *Empirical approaches to social representations* (pp. 90–108). Oxford University Press.

Fife-Schaw, C., and Breakwell, G. M. (1991). The class basis of late teenage voting preferences. *European Sociological Review*, 7(2), 135–147.

Fife-Schaw, C. R., and Breakwell, G. M. (1992). Estimating sexual behaviour parameters in the light of AIDS: a review of recent UK studies of young people. *AIDS Care*, 4(2), 187–201.

Hendy, J., Lyons, E., and Breakwell, G. M. (2006). Genetic testing and the relationship between specific and general self-efficacy. *British Journal of Health Psychology*, 11, 221–233.

Jaspal, R., and Cinnirella, M. (2010). Coping with potentially incompatible identities: accounts of religious, ethnic and sexual identities from British Pakistani men who identify as Muslim and gay. *British Journal of Social Psychology*, 49, 849–870.

Lyons, E., and Breakwell, G. M. (1993). Self-concept, enterprise and educational attainments in late adolescence. *British Journal of Education and Work*, 6 (3), 75–84.

Mavridi, K., and Breakwell, G. M. (2000). Women's coping strategies for workplace gender discrimination: the role of individual differences. In A. Kantas, Th. Velli and A. Hantzi (eds.), *Societally significant applications of psychological knowledge*. Athens, Greece: Hellinika Grammata.

Markowe, L. A. (1996). *Redefining the self: coming out as lesbian*. Cambridge, UK: Polity Press.

Tajfel, H. (ed.) (1978). *Differentiation between social groups*. London: Academic Press.

Timotijevic, L., and Breakwell, G. M. (2000). Migration and threats to identity. *Journal of Community and Social Psychology*, 10, 355–372.

Vignoles, V. L. (2000). Identity, culture and the distinctiveness principle. Ph.D. thesis, University of Surrey, UK.

Vignoles, V. L. (2011). Identity motives. In S. J. Schwartz, K. Luyckx and V. L. Vignoles (eds.), *Handbook of identity theory and research* (pp. 403–432). New York: Springer.

Vignoles, V. L., Chryssochoou, X., and Breakwell, G. M. (2000). The distinctiveness principle: motivation, identity and the bounds of cultural relativity. *Personality and Social Psychology Review*, 4(4), 337–354.

Vignoles, V. L., Chryssochoou, X., and Breakwell, G. M. (2002a). Evaluating models of identity motivation, self-esteem is not the whole story. *Self and Identity*, 1, 201–218.

Vignoles, V. L., Chryssochoou, X., and Breakwell, G. M. (2002b). Sources of distinctiveness: position, difference and separateness in the identities of Anglican parish priests. *European Journal of Social Psychology*, 32(6), 761–781.

Vignoles, V. L., Chryssochoou, X., and Breakwell, G. M. (2004). Combining individuality and relatedness: representations of the person among the Anglican clergy. *British Journal of Social Psychology*, 43(1), 113–132.

Vignoles, V. L., Schwartz, S. J., and Luyckx, K. (2011). Introduction: toward an integrative view of identity. In S. J. Schwartz, K. Luyckx and V. L. Vignoles (eds.), *Handbook of identity theory and research* (pp. 1–27). New York: Springer.

Part II

Methodological issues in Identity Process
Theory research

3   Qualitative approaches to research using Identity Process Theory

Adrian Coyle and Niamh Murtagh

Qualitative research in psychology has had an interesting history over the last couple of decades in terms of its development, standing and popularity (see Howitt, 2010) but its story varies across domains of the discipline and across geographical locations. Social, health and counselling psychology in Europe (particularly in the UK) have been notably open to qualitative work, whereas, with some exceptions, qualitative approaches to psychological research have struggled to make a major impression in North American psychology generally. In places where it has become relatively established, the story of qualitative approaches to psychological research has not been marked by a cumulative upward trajectory of popularity. Even in the UK, for example, where qualitative methods became an increasingly standard presence in psychology degree programs in the 1990s, there may have been a flattening in popularity in recent years associated with a changing research culture and the ascendancy of cognitive neuroscience as a powerful domain within psychology. In the time since its original, most complete presentation within British social psychology (Breakwell, 1986), Identity Process Theory (IPT) has been employed in both quantitative and qualitative research. In this chapter, we examine the contributions that qualitative research located within an IPT framework can make to the understanding of identity and of the theory itself, while also noting some of the challenges associated with using qualitative approaches within IPT research.

In parallel with Vivian L. Vignoles in his chapter on quantitative approaches to IPT research in this volume, we want to make it clear that our chapter should not be seen as suggesting that qualitative research methods are inherently superior to quantitative approaches for studying identity from an IPT perspective. Mindful of critical questions that have been raised about the role and value of qualitative research in the social sciences (e.g. Hammersley, 2008), we advocate a pragmatic approach to methodology. The question is always which research approach – singly or in combination with others – is most useful for achieving the aims and answering the research question of any given study and for maximizing the value of the research, however "research value" might be defined. We agree that some research aims are best suited to quantitative approaches, such as testing theoretical predictions, and other research aims are best achieved through qualitative approaches, such as developing rich, contextualized understandings of phenomena.

To contextualize our discussion of qualitative approaches to research using IPT, it will be useful first to explain what we mean by "qualitative psychological research" and to examine some relevant features and considerations.

Context, epistemology and theory in qualitative psychological research

At its most basic, qualitative psychological research may be regarded as involving "the collection and analysis of non-numerical data through a psychological lens (however we define that) in order to provide rich descriptions and possible explanations of people's meaning-making – how they make sense of the world and how they experience particular events" (Coyle, 2007, p. 11). Willig (2008, p. 8) has observed that qualitative researchers "aim to understand 'what it is like' to experience particular conditions (e.g. what it means and how it feels to live with chronic illness or to be unemployed) and how people manage certain situations (e.g. how people negotiate family life or relations with work colleagues)." Such approaches can help researchers to produce thoroughly contextualized understandings of their research topics, with "context" understood not as mere "background" but as a constituent of the phenomena being researched. Context can refer to a person's partnerships, family relationships, occupational networks and friendship networks in the present and the past for example, and their location within social systems of gender, class, ethnicity and sexuality. In the hands of skillful researchers, many qualitative methods allow the operation of contextual considerations to be traced through the subjectivities of research participants.

This is an important consideration in research with IPT. Whether it is qualitative or quantitative (or adopts a mixed-methods approach), research that uses or that seeks to test IPT needs to be able to identify and distinguish key aspects of the theory with credibility. This may not be feasible without sufficient contextual data. For example, if a researcher were to place someone's diverse statements about their self-worth into the category of "self-esteem" in an undifferentiated way, this could be misleading. It may be important to identify self-esteem that represents a sense of confidence based on a considered assessment of strengths and weaknesses and to distinguish this from a defensive attempt to "talk up" the self to maintain a positive identity in the face of threat to self-esteem. Both dimensions are of interest to IPT researchers but they may carry different meanings and implications for identity and well-being over time. Within a qualitative interview context, a skillful researcher can encourage participants to elaborate thoroughly contextualized accounts of self-esteem that permit data-grounded interpretations of its nature and identity implications to be offered with confidence. This is not to suggest that an "objective" picture of a person's self-esteem can be obtained: by its very nature, a person's self-esteem is their subjective self-evaluation. What a skillful qualitative researcher can elicit through a focus on context is a detailed sense of the nature of a person's self-esteem, the resources upon which they draw in their self-evaluation and the identity functions that this evaluation performs for them.

The broad definitions of qualitative research presented above capture the purposes of much qualitative research in psychology, particularly research from a phenomenological perspective, which uses methods such as interpretative phenomenological analysis (IPA) to explore in detail how people make sense of aspects of their personal and social worlds (Smith *et al.*, 2009). However, other qualitative methods used in psychology have a different focus. The most notable examples are the various forms of discourse analysis which are more commonly encountered in European psychology than in North American psychology. These critically interrogate dimensions of social life, examining how social categories are worked up, how social situations are linguistically managed and the implications of this for social life, with a particular focus on power relations (Coyle, 2012).

The differences between various qualitative approaches (and the differences between qualitative and quantitative approaches) tend to be concerned with epistemology. This refers to assumptions about what knowledge is, how we generate knowledge, what we know and how we know what we know. Epistemology is often discussed alongside "ontology," which refers to the assumptions we make about the nature of being, existence or reality. It is important to bear this in mind and not to assume that qualitative research in psychology is a homogeneous category except at the most general level. When we consider qualitative identity research in this chapter, we shall do so from the vantage point of different qualitative methods based on different epistemological assumptions, including assumptions about the nature and scope of identity.

IPT itself is based on particular epistemological assumptions. In its original exposition in 1986, the theory was located largely within a realist perspective. With some caveats, data generated by identity-relevant research are held to provide insights into the psychological realities of identity and to offer the possibility of advancing evidence of cross-contextual, universal identity processes. This positivist–empiricist, realist epistemology accorded with the cognitive, information-processing framework to which the original presentation of the theory is indebted. The subsequent allying of IPT with Social Representations Theory (see Breakwell, 2001) broadened IPT's epistemological scope, largely because social representations are seen as functioning on different levels and in different forms. Social Representations Theory is best seen as embodying an epistemology of dialogicality. The individual is regarded as living in a world of others' words and the limits of the self are crafted by the individual in interdependent, communicative relationships with others (Marková, 2003); social representations are filtered through other people, groups and communities. By invoking social representations to develop an understanding of how "the social" frames and shapes identity content, value and processes, IPT could be seen as having been opened up in principle to forms of social constructionism. This epistemological stance, which characterizes discourse analysis, conceives of the ways in which we understand the world and ourselves as having been built up through social processes, particularly through language (see Burr, 2003). It can be seen as a more radical social extension of dialogicality, although the relationship between the two can be contested (Marková, 2003).

Elaborations of IPT have not oriented toward accommodating a social constructionist stance explicitly. This may be because the theory needs to retain ideas of psychological processes that (largely) transcend the (local) social context – appropriately so because such psychological processes are necessarily involved in managing the social constructionist processes that produce contextualized realities. The use of social constructionist analyses in research framed within IPT would not be an entirely epistemologically alien importation. It could usefully extend the ways in which the theory engages with macro-social considerations, such as the social construction of desirable functions or principles for identity. Questions arise, though, about what sorts of social constructionist analyses might contribute usefully to the theory's resources and how exactly such analyses would fit with the theory's cognitive commitments.

Within social constructionism, identity can be understood in terms of taking up, according, resisting and otherwise negotiating subject positions within discourses (Davies and Harré, 1990). Subject positions are understood as sets of images, metaphors and obligations about the sort of responses people can make in interactions that are informed by associated discourses. For example, within a biomedical discourse, people who are ill are placed in the subject position of "the patient," with its obligation to act as a passive recipient of care from those who are placed in the subject position of "medical experts." This gives rise to a more fluid, context-specific conceptualization of identity than is found in IPT. Hence qualitative researchers who use IPT, who are interested in exploring the potential value of social constructionist analysis in their work and who want to produce coherent analytic accounts might regard analyses in terms of subject positions as too fundamentally problematic in epistemological terms to be useful. Additionally there is the problem that an analysis in terms of subject positions is most readily undertaken with interactive data involving more natural conversational turns than those afforded by research interviews, which have been the usual form of data in qualitative IPT research. However, if we accept that identities are not just located within individual psyches but are negotiated in social relationships, a case could be made for studying identity negotiation through naturally occurring data generated in identity-relevant settings.

We shall return to the question of social constructionist analyses in qualitative research with IPT later but it is worth noting that research on identity from a social constructionist perspective does not necessarily involve an analysis exclusively in terms of subject positions. Narrative analysis is a qualitative research method routinely concerned with self and identity that is often thought of as embodying social constructionist commitments (see Crossley, 2000). It conceptualizes identity in terms of narratives that people craft and enact about themselves to achieve coherence over time, social relevance and comprehensibility; identity change is seen as occurring through the renegotiation or restructuring of narratives (Breakwell, 2012; for more on narrative analysis, see Howitt, 2010). The overlaps with IPT are evident in terms of the emphasis on coherence, which can be seen as related to (but not isomorphic with) continuity, and on the restructuring of narratives, which can be posited to occur through identity processes. Yet narrative analytic studies have tended not to use IPT as their theoretical framework, sometimes because researchers frame their work primarily within theories of narrative. There are a few exceptions, though. In her narrative analytic study of non-resident mothers in the UK, Kielty (2008) invoked IPT as one resource in interpreting data relating to identity threat. Brygola (2011) made greater use of IPT in studying narrative sequences on threatened identity but the research used mixed methods rather than an exclusively narrative analytic approach and questions could be raised about the emphases within her use of IPT.

This raises a final important introductory consideration in this chapter concerning the role played by theory in qualitative psychological research. Some qualitative methods seek to avoid having pre-existent theory shape the research in an explicit way. For example, research employing a grounded theory approach usually addresses topics on which existing theory is judged to be incomplete or inadequate and, in its comprehensive form, seeks to create new theory through the systematic generation and analysis of qualitative data (see Charmaz, 2006, for a popular contemporary account of the approach). Thus it would not be appropriate to frame an identity-relevant research question in terms of IPT at the outset of a grounded theory study. Interpretative phenomenological analysis would also avoid such early theoretical framing because of the method's concern with exploring the meaning-making of participants as far as possible on their own terms. Some researchers have used IPT in interpretative phenomenological analytic studies in quite an active, explicit way (see Timotijevic and Breakwell, 2000); others have claimed that the theory was used to inform rather than drive their analyses (see, e.g., Coyle and Rafalin, 2000). As practitioners of this method have sharpened their phenomenological focus over the course of its short history, such work might not be regarded as sufficiently phenomenological to qualify as IPA today (another example of such a study is provided later when we consider the research of Turner and Coyle, 2000). Pre-existing theory can be used to interpret findings in a post-hoc way in research involving this class of inductive qualitative methods, usually in a discussion section.

Other qualitative methods with greater flexibility can readily accommodate the use of theory in an explicit, a-priori way to shape research. For example, Braun and Clarke (2006) have advanced a version of thematic analysis oriented toward discerning, analyzing and reporting patterns within qualitative data that does not require researchers to use theory (or not) in a particular way or to adopt a specific epistemological stance. Instead it is up to the researcher to decide whether and how they will use theory (in an inductive or deductive way or in some "both/and" fashion) in their research and how their research will be framed epistemologically: these decisions will be shaped by the research aims and questions. For examples of research in which IPT has been used in explicitly deductive and quasi-deductive ways to inform thematic analyses of data, see Twigger-Ross and Uzzell's (1996) study of place identity with residents of an area of London that had undergone major change and Jaspal and Cinnirella's (2010) study with British Muslim gay men. (The analytic method used in the former study predated Braun and Clarke's exposition of thematic analysis but overlaps with it.) The version of thematic analysis presented by Braun and Clarke (2006) has proven very popular within psychology in the UK and beyond. Given its flexibility and the possibility it affords for making active use of theory, it can now be considered the preferred qualitative method for research using IPT.

Having outlined some considerations relevant to the use of qualitative approaches within IPT research, our attention now turns to what can be gained through these approaches, as well as some further challenges that may be presented by the use of qualitative methods in IPT work. We shall begin by considering one challenge relevant to any consideration of what might usefully be gained from using qualitative research.

Value and challenges of using qualitative approaches within Identity Process Theory research

Telling what we cannot consciously know?

A challenge faced by any research that invites people to think about and provide accounts of identity motivations and processes is that it requires them to verbalize psychological features that may have originally unfolded outside conscious awareness. This applies to quantitative research that involves retrospective self-report in the form of numerical responses to questionnaire items on identity as much as to qualitative research that involves retrospective verbal self-reports of identity. While a qualitative researcher can obtain a person's *understandings* of their identity motivations and processes from retrospective self-report data, it is open to debate whether they can obtain valid insights into the *actuality* of the person's identity motivations and processes. If we accept that this is possible in principle – and counselling and psychotherapeutic practitioners have long assumed it possible to gain meaningful insights into unconscious motivations and processes relevant to past events from people's verbal accounts – a researcher's success in obtaining such insights will depend on the questions they ask and the exploratory skill with which they pose those questions. There is much to be said for adopting some modes of inquiry and questioning from counselling and using modified versions of these in research contexts to elicit rich data, although for ethical reasons it is vital that the interviewer and especially the participant should not become confused about the roles of researcher and counsellor (see Coyle, 1998).

To take a simple example, when exploring the relevance of potential motivators of identity change in a given situation, it may sometimes be best not to ask interview questions directly about how that situation affected someone's self-esteem, sense of distinctiveness, and so forth. We do not rule out the potential value of direct questions per se: people will vary in their awareness of their own psychological processes and some contexts may render identity processes more visible than others. Researchers could opt for a fairly direct approach to questioning at first and monitor the effectiveness of this. An alternative data generation strategy would be to ask more general questions about whether the person thinks that a particular identity-relevant situation had any effect on how they thought and felt about themselves. If the person indicates a belief that there *was* some effect, this can then be explored, for example, by inviting them to consider their thoughts and feelings at the time in a quasi-"free association" way before tracing their implications for identity-relevant action. It may also be useful to invite the person to reflect on how other people might have regarded their actions and motivations at the time when they negotiated situations of identity threat and identity change. These strategies are oriented toward opening up positions from which the interviewee might offer an account other than the position of a consciously aware agent of their identity.

Having said this, it must be conceded that, even with creative approaches to data generation, some aspects of identity processes that may occur largely outside conscious awareness will remain beyond the reach of qualitative self-report data, such as changes in pre-existing identity structure that occur to accommodate new identity content. Such phenomena may need to be accessed through other forms of data or inferred from qualitative self-report data. Inferential readings could be located at least partly within a "hermeneutic of suspicion." This involves not taking self-reports at face value but seeing data as pointing to (unconscious, ideological and/or institutional) phenomena that may be constitutive of the data but are not usually (explicitly) oriented to by participants. Within psychology, such "suspicious" readings of identity-relevant self-reports are usually associated with discourse analysis, with its focus on how versions of events are crafted, the functions these versions perform and the power relations they facilitate or query (e.g. see Merino and Tileagă, 2011, on interviews on ethnic identity). Yet the application of a hermeneutic of suspicion to identity-relevant texts is standard in other disciplines. To take an example, at the end of the fourth century, when he was in his forties, Saint Augustine of Hippo wrote his *Confessions* (1961), in which he recounted his sinful early life and conversion to Christianity in a vivid, compelling and psychologically sophisticated way. Within philosophy, writers have applied a hermeneutic of suspicion to the text and have considered how it operates as a purposeful self-presentation of Augustine (e.g. as a man of interiority, driven by philosophy) that frames his life in particular ways for particular ends (see O'Donnell, 2001). We cannot know whether Augustine would have recognized these as motives for his self-presentation. In this case the hermeneutic of suspicion can operate with the hindsight of centuries of analysis and so, with a richness of contextualizing considerations, can tell *more* than Augustine could have known in his self-story.

Examples of the "(added) value" of qualitative analyses

Having briefly considered some of the challenges of using qualitative approaches in research with IPT, we turn now to look at how such approaches can offer insights over and above what can be yielded by quantitative perspectives. To illustrate this, we shall first examine two studies that used quantitative approaches to explore aspects of identity that are recognizable as identity principles. We shall consider how qualitative approaches might have made additional valuable contributions to the exploration of similar questions. The two studies have not been chosen owing to any weakness or omission in their approach but because of their potential for readily illustrating what might be gained through qualitative analyses. Both are examples of high-quality, topical identity research that is theoretically grounded, well-designed and well-executed and makes novel contributions to the literature.

In the first study, Morrison and Wheeler (2010) investigated self-concept clarity in minority-opinion groups. Drawing on the distinctiveness principle from IPT and on Social Identity Theory, they postulated that holding a minority opinion may help to distinguish oneself from others and that non-conformity may help to define the self. In three elegantly designed experiments, the researchers showed that a manipulation to ensure that one group of participants believed they held a minority opinion was related to increases in self-concept clarity. Furthermore, they showed that the extent to which the opinion reflected participants' personal values and the extent to which participants identified with their group moderated the effect of minority opinion on self-concept clarity. The findings were said to show that holding a non-conforming opinion may function to increase certainty in "who one is." The results may be interpreted as evidence that different principles of identity may influence behavior beyond the well-researched effects of self-esteem and affiliation. They also suggest a mechanism of identity construction and maintenance: distinctiveness may be enhanced through particular forms of non-conformity.

If a qualitative methodology were used to explore the distinctiveness principle, how would such research be approached? A semi-structured interview could explore general questions such as "What makes you *you*?," "Tell me about a time when you have felt particularly strongly 'you,'" or it could adopt a more direct questioning approach such as "Have you ever been in a situation where you were proud that your views differed from most other people?" Allowing the participant to select their personal circumstances of distinctiveness obviates the need to pre-select scenarios in which people may (or may not) feel a sense of positive distinctiveness. In addition, the participants' description of events or situations of salience may reveal how processes of identity maintenance proceed. Does an unsolicited event which activates a sense of distinctiveness also engender insight into identity content with a possibly lasting effect on the self-concept? Or do people seek out circumstances in which their distinctiveness is made salient? IPT proposes that "identity directs action" (Breakwell, 1986, p. 43) but much remains to be explored about how identity motivations guide behavior. A thematic analysis of responses to the sample questions could show the operation of other identity principles as well as pertinent contextual factors: both are central in IPT's exposition of the mechanisms of identity. Patterns in context could be studied across a sample of participants to explore whether there are types of situation in which people commonly experience a threat to or a reinforcement of their sense of distinctiveness. Analyses informed by critical psychology may draw out issues of power that may be crucial to individuals' responses to a majority or minority position (Fox et al., 2009). Power wielded by others or power sought by the individual may influence or even determine conformity or non-conformity. IPT proposes identity as a dynamic social construct and, mindful of the epistemological challenges mentioned earlier, a discursive analysis could explore interaction and transaction within a discussion or account of distinctiveness-salient situations. Questions could be asked such as how the participant's position shifts over time within the interview transcript (or within an account generated through other means) in discussion with the interviewer or, in the case of focus groups, with other participants. Is there initially a strong opposition which activates the distinctiveness principle or does the difference between self and others appear to strengthen or weaken over time in the qualitative account?

Many methodologies could be applied to research on distinctiveness and other identity principles and not all can be explored in the current discussion. Sample approaches have been used here to demonstrate that qualitative research could usefully be employed to explore dimensions proposed by IPT as salient in identity construction and maintenance, including context, identity motivations and time. A question arises about how our suggested approaches might fit together in epistemological and other terms. An emerging development within qualitative psychology in the UK offers a potentially fruitful response. Frost (2011) has explored the value of applying different qualitative methods with different ontologies and epistemologies to the same data set in what she has termed a "pluralist" approach to qualitative research. The aim is to produce rich, multi-layered, multi-perspective readings of any qualitative data set, with the depth and scope of the analysis taking precedence in a pragmatic way over concerns about epistemological coherence. This can be seen as a (restrained) version of what has been termed "bricolage" in other social sciences (Levi-Strauss, 1966), a stance focused on "learning from the juxtaposition of divergent ideas and ways of seeing" (Kincheloe, 2005, p. 344). In the suggestions that we offered above for extending Morrison and Wheeler's (2010) analysis, the resultant qualitative analyses could be juxtaposed with the quantitative analysis to provide diverse insights into the operation of distinctiveness in this identity context. What comes to mind here is a comment on methodology in relation to IPT that Breakwell (1986, p. 44) made in the original, elaborated exposition of the theory: "Methodological liberation [lies] in the acceptance that it is legitimate to use different approaches in unison." We should point out, though, that undertaking a pluralist analysis is a demanding endeavor. The quality of the analytic outcome has as much to do with the creativity of the analyst(s) as with the range of methods involved.

In the second study under consideration, Phinney *et al.* (1997) conducted a large-scale survey to investigate the relationship between ethnic and national (American) identity components and self-esteem among African American, Latino/a and white teenagers. Using Social Identity Theory (Tajfel and Turner, 1986) as a theoretical framework, they argued that the proposition that an individual's self-esteem may be enhanced through group membership holds ambiguous implications for members of ethnic minority groups, which may be generally regarded as being of lower social status to ethnic majority groups. The study found ethnic identity to be a small but significant predictor of self-esteem in each group but an American identity contributed to the measured self-esteem of white participants only. The authors recognized that the relationship between ethnic identity and self-esteem may be made more salient in a minority setting, citing Breakwell (1986). The acknowledgment of the contextual nature of identity components and of self-esteem carries the implication that the findings may not generalize. The critical role of contextual data in understanding the nature of self-esteem for the individual and the identity functions it performs have been discussed earlier.

As the authors linked their findings to IPT and identity threat in their discussion and explored theoretically important questions on the relative salience of ethnic and national identities and their relationship with self-esteem, the study offered a fertile example to explore how similar research questions could be studied qualitatively, informed by IPT. Focus groups of participants with shared ethnic backgrounds could provide data and ethnic and national identity aspects could be examined. Open questions could include: "What does it mean to be Latina/American?," "How do you feel about being a Latina American?," "What makes you feel proud/ashamed of being a Latina/American?," "What role, if any, does wealth play?," "What about where you live?" Responses to these questions would provide data on the content and value dimensions of identity. A particular strength of pursuing a qualitative approach would be the potential to highlight individuals' perceptions of their national identity. As a multifaceted construct, participants' descriptions are likely to be nuanced and may elucidate more complex national identity elements, such as Irish-American, Italian-American or African American and interactions with other salient identity commitments. A temporal dimension may also emerge: is an American national identity more salient for individuals at particular times, such as on the American national holiday of July 4th?

Additional data generation strategies could be used to supplement interview data and perhaps to generate different insights. For example, participants who are recruited to focus groups could be invited to take photographs of contexts in which they are most aware of their ethnic identity and contexts in which they are most aware of their national identity and to email these to the researchers in advance of the interviews. It would be interesting to see how white participants respond to this when "whiteness" is rendered salient as an identity dimension by the research (see Frankenberg's, 1993, classic work on this). The researchers could print out the photographs which could subsequently be analyzed in light of identity-focused research questions using visual methodologies (Rose, 2012), although their primary purpose would be to act as a catalyst for interview discussions about place, identity and identity salience, with the participants presenting rationales for their selection of the photographed contexts and discussing these contexts with other participants.

The significance of place to national identity has been studied through the medium of IPT (Devine-Wright and Lyons, 1997) and raises critical theoretical questions about the interaction between ethnic and national identity components and identity principles including self-esteem. In many countries, immigrant communities have formed in particular geographic locations. The East End of London, for example, is home to a Bangladeshi community and a Nepalese Gurkha settlement in England has centered on Hampshire. Within such immigrant communities, in what ways do individuals perceive themselves to be part of an ethnic minority? How is this related, if at all, to their sense of self-esteem and distinctiveness? Do identity processes and threats to identities differ for immigrants living in extensive and cohesive immigrant communities, immigrants living amongst other ethnic groups (such as a person of Hispanic identity living amongst African Americans) and immigrants living in communities with the majority ethnic population? History too will have bearing on the experience of ethnic and national identity aspects – personal history of family experience and culturally shared histories (see Jaspal and Yampolsky, 2011), together with experiential histories of social representations or constructions of their ethnic communities. These considerations will have provided content and value for ethnic and national identity components, shaping self-esteem possibilities.

This treatment of qualitative research questions and themes around the relative salience of ethnic and national identity elements illustrates the potential for a qualitative approach to incorporate a multiplicity of identity aspects and meanings, individual circumstances and the geographic, social, cultural and historic contexts of identity aspects based on ethnicity and nationality.

Further insights into the possible contribution of qualitative approaches to exploring identity-related research questions can be gained by taking an example of qualitative IPT work and considering what other qualitative analyses might impart to the picture of identity phenomena yielded by that research. The qualitative study that we have selected was conducted by Turner and Coyle (2000): it examined identity among sixteen people who learned in adulthood that they had been conceived by donor insemination and that the man who had raised them was not their biological father. Participants were recruited through donor insemination support networks in the UK, USA, Canada and Australia and were mailed or emailed a questionnaire with mostly open questions, which they completed and returned by email or post. Today "face-to-face" interviews with geographically distant participants have been rendered feasible through Skype but this had not been developed when the study was conducted. The data were analyzed using IPA, with the analysis informed by IPT. Participants consistently reported experiencing mistrust toward their family after the revelation, a sense of negatively evaluated distinctiveness, a perceived lack of genetic continuity, frustration at being thwarted in their search for their biological father and a need to talk to someone who would understand. This study has been selected because the data reported in the paper readily lend themselves to social constructionist analysis that could have extended the analysis reported by the researchers. As it stands, though, the study provides an example of impactful qualitative identity research using IPT. It has been cited much more frequently than any other qualitative identity research that either of us has undertaken to date, including in a 2003 report from a statutory body which advised on the provision of counseling to people

conceived through donor insemination who might apply for information about their donor fathers in the UK (HFEA Register Counselling
Project Steering Group, 2003): in 2004, legislation was enacted which
permitted this from 2005 onward.

In the data presented in the paper, participants can be seen to draw
upon culturally available tropes related to need and entitlement within
social constructions of the self and self-knowledge. Participants referred
to the "need to know who I was and how I came to be" (2003, p. 2046)
and the need to "feel complete" (p. 2047), thereby working up a sense of
a fractured identity with important elements missing. These are standard cultural tropes that are often used, for example, by people seeking
long-lost relatives in television programs that aim to reunite them. They
constitute a recognizable and powerful resource for working up a problem in relation to self and, within the psychologically literate accounts
that participants offered, for justifying actions (or, in IPT terms, coping responses) that are presented as addressing this unfulfilled perceived
need. Within the analysis, Turner and Coyle interpreted this expressed
need in terms of implications for self-esteem and negative distinctiveness
but it can also be seen as mobilizing a sense of discontinuity in and a crisis
of meaning for identity. The rationales that participants offered for the
most obvious coping response (of seeking to find out who their biological father was) also drew upon discourses of entitlement, responsibility
and justice as well as psychological need. For example, "Peter" crafted an
analogy between sperm donors and "'deadbeat dads' and promiscuous
men who father children through random sex" and who are "held responsible to their offspring" (2003, p. 2047). The invocation of what might
be considered extreme cases of fathering children where the fathers are
"held responsible" by the state makes Peter's claim on identifying his biological father seem reasonable and makes it rhetorically difficult to justify
maintaining sperm donors as an exception to claims about responsibility.
In social representational terms, Peter could also be seen here as anchoring the unfamiliar category of "sperm donor fathers" in more culturally
familiar categories, imparting negative valence to the former category, as
part of a meaning-making process for himself and his audience. A broader
anchoring process can be seen where participants locate their speculation
about their biological fathers within a recognizable narrative motif from
fairytales in which a character feels out of place in their parental home
and their true parentage is revealed to be of high social standing. For
example, "Michael" said, "Maybe it [the donor] was a duke or something.
Or Dirk Bogarde. Or Alan Turing" (2003, p. 2046).

We also see a "social representation" being constructed by "Phoebe"
when she talked about how and why "'society' views the whole search

idea [for her biological father] as pathetic" (2003, p. 2047). In elaborating the content of this oppositional account held by the "Other" (loosely specified as "friends, neighbours, etc.") and then providing a rationale for her search in terms of need and entitlement, she positioned herself as acting against local mainstream opinion in an almost heroic way. In terms of IPT, she could be seen as adopting a position within her account that might have been esteem-enhancing and characterized by agency/ self-efficacy. Across accounts, the generalized "Other" was invoked in largely negative ways (e.g. as not understanding "the complexity of the issues" p. 2048), thereby constructing a need for social support by ingroup members and informed, empathic others as a coping resource.

These supplementary analytic observations do not exhaust analytic possibilities, not least because we have restricted ourselves to the data presented in the published paper. Nonetheless, they provide an indication of the potential "added value" of incorporating largely social constructionist analyses, in this case examining the constructive function of language, within qualitative IPT research (although we also invoked social representations in our analyses because the study predated the elaborated linking of IPT to that theory). We have connected our largely social constructionist analyses to the more phenomenological, IPT-focused analyses offered by Turner and Coyle, setting these side by side in a form of pluralist analysis as advocated by Frost (2011).

Using qualitative research to develop Identity Process Theory

The discussion thus far has reviewed how qualitative research can usefully explore questions on identity raised by IPT and can complement or extend existing research analyses. The potential for novel findings grounded in participants' experience and accounts has been considered. The discussion has also addressed the scope for disparate aspects of context to be foregrounded in qualitative analyses. Continuing our exploration of qualitative approaches and IPT, we now consider the potential of qualitative research to contribute to the development of IPT as a theory. Quantitative research can, of course, perform this function through the testing of theoretical predictions. It has also been used to extend the theory through the identification of potential additional identity principles (e.g. Vignoles et al., 2006). When presenting the original principles, Breakwell (1986) acknowledged that these were unlikely to be exhaustive but advised that any additional principles identified in future work would have to function in the manner predicted for the original principles. Here we shall consider how qualitative work has identified additional principles through research with samples drawn from specific populations and has contributed to furthering the under-developed, emotion-oriented aspect of the theory.

Discerning additional identity principles

We would argue that exploratory forms of qualitative research are ideal for discerning additional identity principles that are important in the identity processes of specific groups and that might have at least some transferability across groups. Research in which identity-relevant data are generated through loosely structured or (for the experienced and confident qualitative researcher) unstructured individual or focus group interviews can yield insights that were unanticipated by the researcher, were not indicated by existing literature and may point to principles that inform identity change, identity maintenance and responses to identity threat for that group. Exploratory analysis of quantitative data can do the same but the researcher must work with data that have been framed by the researcher's expectations. In contrast, the qualitative research process can be exploratory at the stages of both data generation and data analysis.

The earliest identification of possible additional identity principles was by Markowe (1996) in her largely qualitative, content-analytic study of "coming out" as lesbian, conducted with lesbian and heterosexual women. She harnessed a range of theoretical perspectives to make a convincing case that coming out should be examined from cultural, historical, social, intergroup, interpersonal and individual perspectives. Whether participants had developed a lesbian identity in their early years or later in life, two salient motivations were evident in the data: the desire for authenticity or integrity and for affiliation. The desire for authenticity or integrity – "being yourself" – predominated in participants' reasons for coming out. It focused on a perceived "need" not to be assumed to be heterosexual, not to have to hide what was represented as an important part of the self and a desire to be open with others. This reflects a similar emphasis on a desire for authenticity discerned by other writers on identity such as Giddens (1991). The related desire for affiliation concerned a perceived "need" to belong with family, friends or a new community. This presaged the proposal of a desire for closeness to others as an additional identity principle by Vignoles (2000), based on interview data with Anglican clergy. In this study, Vignoles also identified a desire for purpose as another identity principle, which overlaps with the meaning principle that he and colleagues identified in a later quantitative study (Vignoles *et al.*, 2006).

In her study of women who had voluntarily changed careers, Murtagh (2009) used IPT as an integrative framework to draw together aspects of identity which appeared salient in phenomenological accounts of career change. She found evidence for threats to self-esteem, continuity, distinctiveness, self-efficacy and meaning in the participants' stories of the early stages in the process of change and she argued that identity threat may be a determinant of voluntary career change. However, further identity-related threats were noted that were not part of the IPT framework. In particular, the analysis of the interview transcripts discerned a thwarted desire for growth to be salient in the preliminary stages of change. A number of theorists have posited a desire or need for growth as a general motivation (Dweck and Molden, 2005; Ryan and Deci, 2000; Summers-Effler, 2004), supporting the argument for a threat to growth as a motivator in change. Murtagh suggested that a threatened desire to grow may constitute an additional type of identity threat and that the findings provided initial evidence for a desire for growth as an additional guiding principle of identity. Further, she noted that IPT, as a theory of identity processes, is highly developed with regard to threat but less so with regard to positive motivations. There remains scope, therefore, to extend IPT to account for positive, constructive and purposeful motivations.

Such purposeful motivations may be examples of what Jaspal and Cinnirella (2012) have termed "identity enhancing strategies," which refer to "active attempts on the part of individuals to enhance the principled operation of identity processes even in the absence of subjectively perceived threat" (p. 236). In our earlier discussion of Turner and Coyle's (2000) data, Phoebe's use of the oppositional "Other" which served as a rationale for her actions could be considered, at some levels, a constructed experience of subjective threat. Drawing together the notion of identity enhancement in the absence of threat, the construction of subjective threat in justifying behavior and Breakwell's (1986) original formulation of coping strategies in response to experiences of threat, a full spectrum emerges of ways in which identity principles may be deployed to serve identity needs. IPT then may be argued to have developed beyond its early focus on protective and defensive processes to encompass proactive and constructive identity motivations.

A third example of potential additional identity principles discerned through qualitative research is provided by Jaspal and Cinnirella's (2010) exploration of the experiences of British Pakistani men who identified themselves as Muslim and gay. Qualitative thematic analysis of interviews showed profound conflict between religious and sexual aspects of identity for some participants. Applying IPT to the accounts provided insight into ways in which participants managed threats to identity at intrapsychic, interpersonal and intergroup levels. The analysis also noted the salience of strategies for maintaining coherence between conflicting elements of identity. As the authors noted, religious and sexual aspects of identity or behavior were experienced as fundamental to the self-concept of most participants, meaning that identity coherence was paramount for safeguarding their psychological well-being. On the basis of this, Jaspal and Cinnirella suggested that a desire for psychological coherence, different from continuity, might be added to IPT's identity principles (see also Amiot and Jaspal, this volume). This is supported by other work, particularly on multiple, salient identity components and commitments, the maintenance of which can carry potential for identity conflict and incoherence (Amiot et al., 2007; Benet-Martinez and Haritatos, 2005; Roccas and Brewer, 2002). Some identity aspects may be perceived as unrelated and therefore unproblematic but some may be experienced as linked and conflicting. Identifying as both Muslim and gay can engender especially fundamental conflict and incoherence, but conflict between identity components that are accepted and lived by the individual may be a widespread and commonplace challenge in identity construction, such as between the identity elements of priest and person (Kreiner et al., 2006) or parent and worker (Pleck, 1985; Thoits, 1992). Psychological coherence speaks to the need to manage compatibility between conflicting identity elements successfully. In proposing psychological coherence between multiple identity components as an additional principle for IPT, Jaspal and Cinnirella have begun to bridge the gap between IPT and sociological and social psychological identity theories which focus on social roles (e.g. Stryker, 1980) and social identities (e.g. Tajfel and Turner, 1979).

Qualitative research with lesbian women, with Anglican clergy, with career changers and with British Asian Muslim gay men has thus yielded proposed developments of IPT. Such studies in themselves do not lead directly to theory extension. Vignoles et al. (2006) have proposed rigorous criteria by which new identity principles should be evaluated, including conceptual and functional distinctiveness from existing principles, applicability cross-culturally and a strong theoretical and empirical case. The studies above begin to establish arguments for theoretical justification and conceptual distinctiveness and provide initial empirical evidence, which should be extended across diverse samples, cultures and methods, although the proposed additional principles do resonate with other identity research. Alongside theoretical extension through deductive reasoning based on existing knowledge, qualitative research offers the potential for inductive extension based on participants' accounts of lived experiences and sense making.

Emotion in Identity Process Theory

A detailed consideration of the role of emotion in identity remains an obvious gap in IPT. In keeping with the prevailing cognitive and information-processing paradigms when it was originally developed, IPT only really considers emotions as components of identity content and, to a lesser extent, in possible responses to identity threat. However, other theoretical perspectives posit emotions as intrinsic to psychological processes and place emotion centrally in models of identity construction and maintenance. For example, Stryker (2004, p. 8, emphasis in original) argued that "emotions have signal functions, not only to others but to self; they are messages not only *from* the self but also *to* the self, informing persons ... about who they really are." Haviland-Jones and Kahlbaugh (2000, p. 294) argued that "the emotional system is the value-making system in identity," which suggests that the evaluation process of IPT may be constituted by emotion processes. However, recent theories of emotion postulate dual dimensions of valence and arousal (see Russell, 2003): IPT's value dimension may map neatly onto emotional valence but the role of level of arousal remains unacknowledged. Burke's (1991) Identity Control Theory proposes emotions as signals for the extent to which an identity is confirmed or disconfirmed within its context. Affect Control Theory (Heise, 1979; Smith-Lovin, 1990) defines emotion as the mechanism by which the alignment of identity and environment is monitored and reported. From such perspectives, emotion is intrinsic to the interplay between identity and context. Current theoretical understanding of emotion proposes that the experience of an emotion requires situated conceptualization that is social and shared (see Feldman Barrett, 2012), interestingly mirroring theoretical understandings of identities as subjectively constructed within social contexts (such as Stryker's). We can suggest that identity processes may form part of the "psychological construction" (Felman Barrett, 2012, pp. 419–420) of emotion, as well as emotion processes signaling to identity processes, as proposed by Smith-Lovin (1990), Burke (1991) and others. The reciprocal, complex interplay between identity processes, emotion processes and context must be accounted for in future developments of IPT. To borrow from Russell (2003, p. 145), "without considering emotion, [theoretical progress will be] about as fast as someone running on one leg."

Many attempts have been made to operationalize and measure emotions, but challenges remain. The definition of emotion remains contested in quantitative research, with mood and emotion often difficult to tease apart as facets of affect. Perhaps the greatest difficulty in measuring emotion in quantitative research is the unavoidable mediating role of cognitive processes: measures of emotion require participants to think about their feelings and to map them to a predefined instrument. Although qualitative research does not escape all of the challenges of exploring emotion, it offers some approaches to affect which depend less on cognition and language than do measures of emotion in the form of quantitative scales. Returning to our earlier point about creative means of data generation, qualitative methods can facilitate indirect approaches to emotion, such as drawing, playing and free association tasks (see, e.g., Davis, 2010). Where language is the basis for analysis, attention can be paid to *how* people tell their stories – to pace, tone, emphasis, fluency, pitch and body language as indicators of emotion. Future theoretical breakthroughs on emotion in identity processes may well come from qualitative studies.

Conclusion

In considering what can be gained and what has been gained from the exploration of identity using qualitative research approaches within an IPT framework, this chapter has demonstrated the capacity of qualitative research to enrich and extend understandings of identity. It is hoped that future qualitative research will continue to make fruitful use of IPT to further this aim and, in particular, will develop our understanding of existing and emergent guiding principles and the role of emotion in identity processes. Advances in qualitative research methodology may assist these endeavors, particularly the refinement of qualitative methods for longitudinal research (see, e.g., Holland, 2011), which will to some extent address concerns about a reliance upon retrospective accounts and the adoption of a pluralist approach to qualitative psychology and to psychological research generally which can enable researchers to do ever-greater justice to a topic as complex and multifaceted as identity.

REFERENCES

Amiot, C. E., de la Sablonnière, R., Terry, D. J., and Smith, J. R. (2007). Integration of social identities in the self: toward a cognitive-developmental model. *Personality and Social Psychology Review*, 11(4), 364–388.

Benet-Martinez, V., and Haritatos, J. (2005). Bicultural identity integration (BII): components and psychological antecedents. *Journal of Personality*, 73(4), 1015–1050.

Braun, V., and Clarke, V. (2006). Using thematic analysis in psychology. *Qualitative Research in Psychology*, 3(2), 77–101.

Breakwell, G. M. (1986). *Coping with threatened identities*. London: Methuen.

Breakwell, G. M. (2001). Social representational constraints upon identity processes. In K. Deaux and G. Philogène (eds.), *Representations of the social: bridging theoretical traditions* (pp. 271–284). Oxford: Blackwell.

Breakwell, G. M. (2012). Diary and narrative methods. In G. M. Breakwell, J. A. Smith and D. B. Wright (eds.), *Research methods in psychology* (4th edn.) (pp. 391–410). London: Sage.

Brygola, E. (2011). The threatened identity: an empirical study. *Psychology of Language and Communication*, 15(1), 63–88.

Burke, P. J. (1991). Identity processes and social stress. *American Sociological Review*, 56 (December), 836–849.

Burr, V. (2003). *Social constructionism* (2nd edn.). London: Routledge.

Charmaz, K. (2006). *Constructing grounded theory: a practical guide through qualitative analysis*. London: Sage.

Coyle, A. (1998). Qualitative research in counselling psychology: using the counselling interview as a research instrument. In P. Clarkson (ed.), *Counselling psychology: integrating theory, research and supervised practice* (pp. 56–73). London: Routledge.

Coyle, A. (2007). Introduction to qualitative psychological research. In E. Lyons and A. Coyle (eds.), *Analysing qualitative data in psychology* (pp. 9–29). London: Sage.

Coyle, A. (2012). Discourse analysis. In G. M. Breakwell, J. A. Smith and D. B. Wright (eds.), *Research methods in psychology* (4th edn.) (pp. 485–509). London: Sage.

Coyle, A., and Rafalin, D. (2000). Jewish gay men's accounts of negotiating cultural, religious and sexual identity: a qualitative study. *Journal of Psychology & Human Sexuality*, 12(4), 21–48.

Crossley, M. L. (2000). Narrative psychology, trauma and the study of self/identity. *Theory and Psychology*, 10(4), 527–546.

Davies, B., and Harré, R. (1990). Positioning: the discursive production of selves. *Journal for the Theory of Social Behaviour*, 20(1), 43–63.

Davis, B. (2010). Hermeneutic methods in art therapy research with international students. *The Arts in Psychotherapy*, 37(3), 179–189.

Devine-Wright, P., and Lyons, E. (1997). Remembering pasts and representing places: the construction of national identities in Ireland. *Journal of Environmental Psychology*, 17(1), 33–45.

Dweck, C., and Molden, D. C. (2005). Self-theories: their impact on competence, motivation and acquisition. In A. J. Elliot and C. Dweck (eds.), *Handbook of competence and motivation* (pp. 122–140). New York: Guilford Press.

Feldman Barrett, L. (2012). Emotions are real. *Emotion*, 12(3), 413–429.

Fox, D., Prilleltensky, I., and Austin, S. (eds.) (2009). *Critical psychology: an introduction* (2nd edn.). London: Sage.

Frankenberg, R. (1993). *White women, race matters: the social construction of whiteness*. London: Routledge.

Frost, N. (2011). *Qualitative research methods in psychology: combining core approaches*. Maidenhead: Open University Press.

Giddens, A. (1991). *Modernity and self-identity: self and society in the late modern age*. Cambridge: Polity Press.

Hammersley, M. (2008). *Questioning qualitative inquiry: critical essays*. London: Sage.

Haviland-Jones, J. M., and Kahlbaugh, P. (2000). Emotion and identity. In M. Lewis and J. M. Haviland-Jones (eds.), *Handbook of emotions* (2nd edn.) (pp. 293–305). New York: Guildford Press.

Heise, D. R. (1979). *Understanding events: affect and the construction of social action*. New York: Cambridge University Press.

HFEA Register Counselling Project Steering Group (2003). *Opening the record: planning the provision of counselling to people applying for information from the HFEA register*. Sheffield: British Infertility Counselling Association.

Holland, J. (2011). Timescapes: living a qualitative longitudinal study. *Forum: Qualitative Social Research*, 12(3), art. 9. http://nbn-resolving.de/urn:nbn:de:0114-fqs110392.

Howitt, D. (2010). *Introduction to qualitative methods in psychology*. Harlow: Prentice Hall.

Jaspal, R., and Cinnirella, M. (2010). Coping with potentially incompatible identities: accounts of religious, ethnic and sexual identities from British Pakistani men who identify as Muslim and gay. *British Journal of Social Psychology*, 49(4), 849–870.

Jaspal, R., and Cinnirella, M. (2012). Identity processes, threat, and interpersonal relations: accounts from British Muslim gay men. *Journal of Homosexuality*, 59(2), 215–240.

Jaspal, R., and Yampolsky, M. A. (2011). Social representations of the Holocaust and Jewish Israeli identity construction: insights from identity process theory. *Social Identities*, 17(2), 201–224.

Kielty, S. (2008). Non-resident motherhood: managing a threatened identity. *Child and Family Social Work*, 13(1), 32–40.

Kincheloe, J. L. (2005). On to the next level: continuing the conceptualization of the bricolage. *Qualitative Inquiry*, 11(3), 323–350.

Kreiner, G. E., Hollensbe, E. C., and Sheep, M. L. (2006). Where is the 'me' among the 'we'? Identity work and the search for optimal balance. *Academy of Management Journal*, 49(5), 1031–1057.

Levi-Strauss, C. (1966). *The savage mind*. Chicago, IL: University of Chicago Press.

Marková, I. (2003). *Dialogicality and social representations: the dynamics of mind*. Cambridge University Press.

Markowe, L. A. (1996). *Redefining the self: coming out as lesbian*. Cambridge: Polity Press.

Merino, M.-E., and Tileagă, C. (2011). The construction of ethnic minority identity: a discursive psychological approach to ethnic self-identification in action. *Discourse & Society*, 22(1), 86–101.

Morrison, K. R., and Wheeler, S. C. (2010). Nonconformity defines the self: the role of minority opinion status in self-concept clarity. *Personality and Social Psychology Bulletin*, 36(3), 297–308.

Murtagh, N. (2009). *Voluntary occupation change: a social psychological investigation of experience and process*. Unpublished Ph.D. thesis, University of Surrey, UK.

O'Donnell, J. J. (2001). Augustine: his time and lives. In E. Stump and N. Kretzmann (eds.), *The Cambridge companion to Augustine* (pp. 8–25). Cambridge University Press.

Phinney, J. S., Cantu, C. L., and Kurtz, D. A. (1997). Ethnic and American identity as predictors of self-esteem among African American, Latino and White adolescents. *Journal of Youth and Adolescence*, 26(2), 165–185.

Pleck, J. H. (1985). *Working wives/working husbands*. Beverly Hills, CA: Sage.

Roccas, S., and Brewer, M. B. (2002). Social identity complexity. *Personality and Social Psychology Review*, 6(2), 88–106.

Rose, G. (2012). *Visual methodologies: an introduction to researching with visual materials* (3rd edn.). London: Sage.

Russell, J. A. (2003). Core affect and the psychological construction of emotion. *Psychological Review*, 110(1), 145–172.

Ryan, R. M., and Deci, E. L. (2000). Self-determination theory and facilitation of intrinsic motivation, social development and well-being. *American Psychologist*, 55(1), 68–78.

Saint Augustine (1961). *Confessions* (trans. R. S. Pine-Coffin). London: Penguin.

Smith, J. A., Flowers, P., and Larkin, M. (2009). *Interpretative phenomenological analysis: theory, method and research*. London: Sage.

Smith-Lovin, L. (1990). Emotion as the confirmation and disconfirmation of identity: an affect control model. In T. D. Kemper (ed.), *Research agendas in emotions* (pp. 238–270). New York: SUNY Press.

Stryker, S. (1980). *Symbolic interactionism: a social structural version*. Menlo Park, CA: Benjamin Cummings.

Stryker, S. (2004). Integrating emotion into identity theory. In J. H. Turner (ed.), *Theory and research in human emotions: advances in group processes* (pp. 1–24). Oxford: Elsevier.

Summers-Effler, E. (2004). A theory of the self, emotion and culture. In J. H. Turner (ed.), *Theory and research on human emotions: advances in group processes*, vol. XXI (pp. 273–308). Oxford: Elsevier.

Tajfel, H., and Turner, J. C. (1979). An integrative theory of intergroup conflict. In W. G. Austin and S. Worchel (eds.), *The social psychology of intergroup relations* (pp. 33–47). Monterey, CA: Brooks/Cole.

Tajfel, H., and Turner, J. C. (1986). The social identity theory of intergroup behaviour. In S. Worchel and W. G. Austin (eds.), *Psychology of intergroup relations* (pp. 7–24). Chicago, IL: Nelson-Hall.

Thoits, P. A. (1992). Identity structures and psychological well-being: gender and marital status comparisons. *Social Psychology Quarterly*, 55(3), 236–256.

Timotijevic, L., and Breakwell, G. M. (2000). Migration and threat to identity. *Journal of Community & Applied Social Psychology*, 10(5), 355–372.

Turner, A. J., and Coyle, A. (2000). What does it mean to be a donor offspring? The identity experiences of adults conceived by donor insemination and the implications for counselling and therapy. *Human Reproduction*, 15(9), 2041–2051.

Twigger-Ross, C. L., and Uzzell, D. L. (1996). Place and identity processes. *Journal of Environmental Psychology*, 16(3), 205–220.

Vignoles, V. L. (2000). *Identity, culture and the distinctiveness principle.* Unpublished Ph.D. thesis, University of Surrey, UK.

Vignoles, V. L., Regalia, C., Manzi, C., Golledge, J., and Scabini, E. (2006). Beyond self-esteem: influence of multiple motives on identity construction. *Journal of Personality and Social Psychology,* 90(2), 308–333.

Willig, C. (2008). *Introducing qualitative research in psychology: adventures in theory and method* (2nd edn.). Maidenhead: Open University Press.

4   Quantitative approaches to researching identity processes and motivational principles

Vivian L. Vignoles

Compared to most perspectives in the identity literature, Identity Process Theory (IPT) is broader and more complex, combining insights about multiple aspects of identity, multiple processes, multiple levels of explanation and multiple motivational principles, not to mention the wide variety of coping strategies that individuals may adopt when identity is under threat. This conceptual richness has obvious appeal for qualitative researchers and IPT has been used extensively as a theoretical framework to guide and inform interpretations in qualitative analyses (Coyle and Murtagh, this volume). However, the same characteristics can make it harder to see how the theory should be tested quantitatively.

Many theoretical claims of IPT were originally informed by previous quantitative studies (e.g. Breakwell, 1978, 1979, 1986b; Breakwell *et al.*, 1984a; Breakwell *et al.*, 1984b) and a number of subsequent studies have tested predictions of IPT (e.g. Bonaiuto *et al.*, 1996; Murtagh *et al.*, 2012; Vignoles *et al.*, 2002). Nevertheless, the social psychological literature still lacks a visible body of basic quantitative research systematically spelling out and testing IPT's core predictions and demonstrating its superiority to other perspectives. This has probably contributed to IPT often being overlooked by mainstream social and personality psychologists.

Hence, my intention in this chapter is not simply to discuss methods, but also to challenge – and, it is hoped, empower – the IPT research community to redress this situation. To this end, I will introduce some quantitative approaches that have been used, or might be used, to examine some of the main theoretical constructs within IPT and to test some of its distinctive predictions. A majority of these constructs and predictions are shared with my current theoretical perspective, Motivated Identity Construction Theory (Vignoles, 2011), which is closely descended from IPT but extends and adapts the original theory in certain respects.

Crucially, I will not argue that quantitative approaches are superior to qualitative approaches for identity research. I believe that quantitative and qualitative approaches each have their own distinctive strengths and that identity researchers should routinely make use of both approaches (Vignoles *et al.*, 2011). However, I also believe that IPT researchers often could make better use of the distinctive strengths of certain quantitative approaches as part of their methodological repertoire. Hence, I will aim here to illustrate the considerable potential that I see for extending quantitative research in IPT, while describing methods for the following: (1) operationalizing identity contents and structures; (2) examining identity processes in action; (3) studying strategies for coping with threats to identity; (4) measuring the influence of motivational principles on identity construction; and (5) addressing potential extensions of IPT, focusing on group processes and identities.

Operationalizing identity contents and structures

IPT is distinguished from many other approaches in the identity literature by its relatively inclusive definition of identity. Other well-known perspectives focus mainly on personal attributes (Sedikides and Strube, 1997), role identities (Serpe and Stryker, 2011), or group memberships (Tajfel and Turner, 1979), whereas IPT conceptualizes identity as encompassing all these characteristics and more. According to IPT, the identity of an individual is composed of multiple aspects (or "identity elements") spanning diverse domains and levels of self-representation. Identity elements are interrelated, rather than separate and are understood to form a structure. Identity structures comprise the emerging and evolving differences among identity elements in their relative centrality or salience ("content dimension") and in their personal and social value ("value dimension"), as well as the patterns of association and connection among them.

Although identity structures are not portrayed as fixed entities, this focus on structural relationships among multiple identity elements is an important feature that differentiates IPT from several other dominant perspectives on identity. For example, Social Identity Theory (SIT: Tajfel and Turner, 1979) pays little attention to the multiplicity of identity, usually focusing attention on one group membership at a time; Self-Categorization Theory (SCT: Turner *et al.*, 1987) recognizes the multiplicity of identity, but seemingly views the salience of different aspects of identity as too contextually variable to be worth thinking of as a "structure" (but see Pehrson and Reicher, this volume).[1]

---

[1] SCT arguably leaves space for the possibility of more enduring dimensions of identity structure within the underdeveloped concept of "perceiver readiness."

Eliciting identity contents

An essential first step toward studying identity structures is to identify the contents that form the structure. Studies in the identity literature often focus on single aspects of identity selected by the researchers; in contrast, studies into identity structure tend to use idiographic approaches, where participants are invited to specify their own identity contents in an open-ended fashion.

The earliest and best-known, method for this is the Twenty Statements Test (TST: Kuhn and McPartland, 1954). Participants ask themselves the question "Who am I?" and write down the first twenty answers that come into their heads, without worrying about logic or importance. This method has been widely used in the identity literature, including IPT research (Vignoles *et al.*, 2002). However, critics have argued that the original TST wording may result in inconsistent and partial descriptions of identity content, dependent on arbitrary features of the context and on participants' interpretations of the rather ambiguous instructions (Wylie, 1974). Moreover, the wording arguably primes a decontextualized and introspective cultural model of selfhood, prevalent in modern Western societies but less relevant in other cultural contexts (Smith, 2011).

An alternative technique was devised by Ogilvie (1987; see also McQuillen *et al.*, 2001). First of all, participants are asked to list "all of their identities, positive and negative." Identities are described as "various 'hats' that people wear in their everyday lives," and numerous examples are provided, including relationships, activities or hobbies, formal roles and social categories. Secondly, participants are asked to list positive and negative "features" or "attributes," defined as adjectives that they currently use, have used in the past, or could potentially use to describe themselves. Unlike the introspective focus of the TST, the "hats" metaphor focuses attention explicitly on contextualized and socially visible manifestations of identity – aspects of the public self, rather than the private self. However, a risk of providing examples is that this may prime participants to give similar answers. Moreover, the "hats" metaphor relies on a particular idiomatic expression that may not be understood in other languages, or by members of groups who do not commonly use this expression.

Recently, Becker *et al.* (2012) developed a new task for eliciting identity content. They adapted the TST to reduce ambiguity and individualistic bias, asking "Who are you?" instead of "Who am I?" and stating explicitly that personal, relational and collective, private and public, and positive and negative aspects of identity are all valid responses – but without insisting on particular types of response or giving specific examples that might bias or constrain participants from thinking of their own answers. This task was used successfully to elicit identity contents among adolescents across nineteen nations.

Although they are most commonly used to elicit "global" identity contents, free-listing methods may also be useful for studying specific domains of identity. Droseltis and Vignoles (2010) asked participants to list freely up to ten places to which they felt linked and Vignoles *et al.* (2007) asked participants to list freely up to 10 possessions that they owned, before responding to further questions designed to elicit the structuring of elements within these specific identity domains.

Approaches to measuring structure

Having identified some relevant content, various approaches can be used to measure identity structures. In some approaches, participants report explicitly on the subjective centrality, salience or value of different aspects of their identities – which Vignoles *et al.* (2002) referred to as *subjective identity structures*. Other approaches use more indirect or implicit methods to measure centrality, salience or value, independently of participants' own judgments or reports about their identity structures (e.g. Batory, 2010; Rosenberg and Gara, 1985). I discuss these two approaches in turn and then consider the information available on the relationship between them.

Perhaps the most obvious way of measuring the positioning of multiple elements within participants' identity structures is simply to ask them. Vignoles *et al.* (2002) used a shortened TST to elicit up to twelve identity elements from each participant and then asked participants to rate each of their identity elements for *perceived centrality* using two questions: "How much do you see each of these things as peripheral or central to your identity?" and "How much does each of these things give you a sense of who you are?" This approach has the advantage of transparency and simplicity (even if it is slightly complex to administer). Moreover, the concept of perceived centrality is applicable to diverse domains of identity, including group identities (see Leach *et al.*, 2008), as well as personal attributes, role identities, material possessions and places.

A potential disadvantage of this direct approach to measuring identity structure is that it assumes that participants have some pre-existing spatial representation of their identity elements that they can report on, or – more radically – it may be creating the dimension that it seeks to measure. Thus, researchers have also attempted to measure "centrality" by more indirect means. Kuhn and McPartland (1954) focused on the

order in which identity elements were listed, assuming that more important elements will have greater cognitive accessibility and thus participants will list them first when asked to describe themselves freely. There
is some evidence that subjectively important identity aspects are more
cognitively accessible (e.g. Aquino *et al.*, 2009). However, this may not
translate directly into order effects on tasks such as the TST. Instead,
people may list particular types of identity elements together (e.g. social
categories first and then personal attributes), or they may list identity
elements in the same life-domain together (Reid and Deaux, 1996).
Some people may list their most important aspects first, whereas others
may take longer to get "warmed up," listing more important aspects as
they go further into the task.

Several researchers have proposed more elaborate approaches to measuring identity structures, based on the interrelationships among identity
elements. These methods assume that aspects of identity that are most
central will have the strongest and most extensive links to other aspects of
identity. One approach was developed by Rosenberg and Gara (1985; see
also McQuillen *et al.*, 2001; Ogilvie, 1987). After listing "identities" and
"attributes" as described earlier, participants are asked to rate how much
each of their "attributes" describes them in the context of each of their
"identities." The resulting matrix is analyzed using a form of hierarchical cluster analysis, to produce parallel tree diagrams for each participant, where those identities sharing more attributes with other identities
appear higher in the identity hierarchy and those attributes sharing more
identities with other attributes appear higher in the attribute hierarchy.
Thus, identities (and attributes) that are more strongly linked to other
identities (and attributes) are considered more central.

A similar, but arguably more elegant, approach was reported by Batory
(2010). After listing identity elements (using a task adapted from Ogilvie,
1987, referring to "faces" instead of "hats"), participants thought about
the "internal dialogues" occurring among the different elements that
they had listed and rated the "frequency of communication" between
each possible pair of elements. Scores were calculated to represent what
Batory called the *dialogical potential* of each identity element, defined as
the average frequency of internal dialogues with the other identity elements. This measure can be interpreted as an index of centrality, in the
sense that more central identity aspects will be more embedded in the
identity structure and thus more closely linked to other identity aspects –
as in the Rosenberg and Gara (1985) method. However, two advantages
of Batory's method are (1) that it is less complex statistically and (2) that
the method does not require generating separate sets of "identities" and
"attributes"; thus placing less restriction on the contents that are listed

and on the kinds of links that are relevant to determining the identity structure.

The cognitive centrality of identity aspects might also be measured using response latencies. For example, Markus and Kunda (1986) tested participants' response latencies for identifying a series of words as "me" or "not me," although the words were adjectives pre-selected by the researchers, rather than identity content generated by participants. Devos *et al.* (2007) used response latencies to measure how strongly female undergraduates associated two identity aspects – college education and motherhood – with the self; participants explicitly claimed that college education was more important to them than motherhood, but implicit associations were stronger with motherhood than with college education and individuals with stronger implicit associations between motherhood and the self also showed a stronger correlation between attitudes to motherhood and self-esteem. These studies suggest that reaction times may be a valuable indicator of cognitive centrality, independent of participants' explicit reports; however, no study to my knowledge has yet used reaction times to measure within-person differences in implicit identification with multiple, freely generated aspects of identity content.

Very few studies have examined the relationship between explicit self-reports and indirect measures of identity structure. Ogilvie (1987) and McQuillen *et al.* (2001) calculated the relationship between centrality of identity elements based on the Rosenberg and Gara (1985) procedure and rankings of the amount of time spent enacting each identity. Both found substantial individual differences in the size and nature of this relationship. Confusingly, Ogilvie reported higher life-satisfaction among those who spent more time enacting relatively central identities, whereas McQuillen *et al.* found the opposite pattern. Batory (2010) found that dialogical potential was moderately correlated with the perceived centrality of identity elements ($r = .3$). Moreover, dialogicality prospectively predicted perceived centrality over two months, although the reverse prediction was not tested.

Whether they are conceived as subjective constructs or as implicit properties to be measured indirectly, one should remember that identity structures are multidimensional. Breakwell (1986a, 1987, 1988) proposed separate "content" and "value" dimensions of identity structure. However, Vignoles *et al.* (2006) distinguished empirically between cognitive, affective and behavioral dimensions: identity definition (~ perceived centrality), identity-related affect and identity enactment. Crucially, the latter dimension implies that identity structures do not exist only in the minds of individuals: they are also negotiated in social relationships (Reicher, 2000; Swann, 1983). Vignoles *et al.* found that identity definition and identity enactment are reciprocally related: over time, people come to enact most those identity aspects that they perceive as most central, but they also come to perceive as most central those identity aspects that they enact most.

Additional structural dimensions may be relevant within particular domains of identity. For example, differences in feelings of solidarity and in perceived similarity with other group members are important dimensions of people's identification with groups (Leach *et al.*, 2008), although there is no analogue of these dimensions for other kinds of identity content. Studying the structure of place identifications, Droseltis and Vignoles (2010) identified three dimensions: attachment/self-extension, self-congruity and environmental fit. The first two dimensions may be relevant to other aspects of the extended self, such as possessions and brand identities; the third seems relevant only to place identity.

Examining identity processes in action

Although the content and structure of identity plays an important role in the theory, IPT is first and foremost a theory of identity *processes*. Breakwell (1986a, 1987, 1988) posits two different classes of identity processes:

1. Over the lifespan, identity is understood to be formed and revised through ongoing processes of *assimilation–accommodation* and *evaluation*.
2. In situations where these processes are unable to satisfy the demands of the identity principles, identity is considered to be *threatened*, leading to the deployment of *coping strategies*.

Studying the "everyday" processes of assimilation–accommodation and evaluation mostly involves looking for evidence of changes in identity over time. Studies of coping strategies can also involve investigating why identity does not appear to change, especially in circumstances where changes might intuitively seem likely.

Investigating change processes

To study identity processes, researchers often investigate people's responses to new information or situations. This can be done using experimental studies. Studies into self-evaluation often involve presenting participants with positive or negative information about themselves and measuring to what extent participants accept, believe, trust or remember the new information (reviewed by Sedikides and Strube, 1997). Social identity researchers often assign their research participants to newly created, artificial "groups" in laboratory studies, and then examine to what extent participants think, feel or act as group members (reviewed by Spears, 2011). Both of these widely used experimental paradigms can be interpreted from an IPT perspective as studying the assimilation (or otherwise) of newly created "content" into identity.

However, IPT researchers have been especially interested in naturally occurring changes in identity, which often span longer periods of time than can be observed in the context of a laboratory experiment. Early studies focused on people who had recently moved into a new social position, such as becoming unemployed (Breakwell, 1986b; Breakwell *et al.*, 1984a) or working in gender-atypical employment (Breakwell and Weinberger, 1987). Until recently, longitudinal studies of identity change were few and far between (for exceptions, see Breakwell, 1992; Ethier and Deaux, 1994; Serpe, 1987). With online data collection, following participants over successive time waves is becoming easier and less expensive.

Recently, Easterbrook and Vignoles (2012) conducted a five-wave online study among new university students, examining the *assimilation* of two new elements into identity: membership of their hall of residence (residence identity) and membership of their flat or floor within the hall of residence (flat identity). In the first wave, participants already reported moderately strong identification with both groups, suggesting that they had assimilated these new identity elements almost immediately on arrival, or perhaps in anticipation. However, different participants showed upward, downward or stable trajectories of identification with both groups over the subsequent 10 weeks. As I describe later, Easterbrook and Vignoles were able to predict these trajectories using hypotheses derived partly from IPT.

An important and distinctive prediction of IPT is that people assimilating new content into their identities will also restructure their pre-existing identity content to *accommodate* (make room for) the new content. Breakwell (1986a, 1987, 1988) describes assimilation and accommodation as so closely intertwined that they should be understood as two sides of a single process. To provide a fuller picture of this double-edged process, it seems important to examine changes in the structuring of pre-existing identity content, rather than just focusing on the assimilation of new content.

Cassidy and Trew (2001) studied changes in the psychological centrality of various identity aspects, including family relationships, friend, student, religious, political and national identities, over one year spanning the transition from school to university among adolescents in Northern

Ireland. On average, friendship, religious and national identities declined in centrality across this period, suggesting that participants accommodated their new student identities by reducing the centrality of other identity aspects. Test–retest correlations for individual differences in the centrality of each identity aspect were mostly low, suggesting that participants also had restructured their identities considerably on a more idiosyncratic level. However, Cassidy and Trew did not examine the relative centrality of the various identity aspects within each participant, as in the studies reviewed earlier.

Manzi et al. (2010) studied the restructuring of identity across two life transitions: moving from school to university and becoming a parent. Participants listed identity aspects and rated their perceived centrality before and several months after the transition. Although the average centrality of identity aspects did not decline, only a quarter of the within-person variance in the perceived centrality of identity elements was stable. Before the transition, participants were asked to imagine their post-transition selves and reported their expected, desired and feared identity structures (after Markus and Nurius, 1986). Expected and desired identity structures predicted the actual shape of post-transition identity structures. Moreover, participants whose post-transition identity structures came closer to their initial desires and expectations reported more positive emotions, whereas those whose identity structures came closer to their initial fears reported more negative emotions. Thus, accommodation is not just a by-product of assimilation: people can formulate goals about restructuring their existing identity content, and achieving these goals predicts their well-being.

Investigating the *evaluation* process is even more complex. Numerous studies have adopted longitudinal methods to examine changes in individuals' levels of self-esteem (e.g. Breakwell, 1992; Trzesniewski et al., 2003). However, the definition of evaluation as "allocation of meaning and value/affect to identity content both new and old" (Breakwell, this volume) points to a richer and more complex set of processes, encompassing how individuals define and experience the meanings of their identity aspects, their implications for satisfying motivational principles (not only self-esteem) and their affective significance. Examining one part of this broad array of processes, Becker et al. (2013) collected longitudinal data predicting the implications of identity aspects for self-esteem among adolescents in seventeen cultural groups. Consistent with IPT's view of identity processes as embedded within social representational contexts, they found that participants came to derive feelings of self-esteem especially from those identity aspects that better fulfilled the value priorities emphasized in their respective cultural groups.

Studies such as these have begun to examine temporal change in identity structures, and yet in many respects they only scratch the surface of the kinds of change process that might be examined from an IPT perspective. Although they provide initial ways of examining the processes of assimilation–accommodation and evaluation, their focus has been limited to selected dimensions of identity structure, all measured using explicit self-reports. To my knowledge, no longitudinal research has yet examined changes in the more indirect measures of identity structure described earlier.

Investigating coping strategies

According to IPT, coping strategies come into play in situations when the processes of assimilation–accommodation and evaluation fail to insulate the individual against threats to identity. Theoretically, these strategies may include any cognition or behavior – as well as the absence of a relevant cognition or behavior – that can be interpreted as responding to a situation of identity threat. This makes it highly difficult to provide generic guidelines for measuring coping strategies within IPT research. However, I will describe some illustrative examples of studies that have examined coping strategies, respectively using correlational, longitudinal and experimental methods.

Correlational (and quasi-experimental) coping studies typically involve comparing the responses of participants who are considered to be occupying more or less threatening identity positions. In an early study, Breakwell (1978) found that young football supporters whose marginal status in their group was made salient rated the supporters of other teams more negatively – thus showing increased intergroup differentiation – compared to those whose status in the group was more secure. Bonaiuto et al. (1996) used a correlational approach to study denial as a strategy for coping with the symbolic threat of having one's local and national beaches labeled as "polluted." They surveyed adolescents in six British seaside resorts with more or less polluted beaches. Participants in more polluted resorts perceived greater pollution of local and national beaches. However, perceptions of beach pollution were also predicted by individual differences in social identification: participants who identified strongly with their town perceived less pollution in their local beaches, and those who identified strongly with Britain perceived that British beaches were less polluted. Bonaiuto et al. proposed that highly identified participants were denying the physical evidence "to cope with the threat to place identity posed by the labeling of local beaches by a powerful outgroup (the EU)" (1996, p. 157). Certainly these results are consistent with IPT, suggesting biased evaluations among those for whom accepting the evidence of pollution would be most threatening. However, the evidence for viewing this as a coping strategy, rather than a more general positive bias, would have been stronger if the effect of local identification had been strongest among participants in resorts that had been categorized negatively by the EU – those who were in the most threatening position. Moreover, as the authors recognized, the correlational design of the study precludes the possibility of drawing strong causal conclusions.

Ethier and Deaux (1994) used a longitudinal methodology to study the coping strategies of Hispanic students during their first year at a high-status university with few Hispanic students. They reasoned that this new environment would threaten the students' ethnic identity, because it lacked the contextual supports for ethnic identification that most participants previously would have been used to: speaking Spanish at home, living in a Hispanic neighborhood and having a significant proportion of Hispanic friends. At first sight, their results appeared to show little evidence of change: average ratings of the importance of Hispanic identity and of Hispanic identification did not change significantly over three time-waves of the study, and test–retest correlations were also high (>.7). However, a finer analysis showed evidence of a great deal of "identity work" underlying this superficial stability. In fact, participants with weaker cultural backgrounds at home tended to perceive the new environment as more threatening, seeing their home/ethnic and university contexts as more incompatible, and this was associated with reduced collective self-esteem and subsequently with reduced Hispanic identification; thus, these participants appear to have re-evaluated their Hispanic identity more negatively, cementing the marginal position of their ethnicity within their identity structures. In contrast, those with initially stronger ethnic backgrounds tended to get involved with Hispanic activities at university, which over time led to higher levels of Hispanic identification; seemingly, these participants were able to maintain their Hispanic identity by "remooring" it within a newly created context of supportive relationships.

A strength of the longitudinal design is that Ethier and Deaux (1994) were able to make stronger causal inferences by testing prospective predictions of changes in collective self-esteem and identification. Moreover, their study shows clearly the role of identity processes in maintenance rather than change of identity structures, offering an important correction to the intuitive view that when something does not change it is therefore fixed and there is nothing happening. However, it is interesting to note that participants who adopted the "remooring" coping strategy did not report any experience of threat during the study: this raises interesting questions about the measurement – and ultimately the conceptualization – of identity threat, to which I return shortly.

Although correlational and longitudinal studies are important for showing the operation of coping strategies in real-world contexts, a majority of research into identity threat and coping has used experimental methods, where participants are placed into threatening situations and their responses are assessed (for an early example, see Breakwell, 1979). Schimel *et al.* (2000) gave participants false feedback that they were (or were not) high in "repressed anger." Participants then read an account, supposedly by a target person with demographic characteristics similar to their own, referring to a recent incident when the target person had (or had not) acted violently. Finally, participants rated themselves on twenty personality dimensions, using a form that already showed the ostensible ratings of the target person. The researchers created a measure of "psychological distancing" based on how dissimilarly participants rated themselves to the supposed profile of the target person. Participants who had been told they were high in repressed anger distanced themselves significantly more from a violent target person, compared to those who had not received the threatening feedback and/or had been exposed to a non-violent target person. This was interpreted as evidence for a "defence mechanism" (i.e. a coping strategy) whereby people distance themselves selectively from others in order to deny characteristics that they fear in themselves.

As well as providing stronger evidence for causal relationships than other approaches, experiments are well suited to studying how participants behave when they are placed in particular situations. Many "person variables" in psychology do not lend themselves readily to experimental manipulation (despite the best efforts of those who believe that experimental methods are the only route to psychological knowledge), but identity threat is fundamentally a situational variable and thus more amenable to manipulation. Indeed, the self and identity literature is replete with identity threat manipulations, often involving false feedback from bogus personality or ability tests, or false information about how the participant, or a group they belong to, is viewed by others (see Leary *et al.*, 2009).

Nevertheless, experimental studies have their limitations. Within an experiment, one cannot represent the range of coping strategies that may be available in naturally occurring situations. Most experiments present participants with one particular threat and make one particular coping strategy available, thus channeling participants' identity processes into a single direction. Thus, although experiments provide important information about how identity processes *can* work, they usually tell us rather less about how identity processes *do* work in naturally occurring contexts.

Evidence for threat

Whatever design is used, a crucial question is how to infer that a threat is present. Only one of the studies described above directly measured perceived threat: Ethier and Deaux (1994) created a measure of "threat perceptions," but participants, on average, reported relatively low levels of threat – especially those with stronger cultural backgrounds who used the "remooring" strategy. Schimel *et al.* (2000) included a manipulation check focusing on the informational content of their manipulation, but they did not ask their participants how threatened they felt about it. Sometimes, participants do report feeling "threatened" following an identity threat manipulation (e.g. Martiny *et al.*, 2012), but IPT predicts that individuals will not always experience their identity threats as "threatening" – either because their coping strategies are working effectively, or because they are in denial (Breakwell, 1988). This raises an obvious problem: if the defining feature of a coping strategy is that it occurs in response to a threat, then how can we claim that a given outcome – such as perceiving one's local beach as clean, or joining the Hispanic society at university – is a coping strategy, when participants show no evidence of feeling threatened?

Rather than asking participants whether they feel threatened, another possibility is to create a theoretically based measure, using items measuring actual or anticipated frustration of identity principles. Korf and Malan (2002) measured ethnic identity threat among Afrikaans-speaking white South Africans, using items measuring perceptions of current and anticipated distinctiveness (e.g. "Afrikaners are going to maintain a unique identity"), continuity (e.g. "Afrikaans is going to disappear slowly but surely") and self-esteem (e.g. "It has become a negative attribute to be an Afrikaner these days"), as well as quality of life (e.g. "I expect my financial situation to deteriorate in the future"). Factor analysis revealed two dimensions, which they named "distinctive continuity" (lack of distinctiveness and continuity) and "well-being" (lack of self-esteem and quality of life). Manzi *et al.* (2006) used twelve items measuring expected satisfaction or frustration of six motivational principles, in a study of UK and Italian adolescents anticipating the life transition from school to university. Example items were "I expect to feel worthless" (self-esteem threat) and "I expect to feel competent and in control" (efficacy satisfaction). Items formed a single factor, which fully mediated the correlational relationships between family processes and well-being in their samples. Neither of these studies focused on coping strategies. However, Murtagh (2009) adapted the Manzi *et al.* scale, finding that participants who perceived greater identity threat at work had more thoughts of changing their occupation, which in turn predicted search behaviors, generation of possible selves in alternative occupations and action to change one's occupation (for a recent experimental study using a similar measure, see Murtagh *et al.*, 2012).

Compared to measures of "feeling threatened," these measures of motive frustration have the advantage of being grounded in a theoretical definition of identity threat. However, they rely on the assumption that the motivational principles examined are relevant and important. This needs testing, as I discuss shortly. Furthermore, because the items are relatively transparent, these measures are not necessarily immune to the same issues affecting "perceived threat" measures: participants may not acknowledge when their self-esteem, continuity or distinctiveness are at risk, or they may cope with threats too quickly to show any effects.

A third possibility is to infer the presence of threat from non-verbal indicators, such as physiological measures. Greenberg *et al.* (1992) found increased skin conductance (evidence of heightened physiological arousal) among participants who had been led to expect painful electric shocks and Strauman *et al.* (1993) found reduced natural killer cell activity and increased cortisol levels in blood samples (evidence of psychological distress), when they primed dysphoric and anxious participants with their ideal and ought selves. Physiological measures have been little used in the identity literature, but they may be useful indicators of threat, especially in situations where explicit measures are likely to be subject to defensive biases or demand characteristics. However, these measures are far from perfect indicators of identity threat, because they provide direct evidence only for physiological arousal or at best for generic anxiety or distress: they cannot show that participants' arousal, anxiety or distress is identity related.

Whichever methodology is used, anyone attempting to measure identity threat must contend with the fact that threat is predicted to be a transient state – at least for those who cope successfully – and in many cases, researchers may simply not catch participants at the right moment to detect when they are threatened. Some coping processes may be virtually instantaneous, or coping may be initiated before the threat becomes "live": thus, some instances of identity threat may be so transient as to be effectively undetectable. This suggests that we should not insist on a significant "threat manipulation check" or that participants necessarily agree that they "feel threatened" in order to justify interpreting a given outcome as a coping strategy.

However, this raises a new problem: if identity threat is potentially unmeasurable, then how can we justify interpreting a given outcome as a coping strategy, without making the theory unfalsifiable? I can offer no definitive answer, but some suggestions are possible. First, one might focus on the *specificity* of coping responses in relation to the threats encountered. Thus, Schimel *et al.* (2000) showed that participants who had been told they were high in repressed anger distanced themselves from a violent target but not from a dishonest target, whereas participants who had been told they were high in repressed dishonesty showed the opposite pattern of effects. Even without any indication that the participants felt threatened, it seems hard to come up with an alternative explanation of this specific pattern of responses without invoking the concept of threat.

Second, it may be useful to focus on the *substitutability* of coping strategies. For example, Tesser *et al.* (2000) reported three studies showing that, after using one strategy to maintain self-esteem, participants showed reduced tendencies to use other self-esteem maintenance strategies. This suggests a "hydraulic" view of coping with identity threat: once a threat has been dealt with using one coping strategy, there is no need to use another strategy. Thus, to the extent that two otherwise unrelated processes both (1) tend to occur under similar circumstances – when identity is believed to be threatened – and (2) appear to be substitutable for each other, this gives stronger grounds for concluding that the two processes serve a common function as coping strategies.

Nevertheless, it may arguably be helpful also to consider adjusting the theory. One possible adjustment could be to understand identity threat as a property of situations, rather than a state of the individual. In this case, one should judge the presence or absence of threat based on analyzing the nature of the situation, rather than expecting to deduce this from individuals' responses. However, this would fail to recognize that the "same" situation may be more threatening to some individuals than to others.

A more radical adjustment could be to remove the theoretical distinction between "normal" identity processes and coping strategies. According to this view, rather than coming into play only when assimilation–accommodation and evaluation run into difficulties, the intrapsychic, interpersonal and intergroup processes that IPT portrays as coping strategies are part of the normal, day-to-day "work" of constructing and maintaining a satisfactory sense of identity. This "identity work" is always a partly defensive enterprise, because there is always the potential for the satisfaction of motivational principles to be undermined. Thus, in situations where one of the motivational principles is relatively frustrated or where there is greater risk of frustration (this is a continuum, not a discrete class of situations), people are expected to intensify their efforts to maintain satisfaction of the frustrated principle (which does not amount to a qualitatively different class of identity processes). To the extent that such efforts are unsuccessful, people may also experience feelings of threat, frustration or other kinds of psychological distress; these feelings are not necessary precursors of identity defence, they are better understood as an indication that the individual's defences are not working effectively, or that they have not yet completed their function.

Testing the effects of motivational principles on identity

At the core of IPT is the idea that identity processes are guided by several *principles* which have a motivational character. Breakwell (1986a, 1987, 1988) proposed that identity processes are guided by principles of maintaining *self-esteem, continuity* and *distinctiveness* and later added a fourth principle of *efficacy* (Breakwell, 1993). Subsequent qualitative research among specific populations has pointed to possible additional principles, including *authenticity/integrity* and *affiliation* (Markowe, 1996), *purpose* and *closeness to others* (Vignoles, 2000) and *coherence* (Jaspal and Cinnirella, 2010). Acknowledging the likelihood of additional principles, Breakwell (1988) suggested a possible *autonomy* principle, although this never became part of the theory. Vignoles (2011) argues theoretically for additional motivational principles of *belonging* and *meaning*.

The fact that so many, and such varied, identity principles have been proposed – even if some of them may be circumscribed to particular populations, and only the principles listed by Breakwell (1993) are consensually acknowledged as part of IPT – raises several important questions for research. One of the most pressing is to determine which identity principles are actually involved in guiding identity processes in a given population or context. This requires demonstrating that each of the four (or more) identity principles has a role in guiding identity processes that is not "redundant" – not reducible to the roles of the other principles. Yet, no consensus exists currently about how to measure identity principles.

Measuring motivational principles

Researchers often attempt to measure identity principles using explicit self-report scales (e.g. the Self-Attributed Need for Uniqueness scale: Lynn and Snyder, 2002). However, people's self-reports of their own motives cannot necessarily be taken at face value. For example, in individualist cultures, a person might attempt to fit in with others by saying how much he or she wants to be different (Jetten *et al.*, 2002; Salvatore and Prentice, 2011). Similarly, in Chinese culture, showing modesty can be a route to higher rather than lower implicit self-esteem (Cai *et al.*, 2011). This suggests that identity principles may be better measured using indirect methods, rather than explicit self-reports.

Instead of asking participants directly how much they want to feel positive, distinctive, continuous or efficacious, Vignoles *et al.* (2008) sought to detect the guiding influence of the four IPT identity principles – and two further motivational principles – within the structuring of participants' desired and feared future identities. Participants freely listed their "possible future selves" (Markus and Nurius, 1986), then completed ratings reflecting (1) the extent to which they desired and the extent to which they feared that each of these possible selves would come to fruition, and (2) the extent to which they anticipated that becoming each of these possible selves would satisfy or frustrate each motivational principle. Using multi-level regression analyses, Vignoles *et al.* (2008) were able to test whether each of the motivational principles in their study contributed uniquely to predictions of within-person variance in desire and fear, while controlling for effects of the other motives – thus aiming to provide evidence for the non-redundancy of each separate principle. Largely supporting IPT, analyses showed that participants desired significantly more and feared significantly less the fruition of those possible selves that promised greater feelings of self-esteem, continuity and efficacy, as well as a sense of meaning in life; possible selves that promised greater feelings of distinctiveness were feared marginally less, but were not desired more.

IPT predicts that identity principles will influence not only people's desires and fears about the future, but also the operation of processes shaping current identity structures. Over a series of studies, Vignoles and colleagues (2002, 2006, 2007, 2013; Droseltis and Vignoles, 2010; Kreuzbauer *et al.*, 2009) have tested the role of the IPT principles, as well as additional motivational constructs, in predictions of subjective identity structures. Recent findings show that men and women from a highly diverse range of cultural groups across the world typically perceive as more central and self-defining those of their identity aspects that provide greater feelings of self-esteem, continuity, distinctiveness and meaning (Vignoles *et al.*, 2013). These results support the original formulation of IPT – with the addition of a "meaning principle" – but seem to contradict the view that identity principles may be culturally relative (cf. Breakwell, 1993).

This methodology has considerable potential for extensions and modifications, opening up interesting new research questions. For example,

Vignoles *et al.* (2006) tested whether the predictive effects of six motivational principles differed across levels of self-representation. Supporting Breakwell's (1986a) arguments against theoretical distinctions between "personal" and "social" identity aspects, they found no significant differences in the effects of each motivational principle across individual, relational and collective levels of identity. Moreover, in a series of studies, Vignoles and colleagues have begun to test whether similar principles predict the structuring of elements of the "extended self," such as material possessions (Vignoles *et al.*, 2007), brand usage (Kreuzbauer *et al.*, 2009) and places (Droseltis and Vignoles, 2010).

Vignoles *et al.* (2006) have also begun to explore the role of motivational principles in predicting other dimensions of identity structure, including participants' happiness with different identity aspects and the extent to which they report enacting different aspects of their identities in everyday life. Whilst predictions of perceived centrality have shown inconsistent support for the efficacy principle and for an additional theorized motive for belonging, these motives appear to have a stronger impact on identity enactment. An important question for future research is whether the motivational principles will play a similar role in shaping further dimensions of identity structure – including dimensions that are measured by indirect or implicit means, rather than using self-reports.

Crucially for IPT, research has begun to examine the role of motivational principles in predicting identity change. Vignoles *et al.* (2006, Study 4) used a cross-lagged longitudinal design to test the prospective effects of motivational principles on the restructuring of identity aspects among university students over a two month period. They found that all four IPT principles, and the meaning motive, were significant prospective predictors of residual change in perceived centrality, whereas the reverse effects were weaker and generally non-significant. In their five-wave study described earlier, Easterbrook and Vignoles (2012) showed that within-person changes in residence and flat identification could be predicted by contemporaneous changes in satisfaction of motivational principles. Interestingly, however, the two different identity aspects were linked to different sets of motivational principles: changes in identification with the broader social category of one's hall of residence were best predicted by satisfaction of motives for self-esteem, distinctiveness and meaning, whereas changes in identification with the interpersonal network group of one's flatmates were better predicted by satisfaction of motives for self-esteem, belonging and efficacy.

Furthermore, studies have begun to measure individual differences in motive strength, based on the strength of within-person associations between satisfaction of the various motivational principles and ratings of subjective identity structures. An advantage of this approach is that individuals are not necessarily aware of the patterning within their responses, circumventing the problems of demand characteristics and response biases inherent in explicit self-report measures. Although this area of research is in its infancy, some initial conclusions are emerging. First of all, studies show little convergence between these implicit measures and explicit self-reports of motive strength (Riketta, 2008). Secondly, implicit measures of different motives show interpretable associations with identity-related outcomes: for example, belonging motive strength uniquely predicts socially desirable responding (Thorpe, 2003) and is uniquely increased by ostracism salience (Kelly, 2004), whereas continuity motive strength is uniquely associated with lower willingness to consider cosmetic surgery (Vignoles and Deas, 2002).

These individual difference measures provide an opportunity to investigate which motivational principles are most involved (or most at stake) in particular identity-related outcomes. Thus, Vignoles and Moncaster (2007) studied correlational relationships between identity motives and national ingroup favoritism among British students. They found that ingroup favoritism was strongest among participants with higher national identification combined with a relatively strong motive for distinctiveness or belonging. In particular, higher identifiers with a stronger belonging motive tended to rate the British more favorably, whereas higher identifiers with a stronger distinctiveness motive tended to rate the Germans (a salient national outgroup) more negatively.

Manipulating motivational principles

Another way of establishing the non-redundancy of effects of motivational principles on identity processes is to use targeted manipulations, designed to affect specific motives rather than others. If effects of the motivational principles included in IPT are not reducible to each other, this should be detectable from patterns of (1) *specificity* and (2) *substitutability* of different kinds of coping responses to particular kinds of identity threats, depending on the motives that are involved. Thus, for example: (1) identity threats that undermine satisfaction of the distinctiveness principle should lead to coping strategies that aim to restore a sense of distinctiveness, but not to strategies that would only be relevant to restoring satisfaction of other motives; and (2) in situations when distinctiveness has been undermined, using a distinctiveness-maintenance strategy, but not using other identity-maintenance strategies, should reduce the need for subsequent distinctiveness-maintenance strategies.

Self-evaluation researchers have usually made little effort to distinguish which motives are undermined in manipulations of identity threat (often termed "ego threat"). Recently, Leary *et al.* (2009) discussed the need to clarify what exactly is threatened in "ego threat" manipulations, arguing that these manipulations often confound threat to self-esteem with threats to public image (belonging threat) or to feelings of competence and control (efficacy threat). Identifying these different kinds of threat paves the way for testing whether they lead to different kinds of coping responses. Following this reasoning, Knowles *et al.* (2010) reported four studies comparing responses to two different threat conditions, designed to undermine either belonging or intelligence; they understood the latter condition as a threat to "general self-esteem," although within IPT it would be viewed as a form of efficacy threat. Participants in the belonging threat condition were more likely to affirm identity aspects relevant to belonging, whereas participants in the intelligence threat condition were more likely to affirm identity aspects unrelated to intelligence. The researchers argued that the need for belonging is regulated separately from the need for self-esteem. This conclusion is consistent with their data, but is weakened by the fact that none of their studies included a no-threat control condition.

Social identity researchers commonly distinguish at least four different types of social identity threat: categorization threat (when a person is labeled based on their group membership against their will), distinctiveness threat (when distinctiveness of the ingroup from one or more relevant outgroups is undermined), value threat (when the competence or the morality of the ingroup is questioned) and acceptance threat (when the position of the individual within the group is insecure). Branscombe *et al.* (1999) have proposed that different kinds of threat will be associated with different sets of coping responses, depending also on individual differences in group identification. More recently, researchers have identified a fifth class of social identity threat: continuity threat, where the self-definition or future existence of the ingroup is perceived to be undermined by changes such as organizational mergers or immigration (Jetten and Hutchison, 2011; Jetten and Wohl, 2012; Smeekes *et al.*, 2011).

These various types of social identity threat are likely to be differentially frustrating to different motivational principles. Most obviously, distinctiveness threat, acceptance threat and continuity threat would be expected to frustrate motives for distinctiveness, belonging and continuity, respectively. Value threat would be expected to frustrate the self-esteem principle, but also the efficacy principle (if the focus is competence) or the belonging motive (if the focus is morality). Categorization threat is more complex, potentially undermining distinctiveness (if the individual is treated as an interchangeable category member), self-esteem (if the category is negatively valued), efficacy (if being viewed as a category member interferes with the individual's activities or desired goals) and/ or belonging (if the individual is rejected by others as a result of their category membership).

Nevertheless, studies to date have tended to focus on single threats and single coping strategies. Thus, they can provide only suggestive evidence for the specificity and the substitutability of links between particular threats and particular coping strategies. Of course, many coping strategies are relevant to more than one motivational principle: for example, an individual might discriminate against a salient outgroup to defend collective self-esteem or distinctiveness, or to affirm their belonging within the ingroup. Nonetheless, where a given coping strategy seems especially relevant to one motivational principle, IPT researchers could test whether this response is triggered especially by threats to that motive.

Studies could test the substitutability of relevant coping responses following threats to a given motivational principle. If the theorized principles are non-redundant, this suggests that coping strategies should be substitutable within the same motivational domain, but not across motives. Especially interesting would be studies into the substitutability of individual- and group-level coping strategies focused on the same motivational principle. Initial evidence comes from studies showing "trade-offs" between interpersonal and intergroup distinctiveness. Threats to individual distinctiveness can lead to increased identification with distinctive groups and tightening of group boundaries (Pickett *et al.*, 2002). Conversely, threats to group distinctiveness can lead some group members to differentiate themselves as individuals (Spears *et al.*, 1997).

The distinction of different types of threat in self-evaluation and social identity research provides a valuable opportunity to test more detailed predictions about which kinds of identity threat will lead to which coping responses, as well as how people will respond when more than one coping strategy is available – as in real-life situations of identity threat and coping. Studies of this kind would help to demonstrate further the nonredundancy of the motivational principles within the theory. Moreover, they would provide a basis for making more precise predictions about threat and coping in applied contexts.

Identity Process Theory and social representation processes

So far, I have aimed to describe and illustrate how various components of the original formulation of IPT can be operationalized in quantitative research: identity contents, structures, processes and the motivational principles that guide them. However, IPT has been extended subsequently with detailed theorizing about the relationship between identity and social representation processes (e.g. Breakwell, 1993, 2001, 2010). Even more than research into IPT, social representations research has typically encompassed a highly diverse range of methods (see Breakwell and Canter, 1993) and it would be impossible to do anything approaching justice here to the multitude of ways in which the two theories might be brought together empirically. Hence, I will restrict myself to illustrating some ways in which social representational ideas can be integrated into the study of identity processes using quantitative research methods. More extensive discussions of the use of quantitative methods in social representation research – which might be integrated with the methods described in this chapter – can be found elsewhere (e.g. Breakwell and Canter, 1993; Doise et al., 1993).

A first sense in which the two perspectives can be integrated is by viewing social representations as providing both a context and content for identity processes. Thus, while IPT describes the structures and processes of identity, the meanings of particular identity aspects are to a large extent socially defined and this may constrain the operation of identity processes (Breakwell, 2001). I will describe two studies examining the effects of social constructions of a particular identity category on attitudes toward social minorities, and a third study examining the effects of wider cultural values and beliefs on the operation of the distinctiveness principle.

Pehrson et al. (2009) analyzed survey data from thirty-one nations to test the prediction that different social constructions of nationhood place different constraints on the identity positions that individuals can occupy – specifically, how possible it is to identify strongly with one's nation while simultaneously holding positive attitudes toward immigrants. In nations where membership was defined to a greater extent in terms of shared language, national identification was correlated with negative attitudes toward immigrants (in these nations, either one could identify with the nation, or one could have a positive attitude toward immigrants); whereas in those nations where national membership was defined in terms of shared citizenship, no such correlation was found (in these nations, the social representational climate made it easier to identify strongly and yet also express positive attitudes toward immigrants). Using multi-level analysis, the authors demonstrated that it was the *average* definition of national membership prevailing in each nation, rather than participants' personal definitions of national membership, that moderated the relationship between national identification and attitudes toward immigrants. Thus, the results appeared to reflect a contextual constraint upon identity processes, irreducible to an individual level of explanation.

The salience of particular social constructions of an identity category can also be primed experimentally. Smeekes *et al.* (2011) tested the effect of priming a construction of Dutch identity as rooted in Christianity on attitudes toward expressive rights for Dutch Muslims. They reasoned that Muslim expressive rights would be seen as threatening to undermine the continuity of Dutch national identity when a Christian representation of Dutch national identity was made salient – leading to greater opposition toward expressive rights even among lower national identifiers. Although they did not measure perceived continuity threat, lower identifiers showed a comparable level of opposition to higher identifiers following a Christian-heritage prime, whereas higher identifiers typically showed greater opposition than lower identifiers when other constructions of Dutch national identity were primed.

Becker *et al.* (2012) sought to test claims that the distinctiveness principle may be stronger in individualist than in collectivist cultures (Triandis, 1995) against the alternative view that the distinctiveness principle should influence identity processes in all cultures, but would be satisfied in different ways depending on prevailing beliefs and values (Vignoles *et al.*, 2000). Using implicit measures of motive strength, they found that the distinctiveness motive was at least as strong in collectivist as in individualist cultures. However, distinctiveness was associated more strongly with difference and separateness in more individualist cultures and more strongly with social position in more collectivist cultures. Multilevel analysis confirmed that the prevailing beliefs and values in an individual's context, rather than the individual's own beliefs and values, accounted for these differences, suggesting that the emphasis on different sources of distinctiveness is a collective process, rather than an individual one.

A second focus for integrating IPT with Social Representations Theory is to explore the role of identity processes in generating, propagating and transforming social representations. Breakwell (2001, 2010) argues that it is especially important to study how individuals "personalize" the social representations that are available to them, depending on their social positions. What is the role of identity dynamics in individuals' internalization or resistance of particular social representations, or their use in communication?

Evidence for the role of identity dynamics in individuals' internalization or resistance of social representations comes from an experimental study by Breakwell *et al.* (2003) into young adolescents' perceptions of an imaginary girl and an imaginary boy who were portrayed either as liking or not liking science. The authors tested the extent to which participants reflected a social construction of science as "masculine" in their ratings of these imaginary targets. Results showed a small tendency for the female target to be rated as less feminine if she was portrayed as liking rather than not liking science. However, the effect was slightly reversed for the male target – he was rated as marginally *more* feminine if he was portrayed as liking science. Moreover, the de-feminized perception of the girl who liked science was strongest among girls in the sample who liked science less. Thus, far from reflecting the consensual application of a de-feminized social construction of science, it seemed that girls who did not like science were using this social construction selectively and strategically to claim superiority for their own identity position.

Evidence for the role of identity processes in people's communicative use of social representations comes from a study into adolescents' use of "status symbols" in self-presentation. Carr and Vignoles (2011) asked their participants to list ten possessions, to rate each possession for its "status value," and finally to choose five possessions to discuss in an anticipated interaction with another participant. Overall, participants chose especially those possessions that they had rated higher in status value, seemingly basing their communicative choices on the socially constructed meanings of the possessions. Moreover, this effect was stronger among those with greater identity insecurity, providing evidence for the role of identity concerns in the decision to utilize the social representation of certain possessions as status symbols in their self-presentational choices.

Although none of the studies reviewed in this section was explicitly framed in terms of integrating IPT with Social Representations Theory, they hopefully provide an idea of the considerable potential for future quantitative research in this area, illustrating various methods that can be used to explore and to test predictions from this rich area of ongoing theoretical synthesis and development.

Conclusions

I began this chapter commenting on the need for a visible body of quantitative research identifying and systematically testing the key theoretical claims of IPT and demonstrating its advantages over competing perspectives. I have described here studies that have tested some of the key predictions of the theory, but I have also identified some important predictions that to my knowledge have yet to be tested, while illustrating the range of quantitative methods that IPT researchers could use to conduct such research.

An important strength of IPT over many competing perspectives in the identity literature is its greater breadth and richness. Especially distinctive is its attention to issues of multiplicity within identity. IPT can be used to understand multiple kinds of identity content, multiple processes and multiple motivational principles. Correspondingly, it may be best addressed empirically using multiple methodological approaches. The methods I have reviewed can be used to test predictions about the personal and social processes involved in constructing, maintaining and defending a sense of identity. These methods treat identity as a "work in progress" and not as an essentialized "object" and so they are epistemologically compatible with many qualitative approaches to identity research (see Coyle and Murtagh, this volume). I hope that this chapter – and this volume – will contribute to further dialogue between identity researchers using qualitative and quantitative methods.

REFERENCES

Aquino, K., Freeman, D., Reed II, A., Lim, V. K. G., and Felps, W. (2009). Testing a social-cognitive model of moral behaviour: the interactive influence of situations and moral identity centrality. *Journal of Personality and Social Psychology*, 97, 123–141.

Batory, A. M. (2010). Diaologicality and the construction of identity. *International Journal for Dialogical Science*, 4(1), 45–66.

Becker, M., Vignoles, V. L., Owe, E., Brown, R., Smith, P. B., Easterbrook, M., … and Yamakoğlu, N. (2012). Culture and the distinctiveness motive: constructing identity in individualistic and collectivistic contexts. *Journal of Personality and Social Psychology*, 201, 833–855.

Becker, M., Vignoles, V. L., Owe, E., Easterbrook, M., Brown, R., Smith, P. B., … and Koller, S. H. (2013). *Cultural bases of self-evaluation: seeing oneself positively in different cultural contexts*. Manuscript submitted for publication, University of Sussex, UK.

Bonaiuto, M., Breakwell, G. M., and Cano, I. (1996). Identity processes and environmental threat: the effects of nationalism and local identity upon perception of beach pollution. *Journal of Community and Applied Social Psychology*, 6, 157–175.

Branscombe, N. R., Ellemers, N., Spears, R., and Doosje, B. (1999). The context and content of social identity threat. In N. Ellemers, R. Spears and B. Doosje (eds.), *Social identity: Context, commitment, content.* (pp. 35–58). Oxford: Blackwell.

Breakwell, G. M. (1978). Some effects of marginal social identity. In H. Tajfel (ed.), *Differentiation between social groups* (pp. 301–336). London: Academic Press.

Breakwell, G. M. (1979). Illegitimate group membership and inter-group differentiation. *British Journal of Social and Clinical Psychology*, 18, 141–149.

Breakwell, G. M. (1986a). *Coping with threatened identities*. London: Methuen.

Breakwell, G. M. (1986b). Political and attributional responses of the young short-term unemployed. *Political Psychology*, 7, 575–586.

Breakwell, G. M. (1987). Identity. In H. Beloff and A. Coleman (eds.), *Psychology Survey No. 6.* (pp. 94–114). British Psychological Society.

Breakwell, G. M. (1988). Strategies adopted when identity is threatened. *Revue Internationale de Psychologie Sociale*, 1, 189–203.

Breakwell, G. M. (1992). Identity and self-concept. In M. Banks, I. Bates, G.M. Breakwell, J. Bynner, N. Emler, L. Jamieson and K. Roberts (eds.), *Careers and Identities* (pp. 109–126). Buckingham, UK: Open University Press.

Breakwell, G. M. (1993). Social representations and social identity. *Papers on Social Representations*, 2, 198–217.

Breakwell, G. M. (2001). Social representational constraints upon identity processes. In K. Deaux and G. Philogene (eds.), *Representations of the social: bridging theoretical traditions* (pp. 271–284). Oxford: Blackwell.

Breakwell, G. M. (2010). Resisting representations and identity processes. *Papers on Social Representations*, 19, 6.1–6.11.

Breakwell, G. M., and Canter, D. V. (eds.) (1993). *Empirical approaches to social representations.* Oxford University Press.

Breakwell, G. M., Collie, A., Harrison, B., and Propper, C. (1984a). Attitudes towards the unemployed: effects of threatened identity. *British Journal of Social Psychology*, 23, 87–88.

Breakwell, G. M., Harrison, B., and Propper, C. (1984b). Explaining the psychological effects of unemployment for young people: the importance of specific situational factors. *British Journal of Guidance and Counselling*, 12, 132–140.

Breakwell, G. M., Vignoles, V. L., and Robertson, T. (2003). Stereotypes and crossed-category evaluations: the case of gender and science education. *British Journal of Psychology*, 94, 437–455.

Breakwell, G. M., and Weinberger, B. (1987). Young women in 'gender-atypical' jobs: the case of trainee technicians in the engineering industry. Department of Employment Research Reports (No. 49).

Cai, H., Sedikides, C., Gaertner, L., Wang, C., Carvallo, M., Xu, Y., O'Mara, E. M., and Jackson, L. E. (2011). Tactical self-enhancement in China: is modesty at the service of self-enhancement in East-Asian culture? *Social Psychological and Personality Science*, 2, 59–64.

Carr, H., and Vignoles, V. L. (2011). Keeping up with the Joneses: status projection as symbolic self-completion. *European Journal of Social Psychology*, 41, 518–527.

Cassidy, C., and Trew, K. (2001). Assessing identity change: a longitudinal study of the transition from school to college. *Group Processes and Intergroup Relations*, 4, 49–60.

Devos, T., Diaz, P., Viera, E., and Dunn, R. (2007). College education and motherhood as components of self-concept: discrepancies between implicit and explicit assessments. *Self and Identity*, 6, 256–277.

Doise, W., Clémence, A., and Lorenzi-Cioldi, F. (1993). *The quantitative analysis of social representations.* London: Harvester Wheatsheaf.

Droseltis, O., and Vignoles, V. L. (2010). Towards an integrative model of place identity processes: dimensionality and predictors of intrapersonal-level place preferences. *Journal of Environmental Psychology*, 30, 23–34.

Easterbrook, M., and Vignoles, V. L. (2012). Different groups, different motives: identity motives underlying changes in identification with novel groups. *Personality and Social Psychology Bulletin*, 38, 1,066–1,080.

Ethier, K. A., and Deaux, K. (1994). Negotiating social identity when contexts change: maintaining identification and responding to threat. *Journal of Personality and Social Psychology*, 67, 243–251.

Greenberg, J., Solomon, S., Pyszczynski, T., Rosenblatt, A., Burling, J., Lyon, D., Simon, L., and Pinel, E. (1992). Why do people need self-esteem? Converging evidence that self-esteem serves an anxiety-buffering function. *Journal of Personality and Social Psychology*, 63, 913–922.

Jaspal, R., and Cinnirella, M. (2010). Coping with potentially incompatible identities: accounts of religious, ethnic and sexual identities from British Pakistani men who identify as Muslim and gay. *British Journal of Social Psychology*, 49, 849–870.

Jetten, J., and Hutchison, P. (2011). When groups have a lot to lose: historical continuity enhances resistance to a merger. *European Journal of Social Psychology*, 41, 335–343.

Jetten, J., Postmes, T., and McAuliffe, B. J. (2002). "We're all individuals": group norms of individualism and collectivism, levels of identification and identity threat. *European Journal of Social Psychology*, 32, 189–207.

Jetten, J., and Wohl, M. J. A. (2012). The past as a determinant of the present: historical continuity, collective angst and opposition to immigrants. *European Journal of Social Psychology*, 42, 442–450.

Kelly, T. L. (2004). *Ostracism and identity motives*. Unpublished BSc dissertation, University of Sussex, Brighton, UK.

Knowles, M. L., Lucas, G. M., Molden, D. C., Gardner, W. L., and Dean, K. K. (2010). There's no substitute for belonging: self-affirmation following social and nonsocial threats. *Personality and Social Psychology Bulletin*, 36, 173–186.

Korf, L., and Malan, J. (2002). Threat to ethnic identity: the experience of White Afrikaans-speaking participants in post-apartheid South Africa. *Journal of Social Psychology*, 142, 149–169.

Kreuzbauer, R., Vignoles, V. L., and Chiu, C.-Y. (2009). *Motivational foundations of brand identification*. Unpublished manuscript, University of Illinois at Urbana Champaign, USA.

Kuhn, M. H., and McPartland, T. S. (1954). An empirical investigation of self-attitudes. *American Sociological Review*, 19, 68–76.

Leach, C. W., Van Zomeren, M., Zebel, S., Vliek, M., Pennekamp, S. F., Doosje, B., Ouwerkerk, J. W., and Spears, R. (2008). Collective self-definition and self-investment: a two-dimensional framework of group identification. *Journal of Personality and Social Psychology*, 95, 144–165.

Leary, M. R., Terry, M. L., Allen, A. B., and Tate, E. B. (2009). The concept of ego threat in social and personality psychology: in ego threat a viable scientific construct? *Personality and Social Psychology Review*, 13, 151–164.

Lynn, M., and Snyder, C. R. (2002). Uniqueness seeking. In C. R. Snyder and S. J. Lopez (eds.), *Handbook of positive psychology* (pp. 395–410). New York: Oxford University Press.

Manzi, C., Vignoles, V. L., and Regalia, C. (2010). Accommodating a new identity: possible selves, identity change and well-being across two life-transitions. *European Journal of Social Psychology*, 40, 970–984.

Manzi, C., Vignoles, V. L., Regalia, C., and Scabini, E. (2006). Cohesion and enmeshment revisited: differentiation, identity and psychological well-being in two European cultures. *Journal of Marriage and Family*, 68, 673–689.

Markowe, L. A. (1996). *Redefining the self: coming out as lesbian*. Cambridge: Polity Press.

Markus, H., and Kunda, Z. (1986). Stability and malleability of the self-concept. *Journal of Personality and Social Psychology*, 51, 858–866.

Markus, H. R., and Nurius, P. (1986). Possible selves. *American Psychologist*, 41, 954–969.

Martiny, S. E., Kessler, T., and Vignoles, V. L. (2012). Shall I leave or shall we fight? Effects of threatened group-based self-esteem on identity management strategies. *Group Processes and Intergroup Relations*, 15, 39–55.

McQuillen, A. D., Licht, M. H., and Licht, B. G. (2001). Identity structure and life satisfaction in later life. *Basic and Applied Social Psychology*, 23, 65–72.

Murtagh, N. (2009). *Voluntary occupation change: a social psychological investigation of experience and process*. Doctoral thesis, University of Surrey, UK.

Murtagh, N., Gatersleben, B., and Uzzell, D. (2012). Self-identity threat and resistance to change: evidence from regular travel behaviour. *Journal of Environmental Psychology*, 32, 318–326.

Ogilvie, D. M. (1987). Life satisfaction and identity structure in late middle-aged men and women. *Psychology and Aging*, 2, 217–224.

Pehrson, S., Vignoles, V. L., and Brown, R. (2009). National identification and anti-immigrant prejudice: individual and contextual effects of national definitions. *Social Psychology Quarterly*, 72, 24–38.

Pickett, C. L., Silver, M. D., and Brewer, M. B. (2002). The impact of assimilation and differentiation needs on perceived group importance and perceptions of ingroup size. *Personality and Social Psychology Bulletin*, 28, 546–568.

Reicher, S. (2000). Social identity definition and enactment: a broad SIDE against irrationalism and relativism. In T. Postmes, R. Spears, M. Lea and S. Reicher (eds.), *SIDE issues centre stage: recent developments in studies of de-individuation in groups* (pp. 175–190). Amsterdam: Royal Netherlands Academy of Arts and Sciences.

Reid, A., and Deaux, K. (1996). Relationship between social and personal identities: segregation or integration? *Journal of Personality and Social Psychology*, 71, 1,084–1,091.

Riketta, M. (2008). Who identifies with which group? The motive-feature match principle and its limitations. *European Journal of Social Psychology*, 38, 715–735.

Rosenberg, S., and Gara, M. A. (1985). The multiplicity of personal identity. In P. Shaver (ed.), *Review of personality and social psychology*, vol. 6 (pp. 87–113). Beverly Hills, CA: Sage.

Salvatore, J., and Prentice, D. (2011). The independence paradox. In J. Jetten and M. J. Hornsey (eds.), *Rebels in groups: dissent, deviance, difference and defiance* (pp. 201–218). Chichester, UK: Wiley-Blackwell.

Schimel, J., Pyszczynski, T., Greenberg, J., O'Mahen, H., and Arndt, J. (2000). Running from the shadow: psychological distancing from others to deny characteristics people fear in themselves. *Journal of Personality and Social Psychology*, 78, 446–462.

Sedikides, C., and Strube, M. J. (1997). Self-evaluation: to thine own self be good, to thine own self be sure, to thine own self be true and to thine own self be better. *Advances in Experimental Social Psychology*, 29, 209–269.

Serpe, R. T. (1987). Stability and change in self: a symbolic interactionist explanation. *Social Psychology Quarterly*, 50, 44–55.

Serpe, R. T., and Stryker, S. (2011). The symbolic interactionist perspective and identity theory. In S. J. Schwartz, K. Luyckx and V. L. Vignoles (eds.), *Handbook of identity theory and research* (pp. 225–248). New York: Springer.

Smeekes, A., Verkuyten, M., and Poppe, E. (2011). Mobilizing opposition towards Muslim immigrants: national identification and the representation of national history. *British Journal of Social Psychology*, 50, 265–280.

Smith, P. B. (2011). Cross-cultural perspectives on identity. In S. J. Schwartz, K. Luyckx and V. L. Vignoles (eds.), *Handbook of identity theory and research* (pp. 249–265). New York: Springer.

Spears, R. (2011). Group identities: the social identity perspective. In S. J. Schwartz, K. Luyckx and V. L. Vignoles (eds.), *Handbook of identity theory and research* (pp. 201–224). New York: Springer.

Spears, R., Doosje, B., and Ellemers, N. (1997). Self-stereotyping in the fact of threats to group status and distinctiveness: the role of group identification. *Personality and Social Psychology Bulletin*, 23, 538–553.

Straumann, T. J., Lemieux, A. M., and Coe, C. L. (1993). Self-discrepancy and natural killer cell activity: immunological consequences of negative self-evaluation. *Journal of Personality and Social Psychology*, 64, 1,042–1,052.

Swann Jr., W. B., (1983). Self-verification: bringing social reality into harmony with the self. In J. Suls and A. G. Greenwald (eds.), *Psychological perspectives on the self*, vol. II (pp. 33–66). Hillsdale, NJ: Lawrence Erlbaum.

Tajfel, H., and Turner, J. C. (1979). An integrative theory of intergroup conflict. In W. G. Austin and S. Worchel (eds.), *Social psychology of intergroup relations* (pp. 33–48). Monterey, CA: Brooks/Cole.

Tesser, A., Crepaz, N., Collins, J. C., Cornell, D., and Beach, S. R. H. (2000). Confluence of self-esteem regulation mechanisms: on integrating the self-zoo. *Personality and Social Psychology Bulletin*, 26, 1,476–1,489.

Thorpe, L. J. (2003). *Awareness of death: does this impact on the processes underlying identity?* BA dissertation, University of Sussex, Brighton, UK.

Triandis, H. C. (1995). *Individualism and collectivism*. Boulder, CO: Westview Press.

Trzesniewski, K. H., Donnellan, M. B., and Robins, R. W. (2003). Stability of self-esteem across the lifespan, *Journal of Personality and Social Psychology*, 84, 205–220.

Turner, J. C., Hogg, M. A., Oakes, P. J., Reicher, S. D., and Wetherell, M. S. (1987). *Rediscovering the social group: a self-categorization theory*. Cambridge, MA: Blackwell.

Vignoles, V. L. (2000). *Identity, culture and the distinctiveness principle*. Ph.D. thesis, University of Surrey, UK.

Vignoles, V. L. (2011). Identity motives. In S. J. Schwartz, K. Luyckx and V. L. Vignoles (eds.), *Handbook of identity theory and research* (pp. 403–432). New York: Springer.

Vignoles, V. L. and 76 members of the Culture and Identity Research Network (2013). *Evidence for the cross-cultural generality of identity motives*. Manuscript in preparation, University of Sussex, UK.

Vignoles, V. L., Chryssochoou, X., and Breakwell, G. M. (2000). The distinctiveness principle: identity, meaning, and the bounds of cultural relativity. *Personality and Social Psychology Review*, 4, 337–354.

Vignoles, V. L., Chryssochoou, X., and Breakwell, G. M. (2002). Evaluating models of identity motivation: self-esteem is not the whole story. *Self and Identity*, 1, 201–218.

Vignoles, V. L., and Deas, C. (2002, September). *Appearance related negative health behaviours and identity motives*. Paper presented at the Annual Conference of the British Psychological Society Social Psychology Section, University of Huddersfield, UK.

Vignoles, V. L., Dittmar, H. E., Langton, T. A. D., Wright, A. E., and Anderson, N. (2007, September). *The material self: identity motives and the symbolic value of material possessions*. Paper presented at the Annual Conference of the British Psychological Society Social Psychology Section, Canterbury, UK.

Vignoles, V. L., Manzi, C., Regalia, C., Jemmolo, S., and Scabini, E. (2008). Identity motives underlying desired and feared possible future selves. *Journal of Personality*, 76, 1,165–1,200.

Vignoles, V. L., and Moncaster, N. (2007). Identity motives and in-group favouritism: a new approach to individual differences in intergroup discrimination. *British Journal of Social Psychology*, 46, 91–113.

Vignoles, V. L., Regalia, C., Manzi, C., Golledge, J., and Scabini, E. (2006). Beyond self-esteem: influence of multiple motives on identity construction. *Journal of Personality and Social Psychology*, 90, 308–333.

Vignoles, V. L., Schwartz, S. J., and Luyckx, K. (2011). Introduction: toward an integrative view of identity. In S. J. Schwartz, K. Luyckx and V. L. Vignoles (eds.), *Handbook of identity theory and research* (pp. 1–27). New York: Springer.

Wylie, R. C. (1974). *The self-concept: a review of methodological considerations and measuring instruments*, vol. I. Lincoln: University of Nebraska Press.

Part III

Integrating theoretical frameworks

5   On the meaning, validity and importance of the distinction between personal and social identity: a social identity perspective on Identity Process Theory

Samuel Pehrson and Stephen Reicher

At first glance, Identity Process Theory (IPT) seems to have a great deal in common with the Social Identity Approach (SIA). Both perspectives share, for example, an appreciation of the multiplicity and fluidity of identity, its embeddedness in broader socio-historical contexts and its centrality to processes of representation and social change. Both perspectives, also, have appealed to researchers seeking to resist the overwhelming tendency for much of psychology (whether in North America, Europe or elsewhere) to reduce social phenomena to de-contextualized mechanisms operating within individual minds. Indeed, SIA and IPT scholars often pursue complementary programs of research and have, to some extent, a common agenda.

Our emphasis in this contribution, however, is on difference rather than similarity. Efforts toward theoretical integration such as that undertaken in this volume are commendable. However, such efforts should not come at the expense of conceptual clarity with regard to the particularities of existing perspectives. We do not want to end up with what Engels once memorably described as "a pauper's broth of eclecticism." Thus, we aim to elucidate what we see as particular insights offered by the SIA and to highlight how these differ from the approach taken by IPT. The SIA comprises Self-Categorization Theory (SCT), Social Identity Theory (SIT) and a number of other theoretical extensions, although our main focus in this chapter is SCT. We cannot, of course, do justice to the full scope of either approach, nor to the large empirical literature each has generated (for recent reviews, see Haslam *et al.*, 2010a, 2010b; Reicher *et al.*, 2010. For a collection of classic articles, see Postmes and Branscombe, 2010). Instead, we concentrate on exploring the implications of one key

The authors thank Vivian Vignoles for his helpful comments on an early draft of this chapter. In particular, the use of the labels "content distinction" and "framing distinction" to clarify our argument are his suggestion.

point: that concerning the concept of social identity itself. Specifically, we will argue that understanding how social identity, as distinct from personal identity, underpins psychological group formation is absolutely indispensable to a social psychology of identity, social action and social change.

Personal versus social identity: two perspectives

If there is one particularly well-known fact about the SIA, it is probably that this family of theories posits that we all possess social identity based on our group memberships on the one hand, and personal identity relating to our individuality on the other. Yet, the implications of this apparently straightforward proposition are often misunderstood. Furthermore, the usefulness of the distinction between personal and social identity is questioned by key presentations of IPT, in which the "distinction between social and personal identity is abandoned" (Breakwell, 2001, p. 227) and rejected as a "misleading detour" (Breakwell, 1986, p. 18). This appears to mark a crucial point of difference between the two approaches that merits closer inspection.

In addressing these contrasting perspectives on the distinction between personal and social identity, let us consider some background to Tajfel's notion of social identity in early accounts of SIT. Many readers will be familiar with the following routinely quoted definition of social identity given by Tajfel (1978): "For the purpose of this discussion, social identity will be understood as that part of an individual's self-concept which derives from his [sic] knowledge of his membership of a social group (or groups) together with the value and emotional significance attached to that membership" (p. 63). Less often quoted, however, are the sentences that immediately follow: "It will be clear that this is a limited definition of 'identity' or 'social identity.' This limitation is deliberate and it has two aims. The first is not to enter into endless and often sterile discussions as to what 'is' identity. The second is to enable us to use this limited concept in the discussions of theory and research which follow" (p. 63).

Thus, it is clear that Tajfel had no interest here in developing a comprehensive theory of "identity" per se. Rather, as he went on to explain, his concern was specifically with understanding intergroup behavior and social change. He was interested in identity insofar as it was instrumental to that goal. Tajfel's most fundamental contention in this work was that, in order to understand intergroup phenomena such as conflict, stereotyping and prejudice, one needs a theoretical perspective that not does assume people to be "randomly interacting individual particles" (Tajfel, 1972, p. 16) and that instead recognizes that they can act on the basis of understanding themselves as group members. For this reason, the notion of social identity was brought into play: people know that they belong to some groups and not to others and this matters to them. Awareness that one is part of a collective allows one to act as part of a collective, and this point is crucial to any convincing account of social change: an issue of paramount concern to Tajfel along with many of his European contemporaries (Israel *et al.*, 1972; see also de la Sablonnière and Usborne, this volume). The notion of "*social* identity" in this early work, defined in terms of group membership, brackets off broader questions about self and identity from those that are directly about the way certain aspects of our identity connect us to others through group membership and therefore underpin intergroup behavior.

SIT, then, is a theory of intergroup relations rather than a theory of self and identity, and we find no specification of the relationship between personal and social identity in Tajfel's work. It is in SCT that the notion of social identity is fleshed out and integrated into a broader and more comprehensive theory of the self and the social group (Turner, 1999; Turner *et al.*, 1987) and where the nature and importance of the distinction between personal and social identity is more thoroughly theorized and explored. It is therefore SCT that will be principal focus in this chapter, even though SIT might appear to have more in common with IPT in certain respects (such as the specification of motivational aspects and on various kinds of identity threat). It is interesting to note that IPT is described as an attempt to replace the "black box" model of identity in Tajfel's work with a more comprehensive theory of identity (Breakwell, 1993). This alone is reason to contrast it with SCT, particularly given that IPT abandons the notion of social identity as conceptually distinct from personal identity.

SCT conceptualizes identity in terms of self-categories that are generated through social interaction. Self-categories are "social contextual definitions of the perceiver" (Turner *et al.*, 1994, p. 458) in that they represent the perceiver in relation to others and do so fluidly in line with the perceiver's changing social reality. At different times a person may self-categorize more as a unique individual, distinguishing between "me" and "not me" (personal identity), or as a group member, distinguishing between "us" and "them" (social identity). Moreover, different groups that individuals belong to become the basis for self-categorization (i.e. become salient) at different times, depending on the immediate context and frame of reference.

Individual and group are different levels of abstraction at which self-categorization may occur throughout the course of this ongoing variation (Turner *et al.*, 1987; Turner *et al.*, 1994). Both are cognitive representations of the perceiver's social relationships generated through an interaction between the social world and the principles of normative and comparative fit. Detailed accounts of these principles can be found elsewhere (e.g. Turner, 1999, Turner and Reynolds, 2001) but, in short, comparative fit maximizes what is called the "meta-contrast ratio" (the extent to which a category maximizes between-category differences and within-category similarities in a given frame of reference), while normative fit refers to the extent to which between-category differences are congruent with expectations, stereotypes and so forth about the groups involved. Both personal and social identity, then, are "social" in a broad sense: they are contextually generated, relational, interpretations of self (Turner et al., 1994).

The distinction that SCT draws between different levels of inclusiveness or abstraction at which self-categorization takes place should not be confused with one between identity "elements" (Vignoles et al., 2006) that are based on group labels ("female," "Scottish") on the one hand and those that refer to traits or idiosyncratic descriptors of an individual ("tall," "big-eared") on the other. The latter could be termed a *content* distinction, which is different from the *framing* distinction that is emphasized by SCT (Turner et al., 1994). "Scottish," for example, may serve to categorize either a group (in contrast to other groups) or an individual (in contrast to other individuals) depending on the frame of reference. Though referring to group membership, as part of a constellation of identity elements (e.g. Scottish, female, young, short sighted, British, Dundee United supporter), "Scottish" informs a representation of "me" in contrast to others. Similarly, as Simon (1997) points out, almost any attribute could function hypothetically as a group-level self-categorization. For example, wearing spectacles could do so if it became a signifier of a dangerous intellectualism that merits persecution. Thus, any of a person's numerous characteristics may become the basis for either personal or social identity, depending on how they position that person in relation to others in a particular social reality and how these social positions and relationships interact with the principles of comparative and normative fit. In this vein, it has been argued that the collective self involves a single self-aspect becoming dominant, while personal identity entails the combination of many such aspects into a unique configuration (Simon, 1997, 2004). The diminution in salience of all but one aspect corresponds to a representation of self in which intra-category differences become secondary to intra-category similarities. In contrast, a configuration of many self-aspects specifies the individual as unique, corresponding to personal identity.

Early accounts of SCT imply a variable activation of stored categories within a hierarchically organized cognitive structure, that is, a "self-concept," with different categories being activated in turn as the social environment changes (e.g. Turner *et al.*, 1987). However, subsequent accounts of SCT dispense with the notion of an enduring self-concept by arguing explicitly that self-categorization is an ongoing interpretative process rather than a "switching on" of stored categories (e.g. Turner *et al.*, 1994). In SCT, then, self can be defined as situated, reflexive cognition rather than as an enduring cognitive structure.

This does not mean that we simply forget about categorizations that are no longer salient, nor does it deny that some categories have more prior importance and meaning to some people than to others. People do not engage in every moment of categorization with total amnesia and detachment (Reicher *et al.*, 2010). These points are represented in SCT by the notion of "perceiver readiness" (sometimes referred to as "accessibility"), which constitutes all the factors from the perceiver's side that constrain categorization in a given context (Turner, 1999; Turner *et al.*, 1987, 1994). The concept of perceiver readiness has rarely been fully unpacked in SCT, because the main concern of the theory is with how categorization is responsive to contemporaneous social reality and the role of social identity in group processes. Perceiver readiness is more linked to one's history of social relations, although perhaps the various identity motives that have been proposed over the years (for an overview, see Vignoles *et al.*, 2006) including the "identity principles" included in IPT could help explain what elements of the past are retained for the present. That is, elements that satisfy an individual's motives for distinctiveness, continuity and so forth may be more likely to retain chronic importance and thus be more "accessible" in the categorization process.

Still, whatever cognitive structures, processes and motives underlie self-categorization, these are not "self" or "identity" in SCT terms unless and until they function as self-categories in context. In other words, self is defined functionally rather than structurally: what qualifies a given cognition as self is its reflexive quality, i.e. being a representation of the perceiver, rather than whether it arises from a particular kind of mental activity or resides within a particular knowledge structure (Turner *et al.*, 1994, 2006).

This understanding contrasts markedly with IPT, in which "identity structure" is a core theoretical construct (Breakwell, 1986, 2001). Identity structure comprises a content dimension, consisting of an array of self-defining attributes ("identity elements") organized hierarchically and in terms of their relative centrality and so forth, as well as a value dimension, which refers to the positive or negative value associated with each of these elements. IPT emphasizes that these identity elements, their organization and their valence undergo revision throughout the lifespan as a result of changing social structures and social influence.

It is this identity structure and the "identity processes" through which such revision takes place that together constitute "identity" in IPT terms (Breakwell, 1986). Thus, identity is conceived as an enduring cognitive structure that moves through time, subject to development and change along the way. In short, in IPT, particular cognitive structures and processes constitute identity (Breakwell, 1986), while for SCT, the cognitive system as a whole functions to produce identities in context (Turner et al., 1994).

This theoretical difference may seem arcane, but it has some important corollaries. Not least, it helps us to understand why IPT views the theoretical distinction between personal and social identity to be ultimately unsustainable, while in SCT it is crucial. When conceptualized as a person's defining properties held within a cognitive structure, personal and social identity elements indeed cannot be straightforwardly distinguished because the distinction depends not on the elements themselves (a content distinction), but on the abstractness of categories in context (a framing distinction). Because SCT defines identity in terms of situated interpretations of self (as "me" or "us"), rather than as elements of a stored self-concept, the framing distinction does not depend on a content distinction: a point that has become clearer as the specification of SCT has developed (e.g. Simon, 1997; Turner, 1994 et al.). Thus, Breakwell's (1986) critique of the *content* distinction between personal and social identity does not require us to discard the *framing* distinction that unpins the Social Identity Approach. It is within SCT's functional conception of identity, rather than IPT's structural conception, that the distinction between personal and social identity is valid.

But why insist on the conceptual distinction between personal and social identity if these are merely different levels of inclusiveness at which the on-going process of self-categorization can occur? Our answer entails two related arguments. First of all, it is social identity, not personal identity, that makes group behavior possible (Turner, 1982). Secondly, understanding group processes is indispensable to understanding society. These arguments are not new, having been made throughout the history of the SIA (Reicher et al., 2010). However, our aim in the remainder of this chapter is to bring together and explicate their implications for the main focus of this volume: identity, social action and social change.

Social identity makes group behavior possible

SCT's account of the consequences of social identity salience begins with the notion of depersonalization, which is the process whereby people come to perceive themselves and others more in terms of their group membership and less in terms of their individuality (Turner et al., 1987). This entails a perceptual shift in that category members are seen as more similar to one another and more different from outgroup members, than is the case when personal identity is salient. This also means that we see group members, including ourselves, in terms of the characteristics and norms associated with that category – a process referred to as self-stereotyping – and that we will seek to conform to these norms. It is through these processes of depersonalization and self-stereotyping that some level of behavioral uniformity can emerge, although of course this uniformity will rarely be total. There is no claim that members' awareness of their individually or differences between them are obliterated by self-categorization as a group member – although the differences that interest people in such circumstances are those which relate to group concerns. To what extent do people accord with group norms? Such a focus is associated with increasing conformity to group norms.

Of course, conformity to norms would not lead to collective behavior unless those norms really are shared between group members. We therefore need to ask how group members arrive at a common understanding of what is normative within the group and what kind of action should follow from this. According to SCT, group members are not only interested in but also expect to agree on matters that are relevant to the group, so depersonalization introduces a dynamic toward seeking consensus (Turner, 1991). Thus, we look to fellow ingroup members in order to validate our own perspective. And, in particular, we look to prototypical members of the group because it is their judgments and actions that should be most indicative of how group members in general should respond (Haslam et al., 2011).

The group prototype here is not some fixed essence or set of traits that somehow resides either within the group or as an inflexible stereotype in the minds of its members. Category prototypes are generated in context not only intra- but also inter-psychically: through debate and discussion. And the balance of discussion is responsive to features of that context. A particularly striking example of this can be found in crowd research; where the relationship between a crowd and the police is antagonistic, it is the most confrontational members of the crowd who are seen as prototypical and therefore influential (Reicher, 1996). Conversely, where police are able to position themselves as facilitators of legitimate goals of the crowd (such as to hold a demonstration or enjoy a football match) then confrontational individuals or subgroups within the crowd will be viewed as peripheral and hence unable to influence others (Stott et al., 2007). Prototypicality, then, is a function of the wider intergroup context within which the categories are embedded.

The idea that social identity salience opens the door to these processes of social influence, rather than mechanistically activating stored attributes in a person's head as in social cognition theories of the self (e.g. McConnell, 2011), is crucial to understanding how the SIA views a range of social phenomena.

A further piece of the jigsaw in accounting for how social identity makes group behavior possible concerns solidarity. To the extent that people share a social identity, they will be more inclined to act in cooperation and support of one another (Haslam *et al.*, 2011a) and also to develop organization and leadership which ensures effective and efficient coordination (Haslam *et al.*, 2011b). In short, social identity is at the root of the processes that turn an aggregation of individuals into psychological group: people who have a shared view of reality, who work toward the same goals and who assist and cooperate with one another.

There may be further pieces still to be developed. For instance there is emerging evidence that shared social identity may not only accentuate the factors which allow people to come together and coordinate their activities but also attenuate the factors which keep people apart and impede co-action. At the very simplest levels, social identity overcomes the barriers of personal space (Novelli *et al.*, 2010). As our on-going research suggests, it may do this by lessening one's disgust at the smells and secretions of ingroup members. We have not yet exhausted the ways in which shared social identity makes group behavior possible (Turner, 1982; Turner *et al.*, 1987).

Identity, social action and social change

To bring together the points that we have discussed so far, the processes described by SCT lead us to a view of social identity as being simultaneously a *product* of our social reality – our lived social relations – and a *means to shape* that reality. Categorization is not merely a way to interpret one's social world, to simplify it in some way or to satisfy individual psychological needs. Rather, it has the potential to transform social relations. Categorization can therefore be seen as a way of acting on the world, directed toward future desired realities (Reicher and Hopkins, 2001a, 2001b). This dynamic, bi-directional relationship between categorization and social reality has broad implications for the study of social action and social change. As we aim to show in the eight points below, the processes flowing from self-categorization as "us" rather than as "me" are at the heart of a number of key issues that any social psychology of social action and social change must address. As a result of discarding these, we argue, IPT will struggle to expand from its concern with personal change to a consideration of collective social change (see de la Sablonnière and Usborne, this volume).

Identity links social structure to social action

The first point is foundational to the social identity tradition as initiated by Tajfel in his Social Identity Theory (Tajfel, 1978; Tajfel and Turner, 1979). Put simply, identity is what enables us to act in terms of our social position, because it is a representation of ourselves in social relations. Thus, feeling and acting in terms of group membership is underpinned by an interpretation of oneself as a member of a group in relation to other groups. This means that intergroup relations, whether they are relations of conflict, hierarchy or cooperation, become something that matter to us.

The SIA is not the only perspective in social psychology to recognize the significance of group memberships and intergroup relations in underpinning human experience and action. Other notable examples include Realistic Group Conflict Theory (Esses et al., 1998; Sherif et al., 1961) and Social Dominance Theory (Pratto et al., 2006; Sidanius and Pratto, 1999). However, these tend to assume that sociological categories and designations are equivalent to social identities, with no examination of the social processes through which the former lead to the latter. Researchers working from an IPT perspective, too, have incorporated groups into their theorizing and similarly seem to adhere to an instrumental model of groups, whereby groups are structural entities entailing various kinds of interdependence between their members (e.g. Breakwell, 1993; Lyons, 1996). From this point of view, groups and intergroup relations are seen as part of the structural backdrop that shapes identity processes, while mobilization is understood as one of the coping strategies people use to deal with threatened identities. We would argue, however, that emergent properties of groups, including norms, collective memory, group interests and intergroup relations entail a discontinuity between individual and group behavior that cannot be understood without the very distinction between personal and social identity that IPT discards (Breakwell, 1986, 2001). Without a mechanism for the emergence of psychological groups, one is left with only the extremes of Allportian individualism (whereby groups are the mere aggregation of individual psychology and interpersonal relations) on the one hand, or some variant of the "group mind" thesis on the other (see Asch, 1952).

In contrast, this longstanding question of the emergence of group behavior is precisely what SCT was developed to address (Turner et al., 1987). It is self-categorization that makes the difference, for example, between a category of individuals who are subjugated in the same way and a *group* whose members have a shared understanding of this common subjugation and represent themselves as a group on that basis. It mirrors the famous Hegelian and Marxist distinction between the group in itself and the group for itself. The question of how the transition from the former to the latter occurs is the critical issue of not only psychology but also politics – and perhaps explains why the SIA has proved so successful beyond the boundaries of academic psychology (Haslam *et al.*, 2010b).

Only where a structural position becomes a self-representation can it lead to a sense of group interest and collective action. The concepts of "group" and "group interests" that are so fundamental to all theories of intergroup relations are therefore inseparable from social identity. The argument is not that social identity processes lead to something other than self-interest: it is that self has to be defined before one can even have interests (see Hopkins and Kahani-Hopkins, 2004).

Power is a dynamic product of social identity processes

In turn, the ability to exert one's will through others by influencing or controlling them depends on psychological group formation (Turner, 2005). Turner describes three ways that this can happen: first of all, convincing others that a judgment or course of action is correct (persuasion) is a process of social influence whereby people look to prototypical group members to infer norms and consensual judgments of the group (Turner, 1991). Secondly, group norms are needed to confer legitimate authority on particular positions and individuals, so that people can be directed without necessarily being persuaded. Thirdly, the use of rewards and punishments to coerce those who do not accept one's authority usually still depends on persuasion and authority at least to some degree, because it requires the cooperation of coercive agents and forms of social organization through which rewards and punishments are administered. This puts social identity and group formation at the heart of the operation of power, because the definition and content of social categories will determine who is prototypical and therefore persuasive, as well as who is able to wield legitimate authority (Haslam *et al.*, 2011b; Turner, 2005). This in turn moves us away from overly deterministic conceptions of social power (Reicher, 2004). In contrast, as we elaborate on below in the section "The psychological group enables shared knowledge," by rejecting the distinction between personal and social identity, IPT lacks the conceptual tools necessary for an adequate theorization of power and social influence.

*Category definitions shape those who can be mobilized and the limits
of collective solidarity*

As we have seen, people act as a group when they self-categorize as a
group. This means that the way in which a particular category is defined,
in terms of who is clearly included within it and who is not, will affect the
scope of mobilization. It has been noted frequently that national categories in particular can be defined in multiple ways, giving rise to a range of
exclusive and inclusive national definitions depending on the criteria that
are seen as necessary to count as a national group member (e.g. Pehrson
and Green, 2010). The extent to which people feel committed to a national
group and work toward its goals will therefore depend on whether they
have what are seen to be the necessary criteria for belonging. In Wales, for
example, being unable to speak Welsh is associated with lower identification as Welsh and less support for Welsh political autonomy compared to
people who are fluent Welsh speakers (Livingstone *et al.*, 2011; study 1).
This pattern is strongest in predominantly Welsh-speaking areas, where
language ability is a more important criterion for inclusion in the national
group (study 2). The definition of category boundaries therefore shapes
the scope of mobilization (see also Reicher and Hopkins, 2001a, 2001b).

The inclusiveness of categorization also shapes the scope of group solidarity; that is, definitions of who else belongs in the category will inform
who is able to benefit from group members' cooperation and assistance.
A particularly powerful illustration of this can be found in the example
of Bulgarian resistance to the deportation of Jews during the Nazi period
(Reicher *et al.*, 2006). Bulgaria was unusual among the countries occupied by the Nazis in that attempts to deport Jewish people and transport
them to the death camps largely failed because of collective opposition
to the practice by Bulgarians. Examination of letters and speeches produced at the time by political and religious leaders reveal the extent to
which the population was addressed in terms that stressed the identity
of the Jews as fellow Bulgarians, deserving of Bulgarian help and solidarity. Experimental work also supports the claim that the inclusiveness of
national group definitions affects the extent to which group members
offer assistance to someone in need, depending on whether the definition includes that person as a fellow ingroup member or not (Wakefield
et al., 2011).

Category content shapes how *group members can be mobilized*

While the inclusiveness of social categories shapes who can be mobilized as a category member, the content of the categories – in particular,

the norms associated with them – shape what they can be mobilized to do. As we have said, group norms are not stored behavioral schemas or static group essences: they are generated in context. Of course, leaders and others do not have total freedom to construe anything they like as being normative of the group. One would have a hard time convincing a crowd of Scotland supporters at a football match to cheer for England, for example. Clearly, most of the groups that matter to us have histories, common understandings of their central values and so forth. However, these do not work like a script that determines action, but rather as the raw material from which different actions, goals, projects and so forth can be construed as either a way of realizing the group identity or as a subversion of it (Reicher and Hopkins, 2001b).

Research on the issue of voting among British Muslims illustrates this clearly. Analysis of material coming from debates about whether or not Muslims should participate in UK elections demonstrates how voting in a non-Muslim country could be characterized by groups with an anti- or pro-participation position as either forbidden or as a duty for Muslims (Hopkins and Kahani-Hopkins, 2004). Crucially, arguments for *both* positions drew examples from the life of the Prophet in order to construe their position not only as "right" in a general sense, but as an authentic expression of what it means to be a Muslim. Thus, while quite opposite norms were constructed regarding participation in the election, these norms could not be simply plucked out of thin air, but instead had to be grounded in something of authority for Muslims: Prophetic example. These norms were therefore constrained by the existing meanings and history of the group involved, while at the same time involving agency and creativity on the part of those seeking to mobilize British Muslims in a certain way. Similarly, national leaders draw flexibly on national history, heroes, stereotypes and even physical geography in order to construct versions of national identity that are consistent with their political projects (Reicher and Hopkins, 2001b).

Different ways of defining ingroup categories can also give rise to different perceptions of threat constituted by outgroups. For example, essentialist or racialized definitions of national ingroup are integral to a "defensive" racism in which immigration is construed as an existential threat (Hopkins *et al.*, 1997; see also Barker, 1981; Gilroy, 1987). Thus, "ethnic" national ingroup definitions are associated with a stronger relationship between national identification and hostility toward asylum seekers (Pehrson *et al.*, 2009a; see also Pehrson *et al.*, 2009b). Or, to take another example, certain idyllic constructions of the countryside as integral to British identity support an interpretation of a foxhunting ban as an attack on British nationhood itself (Wallwork and Dixon, 2004). All of this means that consequences of social identity processes are contingent on particular meanings and definitions of social categories. One cannot make generic claims about what kind of behavior such processes will produce in isolation from these meanings.

The representation of social categories is an arena for struggles to shape the future

That the representation of social categories plays a purposeful and functional role in intergroup relations has been central to the SIA since the formulation of SIT (Tajfel, 1978; Tajfel and Turner, 1979). For example, Tajfel (1978) describes the social functions of stereotypes, such as explaining and legitimizing hierarchical intergroup relations. Similarly, the social mobility and social change belief systems, comprising perceptions of stability, legitimacy and permeability, are viewed as a function of a "shifting pattern of social contexts, ideologies, beliefs and attitudes in a constantly changing social environment" (p. 267). Thus, the SIA has always emphasized that the operation of social identity processes are contingent on shared representations of social reality. Indeed, attempts to extract de-contextualized psychological mechanisms from the framework (such as ingroup favoritism, for example) have encountered conceptual and empirical difficulties precisely because they ignore the interactionist metatheory of the approach (Oakes, 2002; Reicher, 2004; Turner, 1999).

The arguments we have described above about the role of social categories for leadership, power and social influence build on SIT by contributing toward a more sophisticated account of how social representations can be "world-making," shaping the future as well as reflecting the past and present (Elcheroth et al., 2011). Because of this world-making potential, we can expect the meanings and definitions of social categories to be struggled over, as different category constructions are associated with different agendas to shape group behavior in certain ways. There is no single way that a given social reality will inevitably be categorized. This makes the construction and contestation of categories of paramount importance to both social stability and social change.

The psychological group enables shared knowledge

The acceptance or rejection of social representations by group members has been explored from an IPT perspective by Breakwell (1993), who suggests that groups shape the apparent credibility of sources of information as well as rendering individuals susceptible to group pressures such as the threat of censure and rejection. At a descriptive level, these points are uncontroversial. However, because the IPT account is not grounded in a theory of social influence, its utility in addressing these issues is limited. For example, the notion that "acceptance" may be a means of avoiding censure by the group as well as a result of judging information sources to be credible ignores a critical distinction between persuasion and control, which, whilst formulated in a number of ways, can be found throughout the social influence literature (for reviews, see Turner, 1991, 2005). In contrast, because the SIA incorporates a distinctive understanding of social influence, it provides a helpful basis for addressing how both consensus and divergence are produced through group processes. As we have explained, to the extent that a social identity is salient, group members expect those with whom they share a social identity to agree with them and will actively seek such agreement (Turner, 1991). Self-categorization renders group members responsive to norms, which guide group members as to both what to believe (e.g. "capitalism is immoral") and *who* to believe (e.g. "doctors are an appropriate source of medical advice").

The SCT account does not imply that conformity is inevitable. For example, some individuals may not share a social identity with the majority. They may self-categorize in terms of a dissenting subgroup, for example. This is where it becomes vital to distinguish groups as part of the structural context (as in IPT) on the one hand from psychological groups on the other. Where there is a failure to establish consensus through persuasion alone, control and coercion may enforce some level of conformity, but this risks further diminishing any possibility of persuasion because the arbitrary use of coercion undermines shared identity (Turner, 2005). Meanwhile, group members who do not conform may seek to establish a new consensus through minority influence, by depicting themselves and their position as more prototypical and consonant with high-order norms than that of the majority (Turner, 1991).

In short, psychological group formation underlies the emergence of consensual ways of interpreting and representing the world as well as the means by which majority positions are resisted. Without the notions of social identity and depersonalization that underlie this, IPT runs the danger of accounting for social influence primarily in terms of individual "needs" being met by the group (e.g. a need for information or a need to avoid censure) and treating intra-group power relations as structural givens. Within this kind of "dependency" conception of social influence, there is a unidirectional flow of influence from the knowledgeable and powerful to the ignorant and powerless and social change becomes barely conceivable (see Turner, 1991, 2005).

Social representations are a source of stability in self-categorization and social relations

Because of its emphasis on the contextual variability and fluidity of self-categorization, the Social Identity Approach (particularly SCT) has been portrayed as failing to grasp the enduring importance of certain social identities, such as ethnicity and nationality, or the weight of history in shaping their meaning (Huddy, 2001). To speak of identities being "stable" or not, however, really depends of the kind of timescale that one has in mind. The salience of one's nationality, for example, might vary substantially over just a few minutes of watching the evening news. However, over longer periods of time, it is much more stable as nationality retains its potential to become salient whenever it fits the context. If asked one's nationality every year, one will probably keep giving the same answer (or at least a very limited range of possible answers), so it is stable in that sense. Across the lifespan, it could change, especially if one emigrates. Then again, if we are interested in a macro-level of analysis and consider time periods spanning several generations, we may find some continuity in some national identities, but also significant transformation in their prevalence and meaning. Therefore, to discuss whether identities are stable or variable in the abstract is meaningless. We need to be more specific. We also need to distinguish between theoretical and empirical variability (Turner *et al.*, 1994).

The flux described in SCT refers to the process, not the outcome, of self-categorization. There is no reason why a fluid self-categorization process cannot produce stable self-categories to the extent that the context itself is stable and completely different sources of contextual stability are relevant at micro- and macro-contextual levels and timeframes. To put it slightly differently, if there is fixity in group representations (e.g. stereotypes) it should be understood as deriving from fixities in our social system and not (mis)used to suggest that people have fixed cognitive systems.

We live in a world constituted by socially constructed categories such as gender, ethnicity, "race," nationality and so forth, along with the various institutions and practices that enact and concretize these categories. Ethnicity is a social fact, in that it is a function of other people believing that we have an ethnicity and acting on that basis (Searle, 1995). The practices and institutions that designate people as having particular ethnicities and continue to treat them as such over time could be described as "structural," but we need to take care in what we mean by this. Category memberships, such as ethnicity, are *effectively* objective from the point of view of an individual, but they are what Searle calls "ontologically subjective," meaning they are contingent on social processes and therefore others' subjectivity. The reason our ethnicities will not change the moment we categorize ourselves as something different is that such social facts do not depend on the mental processes of any one individual. Such macro-level categories can and do change, but this requires a collective-level process, such as when a marginalized group acts collectively to challenge the meanings of a social category that stigmatizes or excludes them.

Although expressed in slightly different terms, what we are describing here should be familiar to those acquainted with SIT. Among the ways that members may act collectively as a subordinated group in an unstable, impermeable and illegitimate social system is by challenging the meanings of the categories themselves, including their impermeability (Tajfel, 1978). In other words, while the permeability of group boundaries is a "structural" feature of the societies, it is contingent on representation and subject to transformation through human agency. In short, the fluidity of self-categorization processes do not imply unstable identities, because the context in which self-categorization occurs is underpinned by social representations that are irreducible to the cognitive processes of any one individual. There is therefore no contradiction between the highly fluid psychological process of self-categorization and the empirical reality of stable, consequential social categories across time.

Social power and mobilization give meaning to particular identity combinations

The observation that people have multiple identities – that is, cross-cutting group memberships and relationships that can serve to define who they are – has always been a part of the SIA, as it has to other social scientific theories about identity. One of the more fraught issues is whether people can hold multiple identities in mind at the same time.

IPT has approached this matter with the suggestion that holding multiple identities inoculates individuals against certain forms of identity threat (Breakwell, 1986). On the other hand, certain identity combinations might be experienced as personally threatening where these identities are potentially incompatible. Jaspal and Cinnirella (2010), for example, propose the addition of a psychological coherence principle to the IPT framework as a way of accounting for the way their participants sought to reconcile their gay and Muslim identities.

The SIA has struggled with this matter, sometimes seeming to suggest that there is a strict "either/or" character to the salience of different categories, at other times suggesting that people often think of themselves in different terms in the same context (Turner *et al.*, 1994). Perhaps, though, a more fruitful line of investigation would be to focus on the significance and consequences of identity combinations in terms of intra- and intergroup processes. The social identity literature already contains some strong hints as to the direction this could take (see also Amiot and Jaspal, this volume).

To take one example, Turner (2005) has argued that while persuasion depends on a shared social identity, the use of coercive force against in-group members undermines such shared identity. One way that leaders might seek to prevent their use of coercion from undermining persuasive power is to portray the targets of coercion as belonging to an outgroup. So, politicians seeking to use measures such as heavy surveillance and detention without trial against members of the Muslim community in Britain may seek to call the "Britishness" of their targets into question, thus maintaining their persuasive power among the non-Muslim population, or even enhancing it. Characterizing Muslims as only marginally British (and therefore un-prototypical) is one way they might do this.

Conversely, a minority group may seek to gain the solidarity of the majority by portraying themselves collectively as fellow ingroup members (see Subašić *et al.*, 2008). Thus, they may seek to enact a "dual" or "hyphenated" identity (such as "British Muslim") in order that their minority status is no longer a mark of otherness. Strategies such as the articulation of "being British in a Muslim way" and so forth can be viewed in these terms (Hopkins, 2011). Given that the success of such enactment is likely to depend on a combined effort, we can expect a dual identity like "British Muslim" to itself function as a self-category providing the basis for collective action (Simon and Grabow, 2010), as well as validation by others both within and outside the group (Klein *et al.*, 2007). In short, we suggest processes of leadership, influence, enactment and collective action and not just the need to satisfy intrapsychic identity motives, as fertile ground for research on multiple identities.

Some final remarks: psychology is not enough

Our aim has been to highlight the various ways in which social identity makes a variety of group processes possible and argue that these processes in turn lie at the heart of society itself. We do not deny that IPT may also have wide application and provide valuable insights on a range of topics. In particular, we have said that the notion of "perceiver readiness" is fairly unelaborated in SCT, whereas IPT researchers have taken more interest in intra-individual motivational constraints. What we do argue, however, is that theorizing group processes without distinguishing appropriately between social and personal identity cannot work. Thus, we have critiqued IPT's abandonment of this distinction and argued that, because of this, the approach does not theorize social action and social change adequately. In making this argument, we are emphatically not implying that SCT and related theories offer anything like a final account of the social phenomena they are applied to. On the contrary, the very nature of the approach means that substantive claims about behavior without contextual analysis are inimical to it. In this sense, one could say that the theory is incomplete and deliberately so. By the same token, one could also say that it may act as a bridge between psychology and the other social sciences. As an invaluable guide as to the relationship between social categories and social reality, the SIA is the beginning, not the end, of analysis.

REFERENCES

Asch, S. (1952). *Social psychology*. Englewood Cliffs, NJ: Prentice-Hall.

Barker, M. (1981). *The new racism: conservatives and the ideology of the tribe*. Frederick, MD: University Publications of America.

Breakwell, G. M. (1986). *Coping with threatened identities*. London: Methuen.

Breakwell, G. M. (1993). Social representations and social identity. *Papers on Social Representations*, 2, 198–217.

Breakwell, G. M. (2001). Social representational constraints on identity processes. In K. Deaux and G. Philogene (eds.), *Representations of the social: bridging theoretical traditions* (pp. 271–284). Oxford: Blackwell.

Elcheroth, G., Doise, W., and Reicher, S. (2011). On the knowledge of politics and the politics of knowledge: how a social representations approach helps us rethink the subject of political psychology. *Political Psychology*, 32, 729–758.

Esses, V. M., Jackson, L. M., and Armstrong, T. L. (1998). Intergroup competition and attitudes towards immigration: an instrumental model of group conflict. *Journal of Social Issues*, 54, 699–724.

Gilroy, P. ([1987]2002). *There ain't no black in the union jack: the cultural politics of race and nation*. Abingdon, UK: Routledge.

Haslam, S. A., Ellemers, N., Reicher, S., Reynolds, K. J., and Schmitt, M. T. (2010a). The social identity perspective today: the impact of its defining ideas. In T. Postmes and N. R. Branscombe (eds.), *Rediscovering social identity: core sources* (pp. 341–356). New York: Psychology Press.

Haslam, S. A., Ellemers, N., Reicher, S., Reynolds, K. J., and Schmitt, M. T. (2010b). The social identity perspective tomorrow: opportunities and avenues for advance. In T. Postmes and N. R. Branscombe. *Rediscovering social identity: core sources* (pp. 357–379). New York: Psychology Press.

Haslam, S. A., Reicher, S. D. and Levine, M. (2011a). When other people are heaven, when other people are hell: how social identity determines the nature and impact of social support. In Jetten, J., Haslam, C., and Haslam, S. A.

(eds.), *The social cure: identity, health and well-being* (pp. 157–174). London and New York: Psychology Press.

Haslam, S. A., Reicher, S. D., and Platow, M. J. (2011b). *The new psychology of leadership: identity, influence and power*. London: Sage.

Hopkins, N. (2011). Dual identities and their recognition. *Political Psychology*, 32, 251–270.

Hopkins, N., and Kahani-Hopkins, V. (2004). Identity construction and British Muslims' political activity: beyond rational actor theory. *British Journal of Social Psychology*, 43, 339–356.

Hopkins, N., Reicher, S., and Levine, M. (1997). On the parallels between social cognition and the "new racism." *British Journal of Social Psychology*, 39, 305–329.

Huddy, L. (2001). From social to political identity: a critical examination of social identity theory. *Political Psychology*, 23, 127–156.

Israel, J., Tajfel, H., and Psychology, E. A. E. (1972). *The context of social psychology: a critical assessment*. London: Academic Press.

Jaspal, R., and Cinnirella, M. (2010). Coping with potentially incompatible identities: accounts of religious, ethnic and sexual identities from British Pakistani men who identify as Muslim and gay. *British Journal of Social Psychology*, 49, 849–870.

Klein, O., Spears, R., and Reicher, S. (2007). Social identity performance: extending the strategic side of SIDE. *Personality and Social Psychology Review*, 11, 28–45.

Livingstone, A. G., Manstead, A. S., Spears, R., and Bowen, D. (2011). The language barrier? Context, identity, and support for political goals in minority ethnolinguistic groups. *British Journal of Social Psychology*, 50, 747–768.

Lyons, E. (1996). Coping with social change: processes of social memory. In G. M. Breakwell and E. Lyons (eds.), *Changing European identities: social psychological analyses of change* (pp. 31–40). Oxford: Butterworth-Heinemann.

McConnell, A. R. (2011). The multiple self-aspects framework: self concept representation and its implications. *Personality and Social Psychology Review*, 15, 3–27.

Novelli, D., Drury, J., and Reicher, S. (2010). Come together: two studies concerning the impact of group relations on 'personal space'. *British Journal of Social Psychology*, 49, 223–236.

Oakes, P. (2002). Psychological groups and political psychology: a response to Huddy's "critical examination of social identity theory." *Political Psychology*, 23, 806–824.

Pehrson, S., Brown, R., and Zagefka, H. (2009a). When does national identification lead to the rejection of immigrants? Cross-sectional and longitudinal evidence for the role of essentialist in-group definitions. *British Journal of Social Psychology*, 48, 61–76.

Pehrson, S., and Green, E. G. T. (2010). Who we are and who can join us: national identity content and entry criteria for new immigrants. *Journal of Social Issues*, 66, 695–716.

Pehrson, S., Vignoles, V., and Brown, R. (2009b). National identification and anti-immigrant prejudice: individual and contextual effects of national definitions. *Social Psychology Quarterly*, 72, 24–38.

Postmes, T., and Branscombe, N. R. (2010). *Rediscovering social identity: core sources*. New York: Psychology Press.

Pratto, F., Sidanius, J., and Levin, S. (2006). Social dominance theory and the dynamics of intergroup relations: taking stock and looking forward. *European Review of Social Psychology*, 17, 271–320.

Reicher, S. (1996). The Battle of Westminster. *European Journal of Social Psychology*, 26, 115–134.

Reicher, S. (2004). The context of social identity: domination, resistance and change. *Political Psychology*, 25, 921–945.

Reicher, S., Cassidy, C., Wolpert, I., Hopkins, N., and Levine, M. (2006). Saving Bulgaria's Jews: an analysis of social identity and the mobilisation of social solidarity. *European Journal of Social Psychology*, 36, 49–72.

Reicher, S., and Hopkins, N. (2001a). Psychology and the end of history: a critique and a proposal for the psychology of social categorization. *Political Psychology*, 22, 383–407.

Reicher, S., and Hopkins, N. (2001b). *Self and nation: categorization, contestation and mobilization*. London: Sage.

Reicher, S. D., Spears, R., and Haslam, S. A. (2010). The social identity approach in social psychology. In M. S. Wetherell and C. T. Mohanty (eds.), The *SAGE Handbook of Identities* (pp. 45–62). London: Sage.

Searle, J. R. (1995). *The construction of social reality*. St Ives: Penguin.

Sherif, M., Harvey, O. J., White, B. J., Hood, W. R., and Sherif, C. W. (1961). *Intergroup cooperation and competition: the Robbers Cave experiment*. Norman, OK: University Book Exchange.

Simon, B. (1997). Self and group in modern society: ten theses on the individual self and the collective self. In R. Spears, P. Oakes, N. Ellemers and S. A. Haslam (eds.), *The social psychology of stereotyping and group life* (pp. 318–335). Oxford: Blackwell.

Simon, B. (2004). *Identity in modern society. A social psychological perspective*. Oxford: Blackwell.

Sidanius, J., and Pratto, F. (1999). *Social dominance: an intergroup theory of social hierarchy and oppression*. New York: Cambridge University Press.

Simon, B., and Grabow, O. (2010). The politicization of migrants: further evidence that politicised collective identity is a dual identity. *Political Psychology*, 31, 717–738.

Stott, C., Adang, O., Livingstone, A., and Schreiber, M. (2007). Variability in the collective behaviour of England fans at Euro2004: policing, intergroup relations, identity and social change. *European Journal of Social Psychology*, 37, 75–100.

Subašic', E., Reynolds, K. J., and Turner, J. C. (2008). The political solidarity model of social change: dynamics of self-categorisation in intergroup power relations. *Personality and Social Psychology Review*, 12, 330–352.

Tajfel, H. (1972). Experiments in a vacuum. In J. Israel and H Tajfel (eds.), *The context of social psychology* (pp. 69–119). London: Academic Press.

Tajfel, H. (1978). *Differentiation between social groups*. New York: Academic Press.

Tajfel, H., and Turner, J. C. (1979). An integrative theory of intergroup conflict. In W. Austin and S. Worchel (eds.), *The psychology of intergroup relations* (pp. 33–47). Monterey, CA: Brookes Cole.

Turner, J. C. (1982). Towards a cognitive redefinition of the social group. In H. Tajfel (ed.), *Social identity and intergroup relations* (pp. 15–40). Cambridge University Press.

Turner, J. C. (1991). *Social influence.* Belmont, CA: Wadsworth.

Turner, J. C. (1999). Some current issues in research on social identity and self-categorization theories. In N. Ellemers, R. Spears and B. Doosje (eds.), *Social identity: Context, commitment, content* (pp. 6–34). Oxford: Blackwell.

Turner, J. C. (2005). Explaining the nature of power: a three-process theory. *European Journal of Social Psychology*, 35, 1–22.

Turner, J. C., Hogg, M. A., Oakes, P., Reicher, S. D., and Wetherell, M. S. (1987). *Rediscovering the social group: a self-categorization theory.* Oxford: Blackwell.

Turner, J. C., Oakes, P. J., Haslam, S. A., and McGarty, C. (1994). Self and collective: cognition and social context. *Personality and Social Psychology Bulletin*, 20, 454–463.

Turner, J. C., and Reynolds, K. J. (2001). The social identity perspective in intergroup relations: theories, themes and controversies. In R. Brown and S. L. Gaertner (eds.), *Blackwell handbook of social psychology: intergroup relations* (pp. 133–152). Oxford: Blackwell.

Turner, J. C., Reynolds, K. J., Haslam, S. A., and Veenstra, K. E. (2006). Reconceptualizing personality: producing individuality by defining the personal self. In T. Postmes and J. Jetten (eds.), *Individuality and the group: advances in social identity* (pp. 11–36). London: Sage Publications.

Vignoles, V. L. (2004). Modelling identity motives using multilevel regression. In G. M. Breakwell (ed.), *Doing social psychology research* (pp. 174–204). Oxford: Blackwell.

Vignoles, V. L., Regalia, C., Manzi, C., Golledge, J., and Scabini, E. (2006). Beyond self-esteem: influence of multiple motives on identity construction. *Journal of Personality and Social Psychology*, 90, 308–333.

Wakefield, J. R. H., Hopkins, N., Cockburn, C., Shek, K., Muirhead, A., Reicher, S., and van Rijswijk, W. (2011). The impact of adopting ethnic or civic conceptions of national belonging for others' treatment. *Personality and Social Psychology Bulletin*, 37, 1,599–1,610.

Wallwork, J., and Dixon, J. A. (2004). Foxes, green fields and Britishness: on the rhetorical construction of place and national identity. *British Journal of Social Psychology*, 43, 21–39.

6   Identity and social representations

Glynis M. Breakwell

Why the focus on social representations?

It is necessary to explore how social representation processes relate to identity processes (Breakwell, 2001a, 2001b, 2010a, 2011). Why? Social Representation Theory is a theory about the social construction of meaning – it explains how society explains. It theorizes the ways in which society creates models, narratives, rhetoric and arguments that interpret – make sense of – new information (where information is conceived of in the broadest possible sense, ranging from scientific discoveries to reports of macro-socio-economic or cultural movements). Social representations are the ever-evolving products of this effort to understand the changing world around us. Social representations are an essential, all-pervasive part of the fabric of the social world which individuals experience. Consequently, individual identities are developed in the context of an abundance of social representations.

IPT argues that the individual engages, consciously or unconsciously, in a dynamic process of constructing an identity and that this process is continual. Every new experience is interpreted in relation to the existing identity content and evaluation. Each new experience could potentially call into question the legitimacy of the existing identity structure, challenging whether existing identity elements can remain unmodified. On the other hand, each new experience could potentially justify or enhance the existing identity structure. Social representations are fundamentally important in that they allot meaning and value to experiences. Insofar as the individual is aware of a particular social representation, it has the potential to influence the way in which an experience is interpreted and then affects the identity structure. For example, where the prevailing social representation of smoking is that it is hazardous to the health of the user and others close to the user, the experience of being a smoker and its meaning for identity is different from contexts where smoking has less negative connotations. The changes that have occurred in the social representations of smoking over a period of several decades can be plotted against changes in the role that being a smoker (or, indeed, having stopped being a smoker) has to play in the individual identity. A social representation may also have the power to affect the interpretation of the experience even if the individual is not directly aware of the existence, or content, of a particular social representation since its existence will affect others who may influence the meaning of the experience for the individual. For example, an individual who moves from one cultural milieu to another may not immediately recognize that there are social representations in use that will inform and condition the behavior of others and then impact upon themselves. They may quickly become aware of these social representations but they may perceive the implications of the social representation before they come to understand the nature of the social representation itself. Migrant workers, especially ones who have no fluency in the language of their new host community, will be surrounded by social representations that operate to influence the behavior of others towards them. Some of these social representations may be very specifically about the migrant labor force (e.g. that it is underpricing native workers and explains unemployment levels). Some may be not targeted at the migrant in any way directly but are still alien to the prior experience of the migrant (e.g. concerning the appropriate behavior for women of child-bearing age in public). Very often, these social representations will become tangible when the migrant breaches expectations built upon them. Yet, before they become manifest to the migrant, they will be impacting upon the way in which he or she is treated and, in all probability, as a consequence upon self-evaluation and the assimilation of identity content. The indirect effects of social representations for identity construction and maintenance are more numerous and perhaps as a result more significant, than any direct effects. The indirect effects may be more significant simply in numerical terms but also because the individual has less opportunity consciously to use coping strategies to control them.

While the importance of social representations for identity should be emphasized, it is also important to consider the impact in the reverse direction. Identity processes do influence the operation of social representation processes. This is another reason for IPT researchers to focus upon social representation processes. The rest of this chapter analyses various interactions between identity and social representation processes.

The relationship between social representations and the individual

How does the individual relate to social representations? In Social Representations Theory (SRT; Moscovici, 1988) social representations can be both products and processes. As a product, a social representation is defined as a widely shared set of beliefs, a systematic framework for explaining events and evaluating them. As a process, social representation is the whole package of activity (communication, exchange, argumentation) in which individuals and groups engage to make sense of changes in their physical and social environment. According to Moscovici, social representation operates with two prime processes: objectification and anchoring. Objectification entails translating something that is abstract into something that is almost concrete, gaining a density of meaning which ultimately makes it a common and "natural" part of thinking about the object. Anchoring entails categorizing a new object into pre-existing cognitive frameworks in order to render them familiar (reducing the strange and unfamiliar object to the level of an ordinary object set in a familiar context).

SRT states that objectification and anchoring are not individual processes. They are processes that normally involve social interaction and the establishment of shared meaning and consensus through communication among people. This does not mean that everyone holds absolutely identical social representations (Rose *et al.*, 1995). It suggests, however, that the members of a discrete subculture would share certain common core elements of the social representations current in their subculture. Individuals within the subculture might then hold representations that incorporate some elements that are not shared.

Breakwell (2001a) distinguished between "personal representations" and social representations. A personal representation is used to refer to the manifestation of a social representation at the level of the individual. Social representations are deemed social because they are generated in social interaction, they are shared by a number of individuals, they refer to social phenomena, they are manifested in social artifacts (e.g. norms, rituals or literature) and they serve social functions for the communities that evolve them. They have an existence independent of their presence in any *one* individual's cognitions. However, while their existence is not solely or exclusively dependent upon being present in the thoughts, feelings or actions of an individual, nevertheless, they may be expressed in individual cognitions, emotions and behavior. To the extent that a social representation is present in an individual's cognitions, emotions or behavior, it exists as a personal representation.

Abric (1994) has argued that social representations comprise a central core (an indispensable combination of basic underlying components linked in a specific constellation and tied systematically to a set of values and norms associated with the group espousing the social representation) and the peripheric elements (the way in which the representation is articulated in concrete terms depending upon context). Abric argues that the core is resistant to change but that the peripheric elements are responsive to changing context. By adapting, the peripheric elements can protect the core from having to change. Following Abric might lead one to conclude that individuals will be different from each other in the personal representations which they hold not in the core but in the peripheric elements. Empirically, problems in differentiating core from periphery make testing this hypothesis difficult. It is, however, worth pursuing. To do so, would, of course, demand an operational definition of peripheric elements that does not depend upon the extent to which they are included consensually in the representation.

In any case, the social representational world is complex and dynamic. It may be unproductive in practice to think about the individual in relationship to a single social representation. In reality, the individual would never be affected by a single social representation. Moscovici (1961), in moving away from the Durkheim's notion of collective representation, emphasized the multiplicity of social representations that exist in modern societies and their capacity for change. It would seem reasonable to assume that, in this complex world of different and changing social representations, any one individual would rarely have access to all the social representations that are operating and might not have access in its entirety even to a single social representation. Individuals will have different roles in the social process of construction, elaboration and sharing of the representation. Essentially, this is to suggest that each individual is uniquely positioned in relation to the process of social representation and the constellation of products of social representation.

Why is it that some components of a particular social representation are incorporated into an individual's personal representation and others are not? Breakwell (2001a and 2001b) suggested it might help to think about the individual's relationship to any social representation as being described along a number of dimensions, as follows.

1. *Awareness*: individuals will differ in their awareness of the social representation. Some individuals will simply not know that there is a social representation in existence; others will know only part of its scope; and yet others will be virtually fully aware of its structure and content. For instance, awareness of the available social representations of Superstring Theory (which – for the unaware – is a set of attempts to model in one theory gravitation, electromagnetism, strong nuclear force and weak nuclear force and thus resolve the alleged conflict between classical physics and quantum physics) will differ across people. Awareness is likely to be determined, in part,

by previous personal experience, which, in turn, will be controlled to some extent by membership of different groups or communities. Exposure to a social representation will be affected by social category memberships. But awareness will also be determined by the significance of the object of the representation. If the object changes in significance owing to some change of social or physical circumstances, awareness of existing social representations will alter. For example, news of popular uprisings overseas may raise awareness of alternative social representations of the nature of the regime in power there. So, for instance, the so-called "Arab Spring" protests that began in 2010 may have triggered in Western Europe a different social representation of the political regimes in Egypt, Syria and subsequently in other states.

2. *Understanding*: individuals will differ in the extent to which they actually understand the social representations of which they are aware. There is ample evidence that individuals are capable of reproducing all or part of a social representation even though they cannot explain how or why its elements fit together and, if challenged, they cannot justify it. For instance, people may be aware of some aspects of one or more of the social representations of climate change but a large proportion would not claim to understand the underlying science or arguments surrounding the data on which the social representations rely (Leiserowitz, 2006).

3. *Acceptance*: individuals will differ in the extent to which they believe or accept a social representation even if they are fully aware of it. Typically, people can say: this is what is generally believed but, nevertheless, this is what I believe. For instance, I might know that other people commonly believe that regular physical exercise improves health but I believe that exercise causes more harm than good. The point is that people can know (in the sense of being able to reproduce at will) not only contradictory social representations of the same target but also be able to identify at the same time a separate representation of it which is their own. This personal representation may be unique only in the specifics and may share many of the common features of the social representation but it is personalized. The extent to which the personal representation echoes the social representation reflects in part the degree to which the latter is accepted. The importance of being able to resist wholesale acceptance of the social representation so that it appears individualized should not be ignored. While seeking identification with others through communality of understandings and interpretations at one level, people also simultaneously seek distinctiveness and differentiation through resistance to the social

representation. The personalizing of social representations is part of a process of establishing and protecting an identity. Personalizing may not be possible in the case of some social representations, particularly those that are hegemonic (this is considered later).

4. *Assimilation*: the individual does not accept (to whatever extent it is accepted) the social representation in some clinically detached way. Once accepted, the social representation has to be assimilated. It will be assimilated in an active and agentic manner. It will be assimilated to pre-existent systems of personal representation (developed originally on idiosyncratic cognitive biases and capacities). This substratum of already extant personal representations will differ across individuals and the ultimate shape of the new personal representation will be influenced by it differentially for each individual. Just as social processes ensure that the new social representation is anchored in prior social representations, at the individual level cognitive and emotional processes ensure that it is anchored in prior personal representations. In fact, there must be an intimate connection between the social processes of anchoring and objectification and their parallel individual processes. The social communication that ensures novel events and ideas are interpreted in terms of existing systems of meaning is generated by individuals using prior knowledge mediated through cognitive and conative (i.e. affective) networks. The social exchange can produce understandings that no single participant to the interaction might be able to create but at some level even these emergent representations are limited in some ways by the capacities of the individuals involved to anchor and objectify.

5. *Salience*: the salience of a social representation will differ across people and for the same person across time and contexts. The salience of the social representation, for instance, may increase if the community that generates it is important to the individual. In the case of researchers, if the agencies that provide research funding (and are thus very important to researchers) develop a new way of evaluating research (e.g. perhaps they argue that research has to have social or economic impact to be worthwhile), then the researchers are likely to consider this new representation of "valuable research" salient. Similarly, salience may increase if the social representation becomes relevant to the individual's ongoing activity. For example, in Western industrialized communities there is a complex media representation of "whistleblowers" working in public services. The existence of the social representation of "whistleblowers" would be likely to become more salient for an individual facing the decision about whether or not to report a breach of professional conduct. At the level of the

community, if the object for social representation is non-salient it is likely that the social representation will be difficult to elicit, simple, undifferentiated and relatively unconnected with other components of the community's belief system. At the level of the individual, the salience of the social representation will be likely to influence how accurately and completely personal representation mirrors it. There is, however, no empirical evidence for this yet.

It is notable that some of the dimensions that shape the personal representation are potentially non-volitional (e.g. awareness and understanding), whereas others are volitional (e.g. acceptance). However, this distinction may be rightly regarded as arbitrary. Even those which appear volitional are largely predisposed by prior social experiences and constrained by identity considerations.

Types of social representation

The scope that the individual has for developing an idiosyncratic personal representation depends in part upon the type of social representation concerned from which it is derived. Moscovici (1988) identified three types of social representation:

Hegemonic representations – these are shared by all members of a highly structured group without them having been produced by the group; they are uniform and coercive. Perhaps the simplest example of this sort of representation would be the system of beliefs, attitudes and values that characterize a cult – "doomsday" cults that prophesy catastrophe and destruction commonly have complex hegemonic representations that explain why, when and how the end will come for everyone.

Emancipated representations – these are the outgrowth of the circulation of knowledge and ideas belonging to subgroups that are in more or less close contact – each subgroup creates and shares its own version. These representations are freed in the sense that the subgroup is at liberty to elaborate and shape them based on the access that they have to sources of information. For a single issue, there can be a number of emancipated representations – take, for example, the way different subgroups will interpret a news report that horse meat is being passed off as beef and sold in processed foods. The social representations generated may have many dimensions and each subgroup can select or emphasize different dimensions. These social representations are not necessarily conflicting; they do not serve the interests of conflicting parties directly.

Polemical representations – these are generated in the course of social conflict or controversy and society as a whole does not share them, they are determined by antagonistic relations between its members and intended to be mutually exclusive. Take, as an example, the representations that evolve in a community when a new potentially hazardous construction (e.g. a waste disposal facility) is proposed, subgroups within the community will be active in constructing alternative interpretations of the hazard and the implications it will have for them. Some may be positive about the development, others negative. To the extent that they are reflective of antagonism in the community, they are polemical representations and help to justify the position taken by subgroups.

It is debatable whether these are actually different types of social representation or just different and inevitable phases in the overall lifespan of a social representation. Polemical representations can develop into hegemonic ones over time. Nevertheless, this tripartite classification does suggest that individuals and communities, in some cases, can choose between social representations and use them creatively for their own purposes. The three types of social representation that Moscovici proposes offer differing degrees of freedom for the individual to construct a personal representation. The hegemonic representation supposes little individual variation. The emancipated representation supposes individual variation based upon differential exposure within group contexts. The polemical representation supposes individual variation based upon participation in the prevailing intergroup conflict.

It is the scope for personalizing representations, which emerges when emancipated or polemical representations prevail about an object, that is one of the necessary conditions for innovation and change. This assertion is not meant to trivialize or ignore the real differentials between individuals in their power to maintain or to proselytize their personal representations. One of the things this perspective emphasizes is that personal representations will be perpetually under pressure to change from the social representations that surround them. Individuals that are personally powerful (through position, expertise or some other route) are more likely to be able to retain their own personal representations and to be able to influence the development of social representations. Examples may immediately spring to mind from history – from the same era, one might think of Hitler, Stalin and Churchill – but clearly it is only surmise that these individuals actually maintained personal representations in the face of counter-representations. The evidence is circumstantial not direct. In fact, more generally, the role of the individual in mediating emancipated and polemical representations remains to be examined empirically.

Any examination of the degrees of freedom available to the individual in deriving a personal representation begins to highlight the need to understand the role of the individual in constructing a social representation. Since a social representation is defined as a set of understandings shared by a number of people then, to the extent that any individuals demure from the shared understanding, the status of the social representation changes. It may be that the social representation itself changes in content. It may be that it simply changes its adherents (moving from

one set of people to another). It may be that it changes its significance –
becoming less used and less prominent. The important thing here is that
the processes encircling the creation of personal representations also
flow back to influence the social representations. The intimacy of their
relationship cannot be overestimated.

Stickiness of social representations

Before looking at the effects of identity processes upon the development
of personal representations and participation in social representation
processes, it might be useful to consider another characteristic of social
representations that is important. While the tripartite classification of
social representations as hegemonic, emancipated and polemical emphasizes variability in the processes of their production and descriptions
of core and peripheral elements indicates something of their structure,
there is a more holistic characteristic that differentiates between social
representations. For want of a more elegant descriptor, I would call this
their stickiness. Stickiness is just a shorthand term. Stickiness refers to
their tendency to attract adherents (users/believers/communicators) and
their ability to resist being shaken off or ignored. Stickiness is a descriptor that can apply to all three types of social representation.

   Stickiness may be derived from a host of sources. It could be associated with who promulgates the social representation (e.g. if it is emanating from a community that is distrusted or discredited, it may have low
stickiness – take, for example, representations of food safety that origi-
nate from food-processing manufacturers). It could be associated with
how the social representation is transmitted; that is, the channels through
which it is promulgated or the way in which it is presented (some transmission routes are more trusted than others, e.g. reputable TV channels and programs; some are more immediate, e.g. through family and
friends). It could be tied to how far the social representation has already
achieved saturation in the particular social environment (e.g. in terms of
the number of people accepting it, the length of time it has been active,
the number of channels through which it is communicated, or how many
times it has been presented). Additionally, stickiness could be associated
with the extent to which the social representation is capable of triggering,
or is aligned with, emotional arousal. An example of this later source of
stickiness is provided by the way in which the London 2012 Paralympics
was associated in the UK with a great upwelling of positive feeling for
athletes with disabilities and with a marked shift in the social representation of such athletes – becoming more substantive, differentiated and
evidenced as well as generally more accepting.

It seems likely that the stickiness of a social representation will matter when it comes to the way in which identity processes can work with it. It would still be necessary to assume that the individual interacts with the sticky social representation in a purposive manner – the individual will go through the processes of awareness, acceptance and assimilation and these will be directed by identity construction concerns. The interaction is not just reactive but it seems a logical inevitability that the processes of resistance or reactance will be lower. The penetration of the social representation into personal representation and then into identity structure would seem likely to be greater if the stickiness is greater. It may also be linked to greater permanency and lower transience in the identity structure.

Identity Process Theory and social representations

Although social representations have been defined at one level as being a widely shared set of beliefs, we have also noted that it is not the case that social representations are accepted and used by individuals in their entirety and sometimes they are not accepted or used at all. Among the realm of available social representations, the representations of which an individual is aware, will accept and may use will depend upon the significance they have for identity. IPT (Breakwell, 1993) argues that the individual will have awareness, acceptance and use of social representations and their presence in personal representations, shaped by the requirements of identity processes that act in accordance with the principles of self-esteem, self-efficacy, distinctiveness and continuity. IPT proposes that individual responses to social representations are linked to the ways in which they may threaten or secure the identity principles.

IPT has now generated an extensive series of studies illustrating that individuals in the same social category or community will accept and use (i.e. reproduce or act in accordance with) a particular social representation to differing degrees, depending upon its potential impact upon their identity esteem, continuity, distinctiveness and efficacy (Bonauito et al., 1996; Jaspal and Yampolsky, 2011; Thrush et al., 1997, 1999; Twigger-Ross and Breakwell, 1999). Such studies would suggest that polemical social representations are most obviously correlated with the identity principles insofar as essentially, these studies show that individuals were found to reject social representations that might threaten important aspects of their identity. However, it is probably too simplistic to use the term "rejection" when examining how identity constraints motivate the way in which a social representation is treated. What often happens is that the social representation is subtly modified in personal use – for instance, an element is omitted or changed in emphasis. This is seen often in the way in which politicians from different parties will eliminate in their rhetoric aspects of a social representation that does not fit with their broader ideology upon which their sense of distinctiveness and self-esteem is founded. Alternatively, the social representation can be re-anchored or there is a minor tweak to the objectification (often through use of different exemplars).

In effect, individuals who are actively engaged in identity maintenance and development are also perforce engaged in social representation creation and change. Of course, whether or not their renovation of the social representation gains common acceptance or use is a function of the processes outlined in the theory of social representations itself. The significant point that all the studies have shown is that there is virtually never total consensus upon a social representation. All the research illustrates variety among individuals despite elements of agreement and consensus. Empirical studies emphasize divergence amidst consensus (i.e. the personal representation as well as the social representation). Moreover, the divergence is not random. It is ordered, systematic, and, in part, predictable in terms of IPT expectations concerning the desire to achieve and maintain esteem, efficacy, distinctiveness and continuity for identity.

This whole analysis can, and should, be turned upon its head. Are social representations that support the identity principles of the majority in a community more likely to be accepted and used and become salient? It seems like a silly question. The answer is obvious: social representations that promote a community's esteem, efficacy, distinctiveness and continuity do seem to thrive in that community. The body of empirical studies that would support this emanate from virtually every side of social psychology, rather than just via IPT or SRT research (see, e.g., Bandura, 1997).

This leads to a very clear assertion about IPT and SRT – they offer most when they work together (Breakwell, 2010b). SRT assumes that social representations have an impact on individuals and assumes individual actors have a role to play in evolving, promulgating and reproducing the representation. IPT assumes that social representations populate the realm of the possible identity content and evaluation. Social representations provide the interpretative framework for identity construction and maintenance. Understanding how identity processes affect social representation processes and vice versa is vitally important.

Identity Process Theory and group identity

Moscovici was originally interested in how minorities achieve influence. He developed the theory of social representations against an abiding concern with the way in which groups, from differing power positions, achieve influence. SRT consequently has within it assumptions about the ways in which groups gain and maintain their identities through the operation of social representation. SRT was not formulated as a theory of group identity but it has a lot to say about how group identity is manifested. Similarly, IPT was not formulated as a theory of group identity. Yet, it has been extended to groups and it is easy to see why it has been extended to refer to groups (Oren and Bar-Tal, this volume; Cinnirella, 2010; Jaspal and Cinnirella, 2012; Lyons, 1996). The translation works well. It is possible to see that groups seek distinctiveness, efficacy, esteem and continuity in the identity that they generate or acquire for themselves. However, this raises a hoary old question that has plagued social psychology for decades. When is a group a "group"? "Group" seems to be one of the most porous concepts in social psychology. It seems to be used interchangeably with nation, social category, community, or subculture and covers everything from a gathering of three people to a gender classification comprising millions. It is hardly surprising that theories of group behavior and interrelations are so diverse. Confusions about the status of the concept might also explain why so frequently theories that are supposed to explain how "groups" behave actually explain how individuals behave. There seem to be slippages in the level of analysis applied.

This makes the construction of a theory of group identity processes a real challenge. What would a theory of group identity have to include? Having determined what concept of group was to be employed, it would certainly need to explain how group identity is manifested – its expression and its implications for action of the group. It would have to explain how it is structured – the essential ingredients of an identity that is owned by a group and how they cohere. It would need to explain how group identity is created, maintained and changed. It would have to explain under what conditions change in group identity would occur.

If these requirements are accepted as the basics, it is possible to start to construct a model. For the moment, the difficult task of actually defining the concept of group will be shelved. The model might assume that group identity had two fundamental objectives: maintenance of optimal membership and motivation of membership to action. Maintenance of optimal membership might lead to an identity concerned with cohesiveness, distinctiveness and positive value for members but also selectivity. Motivation of membership to action might lead to an identity concerned with delineation of purpose, values and reward structures. Both routes to identity require the group to have channels for communication and to be responsive to change in context.

If these very simple building blocks for a model were to be accepted as the basis for argument, it would seem that a direct translation of IPT tenets would offer more to explaining how the maintenance of the optimal membership would work than to explaining how the motivation of membership to action might work. Though, insofar as the cohesiveness, distinctiveness and positive value are themselves rewarding, there is an overlap of the two identity routes. SRT offers more with respect to explaining how the motivation of membership to action route to identity might be operationalized. Social representations are flexible vehicles for encapsulating group purpose, values and incentive regimes. Social representations readily become markers of group identities – adherence becomes a sign of membership and content a signal of purpose.

The model thus far outlined is a little too dependent upon a particular notion of why groups exist. It rather assumes that groups exist to act – to achieve objectives beyond mere existence. Of course, this is not a comprehensive explanation for the existence of groups. Sometimes, groups exist simply to exist – they continue because they are there and may have been there for a long time. Such groups have outlived their original purpose and may even have forgotten what it was. Alternatively, some groups exist because they are called into existence by others. They are defined as the alter ego, the photo-negative, of some other group. Identity for these other types of groups is probably structured in a somewhat different way to that of the objective-driven group. There is a question as to whether they have different implications for the identity processes at work for their members. There is also a question about whether they would use social representation resources differently and be affected by them differently.

In thinking about the relationship of IPT and SRT, it is important to consider the role of groups (no matter how defined) and of group membership. The significance of group membership is an intrinsic part of the discussion earlier of the factors that influence individual awareness, use, acceptance, assimilation and salience of social representations. The significance of groups in the process of evolving and communicating social representations should never be ignored. This suggests that researchers who have been pushing to extend IPT into a model of group identity may have been addressing the right question – even though the extension does not offer all the answers. A specific theory of the identity of the group would be a major advance. It could be said to be the missing link in modeling the relationship between individual identity processes and social representation processes.

Affect, identity and representation

IPT talks of the structure of identity as having two dimensions: the content and the evaluation dimensions. The evaluation dimension is understood as encompassing the affect associated with the elements that comprise the content of identity. The identity principles are tied to affect: when breached the principles are hypothesized to arouse an aversive emotional state. The negative emotion aroused can be considered to be the intermediate motivation driving the actions that bring the identity into a new state that complies with the requirements of the identity principles. This assumption is embedded in the original formulation of IPT but it is worth making it explicit. When identity processes cannot operate according to the requirements of the identity principles, they trigger an emotional response. Understanding more about the way in which emotional arousal affects identity maintenance is very important. Empirical work on the topic is needed. One of the reasons that this would be useful is that objective indicators of emotional arousal could be used as a proxy for the subjective experience of identity threat. If this can be done, the irritating circularity in some of the operationalizations of threat and response to threat could be eliminated.

There is a further question concerning the role of affect. Affective elements are common in social representations. For instance, in social representations of hazards, fear and anxiety are often an integral part of the narrative attached to the risk. There is a different question, however and this centers upon the role of affect in the social representation process itself. Affect not as a content component of the representation but as an element in the willingness to participate in developing and communicating the representation. There is every reason to suppose that moderately heightened arousal – whether through fear or joy – may encourage engagement with the social representational process. There is evidence that social representations are used more readily (i.e. reproduced and communicated) when they arouse moderate fear (the social amplification of risk model is fundamentally illustrative of this – Pidgeon et al., 2003). Where arousal becomes extreme there is likely to be less engagement as very high arousal is usually associated with a reduced ability to absorb new information. Under such conditions, the individual may not consciously become aware of the representation or may evince rejection without any evident attempt to access the representation.

The role of affect in social representation processes deserves greater exploration but it seems likely that the emotional content of a social representation will be important in determining how it is re-presented in personal representations and thereafter how it impacts upon identity at the individual level. One way in which the emotional tone of the social representation might be important is in the extent to which it parallels the emotional status of the individual identity. To illustrate it simply, if the social representation carries a narrative which is anxiety-arousing will the individual be more receptive to it if his or her identity is already subject to threat that is generating aversive arousal? There is some evidence in the risk literature that this does happen (Slovic, 2010). Affect could be an important element in the determination of awareness, use, acceptance, assimilation and salience of the social representation.

Putting the pieces together

This chapter has attempted to show why social representation is of fundamental importance to the construction and maintenance of individual identity. Extant social representations provide the fabric of the – sometimes competing – societal interpretations and explanations of the social world in which the individual works to create and defend an identity. Social representations largely set the boundaries for identity change and the routes through which it can be achieved. In fact, social representations are often the origin and vehicle for threats to identity. Yet social representations are not monolithic or comprehensive and the individual can maneuver within them and use them creatively to arrive at personal representations that are idiosyncratic to some extent. Therefore the initial import of a social representation for identity can be resisted and reinterpreted. Furthermore, the individual sometimes has a significant role in the creation and maintenance of the social representation. It is important to see the relationship of the individual identity and the social representation over time as truly dynamic in both directions.

This chapter has raised a number of other questions. What characteristics could be said to differentiate between different types of social representation? What is the role of affect in social representation processes? What model of group identity would help us understand the relationship between the individual and social representation processes? It has offered some indications as to how these questions might be answered. There is, nevertheless, an undercurrent running through the chapter: there is still a paucity of empirical research that systematically examines the relationship between identity and social representation processes. The obstacles to doing good research in this area, of course, cannot be ignored. What is needed is a coherent program of research that uses a multi-method approach. It is a salutary lesson for social psychologists to examine how other sciences go about mounting studies that provide cumulative data on particular phenomena and within delineated conceptual frameworks. It seems that the relationship between identity and social representation processes would be an ideal arena in which to deploy such an approach in social psychology.

REFERENCES

Abric, J.-C. (1994). L'Organisation interne des représentations sociales: système central et système périphérique. In C. Guimelli (ed.), *Structures et transformations des représentations sociales* (pp. 73–84). Neuchatel: Delachaux et Niestle.

Bandura, A. (1997). *Self-efficacy.* New York: Freeman.

Bonaiuto, M., Breakwell, G. M., and Cano, I. (1996). Identity processes and environmental threat: the effects of nationalism and local identity upon perception of beach pollution. *Journal of Community & Applied Social Psychology*, 6, 157–175.

Breakwell, G. M. (1993). Integrating paradigms, methodological implications. In G. M. Breakwell and D. V. Canter (eds.), *Empirical approaches to social representations* (pp. 180–201). Oxford University Press.

Breakwell, G. M. (2001a). Social representational constraints upon identity processes. In K. Deaux and G. Philogene (eds.), *Representations of the social: bridging theoretical traditions* (pp. 271–84). Oxford: Blackwell.

Breakwell, G. M. (2001b). Mental models and social representations of hazards: the significance of identity processes. *Journal of Risk Research*, 4(4), 341–351.

Breakwell, G. M. (2010a). Resisting representations and identity processes. Special Issue: *Papers in Social Representations* 19, 6.1–6.11 (in honour of Gerard Duveen: Social Representations and Social Identities: Inspirations from Gerard Duveen).

Breakwell, G. M. (2010b). Models of risk construction: some applications to climate change. *Wiley Interdisciplinary Reviews: Climate Change* (Editor in Chief Mike Hulme) (e-pub October 2010: doi: 10.1002/wcc.74).

Breakwell, G. M. (2011). Empirical approaches to social representations and identity processes: 20 years on. *Papers on Social Representations*, 20, 17.1–17.4; ISSN 1021-5573.

Cinnirella, M. (2010). The role of perceived threat and identity in islamophobic prejudice: applying Integrated Threat Theory and Identity Process Theory to data from two uk surveys. Paper presented at the BPS Social Psychology Section Annual Conference, University of Winchester, September 7–9, 2010.

Jaspal, R., and Cinnirella, M. (2012). Identity processes, threat and interpersonal relations: accounts from British Muslim gay men. *Journal of Homosexuality*, 59(2), 215–240.

Jaspal, R., and Yampolsky, M. (2011). Social representations of the Holocaust and Jewish Israeli identity construction: insights from identity process theory. *Social Identities: Journal for the Study of Race, Nation and Culture*, 17(2), 201–224.

Leiserowitz, A. (2006). Climate change risk perception and policy preferences: the role of affect, imagery and values. *Climatic Change*, 77, 45–72.

Lyons, E. (1996). Coping with social change: processes of social memory. In G. M. Breakwell and E. Lyons (eds.), *Changing European identities: social psychological analyses of change* (pp. 31–40). Oxford: Butterworth-Heinemann.

Moscovici, S. (1961). *La Psychanalyse: son image and son public.* Paris: Presses Universitaires de France.

Moscovici, S. (1988). Notes towards the description of social representations. *Journal of Social Psychology*, 18, 211–250.

Pidgeon, N., Kasperson, R., and Slovic, P. (eds.) (2003). *The social amplification of risk*. Cambridge University Press.

Rose, D., Efraim, D., Gervais, M.-C., Joffe, H., Jovchelovitch, S., and Morant, N. (1995). Questioning consensus in social representations theory. *Papers on Social Representations*, 4 (2). pp. 150–176.

Slovic, P. (ed.) (2010). *The feeling of risk*. London: Earthscan.

Thrush, D., Fife-Schaw, C., and Breakwell, G. M. (1997).Young people's representations of others' views of smoking: is there a link with smoking behaviour? *Journal of Adolescence*, 20, 57–70.

Thrush, D., Fife-Schaw, C., and Breakwell, G. M. (1999). An evaluation of two school-based interventions to reduce smoking prevalence among 9–13 year olds. *Swiss Journal of Psychology*, 58 (2), 156–173.

Twigger-Ross, C. L., and Breakwell, G. M. (1999). Relating risk experience, venturesomeness and risk perception. *Journal of Risk Research*, 2(1), 73–83.

7　Identity processes in culturally diverse societies: how is cultural diversity reflected in the self?

Xenia Chryssochoou

In this chapter, I aim to discuss how identity, as a concept, can help us understand how cultural diversity is reflected in the self. My main focus is the contribution of Identity Process Theory in this endeavor. To do so, in the introductory section I will discuss the concept of acculturation as a meaning-making process. Then, in the following sections I will link acculturation to identity at different levels of analysis. Finally, in the last two sections I will present the contribution of IPT at a theoretical and empirical level. My main argument is that IPT enables us to theorize how acculturation can be customized at a micro-individual level because of its focus on how identity processes work to incorporate new elements.

Cultural diversity: a new societal project

Following the end of the colonialism after World War II, there was a mass movement of people and European societies became increasingly culturally diverse. The collapse of the Berlin Wall and the subsequent political changes in Eastern Europe, the war in former Yugoslavia, European integration and the wars in Iraq and Afghanistan also led to changes in migratory patterns. For example, many countries in Southern Europe that used to be migrant-sending countries became migrant-receiving societies. Along with globalization trends (Castles and Davidson, 2000), national projects,[1] at least in Europe, have changed and people have needed to deal with the idea that their societies are culturally diverse. It has been argued that there is currently a paradigm change from a society organized around social categories and issues toward a society organized

[1] The idea of "project" will be widely used in this chapter. What is meant here is that nations and more generally societies have developed plans about their organization and their collective aims. Thus, these plans are expressed by contents that justify and lead to specific actions. In that respect they constitute projects. As an example one could mention that a national project might lead to actions in order to create a state. It needs to be mentioned that national projects constitute hegemonic representations and are not necessarily shared by everybody.

around cultural categories (Touraine, 2005). The "battle" between a "social" and a "cultural" representation of society has consequences, amongst other things, for people's perceptions about rights, duties and societal cohesion (Chryssochoou, 2010).

Culturally diverse societies possess a unique form of political organization and propose to their members a particular project of societal cohesion. This project, based on unity and diversity, requires a re-conceptualization of the self and the combination of different identifications especially for cultural minorities (Chryssochoou, 2000). However, there is a, largely ideological, representation that societies cannot manage cultural diversity due to a presumed incompatibility between particular cultural groups (Huntington, 1993). In particular, it is supposed that societal cohesion will be threatened unless there is a hegemonic culture and the assimilation of all people under one cultural umbrella (at least concerning the public space).

As a consequence, the issue of acculturation becomes important in contemporary societies. There is, for instance, social psychological research into intergroup relations depending on the acculturation strategies of both cultural majorities and minorities – this work attempts to predict patterns of societal cohesion (Bourhis *et al.*, 1997; Montreuil and Bourhis, 2004; Pfafferott and Brown, 2006; Piontkowski *et al.*, 2002; Zagefka and Brown, 2002; Zick *et al.*, 2001). The spotlight is directed mainly at migrants and ethnic minorities whose patterns of adjustment are investigated (Abu-Rayya, 2009; Jasinskaja-Lahti and Liebkind, 2007; Vadher and Barrett, 2009). For these groups of people an emphasis is put on how they manage their identities in their new environment (Deaux, 2006; Phinney *et al.*, 2001; Verkuyten, 2005). However, acculturation refers to the changes experienced by all groups as a result of intergroup contact (Redfield *et al.*, 1936) and therefore equally concerns receiving societies.[2] Receiving societies also need to acculturate and revisit their own identities (Condor, 2006). However, acculturation is not, I would argue, the end result of adjustment attempts, codified as different strategies (Berry, 1990, 2001) that reflect people's motivation to maintain and/ or acquire different cultural elements. Acculturation in contemporary societies is more than dealing with the co-existence of different cultural groups within the same socio-political organization.

The presence of culturally diverse groups obliges societies to collectively rethink the parameters of success and re-discuss the criteria that enable people to become recipients of resource distribution

---

[2] The term "receiving" is preferred to the term "host," which conveys the idea that somebody has the position of inviting and hosting foreigners.

(Chryssochoou, 2010). Contemporary nation-states, under a "social" paradigm of society, prioritize success at an individual level depending on personal characteristics and skills. People, regardless of their social origins, were supposed to be able to reach the highest levels of social stratification through personal abilities and efforts. However, the implicit understanding was that this process of individual mobility was available only to people who shared the same nationality, citizenship or race in contexts where social cohesion was maintained through the ideology of meritocracy and individual mobility.

As societies become increasingly culturally diverse, with different cultural groups aiming to succeed in them, distribution based on nationality is challenged. Thus, managing cultural diversity is not just a case of tolerating the existence of different cultural traditions within a nation but rather it entails rethinking the meaning of the superordinate group in order to include in the resource distribution people who were previously excluded on the basis of nationality (economic migrants) or whose ingroup was exploited in the division of labor (e.g. African Americans owing to slavery or ethnic minorities owing to colonization).

However, changing the criteria of resource distribution reshuffles the cards of social stratification and therefore all positions are at stake. People in cultural minorities need to understand what the rules of success are and whether or how their diversity can enable or hinder it. In addition, people in cultural majorities need to understand what their position in the new situation might be and to accept the changes that the new social context entails. Of course, none of these groups are socially homogeneous. Instead, there are different positions and interests involved. This change of social stratification is part of the process of acculturation.

I would like to argue, therefore, that acculturation is a dynamic, meaning-making process whose outcome reflects how people from all communities make sense of their social environment, how they aspire to be part of it and how they position themselves in it (Chryssochoou, 2004; Motti-Stefanidi *et al.*, 2012). Acculturation is not the end result but a dynamic process of change that involves the active participation of individuals and groups. Within this process, society changes, groups change and individuals change. In order to capture the changes at these different levels, we need to study the mechanisms that enable people to internalize societal projects and act in favor or against them. As I will argue below, this happens within the terrain of identity. My aim here is to look at acculturation as a dynamic process of change in relation to identity and to discuss in particular the contribution of Identity Process Theory to customizing at a micro-individual level issues of cultural diversity.

Internalizing societal projects: making sense of new environments and dealing with change

People's own understandings of their position and place within the social structure and the consequences of these understandings have interested social psychologists. A major discussion concerns how social regulations influence people's ways of thinking and impact on their actions (Chryssochoou, 2005; Doise, 1990; Lorenzi-Cioldi and Clemence, 2001; Moscovici, 1961/1976). The conceptualization of this "internalization of society" coupled with an understanding of one's positioning and the subsequent actions that reflect this understanding, is made through the concept of identity. Identity offers the possibility to be a structure[3] that mediates between the individual and the social world (Hogg and Abrams, 1988; Stryker, 1997). It encompasses both collective and individual elements of the self. The potential to theorize the relationship between the individual and the social and its relation to human action has made identity a very popular concept among social psychologists. It has been considered in terms of its role and its relation to intergroup behavior, politicization and action (Mead, 1934; Reicher, 2004; Simon, 2004; Tajfel, 1974, 1981), or in terms of how its content is constructed, developed, challenged and changed (Breakwell, 1986; Deaux, 1992; Duveen, 2001). Whatever the angle from which identity is studied, it is considered the social psychological concept that reflects the ways in which people understand their social environment and their place in it. In other words it is the concept that allows us to discuss how society "continues itself within individuals" (Doise, 1997). I have argued elsewhere that identity is a social representation of the self that reflects and objectifies people's understanding of who they are and what they can claim to be, along with their own aspirations within the framework of their social environment (Chryssochoou, 2003). In order to develop a concept of identity that facilitates an understanding of the relationship between identifications and different behaviors (individual and collective), identity needs to be theorized at multiple levels of analysis (Breakwell, 1986, 2010a; Deaux, 2006; Doise, 1986, 2012; Verkuyten, 2005) and both as a product and a

---

[3] Talking about identity as a structure has not, however, acquired the unanimous agreement of the researchers working with this concept. For example, Turner and Onorato (1999, p. 33) suggest that we should look at the self as a process "a functional property of certain categories." In this perspective a category becomes a self-category not because of the way it is stored but because of the way it is used. Identity structure is not regarded as fixed or immutable. On the contrary, we are interested in the ways in which different elements of identity relate to each other and are used in different contexts. This is one of the aims of Identity Process Theory (Breakwell, 2010a).

process (Breakwell, 2001, 2010a). This theorization needs to incorporate how knowledge about the self is created, how this knowledge becomes meaningful within the context of social relationships and how it becomes internalized and customized.

In that respect, if we are interested in understanding acculturation as a meaning-making process within a changing social environment, inevitably we should investigate how identity deals with these changes. How does identity manage to reflect societal changes proposed by cultural diversity in the self? Which identity processes are involved in dealing with the social changes presented earlier regarding the transformation of contemporary societies into culturally diverse organizations?

Identity can be studied at three levels of analysis. First of all, it can be studied at a *macro-societal* level in order to see how identity-projects are constructed collectively to guide actions. This level concerns the normative aspects of identity along with the ensuing disagreements and conflicts. Secondly, identity processes can be studied at a *meso-interactional* level that concerns the various interactions between individuals and groups which are shaped by the identity-roles that people endorse. Finally, identity processes can be studied at a *micro-individual* level of analysis looking at how new elements are incorporated within the self-concept and how people deal with change without losing their sense of self. In this last level Identity Process Theory (IPT) (Breakwell, 1986, 1988, 1993a, 2001, 2010a), whose various facets are presented in this book, has a unique contribution.[4]

I aim, here, to look at identity processes at these different levels within the context of culturally diverse societies. I will present briefly the macro and meso levels of identity in relation to acculturation and then I will focus on the micro-individual level to discuss how IPT can contribute to our understanding of how people acculturate, deal with and provoke social change. The presentation of the other levels of analysis will allow me to contextualize the contribution of IPT and to discuss possible articulations of these theoretical accounts in order to understand the impact of social change (see also de la Sablonnière and Usborne, this volume).

---

[4] One of the major contributions of IPT is its holistic and integrative approach that combines personal and group characteristics – it is able to theorize multiple identifications both individual and collective. Here, I consider, however, the theory as pertaining to a micro-individual level of analysis because its primary focus is on how individuals incorporate new elements into the self-concept and deal with the threat that change can produce. In that respect, IPT is a theory about identity construction at an individual level. The argument that is presented later is that IPT can help us to understand how identity projects and roles, whose content is part of social representations, are selected and customized at an individual level.

Acculturation and identities at a macro-societal level and at a meso-interactional level

The presence of different cultural groups under the same political organization entails new projects of social co-existence and social cohesion. In other words societies need new founding myths that hold their different parts together and bring people and groups to feel part of a cohesive whole and to work toward common goals. The development of these projects is the outcome of social representational and social influence processes that involve different actors with various degrees of power.

There are, of course, the elites and the decision-makers with their own goals and projects. These people act as "entrepreneurs of identity" (Reicher and Hopkins, 2001), aiming to propose identities that will carry on these projects. Sometimes multiculturalism and diversity is celebrated,[5] whereas at other times it is argued that multiculturalism as a societal project has failed.[6] Because of their material, symbolic and political power in society, elites and dominant groups have the opportunity to convince others of their vision of how a successful society should be and to determine the position of the different groups within the social structure. Acculturation at a macro-societal level corresponds to the development of a hegemonic representation (Moscovici, 1988) of political organization and the position of different groups characterized by their ethnic origins and cultural background. The enaction of this representation requires the development of particular identities seen at the macro-societal level as projects (Reicher, 2004).[7] If people accept these identities and feel committed to them, they are expected to act "in their name" and, accordingly, reproduce or challenge the societal status quo (Azzi et al., 2011; Ellemers et al., 1999; Tajfel and Turner, 1986). The aim of elites and powerful individuals is to create normative identity-projects for all groups within a particular society that create a social

---

[5] Consider Canada, where in 1971 multiculturalism became an official policy and in 1988 the Canadian Multiculturalism Act encouraged "institutions to be respectful and inclusive of Canada's multicultural character."

[6] See, for instance, claims by German Chancellor Angela Merkel that multiculturalism in Germany has "utterly failed" (BBC News Europe, 2010).

[7] Identity categories are not deprived of content. We consider that this content is the outcome of social representational and social influence processes at a macro-level and therefore are not mere descriptions but, more importantly prescriptions to act in a certain way. Each social category might be linked to several identity-projects and which identity-project prevails depends on social influence and power dynamics. Because of their strategic aspect, identity projects lead to particular actions in the name of a particular identity. IPT can help us to understand which identity-project will be embraced at an individual level because of the principled way in which identity processes function.

stratification and an organization that suits their own interests. However, the acceptance of these discourses depends also on the aspirations and threats perceived by the other social groups. These identity-projects are developed around perceptions of the social structure and opportunities to succeed and they lead to particular individual and group strategies (Branscombe and Ellemers, 1998; Mummendey *et al.*, 1999).

Ethnic groups can opt for different strategies of acculturation depending on what they perceive to be the best way to succeed in society. Some groups may opt for assimilation strategies, as, for example, the Albanians in Greece who change their name and baptize themselves Christian Orthodox (Hatziprokopiou, 2003), whereas others in the same society (e.g. the Polish in Greece) might choose to maintain their cultural distinction. These strategies can also be influenced by ethnic leaders with their own projects for their ingroup that sometimes are contradictory. For instance, British Muslim leaders displayed contradictory discourses regarding the participation of the British Muslim community in the general elections: some opting for participation and others preaching for abstention (Hopkins and Kahani-Hopkins, 2004). Moreover, the different generations of migrants and ethnic minorities may diverge in their priorities depending on how they perceive the opportunities offered to them. I have argued elsewhere that immigrant generations might dispute different aspects of the socio-structural context (Chryssochoou, 2009). First-generation immigrants, claiming social mobility at least for their offspring, might challenge the permeability of group boundaries. Second-generation immigrants, born and raised in the country but still facing discrimination because of their origins, might call into question the legitimacy of the system that gives ethnic majorities a better position. Finally, third-generation immigrants could defy the stability of the intergroup system and engage in collective social action to ameliorate their position.

From the point of view of cultural majorities, the different discourses of political organization can be accepted by the different groups, depending on their own understanding of their opportunities within the particular society and their position in it. Cultural majorities might try to present their relationship with immigrants and ethnic minorities as legitimate, stable and non-permeable in order to maintain social cohesion without challenging the criteria for nationhood and a resource distribution that favor them. Like ethnic minorities, ethnic majorities are not socially homogeneous. National elites would like to maintain their distinctiveness both from others in their national ingroup and from ethnic minorities. Their discourses about political organization have, therefore, multiple audiences. This means that identities can be ideologically constrained by discourses, for example, about the incompatibility of different identities (Chryssochoou and Lyons, 2011), in order to stratify society in particular ways at a group level. By emphasizing diversity and cultural difference, elites and dominant classes might succeed in stratifying society in terms of culture, thus keeping satisfied their compatriots who are given priority in terms of material and symbolic resources. At the same time, with this strategy, they avoid a challenge of their position in terms of social class. The boundaries of the groups are kept partially open to allow for individual mobility.

At a macro-societal level, identity-projects are constructed with the same mechanisms of social representations (Clemence, 2001; Doise, 1992; Lorenzi-Cioldi and Clemence, 2001) and diffused through social influence processes (Moscovici, 1976). These identities, as the product of the articulation of ideological beliefs with power issues, have consequences for intergroup behavior and intergroup relations. However, they also shape the different roles that people enact at a meso-interactional level.

Everyday activities, position-taking and social interactions at an interpersonal level enact these macro-social identity-projects through the different roles that people endorse. The discussion of identity as role performance has been prominent within an interactionist perspective (Burke and Stets, 2009; Stryker, 1980). In this approach, individuals are considered agents and have the choice to act as role performers within the limits of the social structure. People internalize different roles within a hierarchically organized structure of the self and negotiate the meanings of these roles within social interactions. At a meso-interactional level of analysis, acculturation is shaped by the exchanges people have at an interpersonal level. Through practices and everyday negotiations people will enact the normative content of the identity-projects they have already embraced. For instance, what does it mean to be an immigrant in everyday life? How should one behave as a parent, a colleague, an employer or an employee and a sports' fan in a culturally diverse environment? How can one express one's participation to different cultural communities? Literature on acculturation, especially regarding second-generation immigrants and ethnic minority individuals show how they deal with their different audiences (Vadher and Barrett, 2009; Wiley and Deaux, 2011). People belonging to cultural majorities need in their everyday interactions to manage their own positions as both, for instance, cultural majority members and co-workers with immigrants. The social and cultural memberships give different roles to people belonging to the different communities and people have to accommodate them within the larger acculturative context reflected in the identity-projects.

It is important to investigate acculturation at a meso-interactional level. For instance, Verkuyten (2005, p. 91) remarks that "status and power differences at a societal level can differ from those at work in local situations in which people are in the process of defining and negotiating relations and positions." These interpersonal negotiations shape identities and make salient different social comparisons that do not need to be only between cultural minorities and cultural majorities. People might compare immigrant generations or different ethnic groups present in the proximal context. An analysis of acculturation at a meso-interactional level can also give us insight into how people deal with discrimination at an interpersonal level (Deaux, 2006). The experience of discrimination at an interpersonal level is found to influence the acceptance of superordinate identities and to enhance the development of oppositional ones (Rumbaut, 2008).

In a macro and meso level of analysis, acculturation corresponds to the different societal projects and their enactment in the everyday lives of individuals and groups. These societal projects are mediated through identities that enable their enactment. These identities concern either identifications with large social categories or commitment to different identity roles. If we acknowledge that the endorsement of a particular identity has consequences regarding action, we should investigate at a micro-individual level how identities are accepted by individuals. We cannot claim that it suffices to be a member of a particular group to endorse the relevant identity and act consequently. There are multiple studies that show that people justify a system that disadvantages them (Blasi and Jost, 2006, Jost and Major, 2001). Moreover, the changes at a societal level that necessitate acculturation and threats at an interpersonal level oblige individual identities to be transformed in order to incorporate new elements without the individual losing a sense of self. This is where the contribution of Identity Process Theory is paramount.

Acculturation and identity at a micro-individual level: the contribution of Identity Process Theory

Acculturation at a micro-level of analysis concerns the reflection of the cultural diversity project at the level of the self. It is about the combination of different identities (projects and roles) at an individual level. How do people incorporate specific identities and how do they deal with change? Would an immigrant identify with the category "immigrants in general" or would he or she prefer to identify with the ethnic, national, religious or cultural group that he or she belongs to? Under which circumstances would an individual identify with the receiving society or with their social class? How would a member of the receiving society incorporate the changes that take place at a societal level in the self-concept? The understanding of identity processes at this level is important not only to explain particular behaviors but also to understand the success and failures of acculturation. Why do some people seem able to function in these new environments? Why do some people embrace extreme, racist and fascist ideologies instead of accommodating culturally diverse societal projects? To answer these questions Identity Process Theory can be a useful tool.

Identity Process Theory (Breakwell, 1986, 1988, 1993a, 2001, 2010a, 2011) postulates that individuals seek to generate a structure of their identity that is characterized by different motivations. Two processes operate for the development of this structure: assimilation–accommodation and evaluation. Assimilation–accommodation absorbs and adjusts the different identity elements into the identity structure and evaluation allocates value and meaning to the different identity elements. These processes interact together, influencing each other in order to manage the structure of identity at any given time and diachronically. The identity structure is not static but changes over time with the incorporation of new elements and the readjustment of the past ones. Identity processes work in order to produce a principled identity structure that in the original theoretical formulation was guided by uniqueness or distinctiveness, continuity across time and situation and a feeling of self-worth. Subsequent formulations of the theory added self-efficacy as another principle that guide the two identity processes and more recently other motives, such as feelings of purpose and closeness to others, are proposed (Vignoles *et al.*, 2002, 2006). Although these principles seem culturally bound it has also been argued that their operation can be cross-cultural even if their meaning changes across cultures (Vignoles *et al.*, 2000).

The theory has been described elsewhere in the volume (Jaspal, this volume). However, one aspect that needs to be highlighted here in relation to acculturation is IPT's theorization of change. According to the theory (Breakwell, 1986, p. 39), "any movement in the social matrix will require the individual to process potential new contents and values for identity." Given that social change is considered the norm and that it is constant, individuals are obliged to deal continuously with information that needs to be assimilated–accommodated and evaluated. These operations may be threatened whenever the identity processes are unable to comply with the identity principles. Whatever obstructs this operation can be considered a threat (Breakwell, 1986) and whenever people face such threats they are expected to engage coping strategies to erase them. The theory, lately, has been particularly useful in looking at how scientific and technical developments and changes can threaten identities and how strategies to cope with this threat emerge (Breakwell, 2007, 2010b).

In relation to our discussion about acculturation, IPT can be useful given its theorization of how people deal with unfamiliar and new events. The identity processes proposed by the theory have a close resemblance with the processes in operation in the formation of social representations. One of the major functions of social representations is to domesticate the unfamiliar (Moscovici, 2000, 2001), thus to deal with the threat that unfamiliarity produces. Social representations are "social" and shared knowledge because through the operation of a meta-system, that guides people's operational cognitive system, social regulations are incorporated within people's existing knowledge. Two processes make this guidance possible: anchoring and objectification. Anchoring incorporates the new and unfamiliar elements into pre-existing frameworks and objectification evaluates and gives flesh to abstract elements by producing relevant images that objectify them. These processes seem to function similarly to the assimilation–accommodation and evaluation processes of IPT. I have argued elsewhere (Chryssochoou, 2003, 2009) that identity can be considered a specific form of social representation, that is, a specific form of social knowledge about the self that includes self-cognitions, self-claims and demands recognition. This knowledge is developed through socialization, is communicated and is subject to processes of social influence in order to be socially recognized. If we are able to communicate something about "who we are," this is possible because there is a socially constructed knowledge of ourselves.

Likewise, IPT suggests that identity is a social construct (Breakwell, 2001). At a subjective level identity could be seen as a personal representation, in other words "the manifestation of a social representation at the level of the individual" (Breakwell, 2001, p. 271). One of the concerns of IPT is to be able to combine "the active subjective conscious self and the objectified known self" (Breakwell, 2010a, p. 6.2). The integration of the subjective self and the socially represented one is theoretically possible through the integration of IPT and Social Representations Theory, an integration that Glynis Breakwell has promoted on many occasions (Breakwell, 1993a, 1993b, 2001, 2010a, 2010b). This articulation can be achieved through the study of identity processes at a micro-individual level. Thus, the identity projects developed at the macro-societal level could be manifested at an individual level through a particular identity structure. Seemingly, the identity-roles performed at the meso-interactional level can be enacted because of the way this structure is organized at the individual level (Breakwell, 2011). It can be argued that people living in the same social environment will have similar identity structures but not, of course, the same. By studying them we would be able to understand both commonalities and individual variation. Thus, we might be able to understand why some people embrace extreme ideologies and others resist them, or why some people manage to combine their different positions and memberships while others do not. In particular, in the case of acculturation, studying the processes involved in producing an identity structure would allow us to understand why and how multiple memberships co-exist sometimes peacefully and sometimes in conflict. Moreover, acculturation can be lived as a threat to identity, given its demands to incorporate novelty in a harsh way and in constrained time. Thus, following IPT, one could try to predict which particular identity principles would be obstructed each time in order to predict peoples' actions and acceptance of cultural diversity as a new social order. In the last section of this chapter I will bring some empirical evidence from IPT research and propose some hypotheses in the domain of acculturation.

Visiting acculturation through Identity Process Theory

Identity Process Theory has informed studies aiming to understand how people deal with threats owing to cultural diversity and changes in identity. These studies provide us with good examples of what one could achieve by using this theoretical framework. For instance, in one of the first studies in this area, Timotijevic and Breakwell (2000) investigated identity construction and threats among people from former Yugoslavia in Britain. Their study shows that people negotiate categories of identity at different levels in order to satisfy different identity principles. In this instance, continuity is salient in category negotiation at an individual level whereas distinctiveness is salient at inter-individual and intergroup levels. The use of IPT in this case enables researchers to navigate between levels of analysis and understand why identities acquire different meanings and can have different consequences for action when they concern the individual or group levels.

In a series of more recent studies, mainly with British Asians, Jaspal and colleagues provide us with other aspects in which IPT can be useful. These studies clearly attempt to articulate IPT with social representations operating at the macro-societal level. Jaspal and Cinnirella (2012a) aim to specify the causes of identity threat. They also show how continuity is challenged between two different temporal selves. This theorization can be useful in understanding identity and other social psychological processes involved in the pre-immigration period which may affect peoples' acculturation (Jasinskaja-Lahti and Yijala, 2011). Moreover, their study highlights the complexity of the positions that people with multiple minority identities have to accommodate. They, also, indicate that social change that is beneficial at an interpersonal level may have negative consequences at an intrapsychic level. Like Timotijevic and Breakwell (2000) their analysis articulates different levels in analyzing identity construction.

Jaspal and Cinnirella (2010) deal with the important issue of multiple identifications and the perceived compatibility of identities. They propose another important principle guiding identity processes – psychological coherence, which they argue motivates individuals to reconcile important identities that are presented as incompatible. Psychological coherence impacts on the evaluation of identities in order to achieve this reconciliation. They remark that, although individuals can be influenced by prevailing social representations, ultimately individuals arrive at their own conclusion regarding the compatibility between identities. This study, informed by IPT, can give us an insight on how minority members, at an individual level, deal with the different beliefs about incompatibility between identities proposed by the societal context (Chryssochoou and Lyons, 2011).

Another issue raised by this series of studies is the fact that minority groups are not homogeneous. This is often forgotten in research that tends to oppose minority and majority groups as if there are no other distinctions among them. In their research into the construction of ethnic identity among British Asians, Jaspal and Cinnirella (2012b) remark the differences between different generations. People in their everyday interactions (but also in self-perception) recognize the heterogeneity within the groups they belong to and more importantly, as in the case of Sikhs in Britain (Jaspal, 2013), they strive to assert their distinctiveness from other ethnic groups. Moreover, when people feel that they risk being homogenized by outgroups they attempt to claim and accentuate their different identities (Jaspal, 2012). The recognition of diversity cannot be solely between majorities and minorities. Very often this homogenization is a way to assert power and to reduce the individuality of minority members, which is prioritized in Western industrialized cultures (Beauvois and Dubois, 1988; Lorenzi-Cioldi, 2002). Immigrants are not all from "immigrant-land." The depth of our analysis suffers when we unwittingly homogenize cultural groups (Iatridis and Chryssochoou, 2011).

These studies deal also with other important issues in culturally diverse contexts such as the ways in which people communicate between their culture of origin and the culture in the society in which they live (Jaspal, 2013) and the ways in which they strategically use language to enhance identity principles (Jaspal and Coyle, 2009). The authors argue that language is a symbolic marker of identity and in some situations its use can constitute a threat to peoples' identity. Often language is treated in literature as a marker of acculturation. This analysis shows that the process is much more complex. Finally, all these studies put emphasis on the agency people have in customizing prevailing social representations and identity projects at the macro-societal level and to use different principles in the intrapsychic, interpersonal and intergroup levels in order to achieve a satisfactory way to see and present themselves. Because of the emphasis of IPT on identity changes owing to societal changes and to societal changes due to identity changes, its articulation of different levels of analysis and the importance it puts on individual agency, acculturation research has much to profit by being informed by this theory.

However, the studies that used IPT as their theoretical framework have concentrated their efforts, legitimately, on minorities. Acculturation research would have much to gain if similar studies are conducted with cultural majorities of different social backgrounds. Those who are likely to pose problems to the coexistence of different cultural groups under the same political entity are not minorities but majorities. Majorities are those feeling threatened by the changes induced by culturally diverse societies. Especially in times of economic crisis majorities are the people at risk from extreme political ideologies. Another point that is acknowledged and discussed by IPT researchers is that IPT research regarding acculturation is mainly qualitative (see Coyle and Murtagh, this volume). This can allow for rich and fine-grained analyses of identity construction that are necessary. However, it is within the epistemological project of the theory (Breakwell, 1993b) to articulate different methods and certainly this should be done in the future. Finally, in working on the way in which identity is structured, one should be very careful not to reify the concept, as was done with personality and intelligence. Identity should remain a social psychological structure operating at different levels of analysis and expressing the ways in which people attribute meaning to their environment through the ways in which they position themselves in it.

Concluding remarks

In this chapter I have argued that acculturation is a collective process of changing social stratification and the criteria of resource distribution in culturally diverse societies and is not a mere process of cultural tolerance. Culturally diverse societies require the transformation of beliefs, attitudes and practices in order to reflect these changes. Inevitably, identities, at different levels, are transformed. At a macro-societal level through processes of social representations and social influence, acculturation is reflected in identity projects. Moreover, at a meso-interactional level identity-roles need to be accommodated in the changing contexts of interactions. The processes at these levels and more importantly their consequences for individual and collective behavior have been studied by social psychologists. However, as Deaux and Burke (2010) recently remarked, identity theories have neglected the person and the relationships between identities. I have argued that in the context of acculturation, we should also investigate the micro-individual level. In this endeavor Identity Process Theory can help us understand what motivates particular identity claims, their meaning and their demands for recognition. Jaspal (2010) claims that in the Indian caste system different identity principles operate for the different castes. What happens in culturally diverse societies? My hypothesis (Chryssochoou, 2010) is that currently there is an attempt to establish a "caste system" based on ethnicity and culture that within an ideological framework of meritocracy will keep ethnic minorities at the bottom of the social ladder. If this happens in the social context how will this be reflected in the identity-projects, the identity roles and the ways in which individuals of all communities view themselves? Theoretical integration at different levels is needed. However, in a moment of great uncertainty produced from the economic crisis, being able to articulate the different levels of acculturation and the identities that they generate is not just an academic exercise. A politically engaged social psychology appears to be a necessity.

REFERENCES

Abu-Rayya, H. M. (2009). Acculturation and its determinants among adult immigrants in France. *International Journal of Psychology*, 44 (3), 195–203.

Azzi, A. E., Chryssochoou, X., Klandermans, B., and Simon, B. (2011). *Identity and a multidisciplinary perspective*. Oxford: Wiley-Blackwell.

BBC News Europe (2010). Merkel says German multicultural society has failed. www.bbc.co.uk/news/world-europe-11559451.

Beauvois, J.-L., and Dubois, N. (1988). The norm of internality in the explanation of psychological events. *European Journal of Social Psychology*, 18, 299–316.

Berry, J. W. (1990). Psychology of acculturation: understanding individuals moving across cultures. In R. W. Brislin (ed.), *Applied cross-cultural psychology* (pp. 232–253). Newbury Park, CA: Sage.

Berry, J. W. (2001). A psychology of immigration. *Journal of Social Issues*, 57, 615–631.

Blasi, G., and Jost, J. T. (2006). System Justification theory and research: implications for law. Legal advocacy and social justice. *California Law Review*, 94, 1119–1168.

Bourhis, R. Y., Moise, L. C., Perreault, S. L., and Senécal, S. (1997). Towards an interactive acculturation model. A social psychological approach. *International Journal of Psychology*, 32, 368–386.

Branscombe, N. R., and Ellemers, N. (1998). Coping with group-based discrimination. Individualistic versus group level strategies. In J. K. Swim and C. Stangor (eds.), *Prejudice. The Target's perspective* (pp. 244–266). San Diego, CA: Academic Press.

Breakwell, G. M. (1986). *Threatened identities.* London: Methuen.

Breakwell, G. M. (1988). Strategies adopted when identity is threatened. *Revue Internationale de Psychologie Sociale,* 1, 189–203.

Breakwell, G. M. (1993a). Social representations and social identity. *Papers on Social Representations,* 2, 198–217.

Breakwell, G. M. (1993b). Integrating paradigms, methodological implications. In G. M. Breakwell and D. Canter, *Empirical approaches to social representations* (pp. 180–201). Oxford University Press.

Breakwell, G. M. (2001). Social representational constrains upon identity processes. In K. Deaux and G. Philogene (eds.), *Representations of the social* (pp. 271–284). Oxford: Blackwell.

Breakwell, G. M. (2007). *The psychology of risk.* Cambridge University Press.

Breakwell, G. M. (2010a). Resisting representations and identity processes. Special issue of *Papers on Social Representations,* 19, 6.1–6.11 (in honour of Gerard Duveen: Social Representations and Social Identities: Inspirations from Gerard Duveen).

Breakwell, G. M. (2010b). Models of risk construction: some applications to climate change. *Wiley Interdisciplinary Reviews: Climate Change,* 1(6), 857–870.

Breakwell, G. M. (2011). Empirical approaches to social representations and identity processes: 20 years on. Special issue of *Papers on Social Representations,* 20, 17.1–17.4.

Burke, P. J., and Stets, J. E. (2009). *Identity theory.* New York: Oxford University Press.

Castles, S., and Davidson, A. (2000). *Citizenship and migration: globalization and the politics of belonging.* London: Macmillan.

Chryssochoou, X. (2000). Multicultural societies: making sense of new environments and identities. *Journal of Community and Applied Social Psychology,* 10(5), 343–354.

Chryssochoou, X. (2003). Studying identity in social psychology. Some thoughts on the definition of identity and its relation to action. *Language and Politics,* 22, 225–242.

Chryssochoou, X. (2004). *Cultural diversity. Its social psychology.* Oxford: Blackwell.

Chryssochoou, X. (2005). Social representations. *Encyclopaedic dictionary of psychology.* London: Hodder Arnold.

Chryssochoou, X. (2009). Identity projects in multicultural nation-states. In I. Jasinskaja-Lahti and T. A. Mahonen (eds.), *Identities, intergroup relations and acculturation. The cornerstones of intercultural encounters.* Helsinki: Gaudeamus Helsinki University Press.

Chryssochoou, X. (2010). Representations of the social and of the cultural in the meaning making of the co-existence in multicultural environments: a social psychological analysis of ideological opposition to migration In S. Papastamou, G. Prodromitis and V. Pavlopoulos, *Social thought, cognition and behavior* (pp. 491–523). Athens: Pedio. (In Greek) Αναπαραστάσεις του κοινωνικού και του πολιτισμικού στις νοηματοδοτήσεις της κοινής συνύπαρξης σε πολυπολιτισμικά περιβάλλοντα: μια κοινωνιοψυχολογική ανάλυση της αντίθεσης στη μετανάστευση σε ιδεολογικό επίπεδο Στο Σ. Παπαστάμου, Γ. Προδρομίτης, Β. Παυλόπουλος Κοινωνική Σκέψη, Νόηση και Συμπεριφορά (491–523) Αθήνα: Πεδίο.

Chryssochoou, X., and Lyons, E. (2011). Perceptions of (in)compatibility between identities and participation in the national polity of people belonging to ethnic minorities. In A. E. Azzi, X. Chryssochoou, B. Klandermans and B. Simon (eds.), *Identity and participation in culturally diverse societies* (pp. 69–88). Wiley-Blackwell, Oxford.

Clemence, A. (2001). Social positioning and social representations. In K. Deaux and G. Philogene (eds.), *Representations of the social* (pp. 63–95). Oxford: Blackwell.

Condor, S. (2006). Temporality and collectivity: diversity, history and the rhetorical construction of national entitativity. *British Journal of Social Psychology*, 45, 657–682.

Deaux, K. (1992). Personalizing identity and socializing self. In G. M. Breakwell (ed.), *Social psychology of identity and the self-concept* (pp. 9–33). London: Academic Press.

Deaux, K. (2006). *To be an immigrant*. New York: Russell Sage.

Deaux, K., and Burke, P. J. (2010). Bridging identities. *Social Psychology Quarterly*, 73,(4), 315–320.

Doise, W. (1986). *Levels of explanation in social psychology*. Cambridge University Press.

Doise, W. (1990). Les représentations sociales. In R. Guiglione, C. Bonnet and J.-F. Richard (eds.), *Traité de Psychologie Cognitive 3* (pp. 111–174). Paris: Presses Universitaires de France.

Doise, W. (1992). L'ancrage sur les études sur les représentations sociales. *Bulletin de Psychologie*, 405, 189–195.

Doise, W. (1997). Organising social psychological explanations. In C. McGarty and S. A. Haslam (eds.), *The message of social psychology* (pp. 63–76). Oxford: Blackwell.

Doise, W. (2012). The homecoming of society in social psychology. In J. Pires Valentim (ed.), *Societal approaches in social psychology* (pp. 9–34). Bern: Peter Lang.

Duveen, G. (2001). Representations, identities, resistance. In K. Deaux and G. Philogene (eds.), *Representations of the social* (pp. 257–270). Oxford: Blackwell.

Ellemers, N., Spears, R., and Doosje, B. (eds.) (1999). *Social identity*. Oxford: Blackwell.

Hatziprokopiou, P. (2003). Albanian immigrants in Thessaloniki, Greece: processes of economic and social incorporation. *Journal of Ethnic and Migration Studies*, 29(6), 1,033–1,057.

Hogg, M. A., and Abrams, D. (1988). *Social identifications. A social psychology of intergroup relations and group processes*. London: Routledge.

Hopkins, N., and Kahani-Hopkins, V. (2004), Identity construction and British Muslims' political activity: beyond rational actor theory. *British Journal of Social Psychology*, 43, 339–356.

Huntington, S. P. (1993). The clash of civilizations? *Foreign Affairs*, 72, 22–49.

Iatridis, T., and Chryssochoou, X. (2011). Evidence from the Stereotype Content Model: calling them all immigrants hides perceived competition. Poster Presented at the General Meeting of the European Association of Social Psychology, Stockholm Sweden July 12–16, 2011.

Jasinskaja-Lahti, I., and Liebkind, K. (2007). A structural model of acculturation and well-being among immigrants from the former USSR in Finland. *European Psychologist*, 12(2),80–92.

Jasinskaja-Lahti, I., and Yijala, A. (2011). The model of pre-acculturative stress: a pre migration study of potential migrants from Russia to Finland. *International Journal of Intercultural Relations*, 35, 499–510.

Jaspal, R. (2010). Caste, social stigma and identity processes. *Psychology and Developing Societies*, 23(2), 27–62.

Jaspal, R. (2012). 'I never faced up to being gay': sexual, religious and ethnic identities among British Indian and British Pakistani gay men. *Culture, Health & Sexuality*, 14(7), 767–780.

Jaspal, R. (2013). British Sikh identity and the struggle for distinctiveness and continuity. *Journal of Community and Applied Social Psychology*, 23(3), 225–239.

Jaspal, R., and Coyle, A. (2009). Language and perceptions of identity threat. *Psychology and Society*, 2(2), 150–167.

Jaspal, R., and Cinnirella, M. (2010). Coping with potentially incompatible identities: accounts of religious, ethnic and sexual identities from British Pakistani men who identify as Muslim and gay. *British Journal of Social Psychology*, 49, 849–870.

Jaspal, R., and Cinnirella, M. (2012a). Identity processes, threat and interpersonal relations: accounts from British, Muslim, gay men. *Journal of Homosexuality*, 59, 215–240.

Jaspal, R., and Cinnirella, M. (2012b). The construction of ethnic identity. Insights from Identity Process Theory, *Ethnicities*, 12(5), 503–530.

Jost, J. T., and Major, B. (eds.) (2001). *The psychology of legitimacy: emerging perspectives on ideology, justice and intergroup relations*. New York: Cambridge University Press.

Lorenzi-Cioldi, F. (2002). *Les représentations des groupes dominants et dominés. Collections et agrégats*. Grenoble: Presses Universitaires.

Lorenzi-Cioldi, F., and Clemence, A. (2001). Group processes and the construction of social representations. In M. A. Hogg and R. S. Tindale, *Blackwell handbook of social psychology: group processes* (pp. 311–333). Oxford: Blackwell.

Mead, G. H. (1934). *Mind, self and society*. Chicago, IL: Chicago University Press.

Montreuil, A., and Bourhis, R. Y. (2004). Acculturation orientations of competing host communities toward valued and devalued immigrants. *International Journal of Intercultural Relations*, 28, 507–532.

Moscovici, S. (1961/1976). *La psychanalyse son image et son public*. Paris: Presses Universitaires de France.

Moscovici, S. (1976). *Social influence and social change*. London: Academic Press.

Moscovici, S. (1988). Notes towards a description of social representations. *European Journal of Social Psychology*, 18, 211–250.

Moscovici, S. (2000). *Social representations. Explorations in social psychology.* Oxford: Polity Press.

Moscovici, S. (2001). Why a theory of social representations? In K. Deaux and G. Philogene (eds.), *Representations of the social* (pp. 8–35). Oxford: Blackwell.

Motti-Stefanidi, F., Berry, J., Chryssochoou, X., Lackland Sam, D., and Phinney, J. (2012). Positive immigrant youth adaptation in context: developmental, acculturation and social psychological perspectives. In A.S. Mansten, K. Liebkind, D. J. Hernandez (eds), *Realizing the potential of immigrant youth. The Jacobs Foundation series on adolescence* (pp. 117–158). Cambridge University Press.

Mummendey, A., Kessler, T., Klink, A., and Mielke, R. (1999). Strategies to cope with negative social identity: predictions by social identity theory and relative deprivation theory. *Journal of Personality and Social Psychology*, 76, 229–245.

Pfafferott, I., and Brown, R. (2006). Acculturation preferences of majority and minority adolescents in Germany in the context of society and family. *International Journal of Intercultural Relations*, 30, 703–717.

Phinney, J. S., Horenczyk, G., Liebkind, K., and Vedder, P. (2001). Ethnic identity, immigration and well-being: an interactional perspective. *Journal of Social Issues*, 57(3), 493–510.

Piontkowski, U., Rohmann, A., and Florack, A. (2002). Concordance of acculturation attitudes and perceived threat. *Group Processes Intergroup Relations*, 5, 221–232.

Redfield, R., Linton, R., and Herkovits, M. J. (1936). Memorandum on the study of acculturation. *American Anthropologist*, 38, 149–152.

Reicher, S. (2004). The context of social identity: domination, resistance and change. *Political Psychology*, 25 (6), 921–945.

Reicher, S., and Hopkins, N. (2001). *Self and nation.* London: Sage.

Rumbaut, R. G. (2008). Reaping what you sow. Immigration, youth and reactive ethnicity. *Applied Developmental Science*, 12(2), 108–111.

Simon, B. (2004). *Identity in modern society. A social psychological perspective.* Oxford: Blackwell.

Stryker, S. (1980). *Symbolic interactionism: a social structural version.* Menlo Park, CA: Benjamin Cummings.

Stryker, S. (1997). Sociological social psychology. In C. McGarty and S. A. Haslam (eds.), *The message of social psychology* (pp. 315–327). Oxford: Blackwell.

Tajfel, H. (1974). Social identity and intergroup behavior. *Social Science Information*, 13, 65–69.

Tajfel, H. (1981). *Human groups and social categories. Studies in social psychology.* Cambridge University Press.

Tajfel, H., and Turner, J. C. (1986). The social identity theory of intergroup behavior. In S. Worchel and W. G. Austin (eds.), *Psychology of intergroup relations.* Chicago, IL: Nelson Hall.

Timotijevic, L., and Breakwell, G. M. (2000). Migration and threat to identity. *Journal of Community and Applied Social Psychology*, 10(5), 355–372.

Touraine, A. (2005). *Un nouveau paradigme pour comprendre le monde d'aujourd'hui.* Paris: Fayard.

Turner, J. C., and Onorato, R. S. (1999). Social identity, personality and the self-concept: a self-categorisation perspective. In T. R. Tyler, R. M. Kramer and O. P. John (eds.), *The psychology of the social self.* (pp. 11–46). Mahwah, NJ: Lawrence Erlbaum.

Vadher, K., and Barrett, M. (2009). Boundaries of Britishness in British Indian and Pakistani young adults. *Journal of Community and Applied Social Psychology*, 19, 442–458.

Verkuyten, M. (2005). *The social psychology of ethnic identity.* New York: Psychology Press.

Vignoles, V. L., Chryssochoou, X., and Breakwell, G. M. (2000). The distinctiveness principle: identity, meaning and the bounds of cultural relativity. *Personality and Social Psychology Review*, 4(4), 337–354.

Vignoles, V. L., Chryssochoou, X., and Breakwell, G. M. (2002). Evaluating models of identity motivation. Self esteem is not the whole story. *Self and Identity*, 1, 201–218.

Vignoles, V. L., Regalia, C., Manzi, C., Golledge, J., and Scabini, E. (2006). Beyond self-esteem: influence of multiple motives on identity construction. *Journal of Personality and Social Psychology*, 90, 308–333.

Wiley, S., and Deaux, K. (2011). The bicultural identity performance of immigrants. In A. E. Azzi, X. Chryssochoou, B. Klandermans and B. Simon (eds.), *Identity and participation in culturally diverse societies* (pp. 49–68). Oxford: Wiley-Blackwell.

Zagefka, H., and Brown, R. (2002). The relationship between acculturation strategies and relative fit and intergroup relations: immigrant-majority relations in Germany. *European Journal of Social Psychology*, 32, 171–188.

Zick, A., Wagner, U., Van Dick, R., and Petzel, T. (2001). Acculturation and prejudice in Germany: majority and minority perspectives. *Journal of Social Issues*, 57, 541–557.

8 Identity integration, psychological coherence and identity threat: linking Identity Process Theory and notions of integration

Catherine E. Amiot and Rusi Jaspal

We currently live in increasingly diversified and fluctuating societies. Organization changes, climate changes and immigration are prime examples. With respect to immigration specifically, approximately 175 million people were living outside their country of birth in 2002 (United Nations, 2002). Individuals are also more likely than they were to change jobs and careers, with an estimated average of eleven changes in jobs in one career (Bureau of Labor Statistics, US Department of Labor, 2010). Changes in social networks and in family structure are also noticeable, with approximately 40 percent of individuals likely to divorce in Canada (Statistics Canada, 2011). Moreover, scholars have observed changes in patterns of social connectivity among US citizens; for instance, the percentage of survey respondents who reported having a friend, rather than a family member, as a close confidant has decreased from 73 percent to 51 percent over two decades (McPherson *et al.*, 2006). Such changes in social networks and family structure typically have implications for self and identity, given the associated accentuation or attenuation of particular elements of the self-concept. At a more macroscopic level, many countries – such as Egypt and Libya – are also currently experiencing important changes in their political structure (BBC News Africa, 2011), and recent campaigns worldwide (e.g. Occupy Wall Street Movement) suggest a deep questioning of – and even an upsurge against – the current economic system (see also de la Sablonnière and Usborne, this volume). In the present chapter, we raise the following questions: how do individuals make sense of these changes and come to develop a sense of identification with new social groups (e.g. organizational groups, political groups, friendship groups, family)? As these new identifications develop over time, what needs and principles will these new groups fulfill for individual group members? How do individuals negotiate their different and potentially conflicting group memberships?

We argue in this chapter that such life transitions and social changes – originally external to people – have repercussions for how people perceive their own sense of self. Although humans are active agents with a sense of free will who can actively block some of these external influences (Baumeister, 2008) and choose what dimensions to display and play up or down, these actions and choices are also constrained by powerful situational forces (Zimbardo, 2007). Individuals realize fully the extent of these external constraints when they experience situations over which they have little or no control, such as being a victim of discrimination or when feeling that some of the dimensions of themselves are socially devalued (Crocker and Major, 1989) and that their integrity is compromised.

The goal of the current chapter is threefold, namely: (1) to explain how individuals, in times of change, come to integrate new identities intra-individually in their sense of self and maintain a feeling of psychological coherence in this process; (2) to highlight how the identity principles proposed by identity process theory (IPT) come into play throughout this change process and how the satisfaction of these principles may actually facilitate the integration of new and multiple social identities in the self; and (3) to identify some factors that may actively block the integration of these identities, namely feelings of identity threat and the social devaluation of certain identities relative to others. We base ourselves on different strands of research to make these points and more specifically, the cognitive-developmental model of social identity integration (CDMSII; Amiot et al., 2007a), IPT (Breakwell, 1986) and the concept of psychological coherence (Jaspal and Cinnirella, 2010). Throughout the chapter, an implicit goal is to build bridges between these different social psychological theories, as they are each relevant to addressing these issues and also to provide a broad and integrative framework to understand how diversity can be reconciled subjectively and intra-individually – within each individual.

Defining the notions of identity integration and psychological coherence

Let us start first by defining what we mean by the terms "identity integration" and "psychological coherence."

Identity integration

According to the CDMSII, when multiple identities become integrated in the self, they are organized within the global self-structure so that they can be simultaneously important to the overall self-concept. When this occurs, connections and links are established between these different self-components so that they do not feel fragmented (e.g. Donahue *et al.*, 1993). As a consequence, the self feels coherent rather than conflicted (Amiot *et al.*, 2007a). Hence, identity integration should have positive consequences for psychological well-being. Because the integration of one's identities enables the individual to draw similarities between the different self-defining characteristics, identity integration allows for a more coherent vision of the self, where differences between one's different identities are considered complementary rather than conflicting (e.g. Amiot *et al.*, 2007a; Benet-Martinez *et al.*, 2002; Downie *et al.*, 2004; Roccas and Brewer, 2002).

This view of identity integration emphasizes the cognitive nature of the self, and, in this sense, it is directly based on principles from the social cognition literature. In the social cognition literature, researchers view the self as a multifaceted cognitive structure (Markus, 1977; Markus and Wurf, 1987), which can be defined as "a collection of at least semi-related and highly domain-specific knowledge structures" (Fiske and Taylor, 1991, p. 182). While social identities deal specifically with group memberships as they derive from our memberships to social groups (Tajfel, 1981), they can also be conceived of as one specific type of self-component composing the global self (Deaux, 1991). Because the same individual can belong to a wide variety of groups (Tajfel and Turner, 1979, 1986), the self-concept is hence composed of multiple social identities. But how is this multiplicity represented and organized cognitively?

Self-schemas are a useful concept to illustrate how the self is organized cognitively and how one's multiple social identities, as specific self-components, are organized within the self. Self-schemas are hierarchical knowledge structures that organize and guide the processing of self-relevant information specifically (Markus, 1977). In terms of structure, self-schemas are organized hierarchically such that the more specific elements are subsumed under more inclusive ones (Kihlstrom and Cantor, 1984; Marsh and Shavelson, 1985). We argue that both self-schemas and social identities – because they are particular cognitive elements – are also capable of both short-term situational activation and long-term structural changes (Amiot *et al.*, 2007b; Markus and Kunda, 1986; Smith, 1996). Concretely, this means that the social context may activate the reliance on one particular group membership – the one that the most cognitively salient and functional in a particular context (in line with self-categorization principles: Turner *et al.*, 1987) and also that as these situational activations accumulate over time, some structural changes will take place in the self-concept such that a new social identity may become a recurrent part of the self

(Markus and Wurf, 1987). To understand how individuals change when undergoing important life transitions and social changes, we focus on the process of intra-individual changes in social identities – that is, how the configuration and the structure of individuals' multiple social identities undergoes significant change over time (e.g. Cervone, 2005). Accounting for this intra-individual process is a main contribution of the CDMSII.

Psychological coherence

Like identity integration, the notion of psychological coherence captures how individuals feel subjectively about the different elements that define who they are as a person. At its most basic level, psychological coherence refers to the individual's need to perceive compatibility and coherence between *interconnected* self-aspects or elements of the identity structure (Jaspal and Cinnirella, 2010). Human beings have multiple identities; multiple identification is the norm, rather than the exception. Hence, the individual is typically presented with a vast amount of information, some of which may be contradictory and incompatible and which becomes subject to the psychological process of assimilation–accommodation and evaluation (Breakwell, 2001). Two or more identity elements may be thought of as being "interconnected" if dominant (i.e. mainstream) social representations construct them as having implications for one another.

Drawing upon IPT, proponents of psychological coherence have hypothesized that individuals are psychologically motivated to enhance feelings of compatibility and coherence between these elements of themselves, especially in contexts of multiple identification with interconnected identity elements (i.e. either group-level elements such as social identities or individual-level traits; Jaspal and Cinnirella, 2010; Jaspal and Coyle, 2009; Jaspal and Siraj, 2011). If the need for psychological coherence is not fulfilled, identity becomes susceptible to threat, inducing the individual to engage in strategies to counteract the threat. In this sense, psychological coherence can be seen as an additional identity principle in the IPT framework.

It is important to note that the perceived coherence among one's identities is both fluid and context-dependent and it is very much subjective: it resides "in the eye of the perceiver and [is] not some objective quality of the identities under scrutiny" (Jaspal and Cinnirella, 2010, p. 866). In a recent study on the management of national and religious identities among British South Asians (Jaspal, 2011), British Pakistanis subjectively perceived far greater connectedness and less coherence between their national and religious identities than British Indians.

Social psychologists have also employed the concept of psychological coherence in order to understand how individuals subjectively personalize and manage multiple (and potentially incompatible) social representations. Social representations can be defined in terms of systems of meaning, which can provide explanations and orientations for the surrounding social world (Moscovici, 1988). Social representations are often associated with particular social group memberships. A given social group has its own "system of meaning" and provide its members with access to these systems. The construct of psychological coherence readily acknowledges the influence of prevailing social representations concerning identities, their qualitative nature and their compatibility. For instance, British Muslim gay men may fear "coming out," that is, publicly disclosing membership in the categories "Muslim" and "gay," owing to their awareness of negative social representations of homosexuality within religious circles (Jaspal and Siraj, 2011).

Although psychological coherence has been considered an identity principle (Jaspal and Cinnirella, 2010), some IPT researchers have questioned the distinction between the psychological coherence and continuity principles of identity (e.g. Vignoles, 2011; Breakwell, this volume). While the continuity principle is concerned with maintaining a temporal connection between past, present and future and is, thus, diachronic (Breakwell, 1986), the psychological coherence principle is largely synchronic as it requires feelings of identity compatibility and coherence at a particular point in time (Jaspal and Cinnirella, 2012). Thus, it seems that psychological coherence may be particularly relevant to the present discussion of identity compatibility and identity integration, although – and as we elaborate below – it is fully acknowledged that other identity principles are likely, over time, to become active during the process of identity integration.

Supporting the utility of accounting specifically for the principle of psychological coherence and for its synchronic nature, Jaspal and Cinnirella (2010) found that British Muslim gay men perceived their religious and sexual identities as "pre-existing identities," which were simultaneously primordial in the self-concept at a point in time. Consequently, the threat to identity entailed by the combination of these identities was due to *synchronic* incompatibility. In another study, Jaspal and Cinnirella (2012) discuss threats to identity which result from British Muslim gay men's incipient experiences in gay affirmative social contexts. From a diachronic perspective, starting to be involved in gay space is likely to threaten identity continuity. Yet, even if the individual is successful in overcoming this threat to continuity, the synchronic threat may remain, since the individual is still required to reconcile the two conflicting identities at a particular point in time. In short, we need to account for both the principles of continuity and of psychological coherence, two phenomenologically distinct principles, in order to fully capture the rich and complex identity implications of threats to both of these principles.

Contrasting the notions of identity integration and psychological coherence

The identity integration and psychological coherence concepts share a number of similarities but also some conceptual differences. In terms of similarities, these concepts both focus on the subjective representation of one's multiple self-elements – such as the identities and characteristics that apply to oneself. Both the notions of identity integration and psychological coherence also focus on the notion of cognitive links and the importance of finding ways to "tie" and to cognitively bind one's different identities and self-components. In this sense, both concepts share the assumption that individuals are motivated to reach a state of psychological comfort that is devoid of tensions and intra-individual conflict (see also Festinger, 1957). Finally, both concepts share – at least implicitly – the idea that the social context (e.g. social representations) may influence the individuals' identity configuration, or at the very least, prompt them to position themselves with regards to this environment and decide – if choice is indeed an option – which identity to play up or play down.

In terms of the differences between these concepts, social identity integration focuses on the integration of social identities specifically, whereas psychological coherence applies to a broader range of self-components, including personal and social identities as well as individual traits. Identity integration is mainly cognitive, based on social cognition principles and assumes a hierarchical structure to the self-concept. In contrast, psychological coherence is a subjective notion that applies to different components of the self and which puts less emphasis on the cognitive organization and the structure of these elements per se. Finally, while the psychological coherence principle emphasizes the recurrent and chronic role of identity threat in the process of binding and linking one's different self-elements (Jaspal and Cinnirella, 2010, 2012), the cognitive-developmental model of social identity integration – as we will be discussing below – recognizes the role that threat plays in the identity integration process (e.g. Amiot et al., 2007b, 2012) while also accounting for other antecedents that can facilitate social identity integration – such as coping and social support (e.g. Amiot et al., 2006, 2010). In the current chapter, our goal is to bring together the identity integration, psychological coherence and identity principles concepts together. Within this theoretical integration, we seek to discuss the following: (1) when the different identity principles of self-esteem, continuity, self-efficacy, distinctiveness, meaning, belonging and coherence will become activated as a new social identity is acquired over time; and (2) how social representations and subjective perceptions associated with relevant social groups (e.g. identity threat) may impinge upon identity integration.

Stages and mechanisms through which identities become integrated over time

How do one's multiple identities become integrated in people's sense of self exactly, such that the self feels coherent rather than in conflict? In the CDMSII, we propose four stages of change by which one's different social identities become integrated over time (Amiot *et al.*, 2007a). At each stage, we also outline how the seven basic principles of distinctiveness, continuity, self-esteem, self-efficacy, meaning, belonging and coherence may come into play and become particularly salient (Breakwell, 1986; Vignoles *et al.*, 2002). We propose that, if satisfied, these principles will facilitate the integration of one's different identities and will allow the person to move forward in the identity integration process. By doing so, we also wish to highlight how each principle may become particularly relevant to satisfy at a point in time and to bring a temporal and dynamic perspective to the process of need satisfaction in group settings. Table 8.1 highlights how each stage of the CDMSII is related to each identity principle proposed by IPT.

The role of needs and principles

In prior research, we found that the satisfaction of the needs for autonomy, competence and relatedness – needs that are fundamental according to self-determination theory (Deci and Ryan, 2000) – predicted more active forms of coping and increased identification with new social groups over time (Amiot *et al.*, 2010). Herein, we argue that other types of principles – those proposed by Breakwell (1986), Jaspal and Cinnirella (2010) and by Vignoles *et al.* (2002) – may also fuel the development of new social identities. More broadly, we propose that the extent to which one's needs and principles are satisfied in a particular group context will not only facilitate the recognition, acceptance and endorsement of one's new identity, but it will provide the psychological impetus, the social resources and the energy that are necessary to make the necessary adjustment to one's sense of self and to derive well-being in this process.

Table 8.1. Effects of identity integration for the identity principles

Stages of identity integration	Identity principles enhanced	Identity principles threatened
1. Anticipatory categorization	Continuity Belonging	
2. Categorization	Distinctiveness Self-esteem	Continuity Belonging Self-esteem
3. Compartmentalization	Psychological coherence Belonging Self-efficacy	
4. Integration	Psychological coherence Self-efficacy Self-esteem Meaning Distinctiveness	Self-esteem

Stages of change

Based on developmental principles (e.g. Harter, 1999), the first stage proposed by the CDMSII and involved in the identity integration process takes place as individuals are planning to join a new social group in the future. During this *anticipatory categorization stage*, we propose that a process of self-anchoring operates, where the individual about to join a new social group will project his or her own personal characteristics onto this novel social ingroup (e.g. Otten and Wentura, 2001). For example, a British Muslim gay man planning on frequenting "gay space" such as gay nightclubs could anticipate that some of his personal characteristics also apply to other non-Muslim British gay men who habitually frequent this social space (Jaspal and Siraj, 2011). Seeing gayness as a trait of his own personal identity, the British Muslim gay men may anticipate this commonality in self-definition between himself and other people in "gay space." This projection and self-anchoring process allows one to find similarities between one's personal identity and the new social identity to be integrated. As another example, we could think of an Australian immigrant preparing to arrive in Canada. At the anticipatory categorization stage – just before arriving in his or her new country – they may anticipate that some of their own characteristics will also apply to Canadians in general. Being an extraverted and sociable person, they could foresee that Canadians will also be extraverted.

It is likely that the self-anchoring process – which is central to anticipatory categorization – will enhance the *continuity* principle of identity (Sani, 2008), given that the psychological projection of existing traits and characteristics onto the novel identity can form a psychological bridge between past, present and future. The establishment of cognitive links between a pre-existing social identity and a novel social group in which the individual aspires to acquire membership establishes a temporal bridge. Moreover, it is easy to see how the *belonging* principle may acquire psychological salience at this stage, since the individual is able to foresee acceptance and inclusion in the social group, in which they anticipate membership. These feelings of belonging are facilitated by the process of self-anchoring, given that the individual perceives a "fit" between existing traits and those regarded as being prevalent in the novel social group, which will provide entry in the social group. Clearly, this requires engagement with social representations of the "necessary" self-aspects for membership, acceptance and inclusion in the group (Simon, 2004).

The second stage of social identity integration refers to *categorization*. At this point, group members are in the process of joining their new social group. The contact with this new group also leads the newcomer to realize how different and potentially divergent their new and original group memberships may be. Intergroup dynamics are likely to emerge at this stage. Distinct identities are recognized and differences (in terms of values and norms) among social identities become highly salient. This phenomenon is analogous to the culture clash in the acculturation literature, where immigrants feel conflicted between the cultures as they confront incongruous sets of cultural demands (e.g. Leong and Ward, 2000). Because at this stage, the differences between the identities are particularly salient, the individual undergoing the change cannot yet perceive any similarities or form cognitive links between these groups, nor does he or she yet consider the possibility of being part of these different groups. Going back to the Australian immigrant to Canada, he or she may realize upon arrival that their preconceived ideas about how Canadians would be similar to them are not as accurate as they would have hoped – with certain Canadians being much less extraverted and sociable than what they had expected and some being even annoyed at not being able to understand his or her accent, creating an additional and unforeseen linguistic barrier.

In terms of identity processes (Breakwell, 1986), the actual experience of change has the potential to threaten the *continuity* principle, because the individual makes their transition from anticipatory categorization (which focuses on similarities) to actual categorization (which conversely highlights differences). The unifying psychological thread between past, present and future – which is initially constructed by anticipatory categorization – is potentially jeopardized by the actual experience of change. Conversely, the salience of the differences between the existing group membership and the novel social group renders the *distinctiveness* principle highly relevant and provides scope for the enhancement of this principle. The outcomes for the *self-esteem* principle at that stage are more complex; social representations and social comparison processes dictate the social "status" of one's existing group membership and hence determine whether this distinctiveness between the identities will be positive or negative (Vignoles *et al.*, 2000). Moreover, the perceived differences between one's existing and anticipated group memberships can jeopardize feelings of *belonging* in the novel group. More specifically, not feeling that Canadians are sociable and that some are even closed-minded with respect to foreigners who have a different accent may compromise the Australian immigrant's sense of belonging.

At the *compartmentalization stage*, the new identity stops to be considered as external and foreign to the person's self-concept and instead, increasingly becomes part of the self. As new group members gather experiences in their new social group over time, they will come to develop a sense of identification with his or her new social group. At this point, the individual will also realize that this identity is becoming increasingly part of him or herself. However, cognitively, the different identities are kept in distinct "compartments" within the self at this stage. Concretely, this means that the similarities and the linkages between these identities are not yet completely established; the identities are still perceived as being quite distinct elements. At the compartmentalization stage, the identities are also context-dependent, meaning that they become salient depending on the social context and the situational cues. This context-dependent nature of the social identification process at this stage is analogous to Roccas and Brewer's (2002) compartmentalized representation of multiple social identities – in which one particular social identity becomes primary in a particular social context relative to the other identities and also with Self-Categorization Theory's idea that one particular social identity can become activated if it is the most relevant one to endorse in a specific context (i.e. meta-contrast ratio; Turner *et al.*, 1987). For example, the Australian-Canadian may feel Australian when meeting up with other Australians in Canada for BBQs yet feel Canadian when practicing typically Canadian winter sports. His or her identities are therefore highly contextualized and distinct and are likely to be associated with different thoughts, attitudes and behaviors.

IPT theorists regard compartmentalization as a strategy for protecting identity from threat, that is, for maintaining appropriate levels of the identity principles (Breakwell, 1986). Indeed, potential inconsistencies between particular social group memberships do not enter the psychological forefront, which essentially protects the psychological coherence principle from threat. Furthermore, the salience of social group membership in "appropriate" social contexts (e.g. feeling more Muslim in the mosque and more gay in gay nightclubs in the case of British Muslim gay men) can safeguard the *belonging* principle of identity. The individual is able to derive feelings of acceptance and inclusion from relevant others in social contexts, given that the "problematic" identity is not allowed, at a psychological level, to inhibit a sense of belonging. The compartmentalization of one's social identities clearly elucidates the agency that human beings have in constructing and managing identity. This agency can provide the individual with feelings of control and competence over their life and future. Thus, it can be hypothesized that the *self-efficacy* principle of identity acquires salience during the compartmentalization stage.

The fourth stage is *integration*. At this last stage, the individual will fully realize that conflicts between identities exist and that, if these conflicts are to be resolved, resources must be put forward (e.g. Phinney, 2003). This would take place as the individual realizes that the behaviors that he or she displays are somewhat different to those displayed in another social context. Such contradictions and conflicts could be reconciled by finding similarities and by drawing broader links between one's different social identities. For example, the Australian-Canadian could bridge his or her Canadian and Australian identities by focusing on the founding values that are shared by people of both countries, such as democracy, freedom of speech and liberalism. Engaging in these conflict-resolution strategies will not only allow these two individuals to establish cognitive linkage between their different identities, but it will also maximize the feeling that, even though their behaviors change and adjust across social contexts, they can still experience an overall sense of personal coherence and consistency across these situations and they are still the same person (Amiot and de la Sablonnière, 2010). This integration phase should hence result in the recognition that one's different social identities are no longer (completely) context-dependent and that each identity contributes to the overall self-concept in a unique manner (e.g. Harter, 1999; Harter and Monsour, 1992).

As a specific identity principle (Jaspal, 2011), psychological *coherence* could induce individuals to move toward this integration stage. Although this final stage of identity integration should have positive outcomes for this principle, the impact for the other motivational principles of identity seems to be less straightforward and can vary in accordance with situational context. Like compartmentalization, the integration stage may render salient the *self-efficacy* principle of identity because the *ability* to deploy socio-psychological resources for the minimization of identity conflict and for the reconciliation of social group members can provide the individual with feelings of control and competence. Moreover, the individual can derive a greater sense of *meaning* from belonging in both groups and from their occupancy of their particular identity configuration. This may come to provide a sense of purpose which is beneficial for the meaning principle (Baumeister, 1991).

Furthermore, the perception of belonging to distinct social groups and of possessing self-aspects associated with either group may benefit the *distinctiveness* principle, given that possessing this unique identity configuration can itself highlight one's uniqueness, specificities and strengths. However, as in the case of categorization, the perception of distinctiveness which can result from the integration of distinct social identities may be positive or negative. Being a member of the group "Canadian" may be regarded favorably at a social level, while the individual's Muslim identity may be stigmatized by society – a point we elaborate upon later. Although the individual may establish a linkage between these identities at a psychological level, the social stigma of their devalued identity may cause threats to self-esteem at the integration stage (Amiot *et al.*, 2007a; Berry, 2006). Given that this process is dependent upon the immediate surrounding social context and upon which specific combination of identities are being integrated, the outcomes of this process for the self-esteem principle are highly context-dependent. In terms of the self-esteem principle, there is also a cost associated with identity integration. Because links are forged between these identities at the integration stage, each of the person's identities become part of the self-concept and are recognized as components of the person's self, which may in fact perpetuate any threats to the self-esteem principle caused by membership in any one social group.

The *belonging* principle can also become salient at the integration stage, because the individual recognizes that he or she belongs to the different groups and hence may feel comfortable interacting with individuals from these social groups that are integrated within the self-concept. Although the individual reconciles these social group memberships at the psychological level, they have little control over how members of either social group will concretely interact with them as a result of their attachment to different social groups. For instance, although some British Muslim men who come out as gay do manage to reconcile their gay and Muslim identities, many still report ostracization and a lack of belonging in both Muslim *and* gay circles (Jaspal and Cinnirella, 2012; Jaspal and Siraj,

2011). This can be attributed to the stigma attached by other group members to the particular gay–Muslim identity configuration.

Bringing together identity integration from the view of the CDMSII and IPT allows us to specify how the motivational principles of identity operate and have a potent effect at each stage of social identity integration, providing a more detailed insight into the psychological dynamics underlying the process of identity change. More specifically, this theoretical integration shows how the principles may be benefited or undermined during these stages, potentially inducing some individuals to dwell on one particular stage owing to its psychological benefits and others to entirely sidestep other stages owing to their potential psychological disadvantages. For instance, Coyle and Rafalin (2000) have indicated that gay Jews may remain at the compartmentalization stage, without proceeding to the integration stage, due to the more favorable outcomes for identity they derive at that stage. Testing the hypotheses presented above may elucidate how individuals in particular social contexts may engage with the stages of identity integration. Moreover, by integrating IPT and the CDMSII, we can directly test the important role of social representations in determining how individuals might respond socio-psychologically to the various stages leading to identity integration (Breakwell, this volume). For instance, in order to predict levels of belonging within the social groups which one seeks to reconcile in the self-concept, it is necessary to explore the social representations prevalent in either group.

Inhibitors of the identity integration process: stigma and devalued identities

We can now wonder what happens when the different groups the person belongs to differ widely in terms of how socially valued or devalued they are. In fact, more often than not, social groups differ in terms of the status or prestige they hold in a society (Sachdev and Bourhis, 1991). For instance, not all groups of immigrants are evaluated in the same way within a society (e.g. Canada); with some groups (e.g. Australians) being more positively evaluated than others (e.g. Haitians). Going back to our example, if the Australian Canadian feels that both identities are socially valued, he or she may attribute high importance to both of these identities and report higher identity integration and psychological coherence. If he or she came from a country that possesses less social prestige, however, his or her identities may have clashed much more and one of his or her identities – possibly the one that has the highest social status – may have eclipsed the lower status identity in his or her overall sense of self.

In line with these examples and building on an important body of work in acculturation psychology (Berry, 1997, 2006), we suggest that these differential perceptions of the social status of various groups – although they are originally external to the individual – may become internalized in the person's sense of self. In fact, intergroup contexts that are highly stratified – such that the groups differ widely in terms of the status and power they hold in society – should encourage the dominance of one social identity (possibly the one with the highest status or power) over others, thus impeding the identity development process (Phinney, 1993, 2003). Concretely, this means that the person him or herself may come to reproduce this social consensus about what constitutes "valued" versus "devalued" groups. In this process, the person may come to value the social groups he or she belongs to that are of highest social status such that these more prestigious identities may predominate their sense of self and to downplay or even deny the social identities that are associated with socially devalued groups (de la Sablonnière *et al.*, 2012). It is as if the macroscopic intergroup social structure was reproduced intra-individually and microscopically, within the person's own sense of self.

While this process might not be too difficult to deal with if the person belongs to social groups that each have relatively equal levels of social status (e.g. belonging to a good family, working in a respectable organization, being from the mainstream cultural group), we can easily see how these status differentials may become problematic for individuals who belong to multiple groups, some of which are highly socially devalued while some others are devalued. The experiences of many British Muslim gay men seem to exemplify this point. Although at the integration stage British Muslim gay men may reconcile their identities at the psychological level, it is entirely possible that social stigma encountered as a result of social status differentials between the groups could negatively affect identity integration and psychological coherence. More specifically, individuals' engagement with stigmatizing social representations (from their Muslim ingroup) regarding their gay identity may gradually induce the perception that their Muslim and gay ingroups are in fact *incompatible*. This can potentially disrupt the integration stage. In other words, negative social representations concerning an identity configuration may eventually "un-do" the positive steps taken toward identity integration during the integration stage at the psychological level. Identity integration is a desirable goal, but it is also a highly effortful process, which involves engagement with the identities at a psychological level, as well as engagement with dominant social representations concerning the identities at the social level. In order to facilitate the process of identity integration, it is necessary to create a societal context that will encourage this integration (e.g. Roccas and Brewer, 2002), rather than place this (sometimes very heavy) burden on individuals alone.

Future research directions

The present chapter points to some directions that future research could take to investigate the motivational principles of identity – as described in IPT – that surface throughout the identity integration process. First, future research ought to explore empirically the relationships between different configurations of multiple identities within the self with different identity principles by testing the hypotheses tentatively outlined in the chapter (see also Table 8.1 for an overview). This may in turn shed light upon the likelihood of an individual reaching a particular stage of identity integration and of making the transition to further stages. Indeed, this hypothesis is consistent with research that shows that individuals more readily internalize and prioritize elements of the self which provide appropriate levels of the identity principles (Breakwell, 1986; Vignoles et al., 2002). Furthermore, given IPT's concerns with psychological well-being, it is reasonable to examine how different well-being outcomes (i.e. subjective and psychological well-being; hedonic and eudemonic well-being) may be associated with the stages of social identity integration, as well as each identity principles in the context of social identity integration and each configuration of one's multiple identities.

Ideally, these hypotheses could be tested longitudinally, among individuals who are in the process of joining a new social group or developing a new facet of their sense of self. Adolescents or young adults would represent a particularly interesting population to study as their identities and self-structure are in flux (Harter, 1999). Such a study could either focus on individuals' idiosyncratic identities and how they combine and are coherent with one another, or target one particular identity (e.g. sexual orientation) that may also be socially devalued or threatened and test the process of integration of these particular identities among the person's other identities over time. Using statistical analyses such as hierarchical linear modeling – which allow us to test if the associations among particular identity principles, threat and well-being are stronger at some time points relative to some other time points – will allow the testing of these research questions. As well, identity integration versus imbalance could be assessed using newly established statistical procedures that capture the amount of discrepancy among one's different identities (de la Sablonnière et al., 2012; Smith et al., 2012).

Solutions to a lack of identity integration and psychological coherence

More concretely, what is the solution to the lack of identity integration and psychological coherence that are often experienced as individuals' identities are threatened? How can we ensure that one's multiple social identities will be equally valued and will each contribute to defining the person? The solutions we put forward emphasize the agency that individuals have with respect to these social representations and in determining what constitutes a "valuable" social group or not. First of all, intra-individually, individuals who belong to groups that differ widely in their statuses could actively realize what are these groups' particularities, strengths, specificities and how these sets of characteristics can complement one another and bring a different facet to their sense of self. As another strategy, individuals may focus on the self-elements they wish to promote and present to others, such as some of their particular personality traits (Breakwell, 2001). For instance, individuals with a high degree of autonomy from their groups and whose groups encourage them to express their own individuality may be more able to put forward their personal strengths and idiosyncratic characteristics. This could protect them from stigmatizing social representations disseminated regarding the compatibility of identities, shielding their psychological coherence from threat (Jaspal, 2011). Although individuals are influenced by a combination of social and psychological factors, they may also ultimately arrive at their own conclusion about the compatibility of interconnected self-elements.

Other solutions are located at the societal level. Such solutions could aim at directly questioning the superiority and value of some social groups over others and questioning what constitutes right and wrong. For example, by socially challenging the *authority* of Muslim religious scholars, some British Muslim gay men may actively contest the social representation associated with their ethno-religious ingroup that homosexuality is a "sin" in favor of the competing representation associated with their gay ingroup that homosexuality constitutes a "normal" sexual orientation (Jaspal and Cinnirella, 2010).

Conclusion

In this chapter, we brought together different theoretical perspectives on identity integration and psychological coherence and IPT. These perspectives converge by stressing how important it is that individuals feel a sense of intra-individual comfort with their social identities and the different facets of themselves and in their need to regulate proactively these identities and facets, especially in times of threat. To truly bring these theories together, we proposed specific hypotheses about when each identity principle would become more salient throughout the identity integration process. We then proposed future research to test these hypotheses and suggested concrete solutions for how to reconcile one's various and potentially conflicting identities. As reconciling diversity is a major social issue, we are hopeful that these research ideas and solutions will lead to constructive social changes.

REFERENCES

Amiot, C. E., and de la Sablonnière, R. (2010). Integration of cultural identities in the self: a look at the social facilitators of integration. In R. J. Crisp (ed.), *The psychology of social and cultural diversity* (pp. 34–61). London: Blackwell.

Amiot, C. E., de la Sablonnière, R., Terry, D. J., and Smith, J. R. (2007a). Integration of social identities in the self: toward a cognitive-developmental model. *Personality and Social Psychology Review*, 11(4), 364–388.

Amiot, C. E., Terry, D. J., and Callan, V. J. (2007b). Status, equity and social identification during an intergroup merger: a longitudinal study. *British Journal of Social Psychology*, 46(3), 557–577.

Amiot, C. E., Terry, D. J., Jimmieson, N. L., and Callan, V. J. (2006). A longitudinal investigation of stress and coping processes during an organizational merger: implications for job satisfaction and organizational identification. *Journal of Management*, 32(4), 552–574.

Amiot, C. E., Terry, D. J., and McKimmie, B. (2012). Social identity change and integration during an intergroup merger: the role of status, similarity and threat. Basic and Applied Social Psychology. 34(5), 443–455.

Amiot, C. E., Terry, D. J., Wirawan, D., and Grice, T. (2010). Changes in social identities over time: the role of coping and adaptation processes. *British Journal of Social Psychology*, 49(4), 804–826.

Baumeister, R. F. (1991). *Meanings of life*. New York: Guilford.

Baumeister, R. F. (2008). Free will in scientific psychology. *Perspectives on Psychological Science*, 3(1), 14–19.

BBC News Africa (2011). Libya revolution: future scenarios and the West's role. www.bbc.co.uk/news/world-africa-12577484.

Benet-Martinez, V., Leu, J., Lee, F., and Morris, M. W. (2002). Negotiating biculturalism: cultural frame switching in biculturals with oppositional versus compatible cultural identities. *Journal of Cross-Cultural Psychology*, 33(5), 492–516.

Berry, J. W. (1997). Immigration, acculturation and adaptation. *Applied Psychology: an International Review*, 46(1), 5–68.

Berry, J. W. (2006). Acculturation: living successfully in two cultures. *International Journal of Intercultural Relations*, 29(6), 697–712.

Breakwell, G. M. (1986). *Coping with threatened identities*. London: Methuen.

Breakwell, G. M. (2001). Social representational constraints upon identity processes. In K. Deaux and G. Philogène (eds.), *Representations of the social: bridging theoretical traditions* (pp. 271–284). Oxford: Blackwell.

Bureau of Labor Statistics, US Department of Labor (2010). Number of jobs held, labor market activity and earnings growth among the youngest baby boomers: results from a longitudinal survey. Retrieved October 18, 2011: www.bls.gov/news.release/pdf/nlsoy.pdf.

Cervone, D. (2005). Personality architecture: within person structures and processes. *Annual Review of Psychology*, 56(1), 423–452.

Coyle, A., and Rafalin, D. (2000). Jewish gay men's accounts of negotiating cultural, religious and sexual identity: a qualitative study. *Journal of Psychology and Human Sexuality*, 12, 21–48.

Crocker, J., and Major, B. (1989). Social stigma and self-esteem: the self-protective properties of stigma. *Psychological Review*, 96(4), 608–630.

Deaux, K. (1991). Social identities: thoughts on structure and change. In R. C. Curtis (ed.), *The relational self: theoretical convergences in psychoanalysis and social psychology* (pp. 77–93). New York: Guilford.

Deci, E. L., and Ryan, R. M. (2000). The "what" and "why" of goal pursuits: human needs and the self-determination of behavior. *Psychological Inquiry*, 11(4), 227–268.

de la Sablonnière, R., Amiot, C. E., Cardenas, D., Sadykova, N., and Gorborukova, G. L. (2012). Identity integration: a subtractive process. Unpublished manuscript.

de la Sablonnière, R., Aubin, R. M., and Amiot, C. E. (2013). Le Processus d'intégration des identités culturelles: La Réalité des migrants. *Revue Québécoise de psychologie*, 34(1), 249–270.

Donahue, E. M., Robins, R. W., Roberts, B. W., and John, O. P. (1993). The divided self: concurrent and longitudinal effects of psychological adjustment and social roles on self-concept differentiation. *Journal of Personality and Social Psychology*, 64(5), 834–846.

Downie, M., Koestner, R., El Geledi, S., and Cree, K. (2004). The impact of cultural internalization and integration on well-being among tricultural individuals. *Personality and Social Psychology Bulletin*, 30(3), 305–314.

Festinger, L. (1957). *A theory of cognitive dissonance.* Stanford, CA: Stanford University Press.

Fiske, S. T., and Taylor, S. E. (1991). *Social cognition* (2nd edn.). New York: Random House.

Gordon, C. (1968). Self-conceptions: configurations of content. In C. Gordon and K. J. Gergen (eds.), *The self in social interaction*, vol. I (pp. 115–154). New York: Wiley.

Harter, S. (1999). *The construction of the self: a developmental perspective.* New York: Guilford Press.

Harter, S., and Monsour, A. (1992). Developmental analysis of conflict caused by opposing attributed in the adolescent self-portrait. *Developmental Psychology*, 28(2), 251–260.

Jaspal, R. (2011). The construction and management of national and ethnic identities among British South Asians: an identity process theory approach. Unpublished doctoral dissertation, University of London, UK.

Jaspal, R., and Cinnirella, M. (2010). Coping with potentially incompatible identities: accounts of religious, ethnic and sexual identities from British

Pakistani men who identify as Muslim and gay. *British Journal of Social Psychology*, 49(4), 849–870.

Jaspal, R., and Cinnirella, M. (2012). Identity processes, threat and interpersonal relations: accounts from British Muslim gay men. *Journal of Homosexuality*, 59(2), 215–240.

Jaspal, R., and Coyle, A. (2009). Language and perceptions of identity threat. *Psychology and Society*, 2(2), 150–167.

Jaspal, R., and Siraj, A. (2011). Perceptions of 'coming out' among British Muslim gay men. *Psychology and Sexuality*, 2(3), 183–197.

Kernis, M. H. (2006). *Self-esteem issues and answers: a sourcebook of current perspectives*. New York: Psychology Press.

Kihlstrom, J. J., and Cantor, N. (1984). Mental representations of the self. In L. Berkowitz (ed.), *Advances in experimental social psychology*, vol. XVII (pp. 145–177). New York: Academic Press.

Leong, C. H., and Ward, C. (2000). Identity conflict in sojourners. *International Journal of Intercultural Relations*, 24(6), 763–776.

Markus, H. (1977). Self-schemata and processing information about the self. *Journal of Personality and Social Psychology*, 35(2), 63–78.

Markus, H., and Kunda, Z. (1986). Stability and malleability of the self-concept. *Journal of Personality and Social Psychology*, 51(4), 858–866.

Markus, H., and Wurf, E. (1987). The dynamic self-concept: a social psychological perspective. *Annual Review of Psychology*, 38(1), 299–337.

Marsh, H. W., and Shavelson, R. J. (1985). Self-concept: its multifaceted, hierarchical structure. *Educational Psychologist*, 20(3), 107–125.

McPherson, M., Smith-Lovin, L., and Brashears, M. (2006). Social isolation in America. *American Sociological Review*, 71, 353–375.

Moscovici, S. (1988). Notes towards a description of social representations. *European Journal of Social Psychology*, 18, 211–250.

Otten, S., and Wentura, D. (2001). Self-anchoring and ingroup favoritism: an individual-profiles analysis. *Journal of Experimental Social Psychology*, 37(6), 525–532.

Phinney, J. S. (1993). Multiple group identities: differentiation, conflict and integration. In J. Kroger (ed.), *Discussions on ego identity* (pp. 47–73). Hillsdale, NJ: LEA.

Phinney, J. S. (2003). Ethnic identity and acculturation. In K. M. Chun, P. Balls Organista and G. Marín, Gerardo (eds.), *Acculturation: advances in theory, measurement and applied research* (pp. 63–81). Washington, DC: American Psychological Association.

Roccas, S., and Brewer, M. B. (2002). Social identity complexity. *Personality and Social Psychology Review*, 6(2), 88–106.

Sachdev, I., and Bourhis, R. Y. (1991). Power and status differentials in minority and majority group relations. *European Journal of Social Psychology*, 21(1), 1–24.

Sani, F. (2008). Schism in groups: a social psychological account. *Social and Personality Psychology Compass*, 2(2), 718–732.

Simon, B. (2004). *Identity in modern society: a social psychological perspective*. Oxford: Blackwell.

Smith, E. R. (1996). What do connectionism and social psychology offer each other? *Journal of Personality and Social Psychology*, 70(5), 893–912.

Smith, L. G., Amiot, C. E., Callan, V. J., Terry, D. J., and Smith, J. R. (2012). The balancing act: the relationship between nested levels of identification and turnover intentions for newcomers at work. *British Journal of Management,* 23, 45–64.

Statistics Canada (2011). Health Statistics Division, Canadian Vital Statistics, Divorce Database and Marriage Database. http://statcan.gc.ca/pub/85–002-x/2012001/article/11634-eng.htm. Accessed July 1, 2012.

Tajfel, H. (1981). Social stereotypes and social groups. In J. Turner and H. Giles (eds.), *Intergroup behaviour* (pp. 144–167). Oxford: Blackwell.

Tajfel, H., and Turner, J. C. (1979). An integrative theory of intergroup conflict. In W. G. Austin and S. Worchel (eds.), *The social psychology of intergroup relations* (pp. 94–109). Monterey, CA: Brooks-Cole.

Tajfel, H., and Turner, J. C. (1986). The social identity theory of intergroup behavior. In S. Worchel and W. G. Austin (eds.), *Psychology of Intergroup Relations* (pp. 7–24). Chicago, IL: Nelson-Hall.

Turner, J. C., Hogg, M. A., Oakes, P. J., Reicher, S. D., and Wetherell, M. (1987). *Rediscovering the social group: a self-categorization theory.* Oxford: Blackwell.

United Nations (2002). Number of world's migrants reaches 175 million mark: migrant population has doubled in twenty-five years. Retrieved July 22, 2009.

Vignoles, V. L. (2011). Identity motives. In S. J. Schwartz, K. Luyckx and V. L. Vignoles (eds.), *Handbook of identity theory and research* (pp. 403–432). New York: Springer.

Vignoles, V. L., Chryssochoou, X. and Breakwell, G. M. (2000). The distinctiveness principle: identity, meaning and the bounds of cultural relativity. *Personality and Social Psychology Review,* 4, 337–354.

Vignoles, V. L., Chryssochoou, X., and Breakwell, G. M. (2002). Evaluating models of identity motivation: self-esteem is not the whole story. *Self and Identity,* 1(3), 201–218.

Zimbardo, P. G. (2007). *The Lucifer effect: understanding how good people turn evil.* New York: Random House.

9 Values and Identity Process Theory: theoretical integration and empirical interactions

Anat Bardi, Rusi Jaspal, Ela Polek and Shalom H. Schwartz

Identity and values are important driving forces in human lives. Identity Process Theory (IPT; Breakwell, 1986, 2001b) and the Schwartz Value Theory (Schwartz, 1992) focus on distinct but related aspects of the self and have some overlapping propositions particularly with regards to human motivation. Hence, it is surprising that there has been no attempt so far to integrate them theoretically or empirically. This chapter provides the first attempt to address this gap in the literature. After presenting key elements of both theories, the chapter provides a theoretical integration that addresses the links between identity motives and outcomes and provides an empirical examination of the role of personal values as moderators of such links. Finally, we address identity and value change.

Identity Process Theory

Identity Process Theory (IPT; Breakwell, 1986, 1992, 2001a, 2001b, 2010; Jaspal and Cinnirella, 2010; Vignoles *et al.*, 2006) elucidates the socio-psychological processes underlying identity construction and change. It specifies the following: (1) the necessary requirements of a positive identity; (2) the ways individuals cope with threats to identity; and (3) what motivates individuals and groups to defend their sense of self. IPT proposes that the structure of identity should be conceptualized in terms of content and evaluation dimensions. The content dimension of identity consists of a unique constellation of identities derived from social experience. These identities can include group memberships (e.g. British), individual traits (e.g. smart) and physical aspects (e.g. tall). The evaluation dimension of an identity refers to the person's sense of how good or bad this identity is.

The work of Shalom H. Schwartz was partly supported by the HSE Basic Research Program (International Laboratory of Sociocultural Research).

Identity processes

Two universal processes regulate the identity structure: (1) the assimilation–accommodation process and (2) the evaluation process. *Assimilation–accommodation* refers to the assimilation of new information and new identities into the identity structure (e.g. "I am gay"). This sometimes requires accommodation and adjustment of existing components of the identity structure (e.g. "If I am gay, can I still consider myself a Muslim?"). The *evaluation* process refers to the process of evaluating how good or bad the identity is (e.g. "I am not happy that I am gay"). Both individual (e.g. personal goals) and social (e.g. norms) factors play a role in the evaluation process.

Identity motives

Breakwell (1986, 1992) identified four identity motives, which she sees as guiding these universal processes. These motives are desirable end-states for identity. They include (1) continuity across time and situation (*continuity*); (2) uniqueness or distinctiveness from others (*distinctiveness*); (3) confidence and control of one's life (*self-efficacy*) and (4) a sense of personal worth or social value (*self-esteem*). Extending IPT, Vignoles and colleagues (Vignoles *et al.*, 2002, 2006) proposed two additional identity motives, namely (5) *belonging* – maintaining feelings of closeness to and acceptance by other people and (6) *meaning* – finding significance and purpose in one's life. More recently, Jaspal and Cinnirella (2010) introduced (7) a *psychological coherence* motive – establishing feelings of compatibility among one's (interconnected) identities. IPT suggests that identity is threatened whenever the social context frustrates the satisfaction of any of the identity motives. Individuals utilize coping strategies to minimize the threat. For instance, a Muslim man who feels sexually attracted to other men may perceive his Muslim and gay identities as incompatible, thereby threatening psychological coherence. In order to cope with the threat, he may *deny* both to himself and to others that he is gay (Jaspal and Cinnirella, 2010).

Social representation, social change and identity processes

IPT integrates the intrapsychic, interpersonal and intergroup levels of human interdependence. This is especially evident in IPT's explicit recognition of the role of social representations in the psychosocial processes that underlie identity construction (Breakwell, 2001b; Moscovici, 1988). For Breakwell (1986, p. 55), a "social representation is essentially a construction of reality" that enables individuals to interpret the social world and to render it meaningful. Social representations emerge through interpersonal and intergroup communication and shape the content and evaluation dimensions of identity (Breakwell, 2001b).

Furthermore, the social representational aspect of IPT enables understanding of both personal and social change, because individual and public understandings of specific phenomena fluctuate in accordance with contexts. For instance, the historical representation of homosexuality as a criminal and sinful act versus the contemporary representation of homosexuality as a "normal" sexual orientation leads to distinct social and psychological responses. The contemporary representation leads to greater willingness to "come out" because it is less threatening for self-esteem and may no longer be seen as jeopardizing one's sense of belonging in relevant social circles (Jaspal and Siraj, 2011). Hence, changes in social representations are vital for understanding identity processes.

The theory hypothesizes that the impact of social change on identity is contingent on three main factors. The impact is greater the more personally relevant the social change. Thus, the Arab Spring in the Middle East doubtless affected identity continuity more for Egyptians and Tunisians than for citizens of Russia, for example. Secondly, social changes vary in their demands for revising the content and evaluation of particular identities. The "Black is Beautiful" campaign in the USA brought about a re-evaluation of the meaning of being black for black people, transforming it into a source of self-esteem rather than a threat (Ward and Braun, 1972). Thirdly, it is important to consider how people themselves evaluate the change. In rural India, probably as a result of different implications for self-esteem, lower caste group members might evaluate the state-endorsed dismantlement of the caste system as a positive social change, while higher caste group members are generally said to evaluate this negatively (Jodhka, 2004; Ram, 2004).

Social change can radically change the meaning of identities as it can reshape the social representation of a stimulus or social position. For example, social change to the status of a group could transform an identity once experienced as threatening to one's self-esteem into one that enhances it. It thereby impacts the motivations for the self-efficacy, self-esteem, continuity and other identity motives associated with particular identities. In this way, social change affects the degree of centrality of individuals' different identities.

Identity motives and perceived centrality

According to IPT, the identity structure consists of multiple, interconnected identities, which vary in *perceived centrality*. Centrality of an identity includes three dimensions: (1) the importance of the identity; (2)

the affective evaluation of the identity (i.e. the degree to which one is happy about having it); and (3) the enactment of the identity in everyday actions and interpersonal encounters. Vignoles (2011) suggests that enactment of an identity differs from the more cognitive evaluative components (importance and affect). He notes that one can consider an identity to be important and can be happy with it but still refrain from enacting it publicly because of normative pressures or other reasons.

Vignoles et al. (2002) suggest that identities that best satisfy the identity motives are perceived as most central to the identity structure. Thus, the more a given identity is perceived by the individual as a source of self-esteem, self-efficacy, distinctiveness, meaning, continuity, belonging and psychological coherence, the more central it will be in the individual's identity structure. This suggestion has received considerable empirical support (Vignoles et al., 2002, 2006).

Breakwell (2010) suggests that the relative significance of identity motives in affecting identity outcomes may be culturally specific. Social representations are specific to particular social contexts and, thus, it is likely that different motives will be more or less important in particular cultural contexts. For instance, in a study of national and ethnic identity management among British South Asians (Jaspal, 2011), the importance of the ethnic identity was predicted by the continuity and distinctiveness motives but not by the self-efficacy motive. Hence, centrality does not necessarily depend on the extent to which a given identity satisfies *all* of the identity motives. Rather, it may be necessary to identify the motives that are more important individually or culturally and are hence more likely to enhance a person's identity and psychological well-being.

This chapter presents a novel approach to the relationship between identity motives and the centrality of the identities that satisfy these motives. It examines a possible individual-difference dimension to IPT. It tests the hypothesis that individuals' *value priorities* moderate the relationship between satisfying identity motives and the centrality of the identity. We suggest that the importance of the different identity motives depends on individuals' personal values. If the centrality of an identity depends on satisfying an identity motive that an individual considers important because of his or her values and that motive is jeopardized, the identity will be threatened. If, as a result of his or her values, they do not consider an identity motive important, jeopardizing that motive may not translate into identity threat. By testing hypotheses based on this idea, we hope to reveal why identities differ in centrality. This can contribute to debates regarding "core" identities and multiple identification (Deaux, 1993; Hofmann, 1988; Jaspal and Cinnirella, 2010).

The Schwartz Value Theory

To test our suggestion we draw on the Schwartz Value Theory (Schwartz, 1992). It defines basic values as broad life goals that serve as guiding principles in people's lives (e.g. achievement, tradition). Values are relatively stable. They underlie and are expressed in people's evaluations, attitudes, behaviors and specific goals. They therefore have an overarching effect on people's lives.

Schwartz (1992) defined ten distinct broad values, organized in the quasi-circumplex structure portrayed in Figure 9.1. This structure has been validated empirically in seventy-five countries around the world (Schwartz, 2011). Values that are adjacent in the circle express compatible motivations and have positive empirical correlations (Schwartz, 1992). For example, conformity values express the motivation to fulfill others' expectations. Adjacent in the circle are security values that express the motivation to maintain safety of one's self, one's personal relationships and one's society. These two motivations share an emphasis on maintaining order and harmony that makes them motivationally compatible and positively correlated. In contrast, values that emanate from opposite sides of the center express conflicting motivations and have negative empirical correlations. For example, self-direction values express the motivation for independent thought and action, a motivation that conflicts with the motivation to fulfil others' expectations that underlies conformity values. Hence, these two values are conceptually opposed and negatively correlated.

Why are adjacent values correlated positively whereas values from opposite sides of the center are not? Schwartz (1992) explains this by drawing on the implications that values have for evaluations and behaviors. Values that express compatible motivations lead to similar evaluations and similar behaviors. For example, the adjacent values of conformity and security are likely to induce negative evaluations of change and to promote normative and conservative behavior. Values that are located on opposite sides of the circle express conflicting motivations and lead to opposing effects on evaluations and behaviors. Thus, in contrast to the negative evaluation of change and normative behaviors that conformity values induce, self-direction values are likely to induce positive evaluations of change and may lead to non-normative behavior. Not only is it psychologically inconsistent to pursue motivationally opposed values in a single behavior or evaluation, but it is both practically difficult and socially inappropriate. It is more pleasant and easier to act in a motivationally consistent manner that expresses compatible values. Most people therefore hold value priorities that correspond to the circular empirical

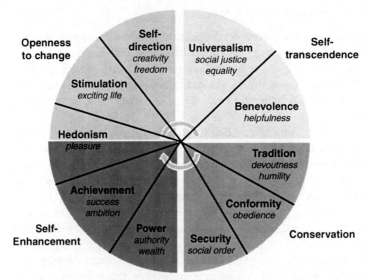

Circle Organized by Motivational Congruence and Opposition

Figure 9.1. Ten motivationally distinct values and their circular motivational structure (adapted from Schwartz, 2012)

structure of associations among values in Figure 9.1. When comparing people to one another, we find that people tend to attribute similar relative levels of importance to adjacent values in the circle and different relative levels of importance to opposing values.

The circle of values can be further divided into four higher order types of values that are ordered as two bipolar dimensions (see Figure 9.1). Conformity, security and tradition values are grouped as *conservation values*. They express a motivation to maintain a stable, harmonious status quo in relationships, in one's surroundings and life and in society. Conservation values conflict motivationally with stimulation, self-direction and, usually, hedonism values that are grouped as *openness to change* values. These values express a motivation for change, variety and challenge in ideas or actions. The second bipolar dimension contrasts *self-enhancement* values (power, achievement and, sometimes, hedonism) with *self-transcendence* values (benevolence and universalism). The former express a motivation to enhance one's self, even at the expense of others; the latter express a motivation to promote the well-being of others and of the natural world.[1]

---

[1] For additional factors that account for the structure of relations among values, see Schwartz (2006).

Value change

A review by Bardi and Goodwin (2011) indicates that values are relatively stable and resistant to change. Values can be seen as core schemas. What people perceive in situations, what they remember and how they behave are all influenced by their core schemas. Ample research (reviewed in Cooper and Shallice, 2006; Janoff-Bulman, 1989) demonstrates that people pay less attention to peripheral schemas than to core schemas, so new values that may be salient in the environment may not enter awareness. All these processes lead to and reinforce the stability of important values and other core schemas. Therefore, a stable state is the default for values. Values start to change only if some exogenous event initiates a process of value change. Even if an event initiates value change, however, the dominance of core schemas sets many factors in motion that can block the change before it reaches completion. Nonetheless, values do change sometimes.

Bardi and Goodwin (2011) suggest that values change through two main routes, an automatic route and an effortful route. In the automatic route, an external event activates new values (e.g. messages of a newly elected government activate conservative values; immigrating to a country in a more individualistic culture activates individualistic values; a baby's cries activate parents' kindness values). Because these values are activated automatically and repeatedly, the person may not be aware that this is happening and may therefore not generate counter-arguments to oppose change. Every time the value is activated, the relevant schema is strengthened until it becomes a core schema, thereby creating value change.

In the effortful route, events make a new value sufficiently salient to draw people's active attention and thought. This happens, for example, when a new group overtly discusses a value, when the government introduces a controversial new policy with clear value implications, or when people are subjected to direct persuasion attempts. If, after consciously thinking about and re-evaluating the value, people are convinced that the value is more (or less) important than they previously thought, then the importance of that value starts to change. And if such re-evaluation is stimulated repeatedly, long-term value change occurs.

Changes in specific values reflect their embeddedness in larger cognitive/affective structures such as people's systems of values and beliefs. Thus, an increase in the importance of one value is accompanied by increases in compatible values (adjacent values in the circle) and decreases in conflicting values (values that emanate from the opposite side of the circle). Both longitudinal studies (Bardi et al., 2009) and a laboratory experiment (Maio et al., 2009) have shown this. Moreover, when beliefs change, values may change to maintain compatibility with those beliefs. A study of migrants' adjustment to a new country (Goodwin *et al.*, 2012) found that prior values predicted changes in beliefs toward more value-compatible beliefs and that prior beliefs predicted value change toward more belief-compatible values. We next integrate IPT with the Schwartz Value Theory in order to advance the understanding and utility of both theories.

IPT and values: theoretical integration and some empirical evidence

Values add an individual-difference dimension to IPT

IPT identifies the processes that all individuals experience in defining and defending their identities, moderated by culture and context. In contrast, the theory of basic values is used to identify differences among individuals in the priority they attribute to motivationally distinct values. Hence, the theory of basic values can add an individual-difference dimension to understanding identity processes and thereby enrich IPT. Because value priorities affect perceptions, social representations and evaluations, it is plausible that values also affect the relations between identity motives (e.g. continuity) and identity outcomes (e.g. identity evaluation) and relations among people's identity motives (e.g. continuity and distinctiveness). We next specify our expectations for effects of values on identity processes and then assess them empirically.

Values, continuity and evaluation Individuals who give high priority to conservation values tend to give low priority to openness to change values. They attribute importance to preserving the status quo in their world, they respect and try to maintain traditions and they try to avoid new ideas and experiences. Therefore, they should consider especially important those identities that provide them with a sense of continuity with the past that promises to stretch into the future. They may also feel happier with such identities. Hence, we expect the value dimension of conservation versus openness to change to moderate the link between the perceived continuity of an identity and the evaluation of that identity.

Values, distinctiveness and evaluation If conservation values enhance the impact of continuity on the evaluation of identities, we might expect openness to change values to enhance the impact of the distinctiveness motive on the evaluation of identities. Openness to change values encourages the pursuit of novel experiences and original and creative ideas and actions that may make one distinctive. Hence, those who value openness to change might evaluate identities that provide a sense of distinctiveness as especially important. However, two aspects of distinctiveness raise problems for this prediction.

One's individual identities are not the only potential sources of a sense of distinctiveness. Rather, the group identities one derives from affiliating with different groups can also provide a sense of distinctiveness, if the group is viewed as having unique qualities, that is, as distinctive (Vignoles et al., 2000). Many identities (e.g. psychologist, dancer, lawyer) can be experienced both as individual difference attributes and as group affiliation attributes. When thinking about such identities, people may seek to satisfy their distinctiveness motive through focusing on either group or individual distinctiveness or both. Secondly, different types of distinctiveness may interact differently with openness versus conservation values. Vignoles et al. (2000) proposed and found three types of distinctiveness motives, being different, being separate, or being in a distinctive (typically high) social position. They found that the motivation to be different is more prevalent in cultures that emphasize openness to change versus conservation values; whereas the motivation to hold a distinctive social position is more prevalent in cultures that emphasize conservation versus openness values. These complexities may prevent a simple moderation of distinctiveness effects by values. Finally, the distinctiveness motive can also be seen as a basic epistemic need, as without knowing what one is *not* it is hard to understand what one *is* (e.g. understanding "kind" is impossible without understanding what is "cruel") (Vignoles, 2011; Vignoles et al., 2000). Although we offer no prediction for how openness to change versus conservation values may affect the relation between the distinctiveness motive and identity evaluation, we assess the possibility of such a moderation effect.

Values, distinctiveness and belonging   As noted above, the distinctiveness motive can find expression through one's individual uniqueness or through the uniqueness of groups to which one belongs. One can have a distinctive individual identity and/or a distinctive group identity. Individuals' value priorities may influence the extent to which people identify with the groups to which they belong. Those who give high priority to conservation values (versus openness) probably tend to think of themselves in terms of group affiliations (Cohen and Shamai, 2010; Meyer et al., 2002). Hence, they may identify more strongly with their membership groups (see evidence in Roccas et al., 2010, regarding national identification). We therefore hypothesize that individuals who attribute more importance to conservation values are more likely to draw their sense of identity distinctiveness from their group belonging. Hence, the conservation versus openness value dimension should moderate the link between distinctiveness and belonging. For those who value conservation, the distinctiveness of an identity should be associated with deriving a sense of belonging from the identity.

Values, belonging and evaluation   As noted, people who value conservation versus openness identify more with groups, presumably because belonging enables them to feel more socially grounded and secure (Roccas *et al.*, 2010). This implies that the sense of belonging that a group identity provides is more important to people who value conservation. Hence, for those who value conservation, their group belonging should relate more strongly to their evaluation of their group identity. We therefore predict that the conservation versus openness value dimension moderates the relation between the sense of belonging an identity provides and the evaluation of that identity.

Conformity values, belonging, self-efficacy and identity enactment   In addition to the evaluation of an identity, Vignoles (2011) suggests that identity enactment is another important outcome of identity motives. Identity enactment refers to displaying the identity through behavior. Vignoles proposed, and found, that the more an identity satisfies identity motives, the more people tend to enact that identity in public. He further proposed that the identity motives of self-efficacy and belonging are particularly important determinants of the extent to which people enact their identities in public. This is because feeling capable (as in self-efficacy) facilitates identity enactment and feeling accepted by others (as in the belonging motive) reduces fear that the enacted identity will be censured.

We suggest that conformity values moderate the relations of identity enactment to self-efficacy and belonging. Of the ten basic values, conformity values seem most relevant to the decision of whether or not to enact an identity in public. This is because conformity values express the motivation to fulfill others' expectations and to avoid confrontations (Schwartz, 1992). Thus, conformity values are especially important guides for public behavior. For those who value conformity highly, the motivation to enact an identity in public should depend especially strongly on the extent to which that identity will provide a sense of competence (self-efficacy) and a sense of acceptance (belonging). We therefore hypothesize that conformity values moderate the association of identity enactment with self-efficacy and belonging.

Empirical investigation

To test our hypotheses we used a varied sample of 156 adults (42 percent men, aged 18–79 years, M = 35.19, SD = 15.32). Participants first completed the most recent version of the Schwartz Value Survey (SVS), in which each of fifty-seven values is followed by a short definition (e.g. "FAMILY SECURITY (safety for loved ones)" measures security values) (Schwartz et al., 2000). Participants rated the importance of each value as a guiding principle in their lives on a scale from −1 (opposed to my principles) to 7 (of supreme importance); 3–8 value items measure each of the broad values (security, conformity, etc.). We computed the value dimension of conservation versus openness to change values by subtracting the mean rating of the self-direction and stimulation values from the mean rating of the conformity, security and tradition values.

Participants then completed the IMQ (Vignoles et al., 2006) which asks them to list eight of their identities and to provide, for each, a rating of nine identity outcomes and motives: importance of the identity, happiness with the identity, how much they show it in public, how much the identity gives them a sense that their life is meaningful, how much the identity provides them with a sense of belonging, self-esteem, continuity, distinctiveness and self-efficacy. The answer scale ranged from 0 (not at all) to 10 (extremely) (Vignoles et al., 2006).

The study design entailed a nested data structure with two distinct levels of analysis: level-1 was the repeated within-person measurement of identity outcomes and motives; level-2 was the between-person measurement of the ten basic values.[2] Following Vignoles (2004), we used multilevel regression modeling. This modeled variance simultaneously on the two levels, thereby providing more accurate and reliable estimates of the nested data structure (Hox, 1995). Following the relevant advice in the literature, prior to all analyses, we centered each level-1 variable around individual's own means (see Vignoles, 2004) and centered values around both individual's means (see Schwartz, 1992) and the sample mean (as required in analyzing interactions between continuous variables; see Aiken and West, 1991).

Table 9.1 reports the Pearson correlations between the level-1 identity outcomes and motives. Note that the significance values in the table reflect the multilevel data structure and may therefore be misleading. Nevertheless, the correlations provide an overall sense of the relations

---

[2] We did not adopt a traditional multiple regression approach because that would ignore the clustering of identity outcomes and motives within individuals and lead to an underestimation of error variance and an increased probability of Type I errors.

Table 9.1. Zero-order correlations between ratings of identity outcomes and motives (N = 1,248) on level-1

	1	2	3	4	5	6	7	8
1. Importance	1							
2. Happiness	.46**	1						
3. Showing	.33**	.28**	1					
4. Meaning	.44**	.60**	.28**	1				
5. Belong	.37**	.50**	.33**	.59**	1			
6. Self-esteem	.41**	.69**	.34**	.61**	.58**	1		
7. Continuity	.31**	.30**	.20**	.39**	.36**	.32**	1	
8. Distinctivness	.31**	.29**	.23**	.29**	.22**	.32**	.28**	1
9. Self-efficacy	.32**	.52**	.26**	.47**	.41**	.58**	.31**	.32**

Note: Significance levels: * $p < 0.05$; ** $p < 0.001$.

among the identity motives and outcomes. As expected by IPT and found previously (Vignoles, 2004; Vignoles et al., 2006), the correlations among all the identity motives and outcomes are positive and moderate to high. This pattern may be owing to the fact that all nine constructs relate to the self and people are likely to see themselves as internally consistent. Moreover, there may be a general positivity factor for identities that may color all of these outcomes and motives. However, such a "halo effect" is only partial. Had it been strong, we would not have obtained the results presented here.

Our hypotheses focus on interactions between values (level-2) and identity motives (level-1). Thus, we expect that the beta slopes in the level-1 regressions of identity outcomes (e.g. centrality, happiness) on identity motives (e.g. continuity) will differ across individuals, depending on the priority they give to particular values (level-2). We therefore estimate cross-level interactions by computing *random effects models* that allow beta slopes to vary across different levels of the level-2 variable (Snijders and Bosker, 1999). To aid in interpreting effects, we follow the common procedure of plotting the results of the cross-level interactions graphically. The graphs display low (below −1 SD), average (between −1 and +1 SD) and high (above +1 SD) values of the level-2 moderator associated with each of the simple slopes of level-1 predictors and dependent variables.[3]

---

[3] Regression lines depicted on Figures 9.2, 9.3 and 9.4 only aid the graphing effects. Interpretation of graphs that show cross-level interactions differs from interpretation of graphs that show interactions in multivariate regression. No inferential tests apply here to test the significance of the simple slopes (Snijders and Bosker, 1999).

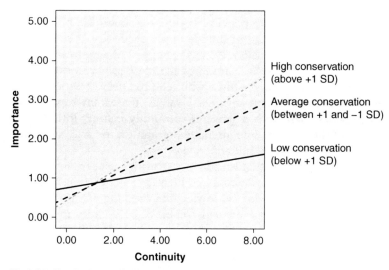

Model 1: Continuity predicting centrality

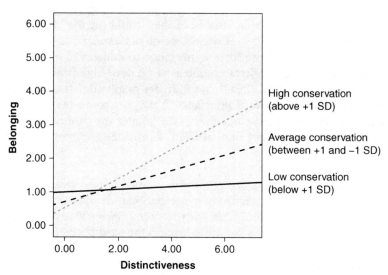

Model 4: Distinctiveness predicting belonging

Figure 9.2. Moderation effect of conservation (vs. openness)

Values, continuity and evaluation   As expected, the conservation versus openness to change value dimension moderated the relations of continuity with evaluation, both for the evaluation component of importance and for the component of happiness with the identity (Table 9.2, models 1 and 2), but it did not moderate the relation of continuity with identity enactment. The top panel of Figure 9.2 shows the moderation in predicting the importance of the identity. Specifically, it shows that, for those who value conservation (versus openness), the more an identity provides them with a sense of continuity, the more important that identity is to them. In contrast, for those who tend to attribute little importance to conservation (versus openness) values, the extent to which an identity provides them with a sense of continuity matters little for the importance of the identity. The interaction graph for the affective evaluation of the identity is very similar.[4]

Although the meaning that an identity provides is seen as an identity motive rather than an outcome of identity motives (e.g. Vignoles, 2011), we believe it is also logical to view the meaning of an identity as an outcome. This is because the satisfaction of an identity motive can also lead to the perception of the identity as providing meaning (see Vignoles, 2011, with regard to continuity and meaning), particularly if it helps people to fulfill their values. Specifically, with regard to continuity and the values of conservation versus openness, we would expect that the more an identity provides people who value conservation (versus openness) with a sense of continuity, the more they would see the identity as providing them with meaning. However, we do not expect this to be the case for those who attribute little importance to conservation (versus openness) values. This moderation effect was indeed significant in the expected direction (model 3 in Table 9.2). Its graph (not shown) was similar to the one shown for importance. Thus, the more people tend to value conservation (versus openness), the greater the positive association between the continuity that an identity provides and its perceived meaningfulness.

Values, distinctiveness and evaluation   Conservation versus openness values did not moderate the relation between distinctiveness and identity evaluation. This converges with Becker *et al.*'s (2012) findings from adolescents in nineteen countries around the world.

Values, distinctiveness and belonging   Conservation versus openness moderated the link between distinctiveness and belonging (see model 4 in Table 9.2). The bottom panel of Figure 9.2 shows that, as expected, distinctiveness and belonging correlated positively among individuals who tend to value conservation (versus openness). In contrast, these identity motives were not correlated among those who tend

---

[4] All graphs are available from the authors.

Table 9.2. Estimated standardized regression weights in multilevel regression in which identity motives and outcomes (level-1) were nested within participants (level-2: N = 1,248). Method: random *slopes*

Level-2 moderator (value)	Tested models (predictor→ dependant)	Model number	Regression estimates			Log-likelihood value ($df =10$)	Variance of dependant variable	Residual variance in dependent variable (level-2)
			Value β	Identity motive β	Value × Identity motive β			
Conservation (vs. openness)	Continuity → Importance	1	−.06*	.08	.05*	−1679.117	1.00	0.03
	Continuity → Happiness	2	.05	−.04	.06*	−1811.538	1.24	0.07
	Continuity → Meaning	3	−.07*	−.01	.09*	−1944.578	1.70	0.08
	Distinctiveness → Belonging	4	−.12**	.08	.09*	−1979.998	1.55	0.05
Conformity	Self-esteem	5	−.10*	.14**	.12*	−1750.819	1.70	0.02
	Meaning	6	−.15**	.34*	.15**	−1745.073	1.70	0.03
	Self-efficacy	7	−.07*	.24*	.12**	−1777.867	1.70	0.02
	Belonging Importance	8	−.08*	.13	.08*	−1638.196	1.00	0.02
	Belonging Happiness	9	−.02	.22 *	.09*	−1675.441	1.24	0.00
	Belonging Meaning	10	−.03	.06	.10*	−1786.488	1.70	0.02
Security	Belonging	11	−.06	.15*	.10*	−1755.654	1.14	0.01
	Continuity	12	−.06	.25**	.10**	−1801.330	1.14	0.01
	Belonging	13	−.03	.15**	.09*	−1756.887	1.14	0.01
	Meaning	14	−.05	.30**	.10*	−1749.33	1.14	0.04

Note: Significance levels: *p <.05, **p <.001.

not to value conservation versus openness. This provides indirect support for the idea that people who value conservation (versus openness) tend to think about themselves in terms of group affiliations and to pursue their distinctiveness motive through the groups to which they belong. Similarly, Vignoles *et al.* (2006) found a stronger positive correlation between these identity motives among church-goers, who are likely to value conservation highly (see Schwartz and Huismans, 1995), compared to school-leavers.

Values, belonging and evaluation   We expected the conservation versus openness value dimension to moderate the relation between the sense of belonging that an identity provides and the evaluation of that identity. We examined this moderation effect for two aspects of evaluation, the importance of the identity and happiness with it. Neither was significant. However, one component of conservation values, namely conformity values, did moderate the relation between the belonging an identity provides and both aspects of its evaluation, importance and happiness (Table 9.2, models 8 and 9, respectively). The top panel of Figure 9.3 shows that the greater the sense of belonging that an identity provided the more important that identity was for people who attribute high or medium importance to conformity values. In contrast, the sense of belonging that an identity provides did not predict the importance of the identity among those who give low importance to conformity values. The bottom panel of Figure 9.3 reveals a similar pattern of interaction for happiness with the identity. In this case, however, a greater sense of belonging derived from an identity was associated with greater happiness with the identity for everyone, but the effect was stronger among those who value conformity highly.

Conformity values, belonging and meaning   In line with our view of meaning as an identity outcome, we examined whether conformity values moderated the links between the sense of belonging and the sense of meaning an identity provides for individuals. We postulated that an identity that provides a sense of belonging to people who value conformity should also provide them with a sense of meaning, because belonging is particularly important to them. This moderation effect was indeed significant and in the expected direction (model 10 in Table 9.2). Specifically, for everyone, a greater sense of belonging derived from an identity was associated with attaching greater meaning to that identity, but this effect was stronger among those who value conformity highly. This is similar to the moderation of the association between belonging and happiness noted above.

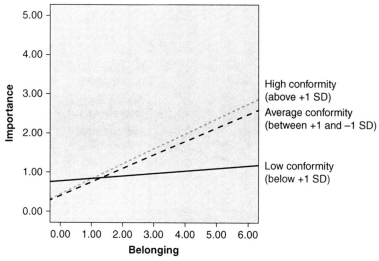

Model 8: Belonging predicting centrality

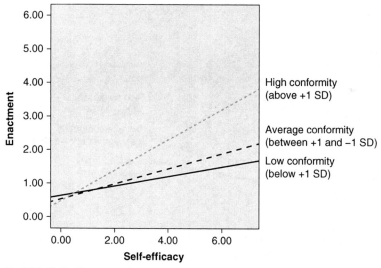

Model 7: Self-efficacy predicting enactment

Figure 9.3a. Moderation effect of conformity

Conformity values, belonging, self-efficacy and identity enact-ment As expected, conformity values moderated the association of self-efficacy and of belonging with identity enactment (Figure 9.3, models 7 and 11, respectively). The bottom panel of Figure 9.3b shows that the

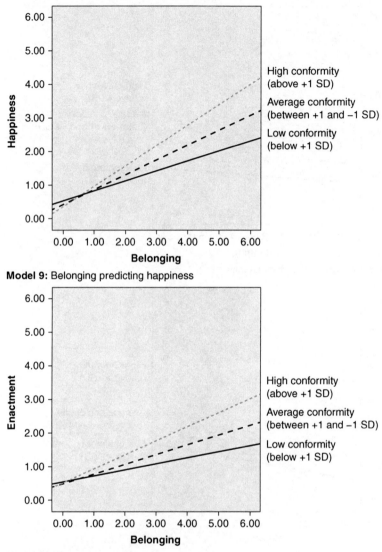

Model 9: Belonging predicting happiness

Model 11: Belonging predicting enactment

Figure 9.3b. Moderation effect of conformity

positive relation between the sense of belonging that an identity provides and enactment of that identity is stronger the more a person values
conformity. Conformity values had a similar moderating effect on relations between self-efficacy and identity enactment (Figure 9.3, bottom

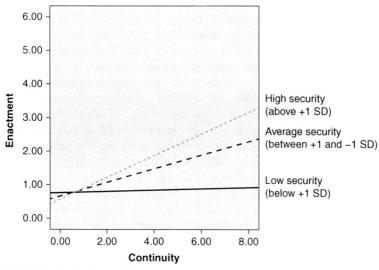

Model 12: Continuity predicting enactment

Figure 9.4. Moderation effect of security

panel). Vignoles (2011) proposed a general link between satisfaction of *all* identity motives and enacting identities in public. We therefore tested whether conformity values also moderated relations between the other identity motives and identity enactment. We found that conformity values had similar moderation effects for both the self-esteem and the meaning motives and the interactions showed a similar shape (models 5 and 6 in Table 9.2, respectively). Thus, we can now add an individual differences perspective to Vignoles' (2011) general proposal that the more an identity satisfies identity motives, the more people tend to show this identity in public. Our findings suggest that, the more people value conformity, the closer the link between the degree to which an identity satisfies various identity motives and the tendency to display that identity in public.

Confirmation of the moderation effects of conformity led us to assess whether the other conservation values, security and tradition, also had such moderation effects. Security values exhibited similar moderation effects on the associations of both belonging and continuity with identity enactment (Table 9.2, models 13 and 12 respectively and Figure 9.4 for continuity). Both the belonging and continuity motives may be particularly important for people who value security highly, because belonging and continuity can provide a sense of being protected and safe in a predictable world. We note, however, that security values had the same moderation effect on the positive link between the identity motive of meaning and identity enactment (model 14 in Table 9.2). Tradition values exhibited no moderation effects. Close examination of the patterns of moderation effects could be a topic for future research.

In sum, we found that personal values moderated links between identity motives and outcomes, suggesting that, although there is universality in links between identity motives and outcomes, there are also individual-differences. Specifically, for individuals who highly value conservation (versus openness to change) values, the feeling that an identity provides them with continuity is particularly important in the evaluation of an identity and for these people distinctiveness is more closely associated with belonging. Furthermore, for individuals who value conformity (one component of conservation values), satisfying the motives of self-esteem, meaning and self-efficacy is particularly associated with their tendency to show the identity in public. Additionally, for people who value conformity, there is a closer association between satisfying the motive of belonging and all aspects of identity evaluation. Finally, individuals who value security highly (another component of conservation values) tend to enact more identities that provide a sense of continuity, belonging and meaning. This suggests that one size does not fit all: values determine which identity motives are more associated with identity outcomes.

Value and identity change

Stability and change are of key importance to the understanding of identities and values. Some of the suggestions and findings from value theory and research could inform IPT and stimulate new research, as we explicate next.

Forces for stability   Bardi and Goodwin (2011) suggested that basic values are embedded in core schemas. This is probably true for identities as well. Hence, as Bardi and Goodwin (2011) suggest with regard to values, core identities may be stable by default, due to the forces that cause stability in core schema reviewed above. That is, for identities to change, something in the environment must change. And indeed, IPT links identity changes with social change (Breakwell, 2001a).

The process of change   As values are embedded in core schemas, any change in values occurs through change to the relevant core schema (Bardi and Goodwin, 2011). Similarly, IPT suggests that identity change involves change to knowledge structures, reflecting the assimilation–accommodation process (Breakwell, 1986). Values and compatible identities are probably associated with the same schema. This implies that they may change together as part of the same process and/or that a change in one may induce a compatible change in the other (see supporting evidence with regard to values and compatible beliefs in Goodwin *et al.*, 2012). Future research can examine whether this holds with regard to values and compatible identities.

IPT suggests that social changes may lead to changes in the centrality of identities. The process by which this could occur can be adapted from Bardi and Goodwin's (2011) suggestions regarding the automatic and effortful routes to value change. Specifically, social change can activate particular values automatically and/or through conscious discussion. For example, messages in the media regarding the threat of Islamic terrorism may automatically activate the identities of "Muslim" and "British" in British Muslims. This activation may lead to an automatic threat to satisfying the motive of self-esteem in of the Muslim identity, because of the negative discourse in the media regarding Muslims. This, in turn, could lead to a reduction in the centrality of Muslim identity. However, the same messages are likely to enter awareness and may cause conscious thought about them. A British Muslim person may disagree with these messages and feel alienated from Britain. This feeling of alienation is likely to reduce satisfaction of the motive of belonging that the British identity provides and therefore lead to a reduction in the centrality of the British identity.

Finally, our empirical research reported above suggests a "values pathway" through which social change may induce identity change. We found that conservation values moderate the links between various identity motives and outcomes. For example, the importance people attribute to conservation values affects the extent to which the sense of continuity that an identity provides influences the evaluation of that identity. If social change leads to an increase or decrease in the importance of conservation values, it is also likely to affect the links between the identity motives and outcomes that these values moderate. To illustrate, consider the sense of continuity that a religious identity can provide. If social change induces increased importance of conservation values, the continuity motive should become more influential and people should experience their religious identities as more important and central and they should be happier with them.

This values pathway could have large-scale ramifications in a society if there were a mass shift in the importance of conservation values that affected the influence of the continuity motive. If conservation values and, consequently, the continuity motive were to become more important, people's identity as adherents of a religion would become more central for them. The role of religious institutions in society might then increase and people might demand changes in government family policies. A decrease in the importance of conservation values and, consequently, of the continuity motive, might have opposite effects. It might weaken religious institutions and lead to more liberal family policies.

Conclusions and future directions

This chapter provided an integration of IPT with the Schwartz (1992) value theory, adding an individual-difference perspective to IPT and demonstrating its importance empirically, as well as integrating ideas and empirical findings regarding changes of identities and values. Our empirical data demonstrated that individual differences in personal values moderate the links between identity motives and identity outcomes, thereby revealing that these links are not the same for everyone. Our hypotheses and findings were focused on conservation values, which express the motivation to maintain stability and thereby to protect the individual from threat. This fits with IPT's focus on identity threat. It suggests that individuals may differ in the level of identity threat that social changes can elicit owing to value-based individual differences in the importance of satisfying certain identity motives. For instance, those individuals who value conservation (and therefore see identities that provide them with feelings of continuity as more important) may be adversely affected if they cease to perceive a sense of continuity, leading to identity threat (Breakwell, 1986).

Future theory and research could expand the contribution of values to IPT by addressing values as determinants of contents of identities that would allow the person to fulfill his or her values (see also Roccas *et al.*, 2010). This is consistent with IPT's recognition that individuals have agency in constructing their identities. Future research could also investigate some of the suggestions put forward regarding value change in the area of identities.

In conclusion, this chapter makes progress in bridging the individual and social levels of cognition. We hope that, by presenting an individual-difference dimension to IPT, we have been able to establish linkage between some of the central tenets of IPT and values theory. This should encourage both IPT and values researchers to consider the theoretical and empirical benefits of further integrating these theories in their work and of acknowledging their respective contributions to understanding the self, change and human motivation.

REFERENCES

Aiken, L. S., and West, S. G. (1991). *Multiple regression: testing and interpreting interactions*. Newbury Park, CA: Sage.

Bardi, A., Lee, J. A., Towfigh, N., and Soutar, G. (2009). The structure of intra-individual value change. *Journal of Personality and Social Psychology*, 97(5), 913–929.

Bardi, A., and Goodwin, R. (2011). The dual route to value change: individual processes and cultural moderators. *Journal of Cross Cultural Psychology*, 42(2), 271–287.

Becker, M., Vignoles, V. L., Owe, E., Brown, R., Smith, P. B., Easterbrook, M., et al. (2012). Culture and the distinctiveness motive: constructing identity in individualistic and collectivistic contexts. *Journal of Personality and Social Psychology*, 201, 833–855.

Breakwell, G. M. (1986). *Coping with threatened identities*. London: Methuen.

Breakwell, G. M. (1992). Processes of self-evaluation: efficacy and estrangement. In Breakwell, G. M. (ed.), *Social psychology of identity and the self concept* (pp. 35–55). London: Academic Press/Surrey University Press.

Breakwell, G. M. (2001a). Promoting individual and social change. In F. Butera and G. Mugny (eds.), *Social influence in social reality*. Goettingen: Hogrefe & Huber.

Breakwell, G. M. (2001b). Social representational constraints upon identity processes. In K. Deaux and G. Philogène (eds.), *Representations of the social: bridging theoretical traditions* (pp. 271–284). Oxford: Blackwell.

Breakwell, G. M. (2010). Resisting representations and identity processes. *Papers in Social Representations*, 19, 6.1–6.11.

Cohen, A., and Shamai, O. (2010). The relationship between individual values, psychological well-being and organizational commitment among Israeli police officers. *Policing: an International Journal of Police Strategies and Management*, 33(1), 30–51.

Cooper, R. P., and Shallice, T. (2006). Hierarchical schemas and goals in the control of sequential behaviour. *Psychological Review*, 113, 887–916.

Deaux, K. (1993). Reconstructing social identity. *Personality and Social Psychology Bulletin*, 19(1), 4–12.

Goodwin, R., Polek, E., and Bardi, A. (2012). The temporal reciprocity of values and beliefs: a longitudinal study within a major life transition. *European Journal of Personality*, 26(3), 360–370.

Hofman, J. E. (1988). Social identity and intergroup conflict: an Israeli view. In W. Stroebe, A. W. Kruglanski, D. Bar-Tal and M. Hewstone (eds.), *The social psychology of intergroup conflict*. New York: Springer Verlag.

Hox, J. J. (1995). *Applied multilevel analysis* (2nd edn.). Amsterdam: TT-Publikaties.

Janoff-Bulman, R. (1989). Assumptive worlds and the stress of traumatic events: applications of the schema construct. *Social Cognition*, 7, 113–136.

Jaspal, R. (2011). The construction and management of national and ethnic identities among British South Asians: an identity process theory approach. Ph.D. dissertation, Royal Holloway, University of London.

Jaspal, R., and Cinnirella, M. (2010). Coping with potentially incompatible identities: accounts of religious, ethnic and sexual identities from British

Pakistani men who identify as Muslim and gay. *British Journal of Social Psychology*, 49(4), 849–870.

Jaspal, R., and Siraj, A. (2011). Perceptions of 'coming out' among British Muslim gay men. *Psychology and Sexuality*, 2(3),183–197.

Jodhka, S. S. (2004). Sikhism and the caste question: Dalits and their politics in contemporary Punjab. *Contributions to Indian Sociology*, 38, 165–191.

Maio, G. R., Pakizeh, A., Cheung, W.-Y., and Rees, K. (2009). Changing, priming and acting on values: effects via motivational relations in a circular model. *Journal of Personality and Social Psychology*, 97, 699–715.

Meyer, P. J., Stanley, D. J., Herscovitch, L., and Topolnytsky, L. (2002). Affective, continuance and normative commitment to the organization: a meta-analysis of antecedents, correlates, and consequences. *Journal of Vocational Behavior*, 61, 20–52.

Moscovici, S. (1988). Notes towards a description of social representations. *European Journal of Social Psychology*, 18, 211–250.

Ram, R. (2004). Untouchability, Dalit consciousness and the Ad Dharm movement in Punjab. *Contributions to Indian Sociology*, 38(3), 323–49.

Roccas, S., Schwartz, S. H., and Amit, A. (2010). Personal value priorities and national identification. *Political Psychology*, 31, 393–419.

Schwartz, S. H. (1992). Universals in the content and structure of values: theory and empirical tests in 20 countries. In M. Zanna (ed.), *Advances in experimental social psychology*, vol. XXV (pp. 1–65). New York: Academic Press.

Schwartz, S. H. (2006). Les Valeurs de base de la personne: théorie, mesures et applications [Basic human values: theory, measurement, and applications]. *Revue Française de Sociologie*, 47, 249–288.

Schwartz, S. H. (2011). Values: individual and cultural. In F. J. R. van de Vijver, A. Chasiotis, and S. M. Breugelmans (eds.), *Fundamental questions in cross-cultural psychology* (pp. 463–493). Cambridge University Press.

Schwartz, S. H. (2012). An overview of the Schwartz Theory of Basic Values. *Online Readings in Psychology and Culture*, 2(1). http://dx.doi.org/10.9707/2307-0919.1116.

Schwartz, S. H., and Huismans, S. (1995). Value priorities and religiosity in four Western religions. *Social Psychology Quarterly*, 58, 88–107.

Schwartz, S. H., Sagiv, L., and Boehnke, K. (2000). Worries and values. *Journal of Personality*, 68, 309–346.

Snijders, T., and Bosker, R. (1999). *Multilevel analysis. An introduction to basic and advanced multilevel modelling.* London: Sage.

Vignoles, V. L. (2004). Modelling identity motives using multilevel regression. In G. M. Breakwell (ed.), *Doing social psychology research* (pp. 184–215). Oxford: BPS Blackwell.

Vignoles, V. L. (2011). Identity motives. In S. J. Schwartz, K. Luyckx and V. L. Vignoles (eds.), *Handbook of identity theory and research* (pp. 403–432). New York: Springer.

Vignoles, V. L., Chryssochoou, X., and Breakwell, G. M. (2000). The distinctiveness principle: identity, meaning and the bounds of cultural relativity. *Personality and Social Psychology Review*, 4, 337–354.

Vignoles, V. L., Chryssochoou, X., and Breakwell, G. M. (2002). Evaluating models of identity motivation: self-esteem is not the whole story. *Self and Identity*, 1, 201–218.

Vignoles, V. L., Regalia, C., Manzi, C., Golledge, J., and Scabini, E. (2006). Beyond self-esteem: influence of multiple motives on identity construction. *Journal of Personality and Social Psychology*, 90(2), 308–333.

Ward, S. H. and Braun, J. (1972). Self-esteem and racial preference in Black children. *American Journal of Orthopsychiatry*, 42(4), 644–647.

Part IV

Identity Process Theory and social change

10 Toward a social psychology of social change: insights from Identity Process Theory

Roxane de la Sablonnière and Esther Usborne

Ideally the central issue of social psychology should be the study of psychological processes accompanying, determining, and determined by social change.

Tajfel (1972, p. 4)

Social psychology is a fascinating field. It examines how people interact with each other and explores internal psychological processes that dictate everyday human behavior. Through rigorous science, complex statistical analyses, creative field research and laboratory experiments, social psychology seeks to understand human behavior in its social context.

Initially, social psychology was born out of a need to comprehend pressing social concerns. Early social psychologists sought an understanding of events characterized by social change such as war, social movements, intergroup relations and racism. They worked to understand the processes associated with people's thoughts and behavior in such challenging contexts. Specifically, after World War II, there was an explosion in social psychological research and a pronounced interest in the field. Important theories were developed in order to achieve a better understanding of human behaviors, particularly those that were difficult to comprehend. Scientists posed research questions that attempted to explain the rise of Nazi Germany, widespread racism and intergroup conflicts. Social psychologists, such as Milgram, Asch, Tajfel, Sherif, Allport and Zimbardo, to name a few, were all influenced by the critical social issues of the day. An important focus of some early work in social psychology was on understanding identity, social action and social change. For example, Tajfel and Turner (1986) sought to understand the adaptation strategies (i.e. collective actions) in which individuals engage as a means to defend minority rights.

Social psychologists were therefore guided by a strong desire to make the world a better place for those who were suffering the most. Theories that would directly impact people's lives were elaborated, tested and debated. Consequently, these theories defined social psychology and helped our discipline make a distinctive contribution to science. At the same time, social psychology began to distinguish itself from other disciplines by employing rigorous methodology and innovative controlled laboratory experiments. One of the main goals of the field was to utilize the scientific paradigm so that social psychology could explore human thought and behavior, using methods that paralleled those used in the hard sciences.

However, after the so-called "Golden Age of Social Psychology," which ended by the mid 1960s (Sewell, 1989), the field has been accused of being simplistic, individualistic and therefore, having a rather weak social impact (Hill, 2006; Kruglanski, 2001). In the first place, most contemporary social psychological findings are based on results from studies with college students performing academic-like tasks in artificial laboratories (Sears, 1986). Henrich and his colleagues claim that behavioral scientists often draw general conclusions about human behavior based only on samples from Western, educated, industrialized, rich and democratic (WEIRD) societies (Henrich et al., 2010). They argue that people from WEIRD societies are not representative of the world's population – they differ on fundamental processes such as visual perception and categorization, as well as on more complex social psychological conceptions of the self-concept and moral reasoning.

Secondly, social psychologists today do not always take into account the context in which the targeted social behavior takes place (Oishi et al., 2009) by conducting studies oriented toward intra-individual processes in simplistic and artificial laboratory conditions (Hill, 2006; Pancer, 1997; Potter and Edwards, 2001; see also Billig, 2009). The results generated in these conditions serve to drive conclusions that lack generalizability and therefore, have little practical use (Allport, 1968; Hill, 2006). Contemporary social psychology emphasizes experimental accuracy at the expense of breakthroughs that are based in a real-world context. Such breakthroughs would serve as the groundwork for concrete action in response to major social issues such as poverty, lack of education and war (Hill, 2006; Kruglanski, 2001; Oishi et al., 2009).

As such, social psychologists seem to have put aside the fundamental objective of "making a difference" in the world in order to become more of a "hard" science. It seems that we have lost sight of the fact that all social behavior is influenced by the sociocultural context in which it takes place and that without considering this context, social psychology cannot answer the most pressing questions. Gergen (1973) argued that social psychology, because it studies social behavior that takes place in a continuously transforming sociocultural context, cannot function on the basis of the accumulation of knowledge like the hard sciences do. Since social behavior varies at the rhythm of this context, so should theories and by extension the research that stems from these theories. Accordingly, social psychological concepts that were "true" in a certain period of human history should undergo constant analyses about whether they remain valid in today's context, a context that continues to be characterized by social change (Weinstein, 2010), or profound societal transformations (e.g. Rocher, 1992). Thus, we argue that because social change is a fundamental contextual element impacting human life, we should take social change into account when developing, generalizing and applying our theories in social psychology.

Taking into account the current criticisms of social psychology, we propose a solution that goes beyond simply conducting Western-designed studies with populations other than Western university students. We argue that the solution requires, at least in part, a new focus on what we call a *social psychology of social change*. We believe that Breakwell's Identity Process Theory (IPT; Breakwell, 1986, 1988, 1993) has an important role to play in the development of a social psychology of social change. Taking social change into account in social psychology represents a concrete way to address the criticisms that were pointed out by many social psychologists over the last decades (e.g. Gergen, 1973; Oishi *et al.*, 2009). For example, a social psychology of social change would do what Gergen (1973) proposed long ago, providing scope for the analysis of constantly changing social environments. The social psychology of social change would include social change as a key component of theories and research, thus allowing for social psychological phenomena to be influenced by and vary according to social change. Instead of presenting research findings as universal truths, we would acknowledge and seek to understand the role of social change for these findings. Therefore, the general goal of the present chapter is to argue that mainstream social psychology needs to return to its roots, and to again become a discipline that is driven by social issues – a social psychology of social change. As societies are changing rapidly and dramatically, we argue that this need is pressing if we want our discipline to further develop its impact and continue having a positive influence on all societies of this world.

First of all, we draw upon both sociological and psychological traditions to define dramatic social change and to describe its pervasiveness and rapidity in today's world. We argue for the necessity of a social psychology that studies human beings as embedded within a constantly evolving social environment.

Secondly, to achieve our general goal, that is to justify the need to move toward a social psychology of social change, we focus on and describe a social psychological theory that does have social change as a central tenet: Identity Process Theory (Breakwell, 1986, 1993). This holistic theory that synthesizes individual and group-level theories conceptualizes social change as fundamental to one's psychological experience. By describing one's identity as constantly changing and by detailing the psychological processes associated with this change, IPT is one of the first and only theories to make change an essential, foundational component of one's psychology.

Thirdly, we argue that although IPT successfully integrates both personal and group levels of analysis, it focuses primarily on "personal" social change, as opposed to "collective" social change. We suggest that there may be additional psychological processes associated with social change processes that are collective.

Finally, we aim to encourage theorists and researchers to construct a social psychology of social change, one that has the capacity to use research to attend to pressing social issues and to improve the well-being of all society members. We call for research that acknowledges the psychological impact of social change that seeks to understand and mitigate its negative well-being effects. Examples from recent advances in Relative Deprivation Theory (e.g. de la Sablonnière et al., 2009b), Goodwin's Adjustment to Change Theory and accompanying research (e.g. Goodwin, 2006; Goodwin et al., 2001) and research on identity integration (e.g. Amiot et al., 2007; Benet-Martinez and Haritatos, 2005; Benet-Martinez et al., 2002; Berry, 2005) will be examined briefly. Future directions in research as well as concrete implications will be discussed.

Dramatic social change

Despite the fact that the study of social change has begun to interest many social scientists, it remains largely understudied (Goodwin et al., 2001; Moghaddam, 1990). Because it is a difficult concept to grasp, both for the laymen and for social scientists, defining social change represents one of the biggest challenges in psychology, which explains why social change is currently understudied.

One particular kind of social change that has been best documented and described by sociologists, because of its considerable impact on individuals' lives, is *dramatic* social change (see Weinstein, 2010). In our previous research, we have defined dramatic social change as "profound societal transformations that produce a complete rupture in the equilibrium of social structures because their adaptive capacities are surpassed" (de la Sablonnière et al., 2009b, p. 325).

Our main argument for why we should move toward a social psychology of social change is that dramatic social change touches all of us, is increasingly rapid, common and affects, or has the potential to affect, every person on our planet. That is, everybody in the world, even those from rich and privileged Western countries, is susceptible to the consequences of dramatic social change (Chirot and Merton, 1986; Fukuyama, 1999; Nolan and Lenski, 2011; Ponsioen, 1969; Sztompka, 1998; Zuck, 1997). This is in line with Smith (1973) who has claimed that "contemporary changes are massive, rapid, continuous yet elusive, varied and apparently unpredictable. They occur at every level of society, they vary in scope and pace, they can be classified as both qualitative and quantitative. Above all, they are global" (p. 60). Because of its enormous possible temporal and spatial scope, dramatic social change should be taken into consideration in social psychological theories. Specifically, given the individual implications of social change, the psychological level needs to be investigated. In addition, by integrating a social psychology of social change, we will enrich current theories by studying individuals in all the complexity of their changing personal and social environment, potentially bridging social psychology and sociology.

Inspired by theory and research from sociology (e.g. Weinstein, 2010; Nolan and Lenski, 2011) and psychology (e.g. Breakwell and Lyons, 1996) we identified six important potential areas of dramatic social change that have a considerable impact on many modern societies: dramatic political and economic events, migration movements, natural disasters, human-made disasters, technology and, finally, dramatic personal social change.

Dramatic political and economic events are dramatic in their very essence, as they can affect the very foundation of societies. Such events can be extensive, affecting several countries at once (e.g. the breakdown of the USSR; Carter, 2000; Gallina, 2011) or at a more localized level (e.g. the Tulip Revolution of 2005 in Kyrgyzstan). Migrant movements are also social changes as they not only affect the migrants and refugees themselves (e.g. Berry, 2005), but also the host society as a whole (Bourhis et al., 1997). For example, waves of non-European immigrants have not only changed the face of many Western countries, but also affected the equilibrium between majority and minority groups in these countries (e.g. Farley, 1997; McBride, 1999; Mercer, 1995).

Natural and human-made disasters represent important social changes because they can dramatically and rapidly transform different aspects of thousands of people's lives (White, 2010). For example, the tsunami that hit Japan affected the Japanese economy, their natural resources and their psychological well-being. Technological changes are also considered to be social changes because, due to technology's prominence and extremely rapid evolution, it has completely transformed us, our interactions and as such, our societies (e.g. Bernardino, 1996; Karoly and Panis, 2004; Marjoribanks, 2000). For example, Facebook and other social networks have revolutionized how people with an array of different backgrounds meet new people for love, for work or for leisure. Lastly, personal social change is an important dimension of social change as it affects the whole community, in addition to the individual personally involved in the change itself. Personal social change differs from *personal change* in that the latter affects only one person and their close circle; whereas, the first influences entire communities, in addition to the one person. For example, in the context of certain Aboriginal communities in Canada, someone committing suicide can be conceptualized as a personal *social* change; everyone in the community will be deeply affected when one suicide takes place because everyone is related to each other (e.g. Kirmayer *et al.*, 2003). We labeled this change "personal *social* change" because it is a change that would be considered just a "personal change" in another context. If one person kills himself in London, that suicide would not disrupt the functioning of the whole city. However, a personal change, like a suicide in a small Aboriginal community, becomes a "social change" when the functioning of the entire community is affected.

In sum, the six types of dramatic social change that we have focused on illustrate the pervasiveness of social change. Its vast, often global, impact on individuals and societies highlights the need for a social psychology of social change. Although it is acknowledged that there are other forms of social change in both Western and non-Western societies, we focus upon these six, as they are among the most salient and publically discussed by both sociologists (e.g. Giddens *et al.*, 2011; Weinstein, 2010) and social psychologists (e.g. Berry, 2005; Tajfel, 1975).

We now turn to a theory that we found epitomizes such a social psychology. IPT is an example of a social psychological theory that integrates, rather than ignores, social change.

Identity Process Theory

Identity Process Theory (Breakwell, 1986, 1988, 1993) is a dynamic and integrative theory that conceptualizes social change as fundamental to one's psychological experience. In IPT, Breakwell describes the structure of one's identity and explains how individuals cope with identity threats, or changes, arising from their social environment. When describing the structure of identity, she outlines two processes – assimilation–accommodation and evaluation – that are thought to regulate the structure of one's identity. Assimilation–accommodation refers to both the absorption of new elements into one's identity (assimilation) and the adjustment that occurs in the identity structure to make room for these new elements (accommodation). Thus, the structure of one's identity is conceptualized not as static, but as constantly adjusting to incorporate new components. IPT takes into account the very real possibility that one's identity will often shift in response to changes in one's social context. For example, as a result of globalization and Americanization in Kyrgyzstan, Kyrgyz students attending an American University show signs that they are integrating the American identity into their self-concept (see de la Sablonnière *et al.*, 2013). Such identity integration necessitates the psychological processes of assimilation and accommodation.

The second process, evaluation, refers to the allocation of value to the identity elements. Individuals will assign a positive or negative worth to these elements. Breakwell acknowledges that one continuously evaluates and re-evaluates the identity structure as it adjusts to social change. For example, in previous research conducted in Russia and Mongolia, it was found that perceiving social changes as rapid and numerous led people to re-evaluate the situation of their group, which in turn affected their positive or negative evaluation of their identity (collective esteem; de la Sablonnière *et al.*, 2009c).

In IPT, Breakwell (1986, 1993) also describes four principles, which guide the processes of assimilation–accommodation and evaluation. These include feelings of continuity across time and situation (continuity), feelings of uniqueness or distinctiveness from others (distinctiveness), feeling confident and in control of one's life (self-efficacy) and feeling personal worth or social value (self-esteem). The search for continuity, distinctiveness, self-efficacy and self-esteem determine when and how the processes of assimilation–accommodation and evaluation occur. The four principles guide the extent to which individuals will incorporate and adjust to new identity elements, and they determine the value that is placed on these elements (Breakwell, 1993). A new immigrant, for example, may find that he or she no longer feels adequate levels of continuity across time and situation after moving to a foreign country and behaving and interacting in new ways. This constitutes a threat to one of IPT's four guiding identity principles – continuity. According to the theory, such a threat will compel the individual to engage in specific coping strategies so he or she can assimilate and accommodate a new identity into his or her identity structure (e.g. a bicultural identity) and thus regain feelings of continuity.

When any of the four principles are threatened by social change, an individual's identity is said to be under threat. Specifically, Breakwell argues that the four identity principles may be threatened at any time by changes in the social context. When there is a threat, the individual engages in specific coping strategies including intrapsychic, interpersonal, intragroup and/or intergroup strategies (see Breakwell, 1988). He or she will seek to remove or modify the threat to identity and restore a sense of balance in the identity principles. Identity threat, or social change, is thus conceptualized in IPT as an essential component of human life. IPT makes predictions based on reactions to social change and its effect on an individual's shifting identity.

Breakwell and her colleagues often use IPT to explore the experiences of people undergoing identity threat or dramatic change. For example, Timotijevic and Breakwell (2000) studied threats to identity experienced by migrants to Britain from the former Yugoslavia. IPT allowed these researchers to analyze the experiences of individuals who had encountered radical social and political upheaval and to examine the identity processes resulting from their migration. Others have used IPT to understand individuals wrestling with potentially incompatible identities (e.g. Jaspal and Cinnirella, 2010). These researchers explored the experiences of British Pakistani men who identified as both Muslim and gay. They found that this overlap of religious, sexual and ethnic identities gave rise to identity threat. Through the lens of IPT, the researchers were able to uncover strategies, such as the use of external attribution, employed by these men to cope with a complex threat to their identities and thus re-establish IPT's identity principles.

By acknowledging identity threat, by describing identity as constantly changing and by detailing the psychological processes and coping mechanisms associated with this change, IPT is one of the first theories to make change an essential, foundational component of one's psychology. Unlike many less comprehensive social psychological theories, IPT not only allows for change, but also makes social change a given for every individual.

Identity Process Theory and collective social change

Although IPT does successfully integrate both personal and group levels of analysis (see Breakwell, 1988), and has the capacity to deal with many forms of social change, we argue here that it has thus far focused primarily on *personal* change, as opposed to *collective* social change. In her seminal book, entitled *Coping with Threatened Identities* (Breakwell, 1986), Breakwell begins by detailing examples of identity-threatening experiences. She describes individuals wrestling with particular concerns such as transsexualism, a diagnosis of leprosy, alcoholism, drug abuse, and the negotiation of conflicting cultural identities. Each of these is a threat to an individual's identity as they cope with some form of dramatic personal change. Accordingly, much of the theory and research conducted in the IPT tradition has examined such personal change – migrating to a new culture (e.g. Timotijevic and Breakwell, 2000), negotiating conflicting identities (e.g. Jaspal and Cinnirella, 2010). We posit that there may be additional psychological processes associated with *collective* social change.

The six social changes that we outlined previously affect large segments of society. IPT does include social change as a foundational component of the model; however, adding a focus on collective social change and examining the impact of collective social change through the lens of IPT could not only broaden the theory but could also improve our understanding of the comprehensive impact of social change.

Identity threat is a central component of IPT. This threat is defined very broadly as when the identity principles of self-esteem, distinctiveness, continuity and self-efficacy are threatened by changes in the social context (Breakwell, 1988). A threat occurs when a person finds that a social change requires modifications in identity. If we adhere to this broad definition of identity threat, it is evident that IPT is capable of taking into account collective social change. A collective social change would undoubtedly threaten some or all of the four guiding identity principles. However, a collective change may threaten identity in a way that is different from a threat stemming from a personal social change and may thus require different methods of coping with it. For example, the norms of the society might be totally disrupted in the advent of dramatic social change, and coping might require a collective intervention, as opposed to an individualistic intervention or strategy. A collective intervention or a collective coping strategy would clarify societal norms that guide behavior in the new social environment (Taylor and de la Sablonnière, 2013). Therefore, we argue that the identity threat in question should be identified in the theory as a personal change versus a collective social change, or some combination of the two. It would then be possible to examine their differential effects on the identity principles outlined in IPT and on the coping mechanisms used to restore the identity principles.

To illustrate this point, we draw upon examples from one of the collective social changes described previously – migration movements. Social psychology has thus far focused primarily on the acculturation processes associated with migration to Western developed nations, and has examined the psychological impact of (im)migration on the individual (im)migrants themselves (e.g. Benet-Martinez and Haritatos, 2005; Benet-Martinez *et al.*, 2002; Berry, 2005; Phinney *et al.*, 2001; Ryder *et al.*, 2000). It has not comprehensively examined collective social change's effect on society in general, even though increasing immigration rates are forcing citizens to redefine what it means to be a member of the majority or mainstream culture. Is a Canadian someone of European descent? Or, can a Canadian be a woman who wears the Islamic veil and speaks Arabic? These questions aptly illustrate the fact that (im)migration constitutes an important collective social change as it triggers key questions about changing the collective and cultural identity of a group, potentially threatening the collective (de la Sablonnière, 2013). We see great potential for IPT to examine the effect of this change *both* on the migrant and on the broader society. By examining identity threat at both an individual and collective level (Lyons, 1996) – the individual wrestling with what it means to be a new member of a particular culture and the society wrestling with what it means to be Canadian – IPT could examine how such threats affect the identity principles and the coping mechanisms applied by individuals to deal with each kind of identity threat. It may be the case that coping with a threat to one's national or cultural identity may require very different, possibly collective, coping mechanisms, compared to the mechanisms employed when reacting to personal migration to a new culture. For example, group-level coping mechanisms, such as the formation of pressure groups or larger social movement may be "effective for the individual because they may either eradicate the source of a threat or change in its social meaning" (Breakwell, 1988, p. 200; see also Breakwell, 1986; Tajfel, 1978).

Another example associated with the social change stemming from migration movements has to do with the migrants themselves and allows one to take into account the collective social changes the migrants may have experienced before coming to their new host country. Timotijevic and Breakwell (2000) used IPT to study threats to identity experienced by migrants to Britain from the former Yugoslavia, migrants who had encountered radical social and political upheaval in their country of origin before moving to a new country. For the most part, these researchers explored the identity processes resulting from migration to a new culture and thus a personal change. However, IPT could also be used to separately examine the identity threat stemming from the collective social change, war and political upheaval, previously experienced by the migrants. It could then help those who face challenges of both collective and personal change, and to understand the differential effects on identity of these types of social change and how they might interact to affect coping and well-being. For example, an immigrant from Rwanda to Canada who has seen his or her country destroyed by genocide faces the double challenge of adapting to Canada and coping with the dramatic social change of his or her country of origin.

More broadly, by taking collective social change into account, IPT could be employed to examine and understand the impact of events for entire segments of a population. Undoubtedly, identity is threatened by such dramatic collective events. IPT therefore has the capacity to understand the psychological consequences of these events and thus help those who are most affected by them.

Toward a social psychology of social change

IPT is an example of a theory that is capable of moving us toward a social psychology of social change. Indeed, it is a theory that has and continues to generate ideas and research pertaining to some of society's most pressing social concerns (Jaspal, this volume). Many other modern social psychological theories however, stop short of a "true" social psychology of social change. We now aim to encourage theorists and researchers to construct such a social psychology, one that has the capacity to attend to pressing social issues and to improve the well-being of all members of society.

Although there may be others, we briefly describe three research domains that have begun to take social change into account and can thus contribute to a social psychology of social change. These are recent advances in Relative Deprivation Theory (e.g. de la Sablonnière et al., 2009b), Goodwin's Adjustment to Change Theory and accompanying research (e.g. Goodwin, 2006; Goodwin et al., 2001) and theory and research on Identity Integration (e.g. Amiot et al., 2007; Benet-Martinez and Haritatos, 2005; Benet-Martinez et al., 2002; Berry, 2005).

Recent advances in Relative Deprivation Theory

Collective relative deprivation is the feeling of dissatisfaction resulting from social or temporal comparisons (Crosby, 1976; Walker and Pettigrew, 1984). Social collective relative deprivation is when group members compare the situation of their own group with that of another group and perceive their own group to be worse off. Temporal collective relative deprivation refers to perceptions of one's group as being currently worse off than it was at a past point in history. Temporal relative deprivation has been found to be especially relevant in the context of social change. During dramatic social change anchor points at the base of social comparison disappear (de la Sablonnière et al., 2009a; see also Albert and Sabini, 1974) and so people rely on temporal comparison to evaluate themselves and their group.

Recent research by de la Sablonnière and her colleagues has described a re-conceptualization of Relative Deprivation Theory in the context of dramatic social change (e.g. de la Sablonnière *et al.*, 2009a, 2010). These researchers examined perceptions of temporal collective relative deprivation in Kyrgyzstan, a country whose history has been marked by dramatic social change including the fall of the Soviet Union and recent revolutions that succeeded in overthrowing the government. Rather than using one particular point in history to which individuals compare their perceptions of current deprivation, as is normally done in relative deprivation research, de la Sablonnière and her colleagues have examined how perceptions of relative deprivation changed across time. They found that the trajectory of relative deprivation across time, across periods of dramatic social change, was better able to predict both personal and collective well-being than was a more traditional measure of relative deprivation. Because the reality of social change was taken into account, they were able to uncover important relationships associated with the well-being of individuals who had lived through very difficult collective events. Instead of assuming that a group's position in society is static, this re-conceptualization of Relative Deprivation Theory inherently included social change. Similar research conducted with Anglophones and Francophones in Quebec (Bougie *et al.*, 2011) as well as with black and white South Africans in South Africa (de la Sablonnière *et al.*, in press), measured relative deprivation across periods of important social change and uncovered psychological relationships between relative deprivation and well-being that would not have been found had the group's changing history not been taken into account. Overall, this research underscores the need to consider historical social changes to understand collective well-being and to take a historical perspective in the face of dramatic social change.

Recent advances in relative deprivation theory go somewhat beyond IPT because they take into account the whole socio-historical context. Specifically, IPT is restrained in the sense that the evaluation process in not always taken in a larger temporal context, where the whole trajectory and history of social change would be taken into consideration.

Adjustment to change theory

Goodwin and his colleagues have explicitly recognized the dearth of psychological research that takes social change into account and have recently developed an integrative model that seeks to examine the impact of dramatic social change on an individual's psychology. These researchers primarily examine the psychological effect of immediate, rapid and substantial social changes. For example, they have conducted research that explores perceptions of social support in the context of former Soviet nations that have undergone rapid and dramatic societal change and have examined the psychological impact of this support (Goodwin, 2006; Goodwin *et al.*, 2001). They have also explored how the 1997 handover of Hong Kong to China affected the marital relationships of those who were living through this change (Goodwin and Tang, 1998). Drawing upon their empirical research in a variety of contexts characterized by social change, they have developed *Adjustment to Change Theory*, which documents collective, personal and interpersonal reactions to dramatic social change (see Goodwin, 2011). They are thus contributing to the beginnings of a social psychology of social change by drawing attention to the prevalence of social change and its collective and individual psychological consequences. A link between IPT and Adjustment to Change Theory can certainly be made. Specifically, the continuity principle may help understand the processes of adaptation as people experience social change. For example, social support is perhaps central in terms of maintaining the continuity between situations and across time in contexts of dramatic social change.

Identity integration

For many, social change means adapting to a new way of living, a new set of values and even a new culture. It also means integrating new identities into one's self-concept (Amiot *et al.*, 2007; Benet-Martinez and Haritatos, 2005; Benet-Martinez *et al.*, 2002; Berry, 2005). Identity Integration Theory (Amiot *et al.*, 2007) is a theory that has recently emerged as having the capacity to document the process of identity integration in the context of social change. Amiot and her colleagues describe four stages of intraindividual change that an individual goes through when integrating a new identity into the self as a result of several social changes, such as immigration, organizational mergers, social political change and important life transitions. These stages include anticipatory categorization, categorization, compartmentalization and finally, integration. This theory therefore sequentially documents the very *process* of identity integration stemming from social change. People in today's world are faced with change and constantly having to integrate new identities into their sense of self, whether they are members of majority or minority groups, business people, or revolutionaries. Identity Integration Theory touches upon the psychological experiences stemming from such change. Finally, it is clear that identity integration is also associated with IPT when it comes to processes such as assimilation–accommodation. A complete discussion can be found in Amiot and Jaspal (this volume).

In the present chapter, we have very briefly outlined research domains that have the potential to contribute to a social psychology of social change. We believe that other mainstream social psychological theories could be similarly transformed or expanded upon to make social change a fundamental component. Only then, will we be able to truly understand the psychological experiences of individuals in our constantly changing social contexts.

Conclusion

When one looks at the history of psychology in general and of social psychology, in particular, one realizes that today's social psychology has, to some extent, lost its roots. Much of current social psychology takes for granted that all humans live in a stable social environment. Moreover, most of our social psychological experiments examine psychological processes among Western, educated, industrialized, rich and democratic (WEIRD) societies (Henrich et al., 2010). However, the reality of Western populations is quite different from that of people fighting for survival in countries at war, for example. The psychological experience of a young teenager growing up in a war zone in Palestine might be very different from that of a Canadian teenager growing up in a suburb of Montreal.

With the six examples of social change that we briefly described – dramatic political and economic events, migration movements, technology, natural disasters, human-made disasters and dramatic personal social change – we underscored the potential of social change to affect dramatically the equilibrium in our daily lives (for more details see de la Sablonnière, 2013). Although social change might appear less dramatic for some in Western societies, it is, nevertheless, very present. It infiltrates all spheres of life – the work place, family life and even questions of national identity and security. Moreover, dramatic social change is amplified for people in social contexts that are underprivileged such as those in poor countries or subgroups in Western nations (e.g. Aboriginal peoples in Canada; see Frideres and Gadacz, 2001).

As a result of this constant and pervasive change, we require a psychology that takes into account change rather than ignores it – a psychology that seeks to understand human beings as embedded within a changing social context. IPT is one of the first theories to have succeeded in making social change a key component of both theory and research, and it continues to be of key importance for the future of a social psychology of social change and social psychology, more generally. Recent advances in other social psychological domains such as relative deprivation theory, adjustment to change theory and identity integration have, like IPT, begun to acknowledge social change. We argue that a synthesis of these theoretical frameworks can make a positive contribution to developing a social psychology of social change.

In terms of coping with dramatic social change, IPT is a useful tool because it provides a general guideline of the possible coping strategies people may use in a context of change (i.e. intrapsychic, interpersonal, intergroup; Breakwell, 1986). However, alternative strategies that use a truly collective approach to collective challenge may also hold some promise in the context of dramatic social change (Taylor and de la Sablonnière, 2013). Specifically, as we have discussed, IPT is mostly grounded in personal change as opposed to collective change. In that context, when a change affects a limited number of people, it might be appropriate to use some intrapsychic or interpersonal strategies of coping. However, when the norms and the social structure are disrupted and sometimes even become dysfunctional, a coping mechanism at the collective level may be necessary to contribute to increasing people's well-being.

We hope that social psychology continues to move toward a social psychology of social change and that IPT researchers will capitalize on the potential that the theory offers. Indeed, as social psychologists, we have a responsibility toward those who are the most gravely affected by our changing world. We therefore require a psychology that seeks to comprehend change and its consequences. By understanding the psychological impact of social change, a social psychology of social change might help in the development of targeted interventions designed to best facilitate coping and build personal and collective resilience. By acknowledging the pervasiveness of social change and its psychological impact, we could return to a form of social psychology that seeks to make the world a better place.

REFERENCES

Albert, S., and Sabini, J. (1974). Attributions about systems in slow vs. rapid change. *Personality and Social Psychology Bulletin*, 1(1), 91–93.

Allport, G. W. (1968). The historical background of social psychology. In G. Lindzey and E. Aronson (eds.), *The handbook of social psychology* (pp. 1–69). Reading, MA: Addison-Wesley.

Amiot, C. E., de la Sablonnière, R., Terry, D. J., and Smith, J. R. (2007). Integration of social identities in the self: toward a cognitive-developmental model. *Personality and Social Psychology Review*, 11, 364–388

Benet-Martinez, V., and Haritatos, J. (2005). Bicultural Identity Integration (BII): components and psychosocial antecedents. *Journal of Personality*, 73, 1,015–1,050.

Benet-Martinez, V., Leu, J., Lee, F., and Morris, M. W. (2002). Negotiating biculturalism: cultural frame switching in biculturals with oppositional versus compatible cultural identities. *Journal of Cross-Cultural Psychology*, 33, 492–516.

Bernardino, A. (1996). *Telecommuting: modeling the employer's and the employee's decision-making process*. New York: Garland.

Berry, J.W. (2005). Acculturation: living successfully in two cultures. *International Journal of Intercultural Relations*, 29, 697–712.

Billig, M. (2009). Discursive psychology, rhetoric and the issue of agency. *Semen* [online]. Accessed September 19, 2012, http://semen.revues.org/8930.

Bougie, E., Usborne, E., de la Sablonnière, R., and Taylor, D. M. (2011). The cultural narratives of Francophone and Anglophone Quebecers: using an historical perspective to explore the relationships among relative deprivation, ingroup entitativity and collective esteem. *British Journal of Social Psychology*, 50, 726–746.

Bourhis, R. Y., Moïse, L. C., Perreault, S. L., and Senécal, S. (1997). Towards an Interactive Acculturation Model: a social psychological approach. *International Journal of Psychology*, 32, 369–386.

Breakwell, G. M. (1986). *Coping with threatened identities*. London: Methuen.

Breakwell, G. M. (1988). Strategies adopted when identity is threatened. *Revue Internationale de Psychologie Sociale*, 1(2), 189–204.

Breakwell, G. M. (1993). Social representations and social identity. *Papers on Social Representations*, 2, 198–217.

Breakwell, G. M., and Lyons, E. (1996). *Changing European identities: socio-psychological analyses of social change*. Oxford: Butterworth-Heinemann.

Carter, R. (2000). The silent crisis: the impact of poverty on children in Eastern Europe and the Former Soviet Union. Accessed October 12, 2013, www.everychild.org.uk.

Crosby, F. J. (1976). A model of egoistical relative deprivation. *Psychological Review*, 83, 85–113.

Chirot, D., and Merton, R. K. (1986). *Social change in the modern era*. New York: Harcourt Brace Jovanovich.

de la Sablonnière, R. (2013). The psychology of social change. Unpublished manuscript.

de la Sablonnière, R., French Bourgeois, L., and Najih, M. (2013). Dramatic social change: a psychological perspective. *Journal of Social and Political Psychology*, 1(1), 253–272.

de la Sablonnière, R., Auger, E., Sadykova, N., and Taylor, D. M. (2010). When the 'we' impacts how 'I' feel about myself: effect of temporal collective relative deprivation on personal well-being in the context of dramatic social change in Kyrgyzstan. *European Psychologist*, 15, 271–282.

de la Sablonnière, R., Hénault, A.-M., and Huberdeau, M.-E. (2009a). *Comparaisons sociales et comparaisons temporelles: vers une approche séquentielle et fonction de la situation unique*. [Social and temporal comparisons: a sequential approach and the role of the unique situation]. *Cahiers internationaux de psychologie sociale*, 83, 3–24.

de la Sablonnière, R., Taylor, D. M., Perozzo, C., and Sadykova, N. (2009b). Reconceptualizing relative deprivation in the context of dramatic social change: the challenge confronting the people of Kyrgyzstan. *European Journal of Social Psychology*, 39, 325–345.

de la Sablonnière, R., Tougas, F., and Lortie-Lussier, M. (2009c). Dramatic social change in Russia and Mongolia: connecting relative deprivation to social identity. *Journal of Cross-Cultural Psychology*, 40, 327–348.

de la Sablonnière, R., Auger, É., Taylor, D. M., Crush, J., and McDonald, D. (in press). Social change in South Africa: a historical approach to relative deprivation. *British Journal of Social Psychology*.

Farley, R. (1997). Racial trends and differences in the United States 30 years after the civil rights decade. *Social Science Research*, 26, 235–262.

Frideres, J. S., and Gadacz, R. R. (2001). *Aboriginal peoples in Canada: contemporary conflicts* (6th edn.). Toronto: Prentice Hall.

Fukuyama, F. (1999). *The great disruption: human nature and the reconstitution of social order.* Touchstone: New York.

Gallina, A. (2011). Human mobility report 2011: migration and human development in ACP countries. Secretariat of the African, Caribbean and Pacific (ACP) Group of States. Accessed October 12, 2013, http://213.246.207.152/acp/sites/default/files/ACPHMR2011ExecutiveSummary(Final).pdf.

Gergen, K. J. (1973). Social psychology as history. *Journal of Personality and Social Psychology*, 26, 309–320.

Giddens, A., Duneier, M., Appelbaum, R. P., and Carr, D. (2011). *Introduction to sociology* (8th edn.). New York: W. W. Norton.

Goodwin, R. (2006). Age and social support perception in Eastern Europe: Social change and support in four rapidly changing countries. *British Journal of Social Psychology*, 45, 799–815.

Goodwin, R. (2011). Changing relations: achieving intimacy in a time of social transition. *Canadian Review of Sociology*, 48, 105–109.

Goodwin, R., Nizharadze, G., Luu, LAN., Kosa, E., and Emelyanova, T. (2001). Social support in a changing Europe: an analysis of three post-Communist nations. *European Journal of Social Psychology*, 31, 379–393.

Goodwin, R., and Tang, C. (1998). The transition to uncertainty: the impact of Hong Kong 1997 on personal relationships. *Personal Relationships*, 5, 183–190.

Henrich, J., Heine S. J., and Norenzayan, A. (2010). The weirdest people in the world? *Behavioral and Brain Sciences*, 33, 61–135.

Hill, D. B. (2006). Theory in applied social psychology: past mistakes and future hopes. *Theory Psychology*, 16, 613–640.

Jaspal, R., and Cinnirella, M. (2010). Coping with potentially incompatible identities: accounts of religious, ethnic and sexual identities from British Pakistani men who identify as Muslim and gay. *British Journal of Social Psychology*, 49, 849–870.

Karoly, L. A., and Panis, C. W. A. (2004). The 21st century at work: forces shaping the future workforce and workplace in the United States. www.rand.org/pubs/monographs/MG164.html.

Kirmayer, L., Simpson, C., and Cargo, M. (2003). Healing traditions: culture, community and mental health promotion with Canadian Aboriginal peoples. *Australasian Psychiatry*, 11, s15-s23.

Kruglanski, A. W. (2001). That 'vision thing': the state of theory in social and personality psychology at the edge of the new millennium. *Journal of Personality and Social Psychology*, 80, 871–875.

Lyons, E. (1996). Coping with social change: processes of social memory in the reconstruction of identities. In G. M. Breakwell and E. Lyons (eds.), *Changing European identities: socio-psychological analyses of social change* (pp. 31–40). Oxford: Butterworth-Heinemann.

Marjoribanks, T. (2000). *News corporation, technology and the workplace: global strategies, local change.* Cambridge University Press.

McBride, M. J. (1999). Migrants and asylum seekers: policy responses in the United States to immigrants and refugees from Central America and the Caribbean. *International Migration*, 37, 289–317.

Mercer, J. (1995). Canadian cities and their immigrants: new realities. *The Annals of the American Academy of Political and Social Science*, 538, 169–184.

Moghaddam, F. M. (1990). Modulative and generative orientations in psychology: implications for psychology in the three worlds. *Journal of Social Issues*, 46, 21–41.

Nolan, P., and Lenski, G. (2011). *Human societies: an introduction to macrosociology* (11th edn.). Boulder, CO: Paradigm.

Oishi, S., Kesebir, S., and Snyder, B. H. (2009). Sociology: a lost connection in social psychology. *Personality and Social Psychology Review*. 13, 334–353.

Pancer, S. M. (1997). Social psychology: the crisis continues. In D. Fox and I. Prilleltensky (eds.), *Critical psychology: an introduction* (pp. 150–165). Thousand Oaks, CA: Sage.

Phinney, J. S., Horenczyk, G., Liebkind, K., and Vedder, P. (2001). Ethnic identity, immigration and well-being: an interactional perspective. *Journal of Social Issues*, 57, 493–510.

Ponsioen, J. A. (1969). *The analysis of social change reconsidered: a sociological study.* Netherlands: Mouton.

Potter, J., and Edwards, D. (2001). Discursive social psychology. In W. P. Robinson and H. Giles (eds.). *The new handbook of language and social psychology* (pp. 103–118). London: Wiley.

Rocher, G. (1992). *Introduction à la sociologie générale* [Introduction to general sociology]. Ville LaSalle, Québec, Canada: Éditions Hurtubise HMH.

Ryder, A. G., Alden, L. E., and Paulhus, D. L. (2000). Is acculturation unidimensional or bidimensional? A head-to-head comparison in the prediction of personality, self-identity and adjustment. *Journal of Personality and Social Psychology*, 79, 49–65.

Sears, D. O. (1986). College sophomores in the laboratory: influences of a narrow data base on social psychology's view of human nature. *Journal of Personality and Social Psychology*, 51, 515–530.

Sewell, W. H. (1989). Some reflections on the golden age of interdisciplinary social psychology. *Social Psychology Quarterly*, 52, 88–97.

Smith, D. S. (1973). *The concept of social change: a critique of the functionalist theory of social change.* Routledge & Kegan Paul: London.

Sztompka, P. (1998). The cultural imponderables of rapid social change: trust, loyalty, solidarity. *Polish Sociological Review*, 1, 45–57.

Tajfel, H. (1972). Experiments in a vacuum. In J. Israel and H. Tajfel (eds.). *The context of social psychology: a critical assessment* (pp. 69–121). London: Academic Press.

Tajfel, H. (1975). The exit of social mobility and the voice of social change: notes on the social psychology of intergroup relations. *Social Science Information*, 14, 101–118.

Tajfel, H. (1978). The achievement of group differentiation. In H. Tajfel (ed.), *Differentiation between social groups: studies in the social psychology of intergroup relations* (pp. 77–98). London: Academic Press.

Tajfel, H., and Turner, J. C. (1986). The social identity theory of inter-group behavior. In S. Worchel and L. W. Austin (eds.), *Psychology of intergroup relations* (pp. 7–24). Chicago, IL: Nelson-Hall.

Taylor, D. M., and de la Sablonnière, R. (2013). Why interventions in dysfunctional communities fail: the need for a truly collective approach. *Canadian Psychology*, 54, 22–29

Timotijevic, L., and Breakwell, G. M. (2000). Migration and threat to identity. *Journal of Community and Applied Social Psychology*, 10, 355–372.

Walker, I., and Pettigrew, T. F. (1984). Relative deprivation theory: an overview and conceptual critique. *British Journal of Social Psychology*, 23, 301–310.

Weinstein, J. A. (2010). *Social change*. Plymouth, UK: Rowman & Littlefield.

White, J. (2010). Economic impact of Gulf of Mexico oil spill varies by industry. Accessed October 12, 2013, www.nola.com/news/gulf-oil-spill/index. ssf/2010/05/economic_impact_of_gulf_of_mex.html.

Zuck, A. M. (1997). Introduction. *American Behavioral Scientist*, 40, 257–258.

11   Collective identity and intractable conflict

Neta Oren and Daniel Bar-Tal

Intractable conflicts are still prevalent in the world. Bercovitch (2005) identified seventy-five serious interstate conflicts out of 309 occurring in the period of 1945–1995, which were violent and lasted at least 15 years. These conflicts are a truly global problem that can have immensely negative implications for the societies involved in them and often for the international community as a whole. Thus, the scientific community should have a special mission to unveil their dynamics and foundations.

In the present chapter we shed light on one socio-psychological aspect that plays a major role in every intractable conflict, namely the formation, transformation, maintenance and strengthening of collective identity. Specifically, we will show how integrating key elements of the coping dimension of Identity Process Theory (IPT) into the study of a collective identity of intractable conflicts provides scope for enriching our understanding of their eruption, persistence and potential change. First we will present our conceptualization of collective identity that has some overlapping propositions with IPT. Then, we will point to relevant IPT elements that can contribute to this framework of collective identity. In the next sections we will use this framework to make sense of the development of collective identity in contexts of intractable conflict. Our analysis will focus on four main phases of the intractable conflict: eruption, escalation, institutionalization and peacemaking. In each phase we will describe the social context and the coping strategies likely to be drawn upon by individuals/groups, the identity processes and the changes in the content of collective identity as a result of these processes. We will end this chapter with the implications of this analysis for the study of intractable conflicts.

Collective identity and intractable conflict

Our starting point is the David and Bar-Tal (2009) model of collective identity that explores the interrelationship between micro-individual and macro-social meanings of identity. The model covers two levels: micro-socio-psychological and macro-socio-psychological. The micro-individual level describes the nature of self-categorization and identification, which are individual processes (see also Roccas *et al.*, 2008). This level focuses on the individual's organization of social group memberships, that is, to which groups a person thinks that he or she belongs, what he or she thinks about them and how he or she evaluates them. This level includes cognitive aspects of identification (self-categorization and the importance that individuals attribute to their identification with the collective), emotional aspects of identification (attachment to the collective) and motivational aspects (the willingness to belong to a collective and to satisfy needs for positive self-value and security).

These micro-socio-psychological processes are the precondition for the emergence of collective identity and underlie its construction, in that they promote a shared social awareness and recognition that members of a collective share the same social identity. This awareness, which leads to the macro-socio-psychological level in the form of collective cognitive, emotional and behavioral consequences, provides the basis for shared belief systems that illuminate the group's common world-view and then allows continuous communication and negotiation about this common world (see also Melucci, 1989; Polletta and Jasper, 2001; Reicher and Hopkins, 2001). Collective identification goes beyond the individual group member's cognitive-emotional processes to the characterization of the entire collective (see also some of the principles of the Self-Categorization Theory in Turner, 1999; Turner *et al.*, 1987).

The macro level of collective identity is founded on two pillars. One pillar consists of general features that characterize the collective identity, are universal, apply to macro level collectives and allow for a comparison between them. The other pillar is particular and consists of content characteristics that provide the unique features to the collective identity. We will first present the six fundamental features of the first pillar.

1. *Perception of the uniqueness of the collective and its distinction from other collectives* relates to the definition of the collective's selfhood as a unique entity that is different from other collectives.
2. *Commonality of beliefs, attitudes, norms and values* characterizes group members and constitutes the basis for their feeling of uniqueness (Bar-Tal, 2000; Smith, 1991).
3. *Continuity and consecutiveness in the dimension of time* indicates a perceived continuity of the group's past, present and future.
4. *A sense of a common fate* pertains to the sense of unity and the feelings of mutual dependence that prevail among members of a collective.

This is the feeling of "togetherness" – the "cement" that binds individuals and social groups in unity (Brown, 2000), despite potential variability in values, beliefs, attitudes and patterns of behavior. In other words, the significance of shared fate eclipses the variability and instills in the collective's individuals the perception that their own fate depends on the fate of the whole collective.

5. *Concern for the welfare of the collective and mobilization and sacrifice for its sake* refer to group members' interest in the experiences of the collective, a concern for its welfare and a motivation to act on its behalf. The motivation to act is manifested through willingness to join in missions of a collective nature, to contribute personal resources for the benefit of all, to help society members in times of distress and even to sacrifice one's life for the protection of the collective.

6. Mobilization requires the *coordinated activity of the collective's members*. This feature refers to the ability of the different groups and sectors that compose the collective to collaborate with each other to achieve societal goals.

Although all six elements are necessary for the existence of collective identity, some of them may be more powerful than others in different societies and at different times. Moreover, collectives differ with regard to the intensity, pervasiveness and quality of these features. The second pillar of the collective identity is content based and it provides the particular epistemic basis for the collective identity. That is, this pillar provides the specific contents that endow the collective identity with its very particular meaning. For example, in the case of a national collective identity it includes attachment to certain territories, culture and language, collective memory and societal beliefs that characterize the collective. As we will demonstrate below, the collective identity of societies in intractable conflict tends also to include a unique content that is influenced by their long exposure to the conflict context.

The above model shares some fundamental assumptions with IPT. Like IPT it emphasizes motivational aspects of identity such as the need for uniqueness and continuity. In addition, like IPT, it claims that social context and historical perspective have a great influence on the identity of the collective. David and Bar-Tal's model further claims that this is a reciprocal process in which the context shapes the elements of the collective identity and they in turn affect the social context in which the collective resides. David and Bar-Tal describe the social context as a multi-layered context that includes global conditions, the topographic and meteorological contexts in which the collectives reside and the cultural context that consists of tangible and intangible symbols, scripts, habits, rules, narratives, concepts and knowledge relating to one's group and other social categories (this layer corresponds to IPT's *social influence process* or *the ideology component* of social context). Another short-term layer of the sociocultural context that is mentioned by David and Bar-Tal is *transitional context*, which consists of major events and major information that have relevance for the well-being of group members and for the group as a whole (see also Bar-Tal, 2013; Bar-Tal and Halperin, 2013).

David and Bar-Tal's model of collective identity allows monitoring changes in identification within each nation, by measuring the intensity and quality of identification with the collective over time, as well as assessing different types of features that determine type and strength of collective identity at the macro level (e.g. David, 2007). As for the causes of changes in collective identity, David and Bar-Tal note that the social context may change the collective meaning of identity and the content that characterizes it. However, they do not specify the exact processes by which social context may change identity. Without this component their model is less dynamic than IPT. In this chapter we argue that integrating ideas from IPT concerning identity processes into David and Bar-Tal's model of collective identity may address this gap in the model, increase its explanatory power and make it more dynamic.

As was described in Jaspal's introduction to this volume, according to IPT the social context influences identity through the dynamic processes of *accommodation–assimilation* and *evaluation*. In Western industrialized cultures this process is guided by several principles: continuity, distinctiveness, self-efficacy, self-esteem, belonging, meaning and the psychological coherence principle (Amiot and Jaspal, this volume; Breakwell, 1986, 2001a; Jaspal and Cinnirella, 2010b; Vignoles *et al.*, 2002). It is important to note that these principles associated with IPT are not necessarily restricted to the individual level of cognition, but may in fact be applied to the group level (Lyons, 1996). Thus, it is possible to talk about group self-esteem, group continuity and group distinctiveness, and so on. IPT suggests that a threat to identity occurs when the processes of assimilation/accommodation are unable, for some reason, to comply with the principles of continuity, distinctiveness, self-efficacy, self-esteem, belonging, meaning and coherence, which habitually guide their operation.

To minimize the negative impact on psychological well-being, the individuals or the group seek to re-institute the principled operation of the identity processes. Coping strategies can be pitched at different levels (intrapsychic, interpersonal level and the group/intergroup) and include strategies such as denial and revision of the relative salience of the three principles guiding assimilation, isolation and rely upon group action to initiate a change which will minimize the threat (Breakwell, 1986).

In the following sections we will demonstrate the merit of the integration of the above models by applying it to a specific case of collective identity – *collective identity of a society in the context of intractable conflict*. Intractable conflicts are severe conflicts that are characterized by goals that are perceived as existential, viewed as being of a zero-sum nature and unsolvable, are violent, preoccupy a central place in the lives of society members, demand great investments and last at least 25 years (Bar-Tal, 1998, 2007a, 2013; Kriesberg, 1993). The analysis of this interaction will focus on four phases: the eruption of the conflict; its escalation; its institutionalization; and finally its resolution through peacemaking.

Eruption of intractable conflict and collective identity

Conflicts tend to break out when two or more groups believe that their goals or interests are in direct contradiction and decide to act on this basis (Bar-Tal, 2013). Prominent among goals that guide conflicts are those related to countering perceived deprivation of basic needs (Maslow, 1954). Basic needs refer to goods, resources, or wealth, as well as to security with its different aspects. Moreover, deprivation may also pertain to needs that are related to esteem and self-actualization (e.g. positive social identity, or self-determination). The processes of recognizing deprivation, refusing to accept it and setting new goals to ameliorate the situation may lead to conflict. These are complex processes which can take various forms and be manifested differently in different contexts.

Social context of conflict eruption

Intractable conflicts tend to evolve in various contexts and therefore the list cannot be exhaustive (see Thackrah, 2009). But among the most notable are conditions of unequal divisions of wealth, power, or resources; social stratification and barriers to mobility; discriminatory practices; conquest and colonialism; disputes over territories; unfulfilled group aspirations and needs; need of territories, resources, or other valued commodities; or existence of rival ideologies and dogmas. Indeed, as Azar (1990) notes, the basic conditions for the eruption of protracted conflicts often concern the deprivation of basic needs related to collective identity (see also Brewer, 2011; Kelman, 2001; Korostelina, 2006).

Some intractable conflicts may be asymmetrical, characterized by "situations in which there exists a severe imbalance of power between the parties and the more powerful party exploits, controls, or abuses the less powerful" (Coleman, 2003, p. 1). Frequently, systems of beliefs that tend to support and enhance hierarchical relationships and dominant group superiority contribute to the deprivation of basic needs. These beliefs can be found in many channels of societal information, such as school textbooks or the media. As we will see in the next section, such social representations may impact the operation of identity processes in both rival groups that could lead to an eruption of conflict.

Thus, the context of the eruption of conflict includes all the elements that were noted by David and Bar-Tal in their conception of collective identity and by Breakwell in Identity Process Theory as important components of the context for identity processes. They include *structure/material components* and *social influence process/ideology components*. *Transitional context* that was discussed by David and Bar-Tal may also play an important role in identity processes and eruption of conflict. It refers to major events and/or significant information that have relevance to the well-being of group members and of the group as a whole, involve group members and have implications that force group members to reconsider and often change, their view of the situation (Oren, 2005). For example, specific major events can affect the processes of identity construction and the eruption of intractable conflict. Indeed, it is assumed that the events in Northern Ireland on Bloody Sunday in 1972 and in South Africa in Sharpeville in 1960 were major catalysts that increased the group readiness of the respective communities of Catholics and blacks to participate in the conflict. Often a combination of all the components of context mentioned above (structure/material, social influence process/ideology and transitional) stimulates an intractable conflict. For example, the initial context of the Israeli-Palestinian conflict includes structure/material components (territorial dispute, changing of the demographical balance in the area), as well as ideological components in that it also concerns deep clashes of religious, cultural and social ideas, such as Zionism, Judaism and Islam. In addition, numerous violent clashes between Jews and Palestinians living in British-ruled Palestine (i.e. major events) played an essential role in the eruption of this conflict (Sandler, 1988).

Identity processes during conflict eruption

The context mentioned above might influence collective identity processes in a way that can contribute to the eruption of an intractable conflict. It may take place when assimilation–accommodation and evaluation among members of the group and among institutions signal threats to identity. Then the strategies that are used by the group members to cope with this threat lead to the emergence of reframed collective identity or strengthen the salience of existing collective identity. In each case, strong identification with the group results in solidification of the collective identity that is directed to the evolved goals of the group in the conflict (Tajfel, 1982; Brewer, 2011; Roccas and Elster, 2012).

It is important to note that context of deprivation might not necessarily lead to intractable conflict. Groups may become aware of their state of deprivation, but also apply coping strategies, such as the intrapsychic strategy of *denial* or the interpersonal strategy of *compliance*, that will not lead to an eruption of intractable conflict. For example, in the Hindu caste system, the Harijans who were previously referred to as the "Untouchables" were deeply deprived for many generations through segregation, discrimination and exploitation by other castes. While negative social representations of caste groups may plausibly threaten the self-esteem principle among the Harijans, for years they tended to use coping strategies that caused them to internalize social representations of their inferiority and cooperate with these practices. Those strategies include intrapsychic strategies, such as *denial* of the need to change identity structures despite recognizing that the position is threatening when many Harijans in the past perceived their fate as deriving from Hindu scriptures and therefore as ordained by God (Flood, 1996). Another intrapsychic coping strategy that some Harijans use is *salience of principles*. This strategy entails the revision of the relative salience of the identity principles guiding assimilation and rearranges priorities between them (Breakwell, 1986). In the context of the caste system it has been argued that Harijan individuals will resist massive social change of a social system to which they are acutely accustomed because of the continuity principle. In this case, then, the principal of continuity is attributed more importance than the principle of self-esteem (Jaspal, 2011; Vignoles *et al.*, 2006).[1]

Therefore, awareness of ingroup deprivation and a perception of threat to identity is the first condition for the eruption of intractable conflict. In addition, at least one of the parties would have to apply coping strategies that might lead to an eruption of conflict. Such strategies may include the interpersonal strategy of *negativism* and the intergroup strategy of

---

[1] The concept of collective relative deprivation, which indicates that groups compare their state with subjective standards that include comparison to other parties and/or the past situations, very well captures this process (Crosby, 1976; Major, 1994; Olson *et al.*, 1986; Runciman, 1966).

group action that aims to change social order and dominant ideologies in the society.

In the context of asymmetrical conflicts characterized by deprivation, threats to identity may appear among both the dominant and the marginalized groups. In this vein, Jaspal and Cinnirella (2010a) claim that exposure to negative social representations (e.g. negative representations of a minority group in the media and in other societal channels of information deploying terms such as "murderers," "Nazis," "terrorists" or "psychopaths" who wish to annihilate the majority group) may severely compromise the continuity principle of identity among the members of the dominant group; since the implication is that the ingroup risks annihilation and may thereby cease to exist as a distinctive collective entity. It could also threaten the self-efficacy principle of identity, given that the dominant group members may feel that they lack competence or control over their lives in face of the outgroup threat. Media representations of cultural difference between the dominant group and the minority group may also compromise the self-esteem principle of identity.

These perceptions of identity threat among the members of the dominant group may induce several coping strategies that were mentioned by Breakwell (1986), such as the interpersonal coping strategy of *negativism* and the intergroup coping strategy of *group action*. The coping strategy of negativism involves attacking anyone who would challenge the identity structure (attacking the attackers). Group action may occur within a social movement that aims to change the social order and often uses violence. Such practices aim to enhance the self-efficacy principle of identity by "taking control" in contexts of perceived threat.

An example of this process can be found in the conflict in Rwanda between Hutus and Tutsis. Tutsis were portrayed as foreigners interested in gaining power and taking over Hutus' property, as seeking to eliminate Hutus on a massive scale and as hoping to conquer lands of the Hutus (Klinghoffer, 1998). The media, especially The Radio Television Libre des Milles Collines (RTLM), played an important role in disseminating these ideas and images of the Tutsis (Slocum-Bradley, 2008; Rothbart and Bartlett, 2008). The implementation of these actions could have severely compromised their sense of group continuity, as well as the self-efficacy and distinctiveness principles of identity. In view of these perceived threats, the Hutu's actions against the Tutsis can be interpreted as coping strategies – the Hutu engaged in strategies of negativism (acting against the pressures from external source) and widescale social mobilization against the Tutsis. Eventually, as a result of this process, an estimated 800,000 Rwandan Tutsis and Hutus were killed in 100 days in 1994.

Negative dominant media representations of subgroups in a society may also threaten the identity of the marginalized group and affect their collective identity in a way that instigates an intractable conflict. For example, the rise in negative prejudice among the dominant group is likely to pose threats to the belonging principle of identity of the minority group as they may feel excluded from the national category because the practices, norms and values associated with their ethnic identities are widely perceived to be incompatible with the national ethos (Jaspal and Cinnirella, 2010a). Furthermore, if rejection is perceived to be a result of the "negativity" of their membership in the ethnic group, this may have adverse repercussion for the self-esteem principle. In this case an intractable conflict might erupt when the marginalized group employs some of the coping strategies that were mentioned by Breakwell (1986), such as the *formation of consciousness-raising group* by strengthening identification with the ethnic group as motivated by the belonging principle of identity and *group action* in the form of social movements that aim to change the social value attached to the group characteristics or change the characteristics associated with the group. Violence may also be part of the actions of this social movement. As Breakwell (1986) notes, the group action has two audiences: those outside the social category it defends and those inside. An intractable conflict is likely to erupt when the threatened are persuaded but not the broader society.

An example of this process could be found in South Africa. Racially exclusionary attitudes and discrimination policy toward black people had a significant influence on leaders of South Africa's black African population, such as Peter Mda, Nelson Mandela, Walter Sisulu and Oliver Tambo, who during the 1940s transformed the African National Congress (ANC) – a national organization that was established in 1912 and represented the black African population – into a mass movement. As a result of the 1948 victory of the National Party that enforced the apartheid policy, the ANC further campaigned for African self-determination. For example, in 1949 it adopted the Programme of Action (AP) which declared that the ANC's fundamental objective was "to achieve national freedom from white domination and the attainment of political independence" (South African Democracy Education Trust, 2010). Since, their goals were not accepted by the National Party and the broader white society, an intractable conflict erupted.

Identity content during conflict eruption

It follows that the most important generic feature of collective identity at the stage of conflict eruption is *mobilization and sacrifice for the group*. It is this mobilization that stimulates the destructive transformation of disagreement into an active conflict. Mobilization means not only that individuals identify with the group, but also that they accept the goals related to the conflict and are willing to carry out various needed activities on behalf of the group, such as violent actions (Klandermans, 1988). Mobilization to participate in conflict requires individuals to feel and think as if they are part of the group, to have a conviction that group members must comply with the group's rules, orders, or calls and to be willing to contribute to the welfare of the group (Branscombe *et al.*, 1999). In these cases, the social identity takes over much of the personal identity and the personal life is overtaken by the identification with the causes of the group, leading to full and active involvement with the collective goals and aspirations. Conflict erupts when at least a significant number of society members devote their life to its cause.

There are empirical indications that social identity becomes a basis for mobilization. For example, Goodwin (2001) in the wide-scope analysis of intra-societal conflicts, noted that identification with the group and its cause underlined successful mobilization for participation in a conflict. Socio-psychological studies found that strong collective identity leads to solidarity and readiness for action on behalf of the group, including sacrifice (Brewer and Silver, 2000; Swann *et al.*, 2010).

In addition, in times of intractable conflict mobilization is facilitated by the strengthening of other generic characteristics of collective identity that were identified by David and Bar-Tal (2009) such as *sense of a common fate* and *coordinated activity by the collective's members*. Related studies by Rothbart and Korostelina (2006) investgated the impact of collective identity salience on the readiness for conflict in Crimea. They argued that the readiness to begin a conflict with the outgroup reflects the willingness to defend one's own group in situations of real or perceived threat from other groups (a *sense of a common fate*) and to punish or take revenge on members of the other group (*carrying out coordinated activity*). Their results showed that group members with salient ethnic identity, as compared to other group members with non-salient ethnic identity, highly valued and adhered to group goals; focused on negative experiences with an outgroup; tended to stereotype the outgroup negatively and especially viewed it as aggressive and antagonistic; and minimized interaction with this group. The concept of politicized collective identity proposed by Simon and Klandermans (2001) is also of particular relevance to the present analysis. The concept denotes a mindset based on high identification with the group that leads to involvement and engagement in the group's struggle for its goals.

The context of conflict also leads to the emergence of *particular content* that gives meaning to collective identity in relation to the conflict. This includes the articulation of the deprivation, the setting of goals for correcting the situation and of epistemic basis for the goals. The goals of the conflict are often defined in terms of social identity. This means that the group perceives that the goals contradicting those of the adversaries are essential to the group's existence (Korostelina, 2006). The goals may be defined in terms of territory, as a specific territory is considered the homeland of the group and the basis of its existence (David and Bar-Tal, 2009; Smith, 1991). The goals may also be defined in terms of a specific ideology, when segments of the society have contradictory visions about the nature of the political, religious and economic system. Another category of goals focus on the expression of group culture, heritage, tradition, religion and language that are all perceived as reflecting the identity of the group. Groups strive to have freedom and equality in these expressions believing that it is essential for the group's existence. Without their free expression the group believes that it may lose its particular identity.

Escalation of a conflict and collective identity

During this stage of the intractable conflict the parties gradually apply more drastic means in order to achieve their goals. In return, these steps are met with severe reactions and both sides raise the level of confrontation, entering into a spiral of reactions and counter reactions. Our basic premise is that during the escalation phase, in order to cope with the challenges posed to identity by the context, the involved societies become entrenched in their repertoire of beliefs, attitudes and emotional sentiments related to conflict which eventually turn into a well-established and institutionalized socio-psychological infrastructure, consisting of an ethos of conflict and collective memory. This is a circular process in which the context lays the groundwork for the reconstruction of a collective identity with characteristics reflecting the context, as will be described below.

Social context of conflict escalation

Escalation is observed in the context of intensification of violence, including hostile verbal rhetoric and especially physical actions such as killing and maiming civilians and active participants in the violence. Probably the key experience in the situation of intractable conflict is the chronic threat that affects various aspects of human life, in the form of exposure to possible human causalities, loss of territory, resources, economy, power, status, or general welfare, as well as threats to religious, political, moral, and/or cultural system of beliefs, attitudes and values (Stephan *et al.*, 2008).

The identity processes during conflict escalation

This context can potentially threaten identity among individuals and groups, as the processes of accommodation–assimilation and evaluation of information from the context may not be compatible with the principles of continuity, distinctiveness, self-efficacy, self-esteem, meaning and so on. More specifically, during the escalation of conflict stage, society members typically live in a continuous state of uncertainty and ambiguity which might threaten the meaning principle. They do not know when a specific act of violence may occur, when the next war will erupt, when something bad will happen to them or to someone dear to them, what kind of economic effect the conflict will have on them and so on. They live in a world that does not always have a clear meaning for them. They reject the goals of the rival and its violent behavior. But sometimes they may also question goals of the own group and the wisdom of engaging in the conflict. In such a context, individuals may feel that they do not have a control over the situation and they do not have mastery over their own fate, which in turn may threaten the self-efficacy principle. Also, the context of intractable conflict often leads to behaviors that violate moral codes and society members may experience distress as a result of feelings of guilt. These feelings in turn pose a threat to positive social identity as well as to personal self-esteem.

Society members need to somehow satisfy those identity needs that become deprived during this stage of intractable conflicts. One coping strategy that is often employed in this situation is the intergroup coping strategy of *changing dominant ideologies* in the society by constructing an elaborated system of beliefs that explain the conflict and the group's actions within the conflict. This process culminates with the development of a collective memory and an ethos of conflict that eventually give meaning to the collective identity of the society and become central in its characterization (Bar-Tal, 2007a, 2013). In addition, specific beliefs and narratives in the collective memory and ethos of conflict can serve as coping strategies at the intrapsychic and interpersonal levels, such as the intrapsychic strategy of the *redefinition or reinterpretation of a situation* and the interpersonal strategy of *negativism*.

Identity content during conflict escalation

We suggest that the specific content of identity that develops at this stage of intractable conflict includes collective memory of conflict and ethos of conflict. Collective memory constructs the narratives, the symbols, the models and the myths related to the past. Societal beliefs of collective memory, in the case of intractable conflict, evolve to present the history of the conflict to society members (Cairns and Roe, 2003; Halbwachs, 1992; Pennebaker *et al.*, 1997; Wertsch, 2002). Collective memories of intractable conflict are usually organized around narratives of transitional contexts or particular major events, with the focus placed on specific individuals that have played major roles in the conflict. These may be short-term events such as battles, or even parts of battles, or prolonged events such as wars or occupations (Bar-Tal, 2003). The narrative of collective memory touches on at least four important themes, which influence the perception of the conflict and its management. First of all, it provides justification for the eruption of the conflict and the course of its development. Secondly, it presents a positive image of one's group. Thirdly, it delegitimizes the opponent. Fourthly, the narrative of collective memory presents one's group as being a victim of the opponent. These themes overlap the themes of ethos of conflict.

Ethos is defined as "the configuration of central societal beliefs that provide a dominant characterization to the society and gives it a particular orientation" (Bar-Tal, 2000, p. xiv). Ethos of conflict may include eight main themes (see Bar-Tal, 2013):

1. The ethos outlines the existential importance of the conflictive ingroup's goals. At the same time, it discredits the goals of the other side, describing them as unjustified and unreasonable. For, example, in the Israeli ethos, societal beliefs about the justness of the Israeli goals in the Arab–Israeli conflict are based on Zionism and focus around the main goal of establishing a Jewish state in the ancient homeland of the Jews (*Eretz Israel*). Historical, theological, national, existential, political, societal and cultural justifications for these goals of establishment of a Jewish state in *Eretz Israel* were used. Some common motifs are that the Jewish nation was founded in the ancient Land of Israel; that during many years of ancient Jewish history the Land of Israel was the Jews' homeland; that during their exile Jews maintained close spiritual and physical ties with the Land of Israel, continuously aspiring to return to it; and that the persistent experience of anti-Semitism in the Diaspora highlighted the Jewish people's need for a secure existence in their old homeland.

Sometimes the goals in the conflict are defined in broader terms such as "a war between civilizations." At the intrapsychic level this trend can serve as the coping strategy of *redefining the situation* – that is, introducing information that puts the situation in a wider context and modifies the meaning of this situation (Breakwell, 1986), which enables the identity processes to operate again in accordance with identity principles, such as continuity, belonging and self-esteem, which may be threatened by the conflict context.

2. The ethos of conflict details the dangers that the conflict poses to society: threats to the physical existence of the ingroup, to the cherished values, to territory and so on. In addition, it describes the sources of the threats and the conditions that may overcome them. For example, Israeli Jews believe that the security of the country and of its Jewish citizens is under serious threat. Therefore, the achievement of security has become the most central need and value, acquiring the status of a cultural master-symbol in the Israeli Jewish ethos (Bar-Tal *et al.*, 1998; Horowitz, 1984).

3. The ethos delegitimizes the opponent. Delegitimization is defined as the categorization of a group, or groups, into extremely negative social categories that exclude it, or them, from the sphere of human groups that act within the limits of acceptable norms and/or values, since these groups are viewed as violating basic human norms or values and therefore deserve maltreatment (Bar-Tal and Hammack, 2012). In essence delegitimization denies the adversary's humanity and serves as a psychological permit to harm the rival group (Bar-Tal and Teichman, 2005). In addition, the ethos focuses on the rival's violence, atrocities, irrationality, intransigence and lack of concern for human life. Indeed, mutual delegitimization has been one of the bitter manifestations of the long years of conflict between the Israeli Jews and the Arabs (Bar-Tal, 1988; Bar-Tal and Teichman, 2005; Oren and Bar-Tal, 2007). At the interpersonal level these beliefs can also be seen as an example of the coping strategy of *negativism*.

4. In contrast, the ethos of conflict presents a positive image of the ingroup (e.g. Baumeister and Hastings, 1997). It describes events that reflect well on the society, exhibits its positive characteristics and specifically depicts the humane and moral nature of the society (Sande *et al.*, 1989). The Israeli Jews viewed themselves as "new people," reborn in the land of Israel (Hofman, 1970). The positive stereotypes portrayed them as tenacious, hard-working, courageous, modern and intelligent, on the one hand, and as moral and humane, on the other.

5. The ethos presents the ingroup as the sole victim of the conflict and of the opponent (Bar-Tal *et al.*, 2009; Vollhardt, 2012). This is a central belief in the Israeli ethos. In the context of the Israeli-Arab conflict, Israeli Jews perceived themselves as victims of unjust aggression by the Arabs (Bar-Tal and Antebi, 1992; Oren, 2009). According to this view, the conflict was forced upon the Israelis and the reason that Israel is involved in an intractable conflict is that the Arabs have attacked Israel. At the intrapsychic level this belief can also serve as a strategy that Breakwell (1986) calls *redefinition*, which may help Israelis cope with the threats to national image and national esteem as a result of their violation of some moral codes during the conflict.

Another type of victimization belief presents the ingroup as a victim of a very hostile world. This is a central theme in the Israeli ethos and it is frequently linked to both the Jewish experience during the Holocaust and to the Arab-Israeli wars (Bar-Tal and Antebi, 1992). Often this kind of beliefs includes claims that the society is being unjustly criticized by other societies. For example, it may be claimed that criticism of the ingroup's actions in the conflict by other states or international organizations (such as the United Nations) is driven by racism or anti-Semitism. Or that the other states do not understand the situation that the ingroup is facing and would not have acted differently had they been in the same situation. Those are common themes in the Israeli ethos, as can be seen, for example, in leaders' speeches. At the intrapsychic level these kind of beliefs may serve as a coping strategy of *modification in the process of evaluation by challenging legitimacy of other evaluation*. In this strategy ingroup members challenge the right of other people (or groups) to judge them and as a result during the evaluation process are able to confront the value system that threatens their identity (Breakwell, 1986).

6. The ethos of conflict encourages patriotism, including the readiness to make the ultimate sacrifice of life. For example, Israeli patriotic beliefs call for various forms of devotion, including settlement of outlying or desolate areas, volunteering for the security forces and working for society's welfare. These beliefs even call for the ultimate sacrifice of life as part of the violent confrontation with the Arabs. Those who act as models of patriotism are glorified, while those who left the country (called "deserters") or did not fulfill their duties to the state (e.g. by not serving in the army) are stigmatized (see the extensive review by Ben-Amos and Bar-Tal, 2004).

7. Ethos of conflict refers to the importance of maintaining unity, by ignoring internal discords and disagreements, in the face of an external threat. The Israeli ethos highlights the common heritage and

religion and downplays the ethnic differences within Israeli society whose members came from diverse parts of the world.

8. Ethos of conflict refers to peace as the ultimate desire of the society and describes the society as peace loving. In Israeli society peace often was conceived of as a dream, a prayer and a hope in utopian and idyllic images (Oren, 2009; Yadgar, 2003). In this case, beliefs about peace may also serve as a coping strategy at the intrapsychic level of *fantasy* (Breakwell, 1986).

While our discussion above focuses on the Israeli case it is important to note that these eight themes were found to be dominant in many other societies engaged in intractable conflict, such as among the Palestinians (Abu-Harthieh, 1993; Khalidi, 1997), Serbs, Kosovars, Albanians, Croats and Bosnians (MacDonald, 2002), among Hutus in Rwanda (Slocum-Bradley, 2008) and among Greek and Turkish Cypriots (Papadakis *et al.*, 2006).

Eventually, the collective memory and the ethos of conflict provide contents that imbue the collective identity with meaning (Cairns *et al.*, 1998; Gillis, 1994; Oren *et al.*, 2004). At the individual level, the conflict may change the individuals' definitions of social identity and levels of identification, by increasing the importance of both social identity and the will to belong to a collective. On the collective level, it may influence the generic characteristics of the *shared sense of common fate* and *continuity, perception of uniqueness, coordination of activity, extent of sharing beliefs, concern for the welfare of the collective and readiness for mobilization on behalf of the collective.*

Institutionalization of conflict and collective identity

This stage is the climax of the intractable conflict when neither side can win the conflict and achieve its conflict goals. In addition, neither party thinks about compromises in order to settle it peacefully. At this stage, the collective identity with its repertoire of the well-organized system of societal beliefs and attitudes, as described above, filters into institutions and the communications channels and gradually crystallizes into a culture of conflict.

Social context of conflict institutionalization

At the institutionalization stage of the conflict, beliefs about the goals and means in the conflict and other societal beliefs dominate the social context. These beliefs are manifested in interpersonal communication between group members, appear in channels of societal information, such as literature, TV programs, films, theater, visual arts and so on. In other words, at this stage of the conflict, the themes of the ethos of conflict are embodied in social representations circulating in society, becoming hegemonic. Indeed, various lines of research have found dominance of the eight themes of the ethos in different Israeli societal and cultural products such as in Israeli cinema, literature, journalism, political platforms, memorial ceremonies and school textbooks reflecting the emergence of a culture of conflict (see, e.g., Bar-Tal, 2007b; Liebman and Don-Yehiya, 1983; Oren, 2010; Podeh, 2002; Shohat, 2010; Yadgar, 2003; Zerubavel, 1995).

In cases of asymmetrical conflicts, the stronger party often has at its disposal channels of communication and societal institutions to disseminate the epistemic basis for continuing the conflict. Within the weaker side, that does not have access to media and societal formal institutions, the interpersonal networks serve as means to disseminate the themes of the culture of conflict.

In addition, at this stage the entrepreneurs of the conflict actively try to preclude the consideration of information and alternative approaches to the conflict that may initiate the peacemaking process. Thus, the context is often characterized by control of mass media, censorship of information, or delegitimization of alternative information and its sources (for detailed descriptions of the mechanisms and examples from various conflicts, see: Bar-Tal and Halperin, 2011; Bar-Tal and Hammack, 2012; Burns-Bisogno, 1997; Wolfsfeld, 2004).

Identity processes during conflict institutionalization

IPT postulates that the content and processes of identity affect exposure to social representations and also affect the extent to which social representations are accepted and internalized by the individual (Breakwell, 1993, 2001a, 2001b, 2010). In the case of intractable conflict, as we indicated above, society members are extensively exposed to social representations of the ethos of conflict; at home, at school, during leisure activities such as watching movies or TV, and so on. Yet, the extent to which the group members accept, internalize and behave according to these social representations of the ethos is determined by the degree to which these beliefs are compatible with the identity principles. We argue that during the institutionalization stage of intractable conflict, representations of the themes of collective memory and the ethos of conflict as underlying parts of the culture of conflict play a crucial role in satisfying needs of identity and hence are accepted and internalized by the majority of the group. In other words, at this stage acceptance and reproduction of social representations of the themes of culture of conflict become the individual's main strategy to cope with threats to identity (see Breakwell, 2001a; Jaspal and Coyle, 2009 for acceptance and reproduction of social representations as a coping strategy).

First of all, knowledge of the themes is often defined as a prerequisite for authenticity as an ingroup member and hence this knowledge may satisfy the belonging principle. As a result, individuals may be motivated to internalize this knowledge and act accordingly. For example, Jaspal and Yampolsky (2011) found in their study of eleven Israeli-born Jewish students, that Holocaust knowledge was perceived as vital in order to be considered a "real" or "proper" Israeli and to experience a sense of acceptance and inclusion in the Israeli society. Even subgroups in the Israeli society (such as *Beta Israel* – the historical name for the Jewish Ethiopian community) who, in some contexts, where considered by some society members as the "Other," came to be regarded as "Jews like us" when social representations of the Holocaust were invoked. Similarly, Hammack (2011), who interviewed Israeli youth, found that negative beliefs about the Arabs contribute to the sense of belonging and inclusion in the Israeli society. For example, a 15-year-old Israeli boy that participated in this study claimed that "in this country there are problems between the orthodox and the secular, but what makes us all together is that we have the same enemy. They are attacking us both" (p. 132). In his interviews with Palestinian youth, Hammack (2011) also found that the need to internalize the Palestinian master narrative of the conflict was perceived by some Palestinian youth as essential to being recognized as authentic Palestinians.

Secondly, since social representations of the conflict often represent a hegemonic social representation in the society and given their centrality in individuals' meaning-making regarding the world, they may be essential for the continuity principle of identity (Jaspal and Yampolsky, 2011). In addition, specific beliefs about the goals in the conflict, such as the goal of establishing a Jewish state in the ancient homeland of the Jews and victimhood beliefs claiming that enemy outgroups always seek the annihilation of the Jews, may also satisfy the continuity principle and hence be internalized by the individuals.

Thirdly, the themes of collective memory and ethos of conflict as they appear in the context at this stage of the conflict sharpens intergroup differences because they describe the opponent in delegitimizing terms and at the same time glorify and praise their own society, as well as present it as a sole victim of the conflict. This view allows total psychological separation between the ingroup and the rival and creates immense social distance that relegates the rival into inferior spheres of inhumanity. This may be beneficial for the distinctiveness principle.

In addition, fourthly, the themes provide clear-cut, simple and comprehensive knowledge about the conflict – and hence could enhance the meaning principle. They explain the nature of the conflict to group members: why the group is in conflict; what the goals are in the conflict and why they are existential; what challenges the society is facing; how did the conflict erupt?; what the course of the conflict was; why it is so violent; why it still continues and cannot be resolved peacefully?; what the enemy's responsibility for and contribution to the conflict is; how the ingroup acted in the conflict; and so on. Indeed, Jaspal and Yampolsky (2011) found that the participants in their study tended "to consider the Arab-Israeli conflict through the interpretive lens of the Holocaust." And "this provided a meaningful 'anchor' for making sense of the potential consequences of not resolving this conflict, either by allowing Palestinian independence or by retaining control of the Occupied Territories" (p. 223).

Fifthly, the themes that present own goals as justified, the goals of the other group as unfounded, portray the own group as a victim and at the same time in a very positive light as being moral, virtuous and righteous, fulfill an important function of maintaining positive self-image as well as positive personal and collective identity in spite of the violence carried out against the rival. For example, a recent study conducted in connection with the Israeli-Palestinian conflict discovered a strong association between holding societal belief of collective victimhood among Israeli Jewish respondents and reduced group-based guilt over Israel's actions against the Palestinians (Schori-Eyal et al., 2011). Those who had a high sense of collective victimhood expressed less guilt and hence could sustain high self-esteem. Note that some social representations of the ethos such as social representation that one's ethno-religious group is universally and consensually regarded with hostility are likely to be threatening for self-esteem. One strategy to eschew threats to identity in this case is salience of principles – when other principles, such as meaning, distinctiveness and continuity, are attributed more importance than the principle of self-esteem.

As a result of the functional and essential role that the collective memory and ethos of conflict fulfill, society members tend to assimilate and evaluate only conceptions of the group that match the ethos and reject any information that is not consistent with it. Thus, group members tend to search and absorb information that is in line with their repertoire, while ignoring contradictory information, which is viewed as invalid (Bar-Tal and Halperin, 2011). Furthermore, even when ambiguous or contradictory information is absorbed, it is encoded and cognitively processed in accordance with held beliefs through bias, addition and distortion (e.g. Pfeifer and Ogloff, 1991; Rosenberg and Wolfsfeld, 1977; Shamir and Shikaki, 2002). These tendencies are also supported by the psychological coherence principle – that is, the need for compatibility and coherence between representations and one's identity.

Identity content during conflict institutionalization

At this stage the eight themes of the collective memory and ethos of conflict that were developing during the escalation stage and became the foundations of culture of conflict, dominate the collective identity of the society (Bar-Tal, 2013). In addition members of societies involved in intractable conflicts perceive the experiences of the conflict as demarcating boundaries that differentiate them from other collectives (e.g. in the Israeli case; see Merom, 1999). Often they even see themselves as so unique in their conflict experiences that they differentiate themselves even from other societies involved in intractable conflicts. This view may contribute to the collective identity by strengthening their *sense of a common fate* and *perception of the uniqueness* – both are generic features of collective identity.

Peacemaking and collective identity

The analysis of the conflict institutionalization described above explains why it is so difficult to resolve intractable conflicts peacefully. Both sides develop a social identity that is dominated by beliefs about the conflict. As we saw above, the societal beliefs of collective memory and ethos of conflict fulfill essential identity functions and as a result the society members tend to accept and internalize social representations of the ethos and reject any information from the context that does not fit these beliefs (see Bar-Tal and Halperin, 2011). Yet, almost every society engaged in intractable conflict includes societal forces (albeit a small minority in some cases) that advocate and campaign for embarking on a different road – the road of peacemaking. Once these forces grow and become influential, it is possible to say that the process of peace-building has gained momentum. A change in the context can facilitate this process.

Social context of peacemaking

In the phase of peacemaking, the context goes through a dramatic transformation of de-escalating the conflict. The characteristics of the context change, moving toward the tractable end of the continuum. Such significant change in the context can potentially be driven, among other things, by the accumulation of negative conflict experiences, by major events like the eruption of a new harsh conflict with a third, unrelated party, an unexpected conciliatory gesture by the rival, an internal non-conflict related event (recession, famine, etc.) and by the rise of new leaders, who are less committed to the ideology of conflict (see Bar-Tal, 2013).

Peacemaking processes, in order to succeed, must have the support of leaders and societal institutions (see, e.g., Bar-Siman-Tov, 2004; Knox and Quirk, 2000). Of special importance is the role played by the mass media and other societal channels of communication and institutions, which can first promote the formation of a peace orientation and subsequently transmit and disseminate a new system of beliefs and social representations of peace among the society members.

It is also important to note that in the period of peacemaking and, even more so, the first stage following an official settlement, society members move from a well-known and familiar context into an uncertain, ambiguous and risky context. This context has many of the characteristics of conflict, while at the same time possessing characteristics of the emerging context of peace. On the one hand signs of peacemaking appear, reflected in meetings between the rivals, coordination of some activities, moderation of violence, and so on. On the other hand, violent acts may continue, conflict rhetoric continues to be employed, and, most importantly, the culture of conflict and collective identity of conflict remains hegemonic. Adding to the confusion characterizing this period is the fact that the rival parties, are not irreversibly committed to a peaceful resolution at this stage and continue to entertain the possibility that they may be forced to return to the road of violent confrontation. Therefore this period can be seen as a period of duality, where signs of conflict and signs of peace coexist (Rosler, 2012).

The identity process during peacekeeping

The changing context described above may cause some group members to perceive the conflict as a threat to identity. In this case, peacemaking will also be triggered by identity needs.

Some group members, following a major event such as a significant military defeat, may feel that the conflict severely compromises the continuity principle of identity; since the ingroup risks annihilation as a result of the continuation of the conflict. Other members of society may, as a result of information about own group wrong-doing in the conflict, feel that it compromises basic values of their society and hence compromises the self-esteem principle of identity. Among these members of the group who perceived the change of the context as threatening, perceptions of identity threat may induce coping strategies, such as the intrapsychic strategy of *fundamental change*. In this strategy the individual may allow the process of assimilation–accommodation to bring about a fundamental change in the identity (Breakwell, 1986). The person may sacrifice any (e.g. beliefs about the opponent) or all of the beliefs of the ethos of conflict in order to assimilate new components into their identity. In addition, some members of the group may use the intergroup coping strategy of *formation of consciousness-raising group* by establishing a peace movement. Indeed, in many cases the process of peacemaking begins with a minority who believe that it is necessary to end the conflict by negotiating its resolution with the rival. In most cases, peacemaking involves, on the one hand, bottom-up processes in which groups, grass-roots organization and civil society members support the ideas of peace-building and act to disseminate these among leaders as well, and, on the other hand, top-down processes in which leaders join the efforts, begin persuading society members of the necessity of a peaceful settlement of the conflict, and initiate its implementation (Gawerc, 2006). The result is a change in the ethos of conflict.

For example, Oren (2005, 2009) who studied the Israeli ethos of conflict in the period from 1967 until 2006, found that major events in the conflict, such as the unexpected peace process with Egypt and the first *Intifada*, triggered a change in the Israeli ethos of conflict as was held by society members. Her analysis of Israeli public polls and elections platforms indicates that these events triggered concerns among some Israelis (including some Israeli leaders) about the growing cost of the conflict in terms of a threat to Israel's national identity as a Jewish and democratic state. More specifically, following some events in the conflict, Israeli control of the territories captured by Israel in 1967, which are densely populated by Palestinians, was perceived by more and more Israelis as threatening the goals of having a Jewish majority and a Jewish state. This may be interpreted as a threat to the continuity and distinctiveness principles. In addition, the practice of keeping masses of Palestinians under Israeli occupation was also perceived by some Israelis as straining democratic practices, which may be seen as another threat to the continuity principle, since Israelis consider their state as democratic and to the self-esteem principles of identity. As a result, the Israeli ethos of conflict has changed over the years. This change took several forms; first, some of the ethos beliefs (security beliefs, victimhood, negative opponent image, positive self-image and patriotism) weakened over time. In addition, some societal beliefs were dropped while others were added. The early societal belief that the Palestinians were not a nation has been gradually abandoned. Also, some beliefs (such as peace societal beliefs) become more dominant while others become less dominant. However, the events of 2000 with the eruption of the second *Intifada* and its violence reversed the trend and strengthened some of the societal beliefs in the ethos of conflict.

Indeed, it is important to note that the processes of change in the ethos of conflict are gradual and complex because societal change is not a simple matter given that identity related beliefs are well entrenched in the society, and any change of existing identity threatens the continuity principle. Indeed, peace agreements that include accepting some of the rival's claims and compromising over own group goals can induce disruptive change which can threaten the continuity principle of identity, and hence resistance to change of the ethos of conflict may be strong and persistent. The duality of the context at this stage of the conflict, where signs of conflict and signs of peace coexist, also makes it difficult to establish and maintain an ethos of peace.

Identity content during peacemaking

The goal in peacemaking, then, is to promote alternative societal beliefs that promote a peaceful resolution of the conflict (Bar-Tal and Halperin, 2009). The ultimate objective is evolving, acceptance and internalization of a new ethos of peace. This ethos must act as the opposite equivalent of the repertoire of conflict, in terms of content and structure, in a way that will successfully fulfill the same needs and aspirations of the ingroup members (Bar-Tal, 2013).

One necessary condition for the emergence of the new repertoire that supports peacemaking is the development of a new view of the rival. Thus, the emergent view has to include contents that legitimize, equalize, differentiate and personalize the rival group (see Bar-Tal and Teichman, 2005). *Legitimization* allows viewing the opponent as belonging to an acceptable category of groups behaving within the boundaries of international norms, with which it is possible and even desirable to end the conflict and construct positive relations. This allows recognition of the legitimate existence of the other group with its differences. *Equalization* implies perception of members of the other group first and foremost as equals, without superiority, and treating them accordingly. *Differentiation* leads to a new perception of the other group as constituted of various subgroups, which differ in their views and ideologies. Differentiation thus also makes it possible to see that members of the rival group differ in their opinions regarding the conflict and its resolution. *Personalization* allows viewing the rival group not as a depersonalized entity, but rather as made up of individuals with ordinary human characteristics, concerns, needs and goals. This means that the delegitimizing image disappears and instead a new positive image is presented.

The new beliefs that signal an emergence of alternative collective identity should include many other new ideas, such as about the need to resolve the conflict peacefully, about changing the goals that fueled the conflict and defining new goals that can lead to peace, about sharing victimhood with the rival, about history of the conflict and about developing shared beliefs or some shared identity with the rival group (Bar-Tal, 2013). For, example, Hadjipavlou (2007, p. 362) identifies a desire on the part of both rival communities in Cyprus to move away from Greek or Turkish nationalistic identities toward a shared *Cypriot* culture. In contrast, Muldoon *et al.* (2007) found a continuing predominance of national and religious identities among adults and adolescents in Northern Ireland after the Belfast Good Friday Agreement.

Conclusion

This chapter focuses on the particular context of intractable conflict which still plagues the world today and greatly preoccupies civilization. It elucidates the role of collective identity in this long lasting context by integrating two complementary approaches, namely the Theory of Collective Identity and Identity Process Theory. Both theories place social context at the center of the processes and recognize the ongoing interaction between the context and the content.

At each phase of the conflict, changes in context may threaten identity. The strategies that are adopted by individuals and groups to cope with these threats influence the course of the conflict and the content of collective identity on generic and specific levels. The chapter systemically described the context of the four phases of intractable conflict (eruption, escalation, institutionalization and peacemaking) and presented the processes involved in the formation and changes of collective identity as well as its contents. This analysis provides a multifaceted understanding of the complexity of intractable conflict and how members of these societies cope and behave. First of all, it explains how the coping strategies that are likely to be drawn upon by individuals and groups (whether it be denial, compliance, negativism or group action) may determine whether intractable conflicts will erupt at some point or not. Indeed, intractable conflicts first of all require extensive mobilization for action, including readiness to sacrifice one's life. Without this mobilization conflicts cannot take off. Secondly, the above analysis also explains why intractable conflicts tend to last so long; the context of intractable conflict is extremely powerful – imprinting the life of the participants. Societies in intractable conflict develop a collective memory and ethos of conflict as a mechanism that helps the society cope with the threat to identity as a result of this context. During the conflict's institutionalization, the collective memory and ethos become building blocks of the culture of conflict, dominate the social context of conflict and fulfill essential identity functions. For example, they could enhance the meaning principle by providing clear-cut, simple and comprehensive knowledge about the conflict, or can contribute to the belonging and self-esteem principles. As a result, the society members tend to accept and internalize social representations of the culture of conflict and reject any information from the context that does not fit these beliefs. Lastly, the changing of context and coping strategies that are adopted by individuals and groups to deal with new threats to identity can also explain peace processes and their difficulties. A peace process may start when a change in the context induces threat to identity among some of the group members and they adopt coping strategies, such as the intrapsychic strategy of fundamental change (e.g. allow the process of assimilation–accommodation to bring about a fundamental change in the identity). As a result, some or all of the beliefs in the ethos may be changed – thereby changing the content of the collective identity of the group. Yet, this process is long since any change of existing identity can threaten the continuity principle.

Thus, any attempt to resolve peacefully an intractable conflict must pay special attention to collective identity and identity processes as key elements.

REFERENCES

Abu-Harthieh, M. (1993). The right to the development under occupation: the case of Palestine. Dissertation, University of Essex, UK.
Azar, E. E. (1990). *The management of protracted social conflict*. Hampshire, UK: Dartmouth.
Bar-Siman-Tov, Y. (ed.) (2004). *From conflict resolution to reconciliation*. New York: Oxford University Press.
Bar-Tal, D. (1988). Delegitimizing relations between Israeli Jews and Palestinians: a social psychological analysis. In J. E. Hofman (ed.), *Arab-Jewish relations in Israel: a quest in human understanding* (pp. 217–248). Bristol, IN: Wyndham Hall Press.
Bar-Tal, D. (1998). Societal beliefs in times of intractable conflict: the Israeli case. *International Journal of Conflict Management*, 9(1), 22–50.
Bar-Tal, D. (2000). *Shared beliefs in a society: social psychological analysis*. Thousand Oaks, CA: Sage.

Bar-Tal, D. (2003). Collective memory of physical violence: its contribution to the culture of violence. In E. Cairns and M. D. Roe (eds.), *The role of memory in ethnic conflict* (pp. 77–93). Houndmills, UK: Palgrave Macmillan.

Bar-Tal, D. (2007a). Sociopsychological foundations of intractable conflicts. *American Behavioral Scientist*, 50, 1,430–1,453.

Bar-Tal, D. (2007b). *Lihyot besichsooch: nituach psychology-hevratis hahevra hayeoodit beisrael* [Living in a conflict: a psychological-social analysis of the Jewish society in Israel]. Jerusalem: Carmel (in Hebrew).

Bar-Tal, D. (2013). *Intractable conflicts: socio-psychological foundations and dynamics.* Cambridge University Press.

Bar-Tal, D., and Antebi, D. (1992). Siege mentality in Israel. *International Journal of Intercultural Relations*, 16, 251–275.

Bar-Tal, D., Chernyak-Hai, L., Schori, N., and Gundar, Y. (2009). A sense of self-perceived collective victimhood in intractable conflicts. *International Review of the Red Cross*, 91(874), 229–277.

Bar-Tal, D., and Halperin, E. (2009). Overcoming psychological barriers to peace process: the influence of beliefs about losses. In M. Mikulincer and P. R. Shaver (eds.), *Prosocial motives, emotions and behaviors: the better angels of our nature* (pp. 431–448). Washington, DC: American Psychological Association Press.

Bar-Tal, D., and Halperin, E. (2011). Socio-psychological barriers to conflict resolution. In D. Bar-Tal (ed.), *Intergroup conflicts and their resolution: social psychological perspective* (pp. 217–240). New York: Psychology Press.

Bar-Tal, D., and Halperin, E. (2013). The psychology of intractable conflicts: eruption, escalation and peacemaking. In L. Huddy, D. Sears and J. Levy (eds.), *Oxford handbook of political psychology* (2nd edn.) (pp. 923–956). New York: Oxford University Press.

Bar-Tal, D., and Hammack, P. L. (2012). Conflict, delegitimization and violence. In L. R. Tropp (ed.), *Oxford handbook of intergroup conflict* (pp. 29–52). New York: Oxford University Press.

Bar-Tal, D., Jacobson, D., and Klieman, A. (eds.) (1998). *Security concerns: insights from the Israeli experience.* Stamford, CT: JAI Press.

Bar-Tal, D., and Teichman, Y. (2005). *Stereotypes and prejudice in conflict: representation of Arabs in Israeli Jewish society.* New York: Cambridge University Press.

Baumeister, R., and Hastings, S. (1997). Distortions of collective memory: how groups flatter and deceive themselves. In J. Pennebaker, D. Paez and B. Rime (eds.), *Collective memory of political events* (pp. 277–293). Mahwah, NJ: Lawrence Erlbaum.

Ben-Amos, A., and Bar-Tal, D. (eds.) (2004). *Homeland: patriotism in Israel.* Tel Aviv: Hakibbutz Hameuhad (in Hebrew).

Bercovitch, J. (2005). Mediation in the most resistant cases. In C. A., Crocker, F. O. Hampson and P. R. Aall (eds.), *Grasping the nettle: analyzing cases of intractable conflict* (pp. 99–121). Washington, DC: United States Institute of Peace Press.

Branscombe, N. R., Ellemers, N., Spears, R., and Doosje, B. (1999). The context and content of social identity threat. In N. Ellemers, R. Spears, and

B. Doosje (eds.), *Social identity: context, commitment, content* (pp. 35–58). Oxford, England: Blackwell.

Breakwell, G. M. (1986). *Coping with threatened identities*. London: Methuen.

Breakwell, G. M. (1993). Social representations and social identity. *Papers on Social Representations*, 2 (3), 198–217.

Breakwell, G. M. (2001a). Social representational constraints upon identity processes. In K. Deaux and G. Philogene (eds.), *Representions of the social: bridging theoretical traditions* (pp. 271–284). Oxford: Blackwell.

Breakwell, G. M. (2001b). Mental models and social representations of hazards: the significance of identity processes. *Journal of Risk Research*, 4 (4), 341–351.

Breakwell, G. M. (2010). Resisting representations and identity processes. *Special Issue: Papers in Social Representations*, 19, 6.1–6.11 (in honour of Gerard Duveen: Social Representations and Social Identities: Inspirations from Gerard Duveen).

Brewer, M. B. (2011). Identity and conflict. In D. Bar-Tal (ed.), *Intergroup conflicts and their resolution: social psychological perspectives* (pp. 125–143). New York: Psychology Press.

Brewer, M., and Silver, M. D. (2000). Group distinctiveness, social identification and collective mobilization. In S. Stryker, T. J. Owens and R. W. White (eds.), *Self, identity and social movement: social movements, protest and contention*, vol. XIII (pp. 153–171). Minneapolis: University of Minnesota Press.

Brown, R. (2000). *Group processes: dynamics within and between groups* (2nd edn.). Oxford: Basil Blackwell.

Burns-Bisogno, L. (1997). *Censoring Irish nationalism: the British, Irish and American suppression of Republican images in film and television, 1909–1995*. Jefferson, NC: McFarland.

Cairns, E., and Roe, M. (eds.) (2003). *The role of memory in ethnic conflict*. New York: Palgrave Macmillan.

Cairns, E., Lewis, C. A., Mumcu, O., and Waddell, N. (1998). Memories of recent ethnic conflict and their relationship to social identity. *Peace and Conflict: Journal of Peace Psychology*, 4, 13–22.

Coleman, P. T. (2003). Characteristics of protracted, intractable conflict: towards the development of a metaframework – I. *Peace and Conflict: Journal of Peace Psychology*, 9(1), 1–37.

Crosby, F. J. (1976). A model of egoistical relative deprivation. *Psychological Review*, 83, 85–113.

David, O. (2007). Hahitgabshut vehishtanut hazehut hayehuditisraelit: Mechkar al bitui vezehut bemikraot lelimud ivrit bameaha-20 [The crystallization and transformations of Jewish-Israeli identity: a study of identity reflection in Hebrew readers of the twentieth century]. Doctoral dissertation, Tel Aviv University, Israel.

David, O., and Bar-Tal, D. (2009). A socio-psychological conception of collective identity: the case of national identity. *Personality and Social Psychology Review*, 13, 354–379.

Flood, G. (1996). *An introduction to Hinduism*. Cambridge University Press.

Gawerc, M. I. (2006). Peace-building: theoretical and concrete perspectives. *Peace & Change*, 31, 435–478.

Gillis J. R. (ed.) (1994). *Commemorations: the politics of national identity.* Princeton, NJ: Princeton University Press.

Goodwin, J. (2001). *No other way out: states and revolutionary movements, 1945–1991.* Cambridge University Press.

Hadjipavlou, M. (2007). The Cyprus conflict: root causes and implications for peacebuilding. *Journal of Peace Research*, 44(3), 349–365.

Halbwachs, M. (1992). *On collective memory.* Chicago, IL: University of Chicago Press.

Hammack, P. L. (2011). *Narrative and the politics of identity: the cultural psychology of Israeli and Palestinian youth.* New York: Oxford University Press.

Hofman, J. E. (1970). The meaning of being a Jew in Israel: an analysis of ethnic identity. *Journal of Personality and Social Psychology*, 15, 196–202.

Horowitz, D. (1984). Israeli perception of national security (1948–1972). In B. Neuberger (ed.), *Diplomacy and confrontation: selected issues in Israel's foreign relations, 1948–1978* (pp. 104–148). Tel Aviv: Everyman's University (in Hebrew).

Jaspal, R. (2011). Caste, social stigma and identity processes. *Psychology and Developing Societies*, 23(2), 27–62.

Jaspal, R., and Cinnirella, M. (2010a). Media representations of British Muslims and hybridised threats to identity. *Contemporary Islam*, 4(3), 289–310.

Jaspal, R., and Cinnirella, M. (2010b). Coping with potentially incompatible identities: accounts of religious, ethnic and sexual identities from British Pakistani men who identify as Muslim and gay. *British Journal of Social Psychology*, 49, 849–870.

Jaspal, R., and Coyle, A. (2009). Language and perceptions of identity threat. *Psychology and Society*, 2(2), 150–167.

Jaspal, R., and Yampolsky, M. (2011). Social representations of the Holocaust and Jewish Israeli identity construction: insights from identity process theory. *Social Identities*, 17(2), 201–224.

Kelman, H. C. (2001). The role of national identity in conflict resolution. In R. D. Ashmore, L. Jussim and D. Wilder (eds.), *Social identity, intergroup conflict and conflict reduction* (pp. 187–212). New York: Oxford University Press.

Khalidi, R. (1997). *Palestinian identity: the construction of modern national consciousness.* New York: Columbia University Press

Klandermans, B. (1988). The formation and mobilization of consensus. In B. Klandermans, H. Kriesi and S. Tarrow (eds.), *From structure to action: comparing social movement research across cultures*, vol. I (pp. 173–196). Greenwich, CT: JAI Press.

Klinghoffer A. J. (1998). *The international dimension of genocide in Rwanda.* New York University Press.

Knox, C., and Quirk, P. (2000). *Peace building in Northern Ireland, Israel and South Africa: transition, transformation and reconciliation.* London: Macmillan.

Korostelina, K. (2006). National identity formation and conflict intentions of ethnic minorities. In M. Fitzduff and C. E. Stout (eds.), *The psychology of resolving global conflicts: from war to peace*, vol. II (pp. 147–170). Westport, CT: Praeger Security International.

Kriesberg, L. (1993). Intractable conflict. *Peace Review*, 5, 417–421.

Liebman, C. S., and Don-Yehiya, E. (1983). *Civil religion in Israel: traditional Judaism and political culture in the Jewish state*. Berkeley: University of California Press.

Lyons, E. (1996). Coping with social change: processes of social memory in the reconstruction of identities. In G. M. Breakwell and E. Lyons (eds.), *Changing European identities: social psychological analyses of social change* (pp. 31–40). Oxford: Butterworth-Heinemann.

MacDonald, D. B. (2002). *Balkan holocausts?: Serbian and Croatian victim-centred propaganda and the war in Yugoslavia*. Manchester: New York.

Major, B. (1994). From social inequality to personal entitlement. *Advances in Experiamental Psychology*, 26, 295–355.

Maslow, A. H. (1954). *Motivation and personality*, (2nd edn.). New York: Harper & Row.

Melucci, A. (1989). *Nomads of the present: social movements and individual needs in contemporary society*. London: Hutchinson.

Merom, G. (1999). Israel's national security and the myth of exceptionalism, *Political Science Quarterly*, 409–434.

Muldoon, O. T., Trew, K., Todd, J., Rougier, N., and McLaughlin, K. (2007). Religious and national identity after the Belfast Good Friday Agreement. *Political Psychology*, 28(1), 89–103.

Olson, J. M., Hermann, C. P., and Zanna, M. P. (eds.) (1986), *Relative deprivation and social comparison: the Ontario symposium*, vol. IV (pp. 1–15). Hillsdale, NJ: Lawrence Erlbaum.

Oren, N. (2005). The Israeli ethos of the Arab-Israeli conflict 1967–2000: the effects of major events. Dissertation, Tel Aviv University, Tel Aviv.

Oren, N. (2009). *The Israeli ethos of conflict 1967–2005*. Working Paper 27. Fairfax, VA: Institute for Conflict Analysis and Resolution, George Mason University. http://icar.gmu.edu/publication/6403.

Oren, N. (2010). Israeli identity formation and the Arab-Israeli conflict in election platforms 1969–2006. *Journal of Peace Research*, 47(2), 193–204.

Oren, N., and Bar-Tal, D. (2007). The detrimental dynamics of delegitimization in intractable conflicts: the Israeli-Palestinian case. *International Journal of Intercultural Relations*, 31, 111–126.

Oren, N., Bar-Tal, D., and David, O. (2004). Conflict, identity and ethos: the Israeli-Palestinian case. In Y.-T. Lee (ed.), *The psychology of ethnic and cultural conflict* (pp. 133–154). Westport, CT: Praeger.

Papadakis, Y., Perstianis, N., and Welz, G. (eds.) (2006). *Divided Cyprus: modernity, history and an island in conflict*. Bloomington: Indiana University Press.

Pennebaker, J. W., Paez, D., and Rimé, B. (eds.) (1997). *Collective memory of political events: social psychological perspective*. Mahwah, NJ: Lawrence Erlbaum.

Pfeifer, J. E., and Ogloff, J. R. P. (1991). Ambiguity and guilt determinations: a modern racism perspective. *Journal of Applied Social Psychology*, 21, 1,713–1,725.

Podeh, E. (2002). *The Arab-Israeli conflict in Israeli history textbooks, 1948–2000*. Westport, CT: Bergin & Garvey.

Polletta, F., and Jasper, J. M. (2001). Collective identity and social movements *Annual Review of Sociology*, 27, 283–305.

Reicher, S., and Hopkins, N. (2001). *Self and nation*. London: Sage.

Roccas, S., and Elster, A. (2012). Group identities. In L. R. Tropp (ed.), *Oxford handbook of intergroup conflict* (pp. 106–122). New York: Oxford University Press.

Roccas, S., Sagiv, L., Schwartz, S., Halevy, N., and Eidelson, R. (2008). Towards a unifying model of identification with groups: integrating theoretical perspectives. *Personality and Social Psychology Review*, 12, 280–306.

Rosenberg, S., and Wolfsfeld, G. (1977). International conflict and the problem of attribution. *Journal of Conflict Resolution*, 21(1):75–103.

Rosler, N. (2012). Political conflict, social challenges, and leadership: rhetorical expressions of psycho-social roles of leaders in intractable conflict and its resolution process – the Israeli-Palestinian case. Ph.D. dissertation, Hebrew University of Jerusalem (in Hebrew).

Rothbart, D., and Bartlett, T. (2008). Rwandan radio broadcasts and Hutu/Tutsi positioning. In F. M. Moghaddam, R. Harré and N. Lee (eds.), *Global conflict resolution through positioning analysis* (pp. 227–246). New York: Springer.

Rothbart, D., and Korostelina, K.V. (2006). *Identity, morality and threat*. Lexington, MA: Lexington.

Runciman, W. G. (1966). *Relative deprivation and social justice*. London: Routledge & Kegan Paul.

Sande, G. N., Goethals, G. R., Ferrari, L., and Worth, L. T. (1989). Value-guided attributions: maintaining the moral self-image and the diabolical enemy-image. *Journal of Social Issues*, 45(2), 91–118.

Sandler, S. (1988). The protracted Arab-Israeli conflict: a temporal-spatial analysis. *Jerusalem Journal of International Relations*, 10, 54–78.

Schori-Eyal, N., Klar, Y., and Roccas, S. (2011). The shadows of the past: effects of historical group trauma on current intergroup conflicts. Manuscript submitted for publication.

Shamir, J., and Shikaki, K. (2002). Self serving perceptions of terrorism among Israelis and Palestinians. *Political Psychology*, 23, 537–557.

Shohat, E. (2010). *Israeli cinema: East/West and the politics of representation*. London: Tauris.

Simon, B., and Klandermans, B. (2001). Politicized collective identity: a social psychological analysis. *American Psychologist*, 56, 319–331.

Slocum-Bradley, N. R. (2008). Discursive production of conflict in Rwanda. In F. M. Moghaddam, R. Harré, and N. Lee (eds.), *Global conflict resolution through positioning analysis* (pp. 207–226). New York: Springer.

Smith, A. D. (1991). *National identity*. London: Penguin.

South African Democracy Education Trust. (2010). *The road to democracy in South Africa*, vol. I: *1960–1970*. Pretoria: Unisa Press.

Stephan, W. G., Renfro, C. L., and Davis, M. D. (2008). The role of threat in intergroup relations. In U. Wagner, L. R. Tropp, G. Finchilescu, and C. Tredoux (eds.), *Improving intergroup relations* (pp. 55–72). Oxford: Blackwell.

Swann, W. B., Jr., Gómez, Á., Huici, C., Morales, J. F., and Hixon, J. G. (2010). Identity fusion and self-sacrifice: arousal as catalyst of extreme and altruistic group behaviour. *Journal of Personality and Social Psychology*, 96, 824–841.

Tajfel, H. (1982). *Social identity and intergroup relations.* Cambridge University Press.

Thackrah, J. R. (2009). *The Routledge companion to military conflict since 1945.* New York: Routledge.

Turner, J. C. (1999). Some current issues in research on social identity and self-categorization theories. In N. Ellemers, R. Spears and B. Doosje (eds.), *Social identity: context, commitment, content* (pp. 6–34). Oxford: Blackwell.

Turner, J. C., Hogg, M. A., Oakes, P. J., Reicher, S. D., and Wetherell, M. S. (1987). *Rediscovering the social group: a self-categorization theory.* Cambridge, MA: Blackwell.

Vignoles, V. L., Chryssochoou, X., and Breakwell, G. M. (2002). Evaluating models of identity motivation: self-esteem is not the whole story. *Self & Identity,* 1, 201–208.

Vignoles, V. L., Regalia, C., Manzi, C., Golledge, J., and Scabini, E. (2006). Beyond self-esteem: influence of multiple motives on identity construction. *Journal of Personality and Social Psychology,* 90, 308–333.

Vollhardt, J. R. (2012). Collective victimization. In L. R. Tropp (ed.), *Oxford handbook of intergroup conflict* (pp. 136–157). New York: Oxford University Press.

Wertsch, J. (2002). *Voices of collective remembering.* Cambridge University Press.

Wolfsfeld, G. (2004). *Media and the path to peace.* Cambridge University Press.

Yadgar, Y. (2003). From "true peace" to "the vision of the new Middle East": rival images of peace in Israel. *Journal of Peace Research,* 40(2), 177–193.

Zerubavel, Y. (1995). *Recovered roots: collective memory and the making of Israeli national tradition.* Chicago, IL: University of Chicago Press.

12   The role of perceived threat and identity in Islamophobic prejudice

Marco Cinnirella

Background: Islamophobia in the UK

In this chapter I explore social-psychological aspects of prejudice toward Muslims (so-called Islamophobia), with a particular focus on the UK context. In doing so, I also aim to address broader theoretical issues about the social psychological nature of prejudice and in particular, its relation to matters of self and identity. My approach extorts the benefits that can accrue from building a hybrid theoretical perspective drawing upon Identity Process Theory (IPT; Breakwell, 1986), Social Identity Theory (SIT; Tajfel and Turner, 1986), Intergroup Threat Theory (ITT; Stephan *et al.*, 2008), Terror Management Theory (TMT; Pyszcynski *et al.*, 2003) and Social Representations Theory (SRT; Moscovici, 1981). At the heart of my argument is a claim that will not meet with universal approval within social psychology – that some forms of prejudice are sufficiently unique in their underlying causes and manifestation so as to require a theoretically eclectic approach that concedes the poverty of any single theory as an explanation. I strongly believe Islamophobia is one such prejudice. The bulk of the chapter is concerned with outlining the new perspective on Islamophobia and once this has been achieved, an exploratory empirical study is briefly discussed which highlights some potential avenues for developing and testing the model.

While some sociologists and other social scientists continue to debate the social construction of the term "Islamophobia" and even whether Islamophobic prejudice is a problem in need of social scientific investigation, the approach adopted here is more pragmatic. A majority of recent studies exploring prejudice toward Muslims reports strong evidence that (1) such prejudice is prevalent in many Western nations; and (2) Muslims themselves report being the target of prejudiced attitudes and discriminatory practices. For example, in a large-scale survey study of the UK population, Abrams and Houston (2006) found Muslims to be the least accepted minority group in Britain. They were stereotyped as incapable and unfriendly and perceived as the greatest cultural, physical and economic threat. The only group that was targeted with more negative feelings in this British survey was gay people. While Islamophobia probably has a long history in the West (Ansari, 2004), the Rushdie affair and then the rising notoriety of al-Qaeda after 9/11 served to elevate anti-Muslim feelings to new levels in Britain. Since the 9/11 attacks, many British Muslim groups have reported increases in anti-Islamic prejudice and abuse (Islamic Human Rights Commission, 2004). In fact, after 9/11, anti-Islamic reactions were recorded across all member states of the European Union (Allen and Nielsen, 2002), matching data from the USA (Sheridan and Gillett, 2005). Sheridan and Gillett (2005) and Sheridan (2006) report empirical studies amongst ethnic minorities in the UK, comparing levels of self-reported experiences of prejudice and discrimination before and after 9/11. Participants of Bangladeshi and Pakistani background (who were predominantly of Muslim faith) reported the largest increases in discrimination of any ethnic groups.

Along with prejudice toward immigrants and "asylum seekers," it could therefore be argued that Islamophobic prejudice, though far from new, in its current form is one of the fastest growing prejudices in the UK and many Western nations. Indeed, work in the Identity Process Theory tradition has uncovered evidence to suggest Islamophobic attitudes within other ethnic and religious minority communities in Britain (see, e.g., Jaspal's study of British Sikhs: Jaspal, 2013). Having established that there is indeed a problem, let us now turn our attention to deploying theory to help understand its psychological underpinnings.

Psychological antecedents of Islamophobia

The psychological antecedents of Islamophobia have already been explored using a range of methodologies and theories, ranging from qualitative interview studies through to quantitative surveys and laboratory experiments (e.g. Crowson et al., 2006; Hitlan et al., 2007; Park et al., 2007). An interesting observation is that many of the varying theoretical approaches used to understand Islamophobia focus on the role of threat as an antecedent of increasing prejudice. With this in mind, in this chapter I explore the degree to which such theories can be subsumed within a model which has IPT at its heart. The motivation for doing so is a straightforward one: it is my belief that IPT offers a parsimonious and elegant model for understanding the psychological antecedents of Islamophobia at multiple levels of understanding (Doise, 1986) – from the intrapsychic through to the interpersonal, intergroup and societal levels. From its inception IPT was conceptualized with the goal of elucidating and predicting how individuals and groups respond to psychological threats and especially threats to identity. IPT is uniquely placed to offer an understanding of how threats to identity affect identity processes at multiple levels of analysis and this is why I place IPT at the center of the theorizing in this chapter. Furthermore, IPT explores threats within a coherent model of identity structure and processes, something which the other theories drawn upon address only partially.

I will bolster IPT with contributions from ITT, SIT, TMT and SRT, in keeping with the earlier claim that Islamophobia has qualities that render any single perspective incapable of offering a complete understanding. ITT is drawn upon because it offers valuable insights into different types of intergroup threat and possible responses to these threats by individuals and groups. SIT is deployed here since work in the tradition offers insights into how levels of group identity affect responses to threats to social identity. TMT is drawn upon because it offers some unique ideas about how fear of violence and death can feed into prejudice. SRT is viewed as an essential component of the model forwarded in the chapter because it comprises a theoretical model for understanding the nature of shared representations, which are a key source of attitudes and beliefs about social groups in society.

Fear of terrorism and the backdrop of media social representations

It seems that when searching for the antecedents of rising Islamophobia, fear of terrorism must be considered a likely candidate, given the extensive mass media coverage of the airplane attacks on November 11, 2001 in the USA and the bombings in 2004 in Madrid and 2005 in London. Since these incidents, the media in many Western nations has kept the issue of Islamic terrorists on the public agenda through discourses aimed at justifying military action in Afghanistan and Iraq and through reporting of various foiled and planned terrorist activities. It seems likely that there will be an agenda-setting effect of this media coverage (McCombs, 2004), acting to keep the threat of (Islamic) terrorism in the public eye as an important and timely issue and perhaps also elevating fear of terrorism as each terrorism story gains media coverage. Since the prominence of Islamic terrorism in the media agenda will wax and wane, it is likely that levels of Islamophobic sentiment may fluctuate to a degree in line with this fluctuating media coverage. More generally, media content analyses have shown how Muslims have been portrayed negatively in the UK press and how some young Muslim men have been demonized as dangerous and potential terrorists (e.g. Moore *et al.*, 2008; Poole, 2002, 2006). Thus, it has been argued that there is a prevailing social representation of Muslims as threatening, largely as a consequence of their positioning as Islamic terrorists or sympathizers with the latter, but also as a group that may be perceived to threaten mainstream norms and values. Rusi Jaspal and I have argued that these media social representations of Muslims and Islam may be anchored into older, more established social representations of war and conflict, thus facilitating a discourse based around the metaphor of a military "enemy" (Jaspal and Cinnirella, 2010). This may partly explain the reported prevalence of Islamophobia, since the adoption of negative attitudes toward a military opponent tends to be deemed in society as necessary and acceptable and perhaps outside the scope of "politically correct" norms around avoiding prejudice and discrimination. Thus, the deployment of warlike rhetoric and discourse by the British press when discussing Islam, Muslims and terrorism, may, unwittingly, act to legitimatize Islamophobia in the eyes of some British citizens.

Thus individual reactions to Muslims, Islam and terrorism do not occur in a vacuum, but, instead, the degree to which they are perceived to threaten identity principles is at least in part determined by prevailing social representations in society and how these are interpreted by groups and individuals. This issue of interpretation is, of course, important (see, e.g., Breakwell, 2001). Individuals and groups are not slaves to media representations and have the scope to contest them. However, cultivation research (Gerbner *et al.*, 2002) demonstrates that in certain circumstances media representations can have powerful effects on perceivers' world-views. Since acts of terrorism are experienced firsthand by relatively few of us and most are not privy to intelligence from the security services, we rely on the media as "gatekeepers" of knowledge in this domain. For some, who value being fair and avoiding stereotyping, they may resist and question media representations, but for others, media messages may be processed in a less critical manner. The survey research summarized above is evidence for the apparent readiness the British public have to accept media representations which appear to associate Muslims and Islam with terrorism and broader threats to society and culture and in my previous work with Rusi Jaspal it is suggested that this endorsement likely serves identity principles (Jaspal and Cinnirella, 2010).

Terror management

If we therefore postulate that media social representations of Muslims and Islam have, whether deliberately or not, created an association between terrorism and Islam/Muslims, then the question arises as to whether this is directly responsible for rising Islamophobia. One theoretical perspective that may shed light on why fear of terrorism might generate anti-Muslim prejudice, is that offered by Terror Management Theory (TMT). Pyszcynski *et al.* (2003) argue that a fear of terrorism will motivate people to support their own culture and group and to become more hostile to those who are different (see also Greenberg *et al.*, 2001). This is because fear of terrorism is thought to activate and elevate an individual's underlying and inevitable fear of their own mortality, resulting in a defensive tendency toward hostility to outgroup members, in order to bolster self-esteem and confirm one's own world-view (see McGregor *et al.*, 1998; Pyszczynski *et al.*, 2003; Yum and Schenk-Hamlin, 2005). To run with this line of thinking, if Islam and Muslims are associated with terrorism in the eyes of the general public in Western nations (largely as a result of media representations), then TMT would predict increasing prejudice toward Muslims because of the desire to rally to the defence of national security and culture in the face of a terrorist threat that, psychologically, is likely to raise mortality salience. TMT remains controversial within social psychology, despite the fact that there is quite compelling evidence from laboratory experiments that shows how manipulating mortality salience appears to have clear effects on social identity and the perception of outgroups in a way in which TMT theorists have speculated it should (see, e.g., Castano, 2004).

I would like to propose that some of the key effects predicted by TMT can be subsumed within a broader, more flexible theoretical model which I will outline in this chapter. Although TMT offers insight into the role of fear of death in driving intergroup conflict and prejudice, it tends to rely on pseudo-psychodynamic theorizing. However, the findings of TMT can be reinterpreted within an IPT framework that instead proposes that mortality salience induces threat reduction behaviors due to the challenges it poses to identity principles and especially continuity. With the explanation of Islamophobia in mind, the notion that the fear of terrorism acts as a catalyst to this prejudice is one that has much merit. Fear of terrorism, when broken into its constituent elements, can be associated with: fear for one's personal safety and security; fear of damage to property; fear of harm to significant others, including other ingroup members; fear of harm to the infrastructure of the nation. Additionally, terrorism can be perceived to threaten one's world-view or the world-view of a valued social group (such as the nation) and to impact on one's ability to engage in day-to-day activities such as use public transport. While this is quite a varied list, IPT is well equipped as a model to make sense of it. What makes fear of terrorism psychologically potent is how it seems to threaten the entire gamut of identity principles contained in the original version of the model (Breakwell, 1986), as illustrated in Table 12.1. In

Table 12.1. Identity principles potentially threatened by fear of terrorism

	Identity principles threatened			
Fear component	Continuity	Self-esteem	Self-efficacy	Distinctiveness
Death/injury	✓	✓		
Damage to property	✓		✓	
World-view threat	✓	✓		✓
Impact on activities	✓		✓	

the table I speculate which identity principles are primarily threatened by each component of fear of terrorism and though it is possible to debate the assignment of these to specific principles, the take home message is that they all seem to be under threat. Furthermore, what crystallizes and perhaps exacerbates the psychological damage done by fear of terrorism here is that it appears to threaten the identity principles *at multiple levels*, as suggested above. So, for example, while personal safety threatens one's personal identity largely via a threat to continuity, at the same time perceived threats to world-view (e.g. the perception that terrorists wish to overthrow societal norms, values and cultural practices) threatens identity at both the individual and collective levels, since on the one hand it challenges attitudes and beliefs perceived as personal, but on the other it may also be perceived to challenge beliefs and practices perceived to be associated with groups (e.g. national culture).

Intergroup threats and social identity

Terror Management Theory is not the only perspective which has been deployed to make sense of public reactions to Muslims. Intergroup Threat Theory (Stephan *et al.*, 2008) also offers a possible window into understanding the antecedents of Islamophobia. ITT adopts a social-psychological approach to threat which argues that whether or not threats have any basis in reality, the perception of threat in and of itself has consequences at both the intergroup and intraindividual levels. The theory posits that there are two basic types of threat, both of which revolve around the potential harm that an outgroup could inflict on the ingroup. Realistic threats are posed by factors which could cause the ingroup physical harm or loss of resources, and can also be represented as individual-level threats causing potential physical or material harm to individual group members as a result of their membership. Symbolic threats represent threats to the meaning system(s) of the ingroup, such as challenges to valued ingroup norms and values, and at the individual level of analysis may be associated with loss of face, challenges to self-identity and potential threats to self-esteem. As outlined above, the prevailing social representations of terrorism, Islam and Muslims in the UK appear to construe Muslims as an intergroup threat to British non-Muslims on both realistic (e.g. the physical threat of harm from terrorism) and symbolic (e.g. the threat to national culture and belief systems) dimensions (Jaspal and Cinnirella, 2010). As such, ITT would predict negative stereotyping and hostility toward Muslims, especially since the potential threat perceived to come from Muslims is likely to be perceived as both a personal one (e.g. terrorism poses a threat to personal safety) and a collective one (e.g. the perception that Muslims seek to change established belief systems and cultural practices).

ITT as a theory is primarily concerned with predicting and understanding intergroup conflict and prejudice – as such, it shares something with Social Identity Theory (Tajfel and Turner, 1986), which outlines how the basic human drives for positive self-esteem and uncertainty reduction lead to ingroup bias and in some circumstances intergroup conflict. Both SIT and ITT are compatible in that they both predict that group members (e.g. in our case non-Muslim British citizens) will respond negatively to perceived threat to the group (i.e. to the UK). SIT research has established that strength of social identity moderates response to threat, such that high identifiers are most likely to respond with hostility and prejudice directed at the perceived source of the threat (see Branscombe et al., 1999). Ultimately, both ITT and SIT would predict that if Muslims and Islam are perceived to threaten the British nation, then those non-Muslims who identify strongly as British are likely to respond with Islamophobic prejudice. ITT's contribution above that of SIT is in its more nuanced approach to elucidating the role of different kinds of perceived threat. However, where both theories lack detail is in relation to the role of the self and motivation. In contrast, Identity Process Theory speaks clearly to these issues with its focus on the role of identity principles and how individuals will respond to threats to these principles by seeking to remove the threat or develop a coping mechanism for dealing with it. Thus we argue that a hybrid amalgamation of Social Representations Theory, Intergroup Threat Theory, Social Identity Theory and Identity Process Theory has the advantage of providing a theory of Islamophobia which focuses not just on its antecedents in intergroup relations, but also provides a window on its genesis in media social representations and its significance for self and

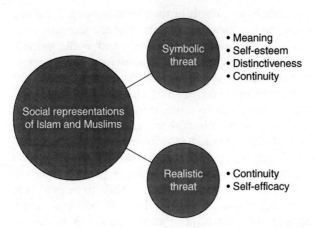

Figure 12.1. Combining ITT and IPT: the identity principles threatened by media social representations of Islam and Muslims

identity. This hybrid theory has at its core the delineation of which identity principles are perceived to be under threat from Islamophobia and what is acting to form an association between Muslims, Islam and these threats. In Table 12.1 I outlined how different elements of fear of terrorism threaten a range of identity principles. Figure 12.1 considers the Intergroup Threat Theory perspective and explores the two main forms of threat in that model and how, in the case of Islamophobia, each seems to threaten certain identity principles.

Jaspal and Cinnirella (2010) argued that British media representations serve to portray Muslims and Islam as a "hybrid" threat to national identity, in both symbolic and realistic terms. This is illustrated in Figure 12.1, which also goes on to postulate which IPT identity principles are likely to be threatened by each kind of threat in this case. In the case of symbolic threat, the media have positioned Islam and Muslims as often wanting to challenge majority British values and traditions. This is a direct challenge to continuity, since it suggests a desire to revise norms, values and traditions. At the same time it challenges the validity of these, thus challenging self-esteem and the degree to which they can be used as a means of being positively distinctive (Tajfel and Turner, 1986) from others. Finally, because it suggests that British traditions and values are incorrect and in need of revision, it acts as a threat to meaning, an identity principle which refers to the need to find significance and purpose in one's life, which was added to IPT by Vignoles and colleagues (Vignoles et al., 2002).

The realistic threat associated with Islam and Muslims, as described in media social representations, is a threat to the nation's infrastructure (e.g. terrorist threats to transport networks), as well as a threat to national security and the safety of citizens. These realistic threats therefore threaten identity principles of continuity (especially linked to perceived threat of death/physical harm) and self-efficacy (especially linked to threats to infrastructure, which in turn reduce the self-efficacy of British citizens). This kind of realistic threat – a threat to national infrastructure and to personal safety – has not been directly addressed in most previous studies of threat and its effects on social identity and prejudice. Instead, some ITT theorists have defined realistic threat more in line with Realistic Conflict Theory (Sherif et al., 1961) and its focus on economic threat over scarce resources. I feel that this misses the point about fear of terrorism and prevailing media social representations of Muslims and Islam – Muslims are not positioned as economic threats by these representations. Thus, as I outline elsewhere (Cinnirella, 2011), while some previous research on anti-Muslim prejudice has found symbolic threat to be a more important predictor of Islamophobia than perceived realistic threat (e.g. González et al., 2008; Hitlan et al., 2007), this may well be because such studies have operationalized realistic threat as economic threat (typically competition for jobs), rather than as the kind of infrastructure and personal safety threat outlined here.

Putting it all together: a new hybrid model of Islamophobic prejudice

The major thrust of my argument in this chapter is that Islamophobic prejudice has sufficient unique properties to challenge the usefulness of any single theoretical perspective and as a consequence I argue that an eclectic combination of IPT, ITT, SIT and SRT is needed. In the preceding sections I have outlined the separate components of this approach and this leaves the task of combining these into a coherent model. This is what I attempt to achieve in Figure 12.2, which represents graphically my proposed new approach, labeled the Identity and Representations Model (IRM). In Figure 12.2 we have as a starting point the media social representations of Islam and Muslims. These social representations, anchored into older ones about Islam and about conflict/war, serve as a backdrop for individual and group constructions of attitudes and stereotypes, though as discussed above, they can be contested and rejected. These media representations, to use the typology offered by Intergroup Threat Theory, position Islam and Muslims as a hybrid threat of both a symbolic and realistic nature (Jaspal and Cinnirella, 2010). Additionally,

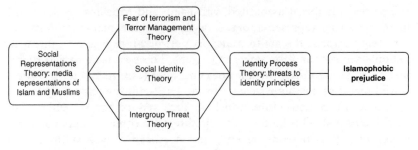

Figure 12.2. The Identity and Representations Model (IRM) of Islamophobia

since media representations of Muslims often include themes of terrorism and security, fear of terrorism and terror management become relevant. Social Identity Theory brings with it the extra nuance that perceived threats to the nation will act to increase Islamophobic prejudice especially when national identity is salient, and particularly in individuals who have a strong sense of national identity. Thus, the degree to which these media representations trigger collective response in defence of national identity is partly dependent on the importance of that identity in an individual's identity repertoire. One can also think of these predictions from SIT as a defense of the identity principles of self-esteem and self-efficacy – SIT (Tajfel and Turner, 1986) stresses positive distinctiveness and its maintenance (driven by a desire for positive self-esteem) along with the motive of making the world more predictable (so-called "uncertainty reduction"), which appears to be serving the self-efficacy principle.

The contribution of the new model is primarily in (1) bridging these theoretical perspectives and exploring their convergence in relation to Islamophobia; and (2) in considering how ITT, SIT, TMT and SRT can be used in the case of Islamophobia to predict threats to the identity principles defined by IPT. Thus, I argue that all of these theories, in their contribution to the understanding of Islamophobia, can be re-conceptualized as outlining a set of threats to identity principles and individual and group responses to these threats. In applying an IPT framework to these disparate theories, a degree of coherence and clarity is offered as well as epistemological simplicity. IPT also offers the advantage of allowing both an individual and intergroup level of analysis. Thus, the threats to the identity principles caused by media representations of Muslims and Islam could be responded to collectively at an intergroup level, by means of shared prejudice and stereotypes, and collective action such as discrimination. However, it is possible to consider also the individual perceiver as a focus, something which social psychology is uniquely placed to do, and evidence of how psychology has a unique contribution to make to the issue at hand, above and beyond that made by sociology. At this level, individuals could respond to threatened identity by adjusting the salience of British national identity in their identity repertoires (e.g. in relation to perceived symbolic threats), or by denying the likelihood of terrorism having an impact on personal safety or national infrastructure. These personal coping mechanisms, which we might call *identity readjustment* and *denial*, might thus prevent the endorsement by an individual of Islamophobic prejudice. However, the prevailing backdrop of social representations would potentially limit an individual's range of coping mechanisms, and perceived group norms might also impact on the chosen coping mechanisms – for example, if it is perceived as normative for non-Muslim Britons to be Islamophobic, then this puts normative pressure on individuals high in British national identity. Furthermore, insofar as media social representations of Muslims present them as a hybrid threat, and one which therefore threatens multiple identity principles, it seems likely that acceptance of these social representations will lead to Islamophobic prejudice since any single coping strategy that might otherwise avoid prejudice is unlikely to protect all principles against attack.

The IRM is not a fully fleshed-out model as yet – it represents the skeleton only of a new hybrid approach that seeks to bridge a range of existing theories and link them to Identity Process Theory via the concept of Islamophobia being driven by a response to the perception of threatened identity principles. IRM is a framework for linking these models together – it is not meant to replace any of its constituent models, and as such it is not offered here as an alternative to these models. Instead, it is forwarded as a way of synthesizing the predictions of the component models into a coherent set of ideas about the antecedents of Islamophobia, though the model may have value beyond the current target prejudice. The IRM model has IPT at its heart since it involves a reformulation of ITT, SIT, TMT and SRT, focusing on the degree to which the predictions of these other frameworks can be reconstituted as predictions about the role of threatened identity principles.

An empirical study

In order to start to explore the IRM and its utility for understanding Islamophobia in the UK I will briefly discuss an exploratory empirical study which will illustrate, explore and expand some of the model's assumptions.

A survey of young British people

The study was a survey of 196 young British people (aged 16–24 years) living in South-East England conducted in 2008 (Cinnirella and Blackwell, 2009). Amongst the measures taken in this study were Likert attitude scales capturing British identity, Islamophobia and perceived personal and collective threats linked to terrorism (all measures developed in-house). Our data suggested that Muslims were perceived significantly more negatively ($p < .001$) than comparison target groups we included (such as the over-seventies and lesbian/gay) and were associated with negative traits such as disgust and anger more than the other groups we asked about. These findings convinced us that there was evidence of Islamophobia in our sample.

In the study we measured fear of terrorism both in terms of its perceived threat to the individual participant's safety (and thus as a "realistic threat" in the language of ITT) and as a perceived collective threat to the nation as a whole (again as a realistic threat to national infrastructure). We found that personal fear of terrorism was predictive of negative stereotyping of Muslims (such as labeling them with the trait "disgust") and of overall prejudice toward Muslims ($r = .351$, $p < .001$, N = 181). Collective threat posed by terrorism was also correlated with negative stereotyping of Muslims and with our overall scale of prejudice toward Muslims ($r = .408$, $p < 0.01$, N = 181). Are there any practical implications of this relationship between fear of terrorism and Islamophobic prejudice? Two of our additional scales shed light on this – we measured desire for future contact with people of a Muslim faith and support for immigration and policing policies that would target Muslims in Britain and reduce their civil liberties (e.g. phone tapping). In both cases, fear associated with perceived threat (personal and collective) was a significant predictor: the higher the levels of fear of terrorism, the lower the reported desire to have contact with Muslims (for personal fear, $r = .215$, $p = .003$, for collective fear, $r = .279$, $p < .001$, N = 192 for both) and the higher the support for policies targeting Muslims (for personal fear, $r = .261$, $p < .001$, for collective fear, $r = .539$, $p < .001$, N = 193 for both; see Cinnirella and Blackwell, 2009, for further detail). Thus realistic threat posed by terrorism (at both personal and collective levels) appeared to be predictive of current prejudice toward Muslims, future contact intentions and support for new policies that would target Muslims. As we operationalized it for the purposes of this study (in terms of personal safety and threat to national infrastructure), we focused mainly on fear of terrorism as a realistic threat in the ITT sense. In terms of IPT and as indicated in Figure 12.1, this represents a threat mainly to the identity principles of self-efficacy (e.g. via restrictions to travel) and continuity (through the threat of death or injury). That the degree of realistic threat perceived correlated with contact intentions suggests an avoidance coping strategy in the face of the threat, which makes sense if continuity is to be retained and Muslims are perceived as potential terrorists. Furthermore, the correlation between fear and support for policies targeting Muslims also makes sense from the point of view of coping mechanisms, since this could be perceived to be a mechanism for reducing the terrorist threat but also for gaining self-efficacy via control over Muslims (of course, at the cost of Muslims' self-efficacy).

We also measured perceived symbolic threats posed by Muslims, asking, for example, if participants felt that Muslims wanted to oppose and replace majority British cultural practices with Islamic ones. This scale correlated with all our measures of attitudes toward Muslims: as perceived symbolic threat increased, so overall attitudes toward Muslims became more negative ($r = .408$, $p < .001$, N = 181), desire for contact with Muslims reduced ($r = .279$, $p < .001$, N = 192) and support for policies targeting Muslims increased ($r = .316$, $p < .001$, N = 193). Multiple regression analyses suggested that in fact symbolic threat was a stronger predictor of our measures of Islamophobia than realistic threat and that strength of British national identity was also an important predictor of Islamophobia, with the latter increasing with increasing levels of British national identity. These findings suggest that national identity remains an important moderator of perceived threats to the nation posed by Muslims and by terrorism. One interesting possibility that we would like to explore in the future, is whether strength and salience of a relevant social identity affect the degree to which threats to identity principles are perceived by individuals to exist at personal and collective levels. We would predict that with stronger social identity, then (relevant) threats are more likely to be perceived at both personal and collective levels (i.e. threatening both the individual and his or her group). Additionally, the finding that the perception of symbolic threats was the most important predictor of Islamophobia may be indicative of how these threats challenge more of the identity principles than realistic threats (see Figure 12.1). Both of these assumptions require further empirical investigation and tackle head-on the interface between SIT, ITT and IPT that lies at the heart of our new perspective, the Identity and Representations Model of Islamophobia.

Conclusion

The IRM represents an attempt to synthesize predictions and observations from a number of separate theories within social psychology, with a specific aim of understanding the antecedents of Islamophobic prejudice. While the IRM is proposed as a framework for understanding anti-Muslim prejudice within the UK context, it is likely to be applicable more broadly to Islamophobia across the Western world and perhaps beyond this to other prejudices. I would argue it is particularly germane to prejudices where there is a strong element of fear and where social representations of the target group in the mass media are predominantly negative. For example, it should be possible to extend the model and apply it to prejudice against asylum seekers and illegal immigrants.

Methodologically, the IRM requires a synthesis of quantitative and qualitative approaches if its promise is to be fully realized. In the IRM, media representations form a key backdrop for group and individual beliefs about the target group and I would argue qualitative approaches such as thematic analysis and discourse analysis are best suited to the study of this element of the model. Both qualitative (e.g. interviews, focus groups) and quantitative (e.g. surveys, experiments) methods could be deployed to explore the role of fear of terrorism, media exposure and perceived threats to identity principles, as well as establish the importance of realistic and symbolic threats. The challenge, of course, is in the effective triangulation of findings from these varied methodologies, some of which draw upon quite different epistemological antecedents. However, I believe there is no *a-priori* reason why such methodological and indeed epistemological pluralism should be avoided and in my view the potential rewards offered to the researcher outweigh the challenges. In my previous work on the interplay between national and European identity (e.g. Cinnirella, 1997; Cinnirella and Hamilton, 2007) I have forwarded similar arguments about the need for methodological pluralism and in that area of social psychology it is now more or less accepted that both qualitative and quantitative approaches offer important and unique insights, albeit with some researchers seeking to establish their preferred epistemological and methodological approaches as preferable.

As it stands, the IRM is only in embryonic form. However I intend to expand and develop it within a program of empirical research on Islamophobic prejudice and its antecedents. In this chapter I hope to have demonstrated that IPT offers a promising way of synthesizing the contribution of other perspectives by using the concept of threats to identity principles as an integrating construct. There is no reason why IRM should be limited to a focus on the antecedents of prejudice – by specifying in greater detail the specific nature of identity threats posed by Islamophobia and associated social representations, there may be hope in time to design innovative new prejudice reduction interventions informed by the IRM. This would be in keeping with the broad scope of Identity Process Theory, which the IRM demonstrates has much to offer the social psychology of prejudice.

REFERENCES

Abrams, D., and Houston, D. M. (2006). *Equality, diversity and prejudice in Britain: results from the 2005 national survey.* Centre for the Study of Group Process, University of Kent.

Allen, C., and Nielsen, J. S. (2002). *Summary report on Islamophobia in the EU after 11 September 2001.* Vienna, Austria: European Monitoring Centre on Racism and Xenophobia.

Ansari, H. (2004). *The Infidel within: the history of Muslims in Britain, 1800 to the present.* London: Hurst.

Branscombe, N. R., Ellemers, N., Spears, R., and Doosje, B. (1999). The context and content of social identity threat. In N. Ellemers, R. Spears and B. Doosje (eds.), *Social identity: context, commitment, content* (pp. 35–58). Oxford: Blackwell Science.

Breakwell, G. M. (1986). *Coping with threatened identities.* London: Routledge.

Breakwell, G. M. (2001). Social representational constraints upon identity processes. In K. Deaux and G. Philogène (eds.), *Representations of the social: bridging theoretical traditions* (pp. 271–284). Oxford: Blackwell.

Castano, E. (2004). In case of death, cling to the ingroup. *European Journal of Social Psychology,* 34, 1–10.

Cinnirella, M. (1997). Towards a European identity? Interactions between the national and European social identities manifested by university students in Britain and Italy. *British Journal of Social Psychology,* 36(1), 19–31.

Cinnirella, M. (2011). Think 'Terrorist', think 'Muslim'? Social-psychological mechanisms explaining anti-Islamic prejudice amongst young people in the U.K. In M. Helbling (ed.), *Islamophobia in the West* (pp. 179–189). London: Routledge.

Cinnirella, M., and Blackwell, C. (2009). The effect of national identity and threat on Attitudes towards British Muslims. Presented at the British Psychological Society Annual Conference, Brighton, UK, April 2009.

Cinnirella, M., and Hamilton, S. (2007). Are all Britons reluctant Europeans? Exploring European identity and attitudes to Europe amongst British citizens of South Asian ethnicity. *Ethnic and Racial Studies,* 30(3), 481–501.

Crowson, H., DeBacker, T., and Thoma, S. (2006). The role of authoritarianism, perceived threat and need for closure or structure in predicting post-9/11 attitudes and beliefs. *Journal of Social Psychology,* 146(6), 733–750.

Dixon, J. A., and Durrheim, K. (2003). Contact and the ecology of racial division: some varieties of informal segregation. *British Journal of Social Psychology,* 42: 1–23.

Doise, W. (1986). *Levels of explanation in social psychology.* Cambridge University Press.

Gerbner, G., Gross, L., Morgan, M., and Signorielli, N. (2002). Growing up with television: the cultivation perspective. In M. Morgan (ed.), *Against the mainstream: the selected works of George Gerbner* (pp. 193–213). New York: Peter Lang.

González, K.,Verkuyten, M.,Weesie, J., and Poppe, E. (2008). Prejudice towards Muslims in the Netherlands: testing integrated threat theory. *British Journal of Social Psychology*, 47(4), 667–685.

Greenberg, J., Schimel, J., Martens, A., Solomon, S., and Pyszcynski, T. (2001). Sympathy for the devil: evidence that reminding whites of their own morality promotes more favorable reactions to white racists. *Motivation and Emotion*, 25: 113–133.

Hitlan, R., Carrillo, K., Aikman, S. N., and Zárate, M. A. (2007). Attitudes toward immigrant groups and the September 11 terrorist attacks. *Peace and Conflict Studies*, 13(2), 135–152.

Islamic Human Rights Commission (2004). *Social discrimination: across the Muslim divide*. London: Islamic Human Rights Commission.

Jaspal, R. (2013). British Sikh identity and the struggle for distinctiveness and continuity. *Journal of Community and Applied Social Psychology*, 23(3), 225–239.

Jaspal, R., and Cinnirella, M. (2010). Media representations of British Muslims and hybridised threats to identity. *Contemporary Islam: Dynamics of Muslim Life*, 4(3), 289–310.

McCombs, M. (2004). *Setting the agenda: the mass media and public opinion*. Malden, MA: Blackwell.

McGregor, H. A., Lieberman, J. D., Greenberg, J., Solomon, S., Arndt, J., Simon, L., and Pyszcynski, T. (1998). Terror management and aggression: evidence that mortality salience promotes aggression against worldview threatening others. *Journal of Personality and Social Psychology*, 74: 590–605.

Moore, K., Mason, P., and Lewis, J. (2008). *Images of Islam in the UK: the representation of British Muslims in the national print news media 2000–2008*. Cardiff School of Journalism, Media and Cultural Studies.

Moscovici, S. (1981). On social representations. In J. P. Forgas (ed.), *Social cognition: perspectives on everyday understanding* (pp. 181–209). London: Academic Press.

Park, J., Felix, K., and Lee, G. (2007). Implicit attitudes towards arab-muslims and the moderating effects of social information. *Basic and Applied Social Psychology*, 29(1), 35–45.

Poole, E. (2002). *Reporting Islam*. London: Tauris.

Poole, E. (2006). The effects of September 11 and the war in Iraq on British newspaper coverage. In E. Poole and J. E. Richardson (eds.), *Muslims in the news media* (pp. 89–102). London: I. B. Tauris.

Pyszcynski, T., Solomon, S., and Greenberg, J. (2003). *In the Wake of 9/11: the psychology of terror*. Washington, DC: American Psychological Association.

Sheridan, L. P. (2006). Islamophobia pre and post September 11th 2001. *Journal of Interpersonal Violence*, 21(3), 317–336.

Sheridan, L. P., and Gillet, R. (2005). Major world events and discrimination. *Asian Journal of Social Psychology*, 8: 191–197.

Sherif, M., Harvey, O. J., White, B. J., Hood, W. R., and Sherif, C.W. (1961). *Intergroup cooperation and competition: the robbers cave experiment*. Norman, OK: University Book Exchange.

Smuts, D., and Westcott, S. (eds.) (1991). *The purple shall govern: a South African A to Z of nonviolent action*. Cape Town: Oxford University Press.

Stephan, W. G., Ybarra, O., and Morrison, R. K. (2008). Intergroup threat theory. In T. Nelson (ed.), *Handbook of prejudice* (pp. 43–60). Mahwah, NJ: Lawrence Erlbaum.

Tajfel, H., and Turner, J. C. (1986). The social identity theory of intergroup behavior. In S. Worchel and W. G. Austin (eds.), *Psychology of intergroup relations* (pp. 7–17). Chicago, IL: Nelson-Hall.

Vignoles, V. L., Chryssochoou, X., and Breakwell, G. M. (2002). Evaluating models of identity motivation: self-esteem is not the whole story. *Self and Identity*, 1, 201–218.

Wetherell, M. (1998). Positioning and interpreting repertoires: conversation analysis and post -structuralism. *Discourse & Society*, 9(3), 387–412.

Yum, Y., and Schenck-Hamlin, W. (2005). Reactions to 9/11 as a function of terror management and perspective taking. *Journal of Social Psychology*, 145(3), 265–286.

13 Places, identities and geopolitical change: exploring the strengths and limits of Identity Process Theory

John Dixon, Kevin Durrheim and Andrés Di Masso

One field to which Identity Process Theory (IPT) has contributed is environmental psychology. Specifically, the theory has enriched our understanding of the nature of person–place bonds, extending theoretical and empirical work on place identity. In the first section of this chapter, we outline IPT research on human–environment relationships, focusing on its relevance for understanding how we evaluate and respond to events of environmental change. We compare this theory with some related perspectives and suggest that its holistic, integrative orientation has enhanced existing knowledge. In the second section of the chapter, drawing on work conducted during South Africa's transition to democracy, we develop this argument by discussing the nature and consequences of "white" resistance to racial desegregation in post-apartheid society. Broadly in line with IPT, we demonstrate how events of desegregation may be associated with threats to identity distinctiveness, continuity, coherence and belonging and thus entail attempts to re-establish intergroup distances and boundaries. We also argue, however, that the dynamics of desegregation (and re-segregation) entail geopolitical processes that have been underspecified by IPT research on human–environment relations. First, they require us to reconceive identity threat as a discursively constructed, contested, strategic and ideological process. Second, they require us to reconnect the study of behavioral responses to environmental change with wider structural relations of intergroup dominance, inequality and political resistance.

Places, identities and social change

Environmental psychological research

The interconnection between places, identities and social change has featured extensively in research on place identity, much of which has been conducted within the sub-discipline of environmental psychology (e.g. see Lalli, 1992; Dixon and Durrheim, 2000). In Proshansky *et al.*'s

(1983) formulation, "place identity" designated the psychological processes through which elements of our everyday physical environments
become integrated within the fabric of the self, forming a subcomponent
of personal identity. Employing an evocative if somewhat nebulous characterization, they described such elements as comprising a "pot-pourri of
memories, conceptions, interpretations, ideas and related feelings about
specific physical settings as well as types of settings" (1983, p. 60).

Though seminal, Proshansky et al.'s work was criticized for being
somewhat vague in its conception of place identity. Adopting a narrower
definition, Korpela conceptualized place identity as an organized set of
"cognitions of those physical settings and parts of the physical environment, in or with which an individual – consciously or unconsciously –
regulates his experience of maintaining his sense of self" (1989, p. 245).
By emphasizing practices of environmental self-regulation, Korpela highlighted how individuals actively appropriate places – especially "restorative" places – as part of an on-going process of sustaining a sense of
self-efficacy (e.g. Korpela, 1989; Korpela and Hartig, 1996). Along similar lines, Sarbin (1983) posited that the organizing principle that links
self to place is "emplotment": the production of a coherent narrative
about "who I am." This process is based around the stories that we tell
about place. By relating where we are from, where we are now or where
we are going, Sarbin proposed, we are able to fashion a cohesive sense of
self, to give meaning and value to our identities.

Although not systematically developed, the idea that individuals' reactions to environmental change are shaped by place-identity processes is
also present in the work of Korpela, Sarbin and Proshansky. After all,
if change reduces the capacity of places to serve as arenas of self-efficacy (Korpela) or if it threatens the coherence of valued narratives of
the self (Sarbin), then it may prompt individual and collective resistance. Proshansky et al. (1983, p. 70) made this point explicitly by highlighting the "mediating change" function of place identity. They argued
that emerging "discrepancies between a person's place identity and the
characteristics of an immediate physical setting arouse relevant and
interrelated cognitions in the individual for reducing if not eliminating
those discrepancies." In other words, they proposed that place identity
enables individuals not only to recognize self-place incongruities (e.g.
resulting from environmental change), but also to resolve such incongruities by, for example, modifying their physical environments (e.g. "I will
hang a picture on the wall"), controlling others' place-related behaviors
(e.g. "I'll put a no-trespass sign at the entrance of my house") or altering their spatial behavior (e.g. "I'll avoid that street-corner because it
frightens me").

Of course, we need to acknowledge here that the impact of environmental change on identity processes was highlighted earlier by Fried (1963), whose classic study inspired later research on the consequences of human *displacement* (e.g. see Dixon and Durrheim, 2004; Fullilove, 1996). Fried's study revealed how the forced removal of residents from Boston's West End – under the auspices of an urban renewal project – provoked a sense of loss so profound, so troubling, that it resembled a form of grief (something akin to a "death in the family"). According to Fried and his colleagues, this case study also revealed the psychological significance of "spatial identity" (see also Giuliani and Feldman, 1993; Fried, 2000): an emotionally charged interconnection between self and place. Although this form of identity often remains tacit in the course of our everyday lives, being only dimly recognized, Fried argued that its influence becomes evident under conditions of sudden environmental change. Loss of place invokes strong reactions precisely because it entails loss of self (e.g. Timotijevic and Breakwell, 2000). It is thus associated with feelings of disorientation, discontinuity and nostalgia for a lost environment; and ultimately, it may even alienate us from a place that has been deprived of its original significance to self.

Identity Process Theory and person–place relationships

The work sketched above barely introduces the complex interrelations between places, identities and social change as formulated within environmental psychology (see also, for relevant examples, the work of Devine-Wright, 2009; Gustafson, 2001; Manzo, 2003). The main value of Identity Process Theory, we shall now suggest, derives from its capacity to provide an *integrative* framework for understanding such interrelations. The basic propositions of IPT have been elaborated in other chapters of this book (see Jaspal, this volume). We focus on its implications for explaining individual and collective reactions to environmental transformation.

To begin with, we note that IPT is one of the few social psychological theories to acknowledge how material environments facilitate identity construction. Whereas other theoretical traditions have typically disregarded the so-called "spatial dimension" of social life (Dixon, 2001), IPT proponents have consistently acknowledged its role in defining our sense of who we are (e.g. Breakwell, 1983; Bonaiuto *et al.*, 1996; Twigger-Ross *et al.*, 2003). That is to say, they have recognized how the characteristics that define identity *content* (e.g. social roles, traits, attributes) and *values* (e.g. pride, shame, distinctiveness) are derived, at least in part, from our relationships to material environments – the places we inhabit, imagine, appropriate and make central to self.

More than this, extending its general perspective on identity threat, IPT has systematized the motivational principles that govern person–place relationships, unifying an array of evidence within a common framework. Specifically, the theory has posited that person–place relations facilitate identity construction via the maintenance of the following.

1. *Distinctiveness*: This refers to our sense of personal uniqueness as well as to our social differentiation from members of other groups – both of which derive partly from our self-in-place relationships. Distinctiveness may be accomplished, for example, via the "territorial personaliza-tion" of local environments. In their seminal study, Greenbaum and Greenbaum (1981) found that Slavic American residents decorated the exteriors of their households in order to express their ethnic iden-tity. They also found that this process was less pronounced amongst renters than amongst home owners – individuals who were presum-ably more thoroughly "grounded" in the neighborhood.

2. *Belonging*: This refers to our sense of being known and accepted by others, a process sustained through relations of spatial inclusion and exclusion. By embedding ourselves within a particular place, for instance, we are able to create what Rowles (1983) once described as a sense of "insideness" – a comforting familiarity with our surround-ings (*autobiographic insideness*) as well as a sense of being known and accepted by others (*social insideness*). Likewise, through this form of place identification, we come to know who or what does *not* belong, another theme that we shall develop later in the chapter.

3. *Esteem*: the motivational principles of distinctiveness and belong-ing are intimately linked to a further principle of identity formation, namely the maintenance of self-esteem. After all, the places in which we feel most "at home" and through which we express our differences from others also tend to sustain our self-worth. At an individual level, our homes may reflect not only who we are, but also how we want to be evaluated by others. At a collective level, communal sites serve as the veritable embodiment of group pride; and, for this reason, their *positive* distinctiveness is often vigorously promoted (e.g. see Bonaiuto *et al.*, 1996).

4. *Continuity*: the stability of person–place relations facilitates another form of identity construction, which is grounded in our sense of con-tinuity over time. Sometimes this sense is based around the perceived durability of our bonds with places that are personally meaningful (so-called *place-referent continuity*). Sometimes it is based around the

perceived durability of the relationship between our individual values and broader categories of place (so-called *place-congruent continuity*) (see Twigger Ross and Uzzell, 1996). Sometimes, too, it is based around our sense that certain "totemic" sites connect us powerfully to the "place traditions" of groups that define our identities, an idea elaborated in Jacobi and Stokol's (1983) strangely neglected chapter (though see Devine-Wright and Lyons, 1997).

5. *Self-efficacy*: Another relevant motivational principle is self-efficacy. As noted already, this principle features centrally in the work of Korpela and colleagues, amongst others (e.g. Gustafson, 2001), who have insisted that environments that enable our unfettered self-expression – either as individual agents or as group members – are typically valued highly. In such places, we can, quite literally, "be" ourselves. We can act in ways that promote the identity projects that express "who we are" and "what we are worth." For this reason, environmental changes that impede self-expression tend to be resisted.

The latter point introduces an additional contribution of IPT. As well as integrating varying processes that are fundamental to identity construction within a common perspective, the theory also shows how place identification shapes our reactions to environmental change. Precisely because such change undermines the capacity of places to act as arenas of self-distinctiveness, belonging, esteem, continuity and efficacy, it also potentially engenders identity threat. And when valued identities are threatened, as other chapters in this book detail, we typically engage in various "coping strategies" (Breakwell, 1983). We reinterpret environmental change so that its threat to identity is diminished; we engage in practices of geographical mobility, distancing ourselves from the source of threat; or we "compartmentalize" threats in order to insulate ourselves psychologically from events that would otherwise be difficult to reconcile with our identities. Likewise, at a collective level, environmental threat may instigate a variety of coping strategies, including a renegotiation of the meaning of group identity or a revision of group boundaries or membership.

A number of studies have used IPT to explore reactions to environmental threat. Bonaiuto *et al.* (1996) studied the influence of local and national identification on the perceived pollution of six British beaches, which had been defined as either "clean" or "not clean" according to European Union standards. They found that respondents who identified more strongly with their home towns tended to view local beaches as less polluted than those who identified less strongly. Correspondingly, respondents who identified more strongly at the national level (as British) tended to view both nation-wide and local beaches as less polluted. The authors concluded that place assessments were informed by a principle of positive self-distinctiveness. By mitigating negative place evaluations, respondents were able to protect valued social identities.

Twigger-Ross and Uzzell (1996) analyzed responses to the development of London's Surrey Docks. Specifically, they showed how local residents' evaluations of their changing environment expressed the identity principles of distinctiveness, self-esteem, self-efficacy and continuity. For example, they found that residents strove to maintain "place congruent" and "place referent" continuity in the face of a radical transformation of their urban environment. They also found that residents' sense of attachment to their local environment shaped their spatial behavior, with more attachment being associated with greater reluctance to leave the area, even under conditions of high identity threat.

Similarly, Speller *et al.* (2002) investigated how residents interpreted a process of relocation from a historical mining town (old Arkwright) to a new settlement (new Arkwright). They focused on changes in two identity principles (continuity and distinctiveness) across five moments of a 6-year relocation process. Amongst other findings, their study documented how relocation dissolved the network of social bonds that had maintained community spirit and distinctiveness in Old Arkwright (see Speller, 2000). In New Arkwright, residents did not meet their former neighbors as often as they once did and knew less about their day-to-day lives. As such, some of them came to base their place identities around the principle of individual rather than communal distinctiveness (e.g. taking greater pride in their personal homes and gardens). Others reported negative experiences of detachment from place, with a corresponding loss of collective identity.

The consequences of place transformation for collective identity were also addressed by Matthews (1983) in a case study of environmental change broadly aligned with the principles of IPT. Investigating the consequences of urban development in a "Housing Action Area," she identified a troubling mismatch between planners' and residents' conceptions of the boundaries of the local community. Specifically, the external boundaries superimposed on the community by the official housing plan did not match residents' internal, subjective perceptions of community membership and territorial organization. People classed as outsiders by residents became insiders according to official criteria; conversely, people classed as insiders were symbolically excluded from community membership and associated decision-making. In short, by enforcing a particular socio-spatial conception of community, the proposed environmental changes threatened the very identity of the established community, notably their sense of collective distinctiveness, continuity and belonging.

The term "enforcing" is chosen deliberately here. Matthew's work sought to expose the role of *power relations* in shaping identity threat under conditions of environmental change. The Local Authority's power, she recognized, was expressed through the non-negotiability of their planning scheme. It was also expressed through strategic modifications of the formal minutes of negotiation meetings, which ultimately established the Local Authority's perspective as the "legitimate" perspective. Environmental change turned, in the final instance, on the power to determine whose version of community "counted."

We see this study as an important transition point toward the kind of perspective that we shall advocate in the rest of this chapter (see also Jaspal, 2011).[1] In the next section, we shall argue that research on the discursive and political practices through which human–environment relations are constructed represents a vitally important direction in which work on IPT must now be developed. We advance this argument by drawing examples from a program of research rooted in the shifting landscapes of post-apartheid South Africa.

"Dislocating identity": exploring white resistance to desegregation in South Africa

The policy of apartheid was officially instituted by the National Party of South Africa in the years following their rise to power in 1948. Although sometimes cast as an anomaly, it effectively extended forms of racial separation that had been introduced during earlier decades, indeed earlier centuries. As is common knowledge, the apartheid system established racial boundaries across varying scales of social life: from the global displacements of the homeland system to the mundane segregation of public parks, toilets, hospital wards and graveyards; from the residential divisions of the apartheid city, with its buffer zones and "natural" boundaries, to the segregation of spaces of leisure, pleasure and entertainment. The grim litany of maps, figures, images and other evidence presented in A. J. Christopher's (1994) "Atlas of Apartheid" records just how far the state was prepared to go in enforcing the ideal of "apartness."

Toward the end of the 1990s, this system of apartheid began to disintegrate. In just a few years, its legal foundations were abolished and the promise of a more integrated society beckoned. Around the same time,

---

[1] Although not focused specifically on environmental change, Jaspal's work is influenced by IPT and highlights the role of power relations in shaping intergroup relations.

the first and second authors of this chapter began a program of research designed to explore lay understandings of the social and political changes that marked the transition to the "new" South Africa. As an emerging theme, we focused on white resistance to desegregation, and, more specifically, on how this resistance was entwined with constructions of place and identity. In this section of our chapter, we draw illustrative material from two of our case studies. The first investigated white reactions to changing leisure relations in the port city of Durban (see Durrheim and Dixon, 2001). The second investigated white reactions to changing residential relations in the village of Hout Bay, located near the "mother city" of Cape Town (see Dixon et al., 1994, 1997). We invoke these case studies in the spirit of theoretical dialogue and exchange. Our aim is to explore – briefly, given our space constraints – how IPT both enriches and obscures our understanding of white resistance to desegregation in South Africa.

White constructions of the desegregation of Durban's beachfront

To an outside observer, it may seem curious that the desegregation of beaches became a focus of the struggle against apartheid. But it did. Under the banner "all God's beaches for all God's people," the Mass Democratic Movement organized a concerted campaign to open up South Africa's beaches to all citizens, regardless of racial classification (see Smuts and Westcott, 1991). Beaches became a site of bitter political protest and conflict between groups. Hence, when Durban's "golden mile"[2] (see Figure 13.1) became increasingly multiracial during the 1980s and early 1990s, many white holidaymakers expressed dismay, if not outrage. Durrheim and Dixon's (2001) analysis of over 400 newspaper reports and letters published in the *Natal Mercury* across that period explored the shifting nature of white reactions to this form of desegregation.

Extract 1
   On occasions during the past few years I have taken my little children to the beachfront paddling-pools and nearby beach and have always come away with a feeling of warmth and contentment. It was my misfortune to expect the same when I ventured there on January 2. We were revolted by the filth and stench around the paddling pool. Garbage was littered on the sidewalk and the water in the pool was brown. Some of the bathers using the pools were half naked, while

[2] This is a prime strip of Durban's beachfront that was reserved for whites during apartheid.

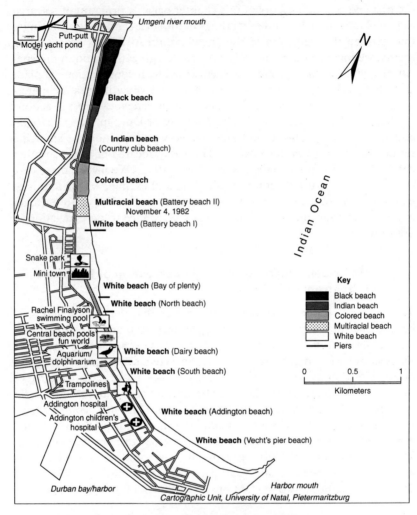

Figure 13.1. Beach apartheid in Durban, 1982

others were fully clothed ... Durban beachfront and the amenities it has to offer are forever lost to whites. *Never again will I take my family near the place.*

(Letter to editor, *Mercury*, January 1, 1986, p. 7; emphasis added)

Extract 2
Durban must hang its head in shame. We invite up-country visitors to enjoy the festive season on our fair (?) beaches [*sic*] and then subject them to the awful experience of being dominated and intimidated by hordes of largely undisciplined black people ... Looking back a few years, one asks what has happened to

the happy family groups that one used to see on our beaches. One certainly does not see such groups of white people on our multiracial beaches.

(D. Rose, letter to editor, *Mercury*, January 13, 1988, p. 10)

Extract 3

I spent New Year's Day on Durban's North Beach and found: (1) Massive over-crowding by blacks. Blacks have completely taken over this beach. (2) The masses of whites who previously flocked to it on holidays were conspicuous in their near total absence, suggesting that they cannot accept what is experienced ... (3) The litter on the beach, the promenade, paddling pools, the garden areas and sur-rounding streets was disgusting. I found rubbish bins empty, but litter strewn everywhere about ... One only need compare the position when whites used the beaches in great numbers. Was the same litter problem found? It wasn't. Most blacks discard rubbish wherever they are irrespective of the facilities provided as will be found wherever they gather in large numbers. (4) The bylaws might not have been written because blacks were camping in the beach area and vehicles nearby; they consumed liquor in the streets and *braais* [barbeques] had been set up on the pavements in the side and back streets to the annoyance of residents and pedestrians. (5) Combi-taxis were jam-packed everywhere and music blared from many. (6) I saw two black children defecating on the beach and their elders covered the mess with sand. And six black children and three black men urin-ating in public places without any regard for discretion (or it being unlawful). (7) One had a chicken tethered to a bush (I wasn't able to establish its fate). (8) Toilets were indescribably filthy due to being used by people illiterate in their use. That when a toilet couldn't take any more the floor was used ...

It would be folly for a woman and children to attend the beach by themselves in these circumstances; indeed a man's presence would hardly help for the arro-gance of many is such that in the event of an altercation it would be foolhardy to remonstrate. An elegant First World area has been transformed into a location by having the standards of the Third World foisted upon it.

(Letter to editor, *Mercury*, January 9, 1990, p. 6)

Desegregation is typically construed as a process that alters the relations between members of different social groups, allowing new forms of con-tact to occur. What extracts 1 to 3 illustrate, however, is that desegregation also entails a transformation of place, altering relations between people and their material environments (see also Dixon and Durrheim, 2004). From the perspective of IPT, these accounts might be read as an expres-sion of (place) identity threat following a process of dramatic environ-mental change, namely the transformation of Durban's beachfront from a "whites only" to a multiracial space. Certainly, their authors lament a loss of place distinctiveness (e.g. "An elegant First World area has been transformed into a location by having the standards of the Third World foisted upon it"), continuity (e.g. "The masses of whites who previously flocked to it on holidays were conspicuous in their near total absence") and belonging ("Durban beachfront and the amenities it has to offer are forever lost to whites"). They also complain that the beachfront's capacity to act as an environment of self-expression has been diminished. In extract 1, for example, a mother suggests that a "restorative" place of fascination and escape (Korpela and Hartig, 1996) has been destroyed: no longer can she and her children experience feelings of "warmth and contentment" there. Extract 2 notes that so-called "up-country visitors" are no longer free to enjoy Durban's "fair" beaches as a result of being "intimidated" by black holidaymakers, while extract 3 ends with the observation that: "it would be folly for a woman and children to attend the beach by themselves in these circumstances."

Under such conditions of (place) identity threat, one might expect individuals and social groups to engage in the kinds of "coping" mechanisms proposed by IPT. The most obvious response would be to avoid an environment that no longer acts as a site of identity; and, in point of fact, this is exactly what occurred in the case of Durban's beachfront during the 1990s and continues to occur to this day. As implied in all of the above accounts, a place that had formerly been a mecca for white tourists – particularly during the peak holiday season when many families made their annual pilgrimage to the coast – became a place to avoid at all costs. Many whites began to holiday "up the coast" in places further removed from KwaZulu-Natal's townships or to take advantage of time share resorts and other privatized spaces of leisure (Durrheim and Dixon, 2005). Moreover, even when they did share beaches with other racial groups, evidence suggests that whites behaved in ways that reproduced racial boundaries at a local scale (e.g. Dixon and Durrheim, 2000, 2004).

As this brief analysis suggests, IPT has the potential to clarify several of the social, psychological and environmental processes that underpinned Whites' resistance to beach desegregation in post-apartheid South Africa. Drawing on discursive and rhetorical psychology (Potter and Wetherell, 1987; Edwards, 2005; Billig, 1987), however, our own analysis of such processes has developed in a different direction, which we shall elaborate on in the rest of the chapter.

A first point of contrast concerns the epistemological status of accounts such as extracts 1 to 3. In general, IPT researchers have treated such accounts as expressions of inner motivations and cognitions, symptomatic of a drive to regulate identity threat in the face of environmental change. By contrast, we treat them as discursive practices designed to *construct* the meaning of changing people–environment relations. The use of the philosophical register of "constructionism" is not incidental here. Crucially, it entails a re-conceptualization of the very nature of place-identity threat. Rather than conceiving of threat as arising from a *perceived discrepancy* between external, objective transformations of place and interior, subjective processes of place identification, we conceive of it as an evaluation that is produced, reproduced and modified through everyday discursive practices (e.g. letter writing). From this perspective, place-identity threat is not so much something that is "perceived," "experienced" or "aroused" as something that is "created" as we jointly make sense of our self-in-place relationships within everyday discourse.

This brings us to a second point of contrast between IPT and our own perspective, which concerns the social and psychological functions of place-identity threat. For IPT researchers, identity threat entails a set of cognitive, affective and behavioral processes that serve to express a kind of "inner trauma" and to motivate behaviors that regulate that trauma in order to maintain identity. An alternative reading of accounts such as extracts 1 to 3 might proceed from a different set of questions about the nature of their social and psychological functions. What are the writers doing in their formulations of place-identity threat in these letters? What discursive and rhetorical goals are they seeking to accomplish and how are constructions of place and identity signaled as relevant to these goals? Above all, what are the broader social and political consequences of varying constructions of place-identity threat under conditions of environmental change?

These questions invite us to replace an "expressive" interpretation of extracts 1 to 3 with an interpretation that prioritizes their "action-orientation" (Edwards, 2005). On the one hand, we would argue that such accounts are designed to normalize particular place-identity relations. As we have elaborated elsewhere, they mobilize the assumption that Durban's beachfront should act, first of all, as a space of (white) family values, activities and norms, and, secondly, as a space of white tourism (Durrheim and Dixon, 2001). By invoking images of "little children" paddling (extract 1) and "happy family groups" (extract 2) and by complaining of the growing absence of "upcountry visitors," the writers are orienting to these normative versions of self-in-place relations. On the other hand, the extracts are designed to construct the presence and behavior of black beachgoers as an unwarranted threat to such relations – something, that is, quite literally, "out-of-place" on Durban's beachfront. The writer in extract 3 is expansive in this regard, presenting a six-point list of the changes through which an "Elegant First World area" has become a "Third World" location.

The latter example introduces a third point of contrast between our perspective and IPT. This concerns our emphasis on the wider geopolitical consequences of local constructions of place threat and the need to recognize their potential role within the "longer conversation of ideology" (Wetherell, 1998). We do not need to explain further, for example, how extracts 1 to 3 perpetuate an ideological system that has deep historical roots in South Africa, recycling the racial symbolism of pollution, danger, disorder and cultural hierarchy. More specifically, we would argue that such accounts instantiate a wider politics of resistance to desegregation during South Africa's transition to democracy, the vestiges of which linger in the post-apartheid era. Interestingly, the nature of this resistance shifted during the movement from the "old" to the "new" South Africa (see Durrheim and Dixon, 2001). In the early 1980s, as struggles to overthrow apartheid inspired organized beach "occupations," the presence of blacks on white beaches was challenged on the grounds it was politically motivated and out of kilter with the "fun-in-the-sun" ethos of beaches. By the late 1980s and early 1990s, when "in principle" resistance to desegregation was increasingly difficult to justify and de-facto desegregation was a material "reality," a new racialized discourse of manners came to dominate. As extract 3 illustrates, desegregation was increasingly challenged on the grounds that black people were incapable of behaving "properly" on formerly white beaches, that they violated dress codes or place norms about how to bathe or use amenities such as toilets, swimming pools and showers. In both cases – and this is our main point here – local constructions of place, identity and environmental change were implicated in broader ideological processes that sought to legitimate, or even naturalize, resistance to racial desegregation. To anticipate the argument in the rest of this chapter, we want to urge IPT researchers to become more attentive to such processes. Our second case study provides even more stark evidence for this idea.

White constructions of residential desegregation in Hout Bay, Cape Town

Like the Jim Crow Laws of the old American South, apartheid legislation became notorious throughout the world. The Group Areas Act, the Immorality Act and the Bantu Education Act, the excesses of "petty apartheid" (can I sit here?; can I queue there?; can I be buried in this grave?) – all these laws met with widespread condemnation. Yet one of the most destructive foundations of apartheid received comparatively limited attention: it was called the Prevention of Illegal Squatting Act. Instituted in 1951, it legalized the forced removal of millions of "non-white" South Africans over a 40-year period, creating a vast number of "surplus" people.

Toward the end of the 1980s, some of those people settled in the coastal village of Hout Bay, located approximately 20 km from Cape Town on the Cape Peninsula. They joined a growing local population

of "squatters" who lived in informal settlements dotted throughout
the town. By August 1989, the local media were reporting an expansion of this population. Estimates recorded some 2,000 homeless people
(Gawith and Sowman, 1992), the majority living at a beachfront site
called Princess Bush.

This expansion of the informal settlement in Hout Bay alarmed
many of the town's legal (white) residents, who called for government
intervention. The Hout Bay Property Rights Association (HPRA), an
anti-squatter action group, was formed to protect residents' interests.
A complicated series of negotiations unfolded between this association, government officials, a liaison group and various representatives
of the squatter communities. The main aim of the HPRA was to expel
squatters from Hout Bay or at least to curtail further influxes into
the town.

Throughout 1990, the HPRA thus pressurized the private owner of the
Princess Bush site to take legal action against squatters. By December of
that year, the courts duly granted an eviction order, and the Princess
Bush squatters were given until February 1991 to vacate the area. Intense
media coverage of events meant that mass removal of "squatters" became
a risky option for the government, particularly during the tense climate
of the transition (Saff, 1998). A local planning firm, MLH, was com-
missioned to survey possible relocation sites. They identified a hillside
on the outskirts of the town, located on a disused Regional Services for-
estry station. The site was officially designated an "Informal Settlement
Area" and most of the town's squatters were located there by April 1991,
in the face of vigorous opposition from local white residents. Originally
called Imizamo Yethu – meaning "through our collective efforts" – the
site became known locally as Mandela Park and is nowadays a thriving
community.

However brief and fragmented, we hope that we have provided sufficient contextual information for readers to begin to evaluate the kinds
of accounts discussed in the next section. Analysis of these varying constructions of the nature of "squatting" as an environmental "threat" in
Hout Bay again develops our exploration of IPT.

The rhetorically contested boundaries of "belonging"

In their manifesto, the HPRA proposed a simple distinction between the
(legitimate) property owners of Hout Bay and the (illegitimate) squatters – a distinction that differentiated insiders (those who *belonged* in
Hout Bay) from outsiders in (those who did *not belong*). This distinction proved difficult to sustain. Indeed, the establishment of Imizamo
Yethu was marked by a fierce struggle to define who belonged in the

village, a rhetorical and ideological "dilemma" (Billig *et al.*, 1988). A key moment in this struggle was a publication issued by MLH (1990), the architects and planners who managed Hout Bay's reorganization. Entitled "A Historical Perspective on the Homeless Families of Hout Bay," this document argued that the town's squatters were victims of apartheid who, far from being alien to the area, had local roots spanning several generations that preceded white settlement in the area.

Extract 4

The facts are that the "other than white" population has not only lived in the Hout Bay valley for considerably longer than the white population but has been gainfully employed. While there are certainly some unemployed people amongst the squatter community they are a minority and do not detract from the fact that the majority of the "other than white" residents have every bit as much right to live there as their more recently arrived white neighbours.

(MLH, 1990, p. 2)

Excerpts from the MLH paper were widely broadcast in local newspapers and aired on the local radio. By inverting the argument that squatters were invaders, it fueled the suspicion that racial privilege was the "real" problem in Hout Bay. The legacy of the Group Areas Act, which had enabled 48 percent of Hout Bay's population ("whites") to occupy 98 percent of the town's residential space, was cited as evidence of how apartheid had predetermined rights of access to land. Current residential patterns, it was pointed out, did not reflect the entitlements of the wider community of Hout Bay (MLH, 1990). In this case, the criteria for "belonging" were not based around individual property rights. Instead, they were based around the rights of an oppressed and indigenous group whose claims to land were as valid as "their more recently arrived white neighbours" (extract 4).

Although dismissed by some as government propaganda, the MLH paper was indicative of the ideological dilemma faced by those arguing that "squatters" had no place in Hout Bay. Any argument supporting the necessity of mass eviction risked summoning the counter-argument that such a policy was racially motivated. Within this ideological climate, the issue of *who truly belonged* in Hout Bay became paramount. An emerging rhetorical construction adopted by anti-squatting groups sought to distinguish between subtypes of "squatters," each possessing different degrees of residential entitlement. With no little cynicism, as extracts 5 and 6 below begin to illustrate, the HBRA increasingly conceded that "historical" squatters "traditional" squatters and "working" squatters might be accommodated in Hout Bay, but that "newcomers" or "recent arrivals" should be removed. By strategically relaxing insider/outsider boundaries, these kinds of accounts allowed representatives to distance themselves from allegations of prejudice while continuing to argue for (selective but mass) exclusion.

Extract 5
The number of squatters in Hout Bay is growing and the problem posed by their presence is growing with it. At the very outset one point must be made: the race of squatters plays no part in the concerns being raised by residents of Hout Bay. People here would feel exactly the same way if squatters happened to be Boerestaters and if their presence posed the same problems to the residents of the valley.

Without commenting in any way on the rights of the landowners and the rights of the squatters, there are are two distinct, virtually geographical problems in this valley and they call for quite distinct solutions.

Problem One: the squatters who have, in effect, become residents of Hout Bay, having lived here for a long time – such as those in Dawidskraal, for example.

Problem Two: the squatters who are *very recent arrivals* and who have *no claim to be treated as Hout Bayers* – those in the Princess Street area, for example.

Again – without prejudice to the rights of those whose land is being occupied without their consent – there is a general view that our *"historical" squatter communities* might be given some help to find permanent homes in the valley, while there is no such obligation on Hout Bay's part as far as the Princess Street squat is concerned.

(*The Sentinel News*, May 1990; our emphasis)

Extract 6
The major standpoints were carefully and strongly discussed with him [The Minister for Housing, Welfare and Works]; that for reasonableness and equity only *traditional* and fully employed people should be settled here and that *recent arrivals* should be settled elsewhere; and that the 1100 *traditional* people living in overcrowded conditions in the harbour should take first priority. These arguments were ignored and by decree, the views of Hout Bay were overridden roughshod. Who is to now bear the cost of settling and servicing the *new citizens* of this Republic?

(*The Sentinel News*, February 1991; our emphasis)

Many fine-grained points could be made about the rhetorical construction of belonging in these extracts. We could highlight, for example, the argumentative functions of denials of racist motivations in the call to exclude (some) squatters and the related, if improbable, comparison with the imagined responses of white property owners to a sudden mass invasion of "Boerestaters" (extract 5).[3] Likewise, we could explore the argumentative functions of appeals to fairness and justice, as well as what is quietly accomplished, via metonymic slippage, by the phrase

---

[3] This term designates a group of (largely Afrikaner) separatists who sought, though never came close to achieving, an exclusively white state during the final years of apartheid.

"the views of Hout Bay were overridden roughshod" (extract 6). Our main point here, however, is that the social and psychological processes that connect people and place are often rhetorically *contested* (and always *contestable;* see also Coyle and Murtagh, this volume). In our view, this insight is of fundamental importance to any theory that is concerned with identity threat under conditions of environmental change. Indeed, events of environmental change are particularly revelatory of the dilemmatic nature of the relationships between places, identities and threat. One might even argue that it is through everyday practices of contestation that threatened place identities are recognized in the first place and come to acquire context-specific meanings and values.

We do not doubt that many IPT researchers would concede this point. However, we do doubt that research conducted to date has adopted a conceptual and methodological approach that is capable of elucidating the contested meanings of environmental transformations. As such, we see a danger that IPT will drift toward the kind of "placid," depoliticized perspective that has characterized much environmental psychological research (see Di Masso *et al.*, 2011, for a further discussion of this theme). We hope not. In that spirit, we shall now outline some related limitations of the IPT concept of "coping strategies" as a way of understanding responses to environmental change.

From desegregation to re-segregation: the re-emergence of landscapes of exclusion

Whereas white holidaymakers could simply choose to bypass Durban's beachfront when it became ever more multiracial, white residents of Hout Bay were locked into comparatively permanent relations of residence and property ownership. Many were also deeply connected to the village itself – in precisely the ways proposed by IPT – and thus invested in the preservation of their self-in-place relations (for detailed discussion see Dixon *et al.*, 1994, 1997). Accordingly, avoidance was both less feasible and less desirable as a reaction to environmental change. Having said that, whites' response to the formal establishment of Imizamo Yethu did not ultimately resemble what would be termed a "coping strategy" by IPT researchers. To the contrary, we feel that to apply this term would be to misrepresent the strategic, politically organized and institutionally sanctioned nature of practices of re-segregation that emerged in Hout Bay. Nor would it capture how such practices were themselves embedded within wider struggles to implement and change intergroup inequality during South Africa's so-called "squatter crisis."

Budow (1976) made two observations about the early history of squatting in Cape Town that remained telling throughout apartheid era. First of all, neither its extent nor its racial character was commensurate with the "normal" pattern of urban growth in industrializing countries, as apologists for racial inequalities sometimes claimed. Secondly, the state's attempts to curb "black" urbanization ultimately proved to be self-defeating. Homeless people displaced by the authorities simply squatted elsewhere in the city: they literally had nowhere else to go. And yet there was a duality in this practice, deeply troubling to the authorities. Squatting was never only a symptom of oppression. It was also a strategy of resistance, a mechanism for contesting the state's monopoly over residential organization and for reclaiming land rights (cf. Smith, 1982). The geopolitical metaphor of a "struggle" for space is in this sense apposite.

We want to suggest that the unfolding pattern of actions and reactions in Hout Bay is better captured by this metaphor of "struggle" than by the metaphor of "coping." "Coping" implies a primarily psychological process of "adjustment" or "accommodation" to a changing environmental reality in which individuals try to "get by" under difficult circumstances. "Struggle," by contrast, implies a primarily *political* process in which historical advantaged and disadvantaged groups actively clash over the nature and direction of environmental change, often in a wider context of inequality. We feel that the latter metaphor better captures what happened in Hout Bay.

Ultimately, competing interest groups engaged in a long, often bitter, battle over space in the town, which shaped and reshaped the human geography of the village. On the one hand, exploiting shifts in government policy surrounding informal settlement and the sensitive politics of South Africa's "transitional" phase to democratic government, squatter groups in Hout Bay won historic rights of residence (see Saff, 1998). They did so in the face of a concerted, well-organized campaign mounted by the HPRA, who pressurized local government for their removal and exclusion. On the other hand, the HPRA and other local residents' groups successfully won concessions over the design and layout of Imizamo Yethu, which effectively enabled a reproduction of racial divisions at a localized scale. Figure 13.2 below illustrates some of the relevant design features. Again, in our view, these features are not best conceived as the outcome of individual or collective attempts to "cope" with the environment threat. Rather, they represent the reinstitution of a particular form of power relations between social groups, achieved through geopolitical practices that are all too familiar to anyone who lived in South Africa during apartheid:

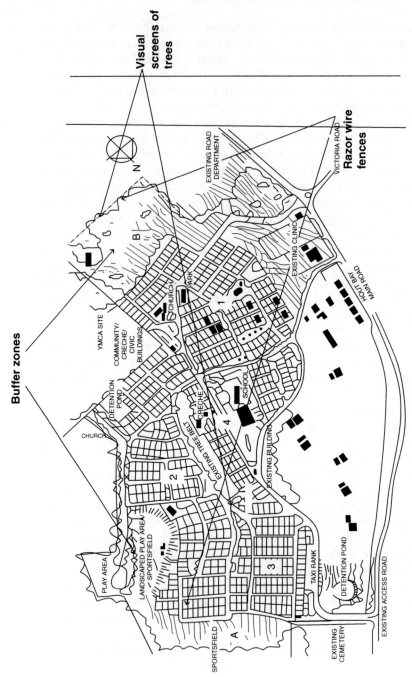

Figure 13.2. Design and layout of Imizamo Yethu

(*Note*: Points A and B indicate the "buffer zones" that divide the settlement from the adjoining estates of Penzance and Hughendon)

1. Although it lies inside village boundaries, Imizamo Yethu was located on the periphery of Hout Bay, distanced from its main centers and disconnected from its infrastructure. Racial division was thus partially reasserted through marginalization (Shields, 1991).

2. This effect was reinforced by the territorial layout of the settlement itself, which implemented buffer zones and boundary fences topped with razor wire. These features were designed to minimize the impact of the township surrounding inhabitants by preventing residents of Imizamo Yethu from crossing into these white neighborhoods, enclosing its residents in a territorially confined space.

3. In addition, visual screens of trees were allowed to flourish at strategic points. As the label "screen" suggests, these trees were intended to act as a sensuous barrier between Imizamo Yethu and surrounding communities.

4. Finally, the infrastructural links that would usually connect a community such as Imizamo Yethu with adjoining neighborhoods are conspicuously absent in Figure 13.2. There is one road in and one road out of the settlement, again re-establishing separation.

Conclusions

Located close to the city's old docklands, District Six is an area of Cape Town that became famous during the apartheid era. In the years prior to the rise of apartheid, it housed a cosmopolitan mixture of residents – mainly "Coloreds" and "Cape Malays," but also some "Xhosas," "Indians" and white "Afrikaners" – and became known for its cultural diversity and richness. During the 1970s, some 60,000 residents were forcibly removed from the area by the apartheid government in one of the most notorious applications of the Group Areas Act. In subsequent decades, the "repatriation" of these inhabitants became the focus of a collective struggle that continues to this day. This struggle is not merely, or even primarily, a matter of economic restitution: it expresses the need, as a matter of social justice, to reconnect people to place. A loss of place and place identity (e.g. see Kruger, 1992) has sustained political activism over several decades because, to echo the lyrics of the music group Amphibious Assault, "You can take the people out of the heart of District Six but you'll never take District Six out of the heart of the people."

We use this example as a counterpoint to the case studies discussed in this chapter, which reveal how rhetorical constructions of place, identity and threat may service a politics of resistance to social change. As the history of District Six illustrates, such constructions may equally inspire a politics of collective action to achieve change, a theme that resonates with arguments presented elsewhere in this book (e.g. see Pehrson and Reicher, this volume).

The value of IPT lies in its capacity to draw together several fundamental principles of person–place relations and to explain how, when and why such principles inform reactions to environmental transformations. As we have shown, the theory has inspired several important studies of the role of place identity distinctiveness, belonging, efficacy, esteem and continuity in shaping responses to urban development and processes of residential relocation. More generally, it has focused social psychologists' attention on the, often neglected, links between self and place. At the same time, we have contrasted IPT research with our own work on the rhetoric and ideology of resistance to racial desegregation in South Africa. Our aim has not been to diminish the contribution of IPT. Rather, we have sought to open up a space for dialogue between researchers working in this tradition and researchers influenced by the so-called "discursive turn" in environmental social psychology (e.g. see also Aiello and Bonauito, 2003; Auburn and Barnes, 2006; Benwell and Stokoe, 2006, ch. 6; Dixon and Durrheim, 2000, 2004; Taylor, 2010). We believe that a shift from a framework based on "perception" or even "social representation" toward a framework based around discursive practice and rhetorical construction offers a promising route forward for research in the IPT tradition – albeit a route that will lead to epistemological, conceptual and methodological tensions that we have not had space to discuss in this chapter. Perhaps most important, if we treat place identities as created rather than perceived or experienced, then threats to such identities are likewise (re)defined as emergent expressions of context specific practices of identity construction. Their specificity of content, action orientation and links to local intergroup dynamics and ideology are highlighted.[4]

As a related theme, our chapter has questioned how IPT conceptualizes behavioral reactions to environmental change. From an IPT perspective, such change produces identity threat and this, in turn, instigates various intrapsychic, interpersonal and intergroup "coping strategies," which are designed to manage or dispel threat. This perspective undoubtedly

---

[4] Contrast, for example, the "nature" of the place-identity threat experienced by the Durban beachgoers studied by Durrheim and Dixon (2000) and the British beachgoers studied by Bonauito et al. (1996). Whereas the Europeans were concerned that the beaches of other nations were viewed as cleaner than theirs, the white beachgoers in Durban constructed specifically racial threats to their identity by complaining about "uncivilized" behavior on newly desegregated beaches.

captures important aspects of our responses to environmental change. However, in our view, it underspecifies something fundamental – their political dimension.

In South Africa, where our own research has been conducted, for example, whites' reactions to the dismantling of apartheid do not simply represent an attempt to "cope" with a changing world. They also reflect wider relations of power and exclusion and, as important, help to recreate such relations in new forms. We are not convinced that the concept of "coping" adequately captures the *geopolitical* nature of this process, which bound up with the ideology of racial difference, entitlement and hierarchy, with politicized assumptions about who belongs where and why and with the power to shape the human geography of a society in ways that maintain racial division and privilege. Of course, we concede that IPT researchers have recognized that threats to power relations are also threats to identity (and vice versa).[5] However, to our knowledge, they have generally not investigated how geopolitical practices of division, exclusion, marginalization and subordination may re-establish spatial inequalities under conditions of environmental change. The core metaphor of "coping," we would conjecture, has not encouraged research in this particular direction.

We would recommend in conclusion, then, that future research adopts a more consistently "critical" perspective on person–place relations. That is, it should seek to "denaturalize" such relations (Kobayashi and Peake, 1994), to interrogate exclusive, parochial or "internalist" histories of place (Massey, 1995) and place identity, and, above all, to recognize how individual and collective reactions to environmental change always express wider relations of power and resistance.

REFERENCES

Aiello, A., and Bonaiuto, M. (2003). Rhetorical approach and discursive psychology: the study of environmental discourse. In M. Bonnes, T. Lee and M. Bonaiuto (eds.), *Psychological theories for environmental issues* (pp. 235–270). Aldershot: Ashgate.

Auburn, T., and Barnes, R. (2006). Producing place: a neo-Schutzian perspective on the "psychology of place." *Journal of Environmental Psychology*, 26, 38–50.

Benwell, B., and Stokoe, E. (2006). *Discourse and identity*. Edinburgh University Press.

---

[5] "[I]f only because a change in power will result in a changed capacity to control the social processes whereby identity is negotiated ... The feedback loop between power and identity is inevitable" (Breakwell, 1983, p. 24).

Billig, M. (1987). *Arguing and thinking: a rhetorical approach to social psychology* (1st edn.). Cambridge University Press.

Billig, M., Condor, S., Edwards, D., Gane, M., Middleton, D., and Radley, A. R. (1988). *Ideological dilemmas: a social psychology of everyday thinking.* London: Sage.

Bonaiuto, M., Breakwell, G. M., and Cano, I. (1996). Identity processes and environmental threat: the effects of nationalism and local identity upon perception of beach pollution. *Journal of Community and Applied Social Psychology,* 6, 157–175.

Breakwell, G. M. (ed.) (1983). *Threatened identities.* New York: John Wiley & Sons.

Budow, M. (1976). Urban squatting in Greater Cape Town, 1939–1948. History honours dissertation, University of Cape Town.

Christopher, A. J. (1994). *The atlas of apartheid.* London: Routledge.

Devine-Wright, P. (2009). Rethinking NIMBYism: the role of place attachment and place identity in explaining place protective action. *Community and Applied Social Psychology,* 6, 426–441.

Devine-Wright, P., and Lyons, E. (1997). Remembering pasts and representing places: the construction of national identities in Ireland. *Journal of Environmental Psychology,* 17, 33–45.

Di Masso, A., Dixon, J., and Pol, E. (2011). On the contested nature of place: Figuera's Well, the Hole of Shame and the ideological struggle over public space in Barcelona. *Journal of Environmental Psychology,* 31, 231–244.

Dixon, J. A. (2001). Contact and boundaries: "locating" the social psychology of intergroup relations. *Theory and Psychology,* 11, 587–608.

Dixon, J. A., and Durrheim, K. (2000). Displacing place-identity: a discursive approach to locating self and other. *British Journal of Social Psychology,* 39, 27–44.

Dixon, J. A., and Durrheim, K. (2004). Dislocating identity: desegregation and the transformation of place. *Journal of Environmental Psychology,* 24, 455–473.

Dixon, J. A., Foster, D. H., Durrheim, K., and Wilbraham, L. (1994). Discourse and the politics of space in South Africa: the "squatter crisis." *Discourse and Society,* 5, 277–296.

Dixon, J. A., Reicher, S., and Foster, D. (1997). Ideology, geography and racial exclusion: the squatter camp as "blot on the landscape." *Text,* 17, 317–348.

Durrheim, K., and Dixon, J. A. (2001). The role of place and metaphor in racial exclusion: South Africa's beaches as sites of shifting racialization. *Ethnic and Racial Studies,* 24, 433–450.

Durrheim, K., and Dixon, J. A. (2005). *Racial encounter. The social psychology of contact and desegregation.* London: Psychology Press.

Edwards, D. (2005). Discursive psychology. In K. L. Fitch and R. E. Sanders (eds.), *Handbook of language and social interaction* (pp. 257–273). Erlbaum.

Fried, M. (1963). Grieving for a lost home. In L. Duhl (ed.), *The urban condition* (pp. 151–171). New York: Basic Books.

Fried, M. (2000). Continuities and discontinuities of place. *Journal of Environmental Psychology,* 20, 193–205.

Fullilove, M. T. (1996). Psychiatric implications of displacement: contributions from the psychology of place. *American Journal of Psychiatry*, 153, 1516–1523.

Gawith, M., and Sowman, M. (1992). Informal settlements in Hout Bay: a brief history and review of socio-demographic trends (1989–1991). Unpublished Environmental Evaluation Unit Report. University of Cape Town, Cape Town.

Giuliani, V., and Feldman, R. (1993). Place attachment in a developmental and cultural context. *Journal of Environmental Psychology*, 13, 267–274.

Greenbaum, P. E., and Greenbaum, S. D. (1981). Territorial personalization: group identity and social interaction in a Slavic-American neighborhood. *Environment and Behavior*, 13, 574–589.

Gustafson, P. (2001). Meanings of place: everyday experience and theoretical conceptualizations. *Journal of Environmental Psychology*, 21, 5–16.

Jacobi, M., and Stokols, D. (1983). The role of tradition in group-environment relations. In N. R. Feimer and E. S. Geller (eds.), *Environmental psychology: directions and perspectives* (pp. 157–159). New York: Praeger.

Jaspal, R. (2011). Caste, social stigma and identity processes. *Psychology and Developing Societies*, 23(2), 27–62.

Kobayashi, A., and Peake, L. (1994). Unnatural discourse: "race" and gender in geography. *Gender, Place and Culture*, 1, 413–434.

Korpela, K. (1989). Place-identity as a product of environmental self-regulation. *Journal of Environmental Psychology*, 9, 241–256.

Korpela, K., and Hartig, T. (1996). Restorative qualities of favourite places. *Journal of Environmental Psychology*, 16, 221–233.

Kruger, D. (1992). District six, Cape Town: an apartheid landscape. *Landscape*, 31, 9–15.

Lalli, M. (1992). Urban-related identity: theory, measurement and empirical findings. *Journal of Environmental Psychology*, 12, 285–303.

Manzo, L.C. (2003). Beyond house and haven: towards a revisioning of emotional relationships with places. *Journal of Environmental Psychology*, 23, 47–61.

Massey, D. (1995). Places and their pasts. *History Workshop Journal*, 39, 182–192.

Matthews, J. (1983). Environmental change and community identity. In G. M. Breakwell, (ed.), *Threatened identities* (pp. 215–237). New York: John Wiley and Sons.

MLH (1990). Assessment of the development potential of various sites in Hout Bay. Unpublished report. Cape Town.

Potter, J., and Wetherell, M. (1987). *Discourse and social psychology*. London: Sage.

Proshansky, H., Fabian, A., and Kaminoff, R. (1983). Place-identity: physical world socialization of the self. *Journal of Environmental Psychology*, 3, 57–83.

Rowles, G. D. (1983). Place and personal identity in old age: observations from Appalachia. *Journal of Environmental Psychology*, 3, 299–313.

Saff, G. (1998). *Changing Cape Town*. New York: University of America Press.

Sarbin, T. (1983). Place identity as a component of self: an addendum. *Journal of Environmental Psychology*, 3, 337–342.

Shields, R. (1991). *Places on the margin: alternative geographies of modernity.* London: Routledge.

Smith, D. M. (1982). Urbanization and social change under apartheid: some recent developments. In D. M. Smith (ed.), *Living under apartheid* (38–44). London: Allen and Unwin.

Smuts, Dene and Shauna Westcott (eds.). (1991). *The Purple Shall Govern: A South African A to Z of Nonviolent Action.* Cape Town: Oxford University Press.

Speller, G. M. (2000). A community in transition: a longitudinal study of place attachment and identity processes in the context of an enforced relocation. Ph.D. thesis, University of Surrey, UK.

Speller, G. M., Lyons, E., and Twigger-Ross, C. (2002). A community in transition: the relationship between spatial change and identity processes. *Social Psychological Review*, 4, 39–58.

Taylor, S. (2010). *Narratives of identity and place.* London: Routledge.

Timotijevic, L., and Breakwell, G. M. (2000). Migration and threat to identity. *Journal of Community and Applied Social Psychology*, 10, 355–372.

Twigger-Ross, C. L., and Uzzell, D. L. (1996). Place and identity processes. *Journal of Environmental Psychology*, 16, 205–220.

Twigger-Ross, C. L., Bonaiuto, M., and Breakwell, G. M. (2003). Identity theories and environmental psychology. In M. Bonnes, T. Lee and M. Bonaiuto (eds.), *Psychological theories for environmental issues* (pp. 203–233). Aldershot: Ashgate.

Wetherell, M. (1998). Positioning and interpretative repertoires: conversation analysis and post-structuralism in dialogue. *Discourse and Society*, 9(3), 387–412.

14   Old age and its challenges to identity

Dario Spini and Daniela S. Jopp

Does the identity of a person remain consistent throughout the course of development from youth to old age? Does a centenarian experience his or her identity as being similar to when he or she was younger? And if this were the case, how can changes and the loss of roles, health and loved ones be without impact on identity when traveling through the different stages of life? Given increasing life expectancy and retirement unfolding into an extended period of life with new opportunities and issues (Neugarten, 1996), studying identity development across the whole life course is one of the future challenges.

In past years, social psychologists have typically investigated identity and many other processes using student samples with a surprising blindness to crucial factors such as age, generations/cohorts and historical change (Sears, 1986; Spini *et al.*, 2008). Given that more and more individuals reach old and very old age these days, studying identity development across the whole life course seems timely and has been called for by various scholars (e.g. Freund and Smith, 1999; Ryff and Marshall, 1999). Lifespan developmental scholars and gerontologists have indeed investigated self-processes in advanced age. However, this research seems to have developed without taking into account some of the important theoretical considerations intensively studied by social psychologists. For example, Krauss Whitbourne's Identity Process Theory proposes that age-associated changes are negotiated through the central processes of assimilation, accommodation and identity balance, without highlighting parallels to Identity Process Theory as posited by Breakwell (1993). Reciprocally, Identity Process Theory could at the same time benefit from expanding its applications into old age, as ageing research is a wonderful laboratory for studying identity processes. For instance, investigating the

This publication results from research works executed within the framework of the Swiss National Centre of Competence in Research LIVES, which is financed by the Swiss National Science Foundation. The authors are grateful to the Swiss National Science Foundation for its financial support.

295

mechanism involved in the development of the self at work as the individual changes over the course of the ageing process represents a natural experiment worth exploring, as it allows us to examine the effectiveness of the mechanisms and may also show their limits.

Given that we believe that both disciplines, social psychology and lifespan developmental psychology/gerontology, could benefit from each other, the present chapter is meant to offer theoretical elements and empirical findings that both disciplines could consider in order to enhance their work. We will start this endeavor by pointing out how the social psychological approach, exemplified by Identity Process Theory, provides opportunities to elaborate new heuristic questions. We will also present research conducted on identity and mechanisms that contribute to the stabilization of self-processes in old age and highlight how Identity Process Theory could benefit from research in gerontology and lifespan psychology (Baltes *et al.*, 1998; Heckhausen, 1999; Sapin *et al.*, 2007). Specifically, we will address three central questions regarding identity development in old age: (1) how adults integrate the threats (and stereotype threats) associated with age into their identity; (2) whether the main principles of identity, such as continuity and distinctiveness, have limits in functionality during later life; and (3) whether identity continuity and distinctiveness, with a relatively satisfying level of well-being, can be maintained despite declines in cognitive capacity, health and autonomy.

Setting the stage: identity principles and ageing

In considering how identity may be influenced by the ageing processes, as well as how individuals react to the threat of ageing, Breakwell's (1986a) theory of identity processes offers a framework which can, at least in part, be readily applied to investigate these questions. First, Breakwell specifies two central mechanisms contributing to identity, namely assimilation and accommodation: "Assimilation refers to the absorption of new components into the identity structure; accommodation refers to the adjustment which occurs in the existing structure so as to find a place into which to fit the new elements" (Breakwell, 1986a, p. 23). These two basic mechanisms are sustained by three essential principles of identity, which are of central relevance in the ageing context: uniqueness or distinctiveness; continuity across time and situation; and a feeling of worth or social value (self-esteem). Later, this list was complemented by other motives, including self-efficacy (Breakwell, 1993), belonging and meaning (Vignoles *et al.*, 2006) and psychological coherence (Jaspal and Cinnirella, 2010).

As acknowledged by a number of authors, identity (or self or personality) represents a phenomenon that is difficult to define, as each conceptualization is related to different traditions in the field of personality and social psychology (Hooker, 2002; Leary and Tangney, 2003; Vignoles *et al.*, 2006). To wit, in their overview of different models of self and identity, Leary and Tangney (2003) describe no less than sixty-six self-related constructs and motives. There is a good deal of conceptual confusion when trying to determine the specific ontological principles of identity processes and research in recent years has shown a shift from the idea of basic principles of identity processes (Breakwell, 1986a) to the study of identity motives (Vignoles *et al.*, 2006). The increase in proposed identity principles and their associated complexity is probably a result of the two-fold (or ambiguous) definition of identity principles offered by Breakwell in 1986: "the fundamental codes which guide the processes [of identity]. Basically, the principles specify the end states which are desirable for identity" (p. 24).

In this chapter we will restrain ourselves to what appears as the necessary and sufficient conditions for defining identity: continuity and differentiation. Although other principles have been discussed and may be worth studying in the context of old age development (e.g. self-efficacy, which may show some change when individuals lose physical capacity), we will concentrate on these two conditions, following the suggestion by Codol (1981) arguing that only these two principles are essential features of identity (see also Jodelet, 2005). Specifically, continuity refers to maintaining one's identity across time and situations, which represents a crucial mechanism in the ageing process (Atchley, 1989, 1999), whereas distinctiveness refers to feeling unique and different from others, which is the result of categorization processes (Brewer, 1991; Turner, 1987). Maintaining or developing positive self-esteem has been recognized as the main motive in social psychology (Baumeister, 1998; Ruble and Goodnow, 1998; Sedikides and Strube, 1997; Tesser *et al.*, 2000). However, self-esteem is not a superordinate or overarching principle of identity above and beyond others. As highlighted by research, individuals can define themselves as members of a group even if this identity is not positive (Vignoles *et al.*, 2000). Some authors have also argued that the centrality of self-esteem as the main identity motive has probably been overestimated (Emler, 2001). However, maintaining and enhancing a positive conception of oneself (or more generally high levels of well-being) represents an end state and a key indicator of the functionality of identity, namely successful adaptation and social integration of the individual. We will therefore discuss distinctiveness and continuity as main principles, while keeping in mind that self-esteem is one motive in establishing identity among many others depending on the social context (Breakwell, 1986a) and its functional role for regulating the self in the environment (Heckhausen, 1999).

Continuity and distinctiveness play a prime role in maintaining and developing an identity over the life course. Given that old age is associated with various loss experiences, which endanger identity and trigger its revaluation, it is likely that both continuity and distinctiveness will be of central importance in modeling identity in older age. Gerontological research shows that ageing individuals are confronted with loss in most if not all central domains of functioning (Lalive d'Epinay and Spini, 2008). Whereas young-old age (i.e. 65 to 79 years) is usually characterized by relative freedom after retirement and participation in (leisure) activities, the balance of gains and losses gets most negative when advancing into very old age (e.g. 80 or 85 and older). This period is characterized for many individuals by a qualitative shift toward frailty, health impairment, chronic diseases and for some by dependence (Baltes and Smith, 2003). Other feared losses include dementia, hospitalization, loss of loved ones and anticipation of one's own death. One of the effects of ageing is the fragilization of the oldest old, which describes the slow age-related process of weakening and deterioration of all bodily system (Lalive d'Epinay and Spini, 2008; Spini et al., 2007). This fragilization typically results in the restriction of one's activities first within his or her environment, then to the household and finally to oneself. Whereas men tend to die younger than women, this process of fragilization is particularly salient for women, who are more likely to live longer, but end their life alone after longer periods of health problems.

However, prior to being affected by these fundamental losses, the identity of a person advancing into old age is usually first put into question when he or she is subjected to the negative stereotypes of others. We will begin by discussing ways in which stereotypes of old age affect identity and then move to the processes of social and temporal comparison, two central processes of continuity and distinctiveness. In addition, we will consider identity in the case of dementia in order to frame the discussion of the limits of the identity paradigm. Finally, we will tackle the question of the possibility of studying and maintaining identity even when memory (and thus the cognitive possibility of ensuring continuity and distinctiveness) disappears.

Identity processes and old age stereotypes

Age, as sex and other phenotypic traits of individuals, is a basic social marker that shapes our perception and attitudes toward others (Cuddy and Fiske, 2002; Montepare and Zebrowitz, 1998). Nonetheless, age is a special social category (compared to more impermeable social categories, such as sex or social class), as the majority of individuals in industrial societies are more or less "condemned" to become very old, especially if they have a high social status and are women (Arber and Ginn, 1993). Another important aspect that makes age a special social category is that we will, if our lives are long enough, grow into this category (Levy, 2003). Whereas individual characteristics such as ethnicity are fixed and thus allow individuals to build up strategies to handle discrimination and distress related to their membership of a particular ethnic group, individuals build up (often negative) attitudes about the old very early in life even as they invariably progress toward becoming part of this group themselves (Levy, 2009). Besides these specific aspects concerning the role of the age category at the individual level, life course theorists have repeatedly argued that society is deeply structured by age and that the life course (Riley and Riley, 1994) is a central institution of society (Kohli, 1986). In this regard, ageing concerns both individual and intergroup processes of identity development. The phenomenon of age stereotyping is of particular interest here, because it is potentially a threat to identity continuity and distinctiveness.

In Western societies, old age stereotypes are ambivalent. Elderly stereotypes have been thoroughly studied and the traits associated with advanced age are mostly negative and related to physical decline, cognitive deterioration and social isolation or exclusion (Kite and Johnson, 1988; Palmore, 1990). At the same time, positive stereotypes have also been repeatedly found with respect to characteristics such as wisdom and dignity (Heckhausen et al., 1989) or certain "young-old" characteristics, such as specific activity patterns and/or friendliness (Hummert et al., 1994). This ambivalence can also be found in the results presented by Cuddy and Fiske (2002), regarding the two classical dimensions of warmth and competence (Asch, 1946): elderly individuals were perceived as high on warmth, but low on competence. Also of interest is the fact that the two groups who were categorized as "alike" were individuals with mental and physical disability.

As proposed by Greenberg et al. (2002), the negative attributes of old age are threatening because they are associated with our fear of mortality and irreversible decline. For many, old age is linked with losing social roles, and physical and cognitive decline. There is empirical evidence that indeed age stereotypes are threatening and have substantial negative effects on cognitive performance, health and even survival (Desrichard and Kopetz, 2005; Hess et al., 2003; Levy, 1996; Levy and Meyers, 2005; Levy et al., 2002; Tettamanti et al., 2009). In order to avoid one's assimilation into a category associated with threats to identity, older adults tend to see themselves as being different from their age category (Greenberg et al., 2002; Martens et al., 2005).

It is also a well-known fact that individuals of all ages tend to declare a younger subjective age or age identity than their chronological age (Westerhof, 2008). Moreover, this tendency increases with advancing age and is particularly pronounced for older adults (Barak and Stern, 1986; Kleinspehn-Ammerlahn et al., 2008; Montepare and Lachman, 1989). Moreover, a younger subjective age was found to be associated with a higher well-being (Barak and Stern, 1986; Filipp and Ferring, 1989; Steverink and Timmer, 2001). This positive effect of the discrepancy between chronological and subjective age is usually interpreted in the sense that people contrast themselves from the negative ageing stereotype or expectancies associated with older individuals or groups, representing a self-enhancing strategy (Westerhof, 2008). However, this discrepancy may also reveal that individuals tend not to feel old. In interviews conducted by Hummel (1998) individuals reported that as long as their cognitive capacities are intact, they would not become old. This statement matches that individuals may not feel that they are getting older when they refer to their inner subjective experience, which Kaufman (1986) called "the ageless self," an expression developed on the basis of interviews about the personal experiences of ageing. When asked what helped them to reach their very advanced age, even centenarians indicated that they were 100 "all of a sudden," as documented in a film portrait by Michel (2010), indicating that they had experienced their ageing as a continuous process despite all obvious qualitative changes in terms of losing health and loved ones and being no longer able to pursue valued activities – a very striking illustration of the continuity/discontinuity principle relying on the age experience.

Although many old adults have a strong sense of continuity that gives the impression that subjectively we remain the same independently of our chronological age or health status (Atchley, 1999), some individuals report ageing to be a more continuous experience than others (Cavalli and Henchoz, 2009). Furthermore, there seem to be limits to this subjective experience of continuity, especially in the context of health decline. Longitudinal research has shown that when the same individuals are followed over time, not all individuals experience an increase in perceived youthfulness; frailer individuals tend to feel less young (Uotinen et al., 2006). Moreover, the content of self-definitions show a less favorable ratio of positive to negative evaluations for individuals aged more than 85 years old (compared to those aged 70 to 84 years) and that older adults with more health-related constraints reported fewer and less rich self-defining domains (Freund and Smith, 1999). This result could suggest that the principle of continuity may no longer hold when confronted with too many difficulties and health declines.

Although this interpretation has not been put forward by scholars interested in age identity, Breakwell's (1986a) Identity Process Theory may help us to understand why distinctiveness is at stake in the processes related to age identity. Many older adults, and especially the oldest ones, do not feel that they belong to the elderly group but instead feel that they are special and different from their same age peers – sometimes even superior. Findings demonstrating this feeling of uniqueness were probably first reported by Johnson and Barer (1997). Very old individuals, who survived compared to most individuals of their cohort, may indeed have the impression that they are more resilient and luckier than the members of their generation. This feeling of being somewhat better off than others is particularly visible in research on social comparison, a topic that we will now turn to.

Social and temporal comparison processes

When individuals experience age-associated changes, specific mechanisms kick in to protect and restore the identity of the individual. Continuity and distinctiveness principles have been studied through social comparison and temporal comparison processes and their relationship to well-being as an indicator of healthy adaptation to ageing. A striking gerontological finding often investigated is the so-called well-being paradox which reflects the observation that well-being in later life is pretty stable (e.g. Charles *et al.*, 2001; Diener and Suh, 1997; Mroczek and Spiro, 2005), despite the fact that old individuals are often affected by loss in all central domains of functioning, including loss of loved ones and social roles, mental capacity and health. Of course the relationship between resources and well-being is complex and loss of resources such as health declines have indeed negative effects on well-being (Kunzmann *et al.*, 2000). Longitudinal and cohort-sequential longitudinal studies on the development of mental health and self-esteem reveal some more variability: values were lowest in young ages and increased until individuals reached 60 years of age and then declined (Jones and Meredith, 2000; Orth *et al.*, 2010). The decline in older ages has been shown to be due mainly to changes in socio-economic status and health (Orth *et al.*, 2010; Smith *et al.*, 2002). However, over shorter periods of time, individual well-being is rather stable, even in old age (Diener and Suh, 1997), although some dimensions of well-being seem to show more independence from health than others (Kunzmann, *et al.*, 2000).

Most scholars argue that self-regulation mechanisms are responsible for the stabilization of self-esteem or well-being in the face of adverse conditions and age-related declines (Baltes and Baltes, 1990; Jopp and Rott, 2006; Jopp and Smith, 2006) and that they are available and well-functioning until very old age (Jopp and Rott, 2006; Jopp *et al.*, 2013). These self-regulatory mechanisms have been discussed under the term psychological strengths and include strategies (e.g. coping, life-management) as well as attitudes and beliefs (e.g. self-efficacy, optimism, meaning in life, will to live; Jopp *et al.*, 2010). Among the numerous self-regulation strategies, identity motives or coping strategies (Breakwell, 1986a), social comparison and temporal comparison are of particular interest in the context of this chapter as they are directly related to well-being stabilization and to the distinctiveness and continuity principles.

Social Comparison Theory (Festinger, 1954) established that individuals have a basic drive to evaluate opinions and abilities through the comparison of oneself to similar individuals (or groups). According to Breakwell (1986a), social comparison processes help individuals to establish their self-worth. However, social comparison as a coping mechanism is also a judgment of (dis)similarity with others (or the stereotyped idea of others) and therefore is also guided by the distinctiveness principle (Breakwell, 1986b). Social comparison enables individuals to position themselves in relation to others in order to optimally regulate their distinctiveness (Brewer, 1991).

Temporal Comparison Theory was first elaborated by Albert (1977) in parallel to Social Comparison Theory. Temporal comparison is the comparison of oneself with respect to two points in time (mostly past/present or present/future). Temporal comparison is directly related to identity continuity and is a "drive to provide and maintain a sense of enduring (as well as coherent and integrated) self-identity over time and to evaluate and adjust to perceived changes in aspects of the self over time" (Albert, 1977, p. 488).

The beneficial effects of social and temporal comparison have been studied extensively and confirmed in old and very old age. Specifically, findings indicate that applying both strategies is related to more positive outcomes (Heckhausen and Krueger, 1993; Heidrich and Ryff, 1993; Rickabaugh and Tomlinson-Keasay, 1997; Robinson-Whelen and Kiecolt-Glaser, 1997; Spini *et al.*, 2007a; Suls *et al.*, 1991; Suls and Mullen, 1983–1984). Most studies also report that downward social comparison is the most effective social comparison strategy; for example, comparing oneself to someone in a worse health has strong positive effects on the individual's sense of well-being (Wills, 1981; Wood *et al.*, 1985). Concerning temporal comparison, believing that no short-term change has occurred seems to be the most functional coping strategy against health or ageing-related threats, highlighting the importance of the continuity principle (Albert, 1977).

However, the beneficial effect of comparison strategies may depend on specific conditions and probably has limits due to frailty, which was investigated most intensively for social comparison (Girardin Keciour and Spini, 2006; Girardin and Spini, 2008). In a study by Frieswijk *et al.* (2004), the relationship among frailty, social comparison and life satisfaction was investigated in order to clarify the links between identity processes and life satisfaction in old age. The extent to which study participants identified themselves with the target of comparison (presented in a bogus interview with a fictive person low or high on frailty) was noteworthy. The main finding was that older individuals with higher frailty benefitted more strongly from downward comparison than less frail older persons, but this was only the case if they had low levels of identification with the fictive interview partner. Interpreted by Identity Process Theory, these results indicate that beneficial effects of downward social comparison are only observed if an individual is able to distinguish him- or herself from a threatening target (i.e. a frailer individual than oneself). If, by contrast, distinctiveness from the fictive interview partner was not given, downward social comparison was less beneficial than upward social comparison. Thus, individuals who feel threatened by frailty can "escape" the negative stereotypes related to old age only by using social comparison, allowing some distinctiveness from dissimilar (with downward social comparison) or similar (with upward social comparison) individuals. This suggests that the functionality of downward social comparison is directly related to the distinctiveness principle.

Additional evidence for limits of the positive function of social and temporal comparisons comes from another line of research. Spini *et al.* (2007a) showed on the basis of the Swiss Longitudinal Study on the Oldest Old data (SWILSOO; Guilley and Lalive d'Epinay, 2008; Lalive d'Epinay and Spini, 2008) that both processes do indeed have a beneficial effect on the oldest olds' subjective health.

A series of analyses addressing potential limits of the functionality of social comparison (Girardin and Spini, 2006, 2008), provided evidence that using downward social comparison (a strategy used by two-thirds of the respondents) was indeed related to higher well-being. Moreover, when taking into account longitudinal data on different health transitions, subgroups emerged that offered different results regarding the role of the comparison strategies and their effectiveness. First of all, well-being was directly linked to health changes. Individuals who were independent across both measurement occasions had a relatively high level of well-being, whereas those (a minority of cases) transiting from frailty to dependence or into a chronic state of dependence expressed rather low levels of well-being – this latter finding stands in contrast to the well-being paradox. Secondly, downward social comparison and well-being were positively related in relatively healthier individuals who were at risk of losing their health (with the exception of the healthiest individuals who did not use social comparison for stabilizing well-being). However, for individuals moving from frailty into dependence, which was marked by a relatively low level of well-being and a reduction of well-being between the two waves of observation, the social comparison strategy had no association with well-being. This latter result may suggest that when having to face the threatening transition into dependency, it is difficult for older individuals to maintain or restore a distinctive positive identity. Surprisingly, although results indicated that some individuals had rather low levels of well-being, downward social comparison was again effective when chronic dependency was observed. All in all, these results indicate that social comparison processes and the underlying principle of distinctiveness (from a negative identity), on the one hand, are effective even in situations of poor health (Girardin *et al.*, 2008), but on the other hand may find limits in very old age and in particularly in threatening health transitions.

Do the same limits exist for temporal comparisons? Two empirical studies suggest that temporal comparison and its underlying principle of continuity, may be very beneficial in very old age. The first set of analysis was again based on SWILSOO data realized by Ryser (2010, study 1) and compared the functionality of social and temporal comparison across two age groups, namely those aged from 80 to 85 years and those aged from 86 to 94 years. In the analysis, variables such as gender socioeconomic status, age and health were controlled for. Results indicate that both downward social and lateral temporal comparisons were positively related to subjective health in the 80–85-year-old group, whereas in the oldest old aged 86 to 94, temporal comparison was the only predictor and had a strong positive effect on subjective health. Further evidence comes from a study comparing three younger age groups (18–39; 40–64 and 65–87 years old; Brown and Middendorf, 1996), in which respondents completed a questionnaire that assessed the preference for temporal or social comparison. Results showed that temporal comparison was preferred to social comparison in every age group, but an interaction effect appeared between age groups and preference. Although young individuals had no preference for either of the strategies, the importance of temporal comparison was stronger in older ages, whereas the importance of social comparison remained constant for all age groups.

Although more research is clearly needed in this area given the limited number of studies (see Robinson-Whelen and Kiecolt-Glaser, 1997; Spini *et al.*, 2007a; Suls *et al.*, 1991), existing empirical evidence suggests at this point that downward social comparison and lateral temporal comparison are two effective processes for maintaining a sense of well-being in old age. Their functionality in maintaining relatively satisfying levels of well-being finds, however, some limits in situations in which frailty is high, notably when a transition to dependency is experienced. Future empirical research is needed to better understand when the continuity or distinctiveness principles can or cannot compensate together or separately, for changes (and notably decline) in the various dimensions of individuals' development.

Testing the limits of identity processes among individuals with dementia

Finally, the end-of-life stage in the developmental cycle poses another challenge to Identity Process Theory. Following Breakwell (1986a), self-awareness and cognitive competencies are central components required for the assimilation–accommodation process, which is responsible for integrating new aspects into identity. According to Identity Process Theory, this process is based on cognitive processes like "memory, learning, consciousness, and, probably, organized construal" (Breakwell, 1986a, p. 26). In the same context, Breakwell also addresses what could happen if these cognitive processes are no longer available: "without memory the whole process of assimilation–accommodation takes place in a vacuum ... The erosion of memory which often accompanies ageing is a central plank in the explanation of identity changes in the elderly" (Breakwell, 1986a, p. 26).

Does this mean that cognitive impairment, which is quite common in very old age, results in individuals losing their identity? What happens to identity, for example, when individuals' short-term memory is impaired, as is the case for patients with dementia or Alzheimer disease? And what are the consequences at an individual and a societal level?

The main threat of ageing that people report in interviews is to "lose one's head." If expectations concerning the physical health can be leveled and adjusted to some extent, maintaining one's cognitive capacities represents the central battle of very old age. The main reason is the threat of losing self-awareness, which can be thought of as going back to infancy or more extremely to losing one's humanity (Kruse, 2009). This anxiety about dementia can also be related to the fact that, as underlined by Breakwell (1986a), the memory system is a necessary framework for maintaining distinctiveness and continuity. Does this then mean that identity can totally disappear if the memory gets lost? To be sure, the damage to the self and identity can be dramatic as dementia progresses. However, there are more and more claims that some elements of the self (personality traits, memories), notably from the past, survive even into advanced dementia (Cohen-Mansfield et al., 2000; Klein et al., 2003; Sabat and Harré, 1992). For instance, individuals with the beginning stages of dementia show complex processing and adjustment to the disease (Stechl et al., 2007). Individuals at later stages of dementia were furthermore found to be able to experience a variety of distinct emotions, including positive as well as negative affect, as assessed via coding of facial expressions (Re, 2003). It was also shown that daily situations of high emotional value can be identified for individuals with dementia via observation (Bär et al., 2006) and that the well-being of dementia patients can be enhanced by allowing them meaningful interactions with volunteers who trigger personally relevant situations through sensual experiences (e.g. looking at a book representing the landscape where a person grew up, by providing the food they used to like most; Ehret, 2009). Thus, there is substantial evidence that individuals living with dementia may have more access to everyday life stimuli and emotional experiences than previously thought.

Research addressing identity processes in the course of dementia and Alzheimer disease are still scarce. There is, for example, evidence that some aspects from the past remain, even in the context of a declining memory (Kitwood, 1993); several scholars claim that these remaining memories are a basis for establishing continuity between the past and present, which is of key importance in maintaining a coherent sense of the self.

Moreover, there is empirical evidence that patients with dementia can still learn and improve their well-being through group activities (Haslam et al., 2012). An individual's memory may not be the only source of identity. As claimed by the tenants of lifespan psychology (Baltes et al., 1998), despite the decline in biological resources in very old age, cultural resources may partially compensate for losses. Such cultural compensation may also apply to identity, given that it is a social representation composed of contents shared by individuals and groups whose value depends on social structures and communication systems (Breakwell, 1993; Doise, 1998). Although Identity Process Theory recognises that social processes contribute to identity, most researchers have focused on individuals' cognitive definition of the self. For example, Vignoles et al. (2006, p. 309) acknowledge that "like all subjective meanings, identity is constructed through a complex interplay of cognitive, affective and social interaction processes, occurring within particular cultural and local contexts." However, their next sentence reaffirms the pre-eminence of the individualist cognitive framework of the original theory, that: "an important assumption of the current studies is that these processes are guided by particular motives or goals of the individual." Is the individual's self-consciousness really the cornerstone of identity in a social system? Are there not other processes based on the emotions, body, or collective practices that could strengthen other parts and processes of our identity as a process? Moreover, could we not also define parts of an individual's identity in his or her environment?

In ancient Egypt, pharaohs used to inscribe their name in cartouches on every important building. This practice was meant to ensure immortality of individual's soul following the belief that if the name of the person survives his or her death, they would overcome death. Would it not be possible to think the same of identity? Identity is also constituted by social relations and interactions (Cooley, 1964; Sabat and Harré, 1992). Other individuals or the groups we belong to help to shape and maintain our self-image, contribute to experiencing continuity and distinctiveness, in their representations and communication. Most current theories of identity have an individualistic and atomistic view of identity. Future theories should also explore ways in which institutions, family and groups can sustain identity processes in order to empower patients (Haslam et al., 2012). In the most extreme cases of dementia, institutions (families, nursing homes, hospitals) should have the duty of maintaining and developing an individual's identity as a distinct and valuable person anchored in temporality within individual and in collective narratives and practices. In these later cases of dementia institutions may acknowledge identity discontinuity and adapt the environment to the person instead of stressing or neutralizing the person in order to behave "normally." It may be a more philosophical or a-priori statement at this stage, but we believe that researchers should go beyond an individual and cognitive definition of an individual's identity and complement it with a social and institutional definition. Articulating different layers that form identity, spanning the person-specific aspects to institutional or societal aspects, is needed to complement the already well-developed study of the self within the so-called social cognition tradition.

Conclusion

This chapter focused on ways in which distinctiveness and continuity principles can be studied in old age and how studies focusing on later stages of life can enrich the field of identity studies. Three fields of study have been developed: (1) stereotypes of old age and their deep impact on the content and value identity of the elderly; (2) the functionality and limits of social and temporal comparisons in maintaining well-being; and (3) the potential impact of studies on individuals with dementia in order to not only understand the limits of what we define as the self or an individual's identity, but also how these studies should push us to overcome the limitations of a cognitive and individualistic definition of identity and to consider more social and collective definitions of identity.

Old age and more specifically what is called the fourth age (Lalive d'Epinay and Spini, 2008), is marked by frailty and losses in different domains. These losses pose serious challenges to individuals' adaptive functioning and identity structure. Research on self-regulation, however, shows that individuals adopt various strategies for defending or keeping a valuable sense of identity, notably using downward comparison and continuity in temporal comparisons.

As there are limits to these beneficial mechanisms, especially with respect to health and cognitive issues typically associated with very old age, future work should seek to address these challenges to identity, given their importance for the individual and society. The debate is already in progress in the field of gerontology: Baltes and Smith (2003), for example, described the fourth age as being characterized by biocultural incompleteness, vulnerability and unpredictability and even by what they called "psychological mortality" (i.e. loss of identity, psychological autonomy and sense of control), referring to individuals with dementia. To be sure, the fourth age is a period of life in which adaptation to losses is not an easy task and identity may indeed be subject to discontinuities. Nevertheless, there is substantial empirical evidence that many very old individuals are able to master the challenges of the fourth age well, as shown by their high levels of resilience, which seems mostly the consequence of adjusting standards and using the adaptive strategies. High levels of such psychological strengths remain effective even in centenarians. Extant research also clearly shows that individuals with dementia are not psychologically "dead," as they maintain important functions such as the ability to experience emotions, to learn and to react to stimuli. Thus, in sum, there seems limited support for the notion of psychological mortality.

However, with respect to identity, major hurdles are still necessary to overcome. This is an urgently needed debate that should involve research, individuals and society. Society and institutions play a crucial role in defining identity and identity may not be composed of the same aspects at different ages. Rather, these characterizations of identity should be adapted to the realities of the different stages of the life course. We hope that we were able to show that identity process theory and the principles of continuity and distinctiveness, can help in this endeavor and that social psychologists interested in identity and health should feel encouraged in their efforts to face the challenges of this exciting field of research.

REFERENCES

Albert, S. (1977). Temporal comparison theory. *Psychological Review*, 84(6), 485–503.

Arber, S., and Ginn, J. (1993). Gender and inqualities in health in later life. *Social Science & Medicine*, 36(1), 33–46.

Asch, S. E. (1946). Forming impressions of personality. *The Journal of Abnormal and Social Psychology*, 41(4), 258–290.

Atchley, R. C. (1989). A continuity theory of normal aging. *The Gerontologist*, 29(2), 183–190.

Atchley, R. C. (1999). *Continuity and adaptation in aging: creating positive experiences*. Baltimore, MD: Johns Hopkins University Press.

Bär, M., Böggemann, M., Kaspar, R., Berendonk, C., Seidl, U., Schröder, J., and Kruse, A. (2006). Demenzkranke Menschen in individuell bedeutsamen Alltagssituationen. *Zeitschrift für Gerontologie und Geriatrie*, 39, 173–182.

Baltes, P. B., and Baltes, M. M. (1990). Psychological perspectives on successful aging: a model of selective optimization with compensation. In P. B. Baltes and M. M. Baltes (eds.), *Successful aging: perspectives from the behavioral sciences* (pp. 1–34). New York: Cambridge University Press.

Baltes, P. B., Lindenberger, U., and Staudinger, U. M. (1998). Lifespan theory in developmental psychology. In W. Damon and R. M. Lerner (eds.), *Handbook of child psychology*, vol. I: *theoretical models of human development* (5th edn.; pp. 1,027–1,143). New York: Wiley.

Baltes, P. B., and Smith, J. (2003). New frontiers in the future of aging: from successful aging of the young old to the dilemmas of the fourth age. *Gerontology*, 49, 123–135.

Barak, B., and Stern, B. (1986). Subjective age correlates. A research note. *The Gerontologist*, 26(5), 571–578.

Baumeister, R. (1998). The self. In B. Gilson, S. T. Fiske and G. Lindzey (eds.), *The handbook of social psychology*, vol. I (pp. 680–740). Boston, MA: McGraw-Hill.

Breakwell, G. M. (1986a). *Coping with threatening identities*. London: Methuen.

Breakwell, G. M. (1986b). Identities at work. In H. Beloff (ed.), *Getting into life* (pp. 43–66). London: Methuen.

Breakwell, G. M. (1993). Social representations and social identity. *Papers on Social Representations*, 2(3), 198–217.

Brewer, M. B. (1991). The social self: on being the same and different at the same time. *Personality and Social Psychology Bulletin*, 17, 475–482.

Brown, R., and Middendorf, J. (1996). The underestimated role of temporal comparison: a test of the lifespan model. *Journal of Social Psychology*, 136(3), 325–331.

Cavalli, S., and Henchoz, K. (2009). L'Entrée dans la vieillesse: paroles de vieux. In M. Oris, E. Widmer, A. De Ribaupierre, D. Joye, D. Spini, G. Labouvie-Vief and J.-M. Falter (eds.), *Transitions dans les parcours de vie et construction des inégalités* (pp. 389–406). Lausanne: Presses polytechniques et universitaires romandes.

Charles S. T, Carstensen, L. L., and McFall, R. M. (2001). Problem-solving in the nursing home environment: age and experience differences in emotional reactions and responses. *Journal of Clinical Geropsychology*, 7(4), 319–330.

Codol, J.-P. (1981). Une approche cognitive du sentiment d'identité. *Social Science Information*, 20, 111–136.

Cohen-Mansfield, J., Golander, H., and Arnheim, G. (2000). Self-identity in older persons suffering from dementia: preliminary results. *Social Science and Medicine*, 51, 381–394.

Cooley, C. H. (1964). The social self. The meaning of "I." In C. H. Cooley (ed.), *Human nature and the social order* (pp. 168–210). New York: Schocken Books.

Cuddy, A. J. C., and Fiske, S. T. (2002). Doddering but dears: process, content and function in stereotyping of elder persons. In T. D. Nelson (ed.), *Ageism. stereotyping and prejudice against older persons* (pp. 3–26). Cambridge, MA: MIT Press.

Desrichard, O., and Kopetz, C. (2005). A threat in the elder: the impact of task-instructions, self-efficacy and performance expectations on memory performance in the elderly. *European Journal of Social Psychology*, 35, 537–552.

Diener, E., and Suh, M. E. (1997). Subjective well-being and age: an international analysis. In K. W. Schaie and M. P. Lawton (eds.), *Annual review of gerontology and geriatrics*, vol. VIII (pp. 304–324). New York: Springer.

Doise, W. (1998). Social representations in personal identity. In S. Worchel, J. F. Morales, D. Paez and J.-C. Deschamps (eds.), *Social identity: international perspectives* (pp. 13–23). London: Sage Publications.

Ehret, S. (2009). *Ich werde wieder lebendig. Personale Geschehensordnung und Daseinsthematische Begleitung bei Demenz.* Saarbrücken: Südwestdeutscher Verlag für Hochschulschriften.

Emler, N. (2001). *Self-esteem. The costs and causes of low self-worth.* Layerthorpe: Joseph Rowntree Foundation.

Festinger, L. (1954). A theory of social comparison processes. *Human Relations*, 7, 117–140.

Filipp, S.-H., and Ferring, D. (1989). Zur Alters- und Bereichsspezifität subjektiven Alterserlebens. *Zeitschrift für Entwicklungspsychologie und Pädagogische Psychologie*, 21, 279–293.

Freund, A. M., and Smith, J. (1999). Content and function of the self-definition in old and very old age. *Journal of Gerontology Series B: Psychological Sciences & Social Sciences*, 54B(1), 55–67.

Frieswijk, N., Buunk, B. P., Steverink, N., and Slaets, P. J. (2004). The effect of social comparison information on the life satisfaction of frail elderly persons. *Psychology and Aging*, 19(1), 183–190.

Girardin, M., and Spini, D. (2006). Well-being and frailty process in later life: an evaluation of the effectiveness of social comparison. *Swiss Journal of Sociology*, 32(2), 389–406.

Girardin, M., and Spini, D. (2008). Fragilité, perception de la santé et bien-être. In C. Lalive d'Epinay and D. Spini (eds.), *Les Années fragiles. La Vie au-delà de quatre-vingts ans* (pp. 281–308). Québec: Les Presses de l'Université Laval.

Girardin, M., Spini, D., and Ryser, V.-A. (2008). The paradox of well-being in later life: effectiveness of downward social comparison during the frailty process. In E. Guilley and C. J. Lalive d'Epinay (eds.), *The closing chapters of long lives* (pp. 129–142). New York: Nova Science.

Greenberg, J., Schimel, J., and Martens, A. (2002). Ageism: denying the face of the future. In T. D. Nelson (ed.), *Ageism, stereotyping and prejudice against older persons* (pp. 27–48). Cambridge, MA: The MIT Presss.

Guilley, E., and Lalive d'Epinay, C. (2008). *The closing chapters of long lives: results from the 10-year Swilsoo study on the oldest old.* New York: Nova Science.

Haslam, C., Jetten, J., Haslam, S. A., and Knight, C. P. (2012). The importance of remembering and deciding together. Enhancing the health and well-being of older adults in care. In J. Jetten, C. Haslam and S. A. Haslam (eds.), *The social cure: identity, health and well-being* (pp. 297–315). Hove, UK: Psychology Press.

Heckhausen, J. (1999). *Developmental regulation in adulthood: age-normative and sociostructural constraints as adaptative challenges.* New York: Cambridge University Press.

Heckhausen, J., Dixon, R. A., and Baltes, P. B. (1989). Gains and losses in development throughout adulthood as perceived by different adult age groups. *Developmental Psychology*, 25(1), 109–121.

Heckhausen, J., and Krueger, J. (1993). Developmental expectations for the self and most other people: age grading in three functions of social comparison. *Developmental Psychology*, 29, 539–548.

Heidrich, S. M., and Ryff, C. D. (1993). The role of social comparisons processes in the psychological adaptation of elderly adults. *Journal of Gerontology: Psychological Sciences*, 48, P127–P136.

Hess, T. M., Auman, C., Colcombe, S., and Rahhal, T. (2003). The impact of stereotype threat on age differences in memory performance. *Journal of Gerontology: Psychological Sciences*, 58, 3–11.

Hooker, K. (2002). New directions for research in personality and aging: a comprehensive model for linking levels, structures and processes. *Journal of Research in Personality*, 36, 318–334.

Hummel, C. (1998). La Tête et les jambes. Représentations de la vieillesse chez des jeunes adultes. *Prévenir*, 35, 15–22.

Hummert, M. L., Gartska, T. A., Shaner, J. L., and Strahm, S. (1994). Stereotypes of the elderly held by young, middle-aged and elderly adults. *Journal of Gerontology: Psychological Sciences*, 49(5), 240–249.

Jaspal, R., and Cinnirella, M. (2010). Coping with potentially incompatible identities: accounts of religious, ethnic and sexual identities from British Pakistani men who identify as Muslim and gay. *British Journal of Social Psychology*, 49(4), 849–870.

Jodelet, D. (2005). Formes et figures de l'alterité. In M. Sanchez-Mazas and L. Licata (eds.), *L'autre: regards psychosociaux* (pp. 23–47). Grenoble: Les Presses de l'Université de Grenoble.

Johnson, C. L., and Barer, M. (1997). *Life beyond 85 years – the aura of survivorship*. New York: Springer.

Jones, C. J., and Meredith, W. (2000). Developmental paths of psychological health from early adolescence to later adulthood. *Psychology and Aging*, 15(2), 351–360.

Jopp, D., and Rott, C. (2006). Adaptation in very old age: exploring the role of resources, beliefs and attitudes for centenarian's happiness. *Psychology and Aging*, 21(2), 266–280.

Jopp, D., and Smith, J. (2006). Resources and life-management strategies as determinants of successful aging: on the protective effect of selection, optimization and compensation. *Psychology and Aging*, 21(2), 252–265.

Jopp, D., Rott, C., and Wozniak, D. (2010). Psychologische Stärken im Alter [Psychological strengths in old age]. In A. Kruse (ed.), *Potenziale des Alters* (pp. 51–74). Heidelberg: Akademische Verlagsgesellschaft.

Kaufman, S. R. (1986). *The ageless self: sources of meaning in late life*. Madison: University of Wisconsin Press.

Kite, M. E., and Johnson, B. T. (1988). Attitudes toward older and younger adults: a meta-analysis. *Psychology and Aging*, 3(3), 233–244.

Kitwood, T. (1993). Towards a theory of dementia care: the interpersonal process. *Ageing and Society*, 13, 51–67.

Klein, S. B., Cosmides, L., and Costabile, K. A. (2003). Preserved knowledge of self in a case of Alzheimer's dementia. *Social Cognition*, 21, 157–165.

Kleinspehn-Ammerlahn, A., Kotter-Grühn, D., and Smith, J. (2008). Self-perceptions of aging: do subjective age and satisfaction with aging change during old age? *Journal of Gerontology Series B: Psychological Sciences and Social Sciences*, 63(6), 377–385.

Kohli, M. (1986). The world we forgot: a historical review of the life course in later life. In V. W. Marshall (ed.), *Later life: the social psychology of aging* (pp. 271–303). London and Beverly Hills, CA: Sage.

Kunzmann, U., Little, T. D., and Smith, J. (2000). Is age-related stability of subjective well-being a paradox? Cross-sectional and longitudinal evidence from the Berlin Aging Study. *Psychology & Aging*, 15(3), 511–526.

Kruse, A. (2009). Demenz – Ethische Überlegungen zur Menschenwürde in Grenzsituationen. In Landesstiftung Baden-Württemberg GmbH (Hrsg.), *Training bei Demenz – Dokumentation zum Kongress "Training bei Demenz" Dezember 2008* (S. 146–171). Stuttgart: Schriftenreihe der Landesstiftung Baden-Württemberg.

Lalive d'Epinay, C., and Spini, D. (2008). *Les Années fragiles: la vie au-delà de quatre-vingt ans*. Québec: Presses Universitaires de Laval.

Leary, M. R., and Tangney, J. P. (2003). The self as organizing construct in the behavioral and social sciences. In M. R. Leary and J. P. Tangney (eds.), *Handbook of self and identity* (pp. 3–14). New York: The Guildford Press.

Levy, B. R. (1996). Improving memory in old age by implicit self-stereotyping. *Journal of Personality and Social Psychology*, 71, 1,092–1,107.

Levy, B. R. (2003). Mind matters: cognitive and physical effects of aging self-stereotypes. *Journals of Gerontology, Series B: Psychological Sciences and Social Sciences*, 58, 203–211.

Levy, B. R. (2009). Stereotype embodiment: a psychosocial approach to aging. *Current Directions in Psychological Science*, 18(6), 332–336.

Levy, B. R., and Myers, L. M. (2005). Relationship between respiratory mortality and self-perception of aging. *Psychology and Health*, 20(5), 553–564.

Levy, B. R., Slade, M. D., Kunkel S. R., and Kasl, S. V. (2002). Longevity increased by positive self-perceptions of aging. *Journal of Personality and Social Psychology*, 83, 261–270.

Martens, A., Goldenberg, J. L., and Greenberg, J. (2005). A terror management perspective on ageism. *Journal of Social Issues*, 61(2), 223–239.

Michel, H. (2010). *Betrifft: 100 Jahre jung*. Film by Hanspeter Michel, aired by SWR Fernsehen on June 22, 2010.

Montepare, J. M., and Lachman, M. E. (1989). "You're only as old as you feel": self-perceptions of age, fears of aging and life satisfaction from adolescence to old age. *Psychology and Aging*, 4, 73–78.

Montepare, J. M., and Zebrowitz, L. A. (1998). Person perception comes of age: the salience and significance of age in social judgements. In M. P. Zanna (ed.), *Advances in experimental social psychology*, vol. XXX (pp. 93–161). San Diego, CA: Academic Press.

Mroczek, D. K., and Spiro, A. (2005). Change in life satisfaction over 20 years during adulthood: findings from the VA Normative Aging Study. *Journal of Personality and Social Psychology*, 88(1),189–202.

Neugarten, B. (1996). The young-old and the age-irrelevant society. In D. A. Neugarten (ed.), *The meanings of age* (pp. 47–55). University of Chicago Press.

Orth, U., Trzesniewski, K. H., and Robins, R. W. (2010). Self-esteem development from young adulthood to old age: a cohort-sequential longitudinal study. *Journal of Personality and Social Psychology*, 98(4), 645–658.

Palmore, E. B. (1990). *Ageism: negative and positive*. New York: Springer.

Re, S. (2003). *Erleben und Ausdruck von Emotionen bei schwerer Demenz*. Hamburg: Verlag Dr. Kovac.

Rickabaugh, C. A., and Tomlinson-Keasay, C. (1997). Social and temporal comparisons in adjustment to aging. *Basic and Applied Social Psychology*, 19(3), 307–328.

Riley, M. W., and Riley, J. W. (1994). Structural lag: past and future. In M. W. Riley, R. L. Kahn and A. Foner (eds.), *Age and structural lag. Society's failure to provide meaningful opportunities in work, family and leisure* (pp. 15–36). New York: Wiley.

Robinson-Whelen, S., and Kiecolt-Glaser, J. (1997). The importance of social versus temporal comparison appraisals among older adults. *Journal of Applied Social Psychology*, 27, 959–966.

Ruble, D. N., and Goodnow, J. J. (1998). Social development in childhood and adulthood. In D. T. Gilbert, S. T. Fiske and G. Lindzey (eds.), *The handbook of social psychology*, vol. I (pp. 741–787). Boston, MA: McGraw-Hill.

Ryff, C. D., and Marshall, V. W. (eds.) (1999). *The self and society in aging processes*. New York: Springer.

Ryser, V.-A. (2010). Importance de la comparaison sociale et temporelle dans la grande vieillesse. Ph.D. thesis, Université de Lausanne.

Sabat, S. R., and Harré, R. (1992). The construction and deconstruction of self in Alzheimer's disease. *Ageing and Society*, 12, 443–461.

Sapin, M., Spini, D., and Widmer, E. (2007). *Les Parcours de vie: de l'adolescence à la vie adulte*. Lausanne: Presses Polytechniques et Universitaires Romandes.

Sears, D. O. (1986). College sophomores in the laboratory: influences of a narrow database on social psychology's view of human nature. *Journal of Personality and Social Psychology*, 51, 515–530.

Sedikides, C., and Strube, M. J. (1997). Self-evaluation: to thine own self be good, to thine own self be sure, to thine own self be true and to thine own self be better. In M. P. Zanna (ed.), *Advances in experimental social psychology*, vol. XXIX (pp. 209–269). New York: Academic Press.

Smith, J., Borchelt, M., Maier, H., and Jopp, D. (2002). Health and well-being in the young old and oldest old. *Journal of Social Issues*, 58(4), 715–732.

Spini, D., Clémence, A., and Ghisletta, P. (2007a). Temporal and social comparisons in the oldest old's appraisals of self-rated health across time. *Swiss Journal of psychology*, 66(2), 79–89.

Spini, D., Elcheroth, G., and Figini, D. (2008). Is there space for time in social spychology publications? A content analysis across five journals. *Journal of Community and Applied Social Psychology*, 19, 165–181.

Spini, D., Ghisletta, P., Guilley, E., and Lalive d'Epinay, C. (2007b). Frail elderly. In J. E. Birren (ed.), *Handbook of aging*, vol. I (2nd edn.; pp. 572–579). Oxford: Elsevier.

Stechl, E., Lämmler, E., Steinhagen-Thiessen, E., and Flick, U. (2007). Subjektive Wahrnehmung und Bewältigung der Demenz im Frühstadium – SUWADEM: Eine qualitative Interviewstudie mit Betroffenen und Angehörigen. *Zeitschrift für Gerontologie und Geriatrie*, 40, 71–80.

Steverink, N., and Timmer, E. (2001). Das subjektive Alterserleben. In F. Dittmann-Kohli, C. Bode and G. J. Westerhof (eds.), *Die zweite Lebenshälfte – Psychologische Perspektiven. Ergebnisse des Alters-Survey* (pp. 451–484). Stuttgart: Kohlhammer.

Suls, J., Marco, C. A., and Tobin, S. (1991). The role of temporal comparison, social comparison and direct appraisal in the elderly's self-evaluation of health. *Journal of Applied Social Psychology*, 21(14), 1,125–1,144.

Suls, J., and Mullen, B. (1983–1984). Social and temporal bases of self-evaluation in the elderly. *International Journal of Aging and Development*, 18, 111–120.

Tesser, A., Crepaz, N., Beach, S. R. H., Cornell, D., and Collins, J. C. (2000). Confluence of self-esteem regulation mechanisms: on integrating the self-zoo. *Personality and Social Psychology Bulletin*, 26, 1,476–1,489.

Tettamanti, M., Ryser, V., and Spini, D. (2009). Les Effets ambivalents des stéréotypes liés au vieillissement chez les personnes âgées. In M. Oris *et al.* (eds.), *Transitions dans les parcours de vie et construction des inégalités* (pp. 268–282). Lausanne: Presse polytechniques et universitaires romandes.

Turner, J. C. (1987). *Rediscovering the social group: a self-categorization theory*. Oxford: Basil Blackwell.

Uotinen, V., Rantanen, T., Suutama, T., and Ruoppila, I. (2006). Change in subjective age among older people over an eight year follow-up: "Getting older and feeling younger?" *Experimental Aging Research*, 32(4), 381–393.

Vignoles, V. L., Chryssochoou, X., and Breakwell, G. M. (2000). The distinctiveness principle: identity, meaning and the bounds of cultural relativity. *Personality and Social Psychology Review*, 4, 337–354.

Vignoles, V. L., Regalia, C., Manzi, C., Golledge, J., and Scabini, E. (2006). Beyond self-esteem: influence of multiple motives on identity construction. *Journal of Personality and Social Psychology*, 90(2), 308–333.

Westerhof, G. J. (2008). Age identity. In D. Carr (ed.), *Encyclopedia of the Life Course and Human Development*, vol. III (pp. 10–14). Detroit, MI: Macmillan Social Science Library.

Wills, T. A. (1981). Downward comparison principles in social psychology. *Psychological Bulletin*, 90, 245–271.

Wood, J. V., Taylor, S. E., and Lichtman, R. R. (1985). Social comparison in adjustment to breast cancer. *Journal of Personality and Social Psychology*, 49, 1,169–1,183.

15   Religion, identity and mental health

Kate Miriam Loewenthal

Religious factors often relate positively to mental health (Koenig *et al.*, 2001; Loewenthal, 2007). There are many relevant religious factors. For example, religious ways of coping with stress (Pargament, 1997, 2002) can improve mental health outcomes, or have negative effects. The help available and sought for stress and mental health difficulties is varied and effects are variable: religious groups may provide social support, to good effect, or religious factors may inhibit professional help-seeking (Leavey *et al.*, 2007; Loewenthal and Brooke-Rogers, 2004). Some studies on religion and mental health have taken identity into consideration. This chapter explores the extent to which identity and identity-related processes might be involved in mediating and explaining the relations between religion and mental health.

Definitions

What is identity? Identity involves a self-aware "I," viewing "me" the object of awareness as comprising characteristics derived from significant others – carers, friends, fellow members of social groups. Sometimes the characteristics will be disowned (a contra-identity), but more commonly, the characteristics have been adopted and/or are aspired to. Here I will be focusing particularly on religious identity and looking at its nature, its construction and its effects. Some identity theories will be outlined in the next section.

Religious identity normally involves alignment with a particular religious tradition. Inner states include: "the belief that there is an unseen order and that our supreme good lies in harmoniously adjusting ourselves thereto" (James, 1902). Religious traditions involve beliefs and behaviors about spiritual reality, the divine, morality, purpose and the communication of these (Loewenthal, 2007). Identity strength may vary, for example, between leaders, members and marginal members (Barker, 1998). A recent important and growing development is the emergence of "spirituality": "an inner path enabling a person to discover the essence of his/her being"; or the "deepest values and meanings by which people live" (Sheldrake, 2007, pp. 1–2). Most people who regard themselves as "religious" also regard themselves as "spiritual" (Zinnbauer *et al.*, 1997), but a growing number of people prefer to define themselves as spiritual rather than religious (Heelas and Woodhead, 2005; Loewenthal, 2012). Spirituality is viewed as individualistic and subjective, whereas religion involves normative group beliefs. Spirituality and religion are clearly not identical and self-identification as "spiritual" may imply an explicit dissociation from any religious group.

Littlewood and Lipsedge (1989) note that religion may play a special role in maintaining and developing cultural norms, suggesting that these are often clothed as unquestionable religious injunctions. Religion and culture can be treated as distinguishable, but in some studies, ethnic/cultural identity is treated as a package involving religion (e.g. Robinson, 2009).

Mental health can be defined "negatively" as the absence of psychiatric illness(es), or low levels of symptoms or distress states. Another view of mental health involves the presence of positive states. This approach recognizes that there is more to health than the absence of illness and involves the assessment of positive states or traits, such as happiness, or purpose in life. In practice the assessment of positive states is much less frequently done than the assessment of negative states. This is a loss, since positive and negative states are often not inversely related to each other and the relations of negative states to religion do not enable us to predict the relations of positive states to religion (Loewenthal *et al.*, 2000, 2009).

Identity theories

Several theoretical perspectives on identity have formed a backdrop to research examining the roles played by identity in the relations between religion and mental health. Breakwell's Identity Process Theory (IPT; 1986, 2010) views identity as a dynamic process, a function of social representations and in turn affecting social representations (Moscovici, 2001). Identity involves constant self-monitoring and assimilation of and accommodation to the social context. Identity involves structured, hierarchical content, with elements varying in centrality and salience and with values appended to elements. The content of identity includes both "social" elements (group memberships, roles, etc.) and "individual" elements (values, beliefs, etc.). The social–individual distinction is not important in IPT when considering individual identity (see Pehrson and Reicher, this volume). Changes in social context can call forth changes in identity, depending on personal relevance, personal involvement, amount of change demanded and how negative the change is considered to be. An important feature of IPT is the notion of threat to identity. Threats to identity are aversive, and this has important implications for well-being: threats to esteem, efficacy, distinctiveness or continuity will trigger coping strategies. Responses to diminish threat may be of any kind (thoughts, actions, etc.) and pitched at intrapersonal, interpersonal, intragroup or intergroup levels. For example, Jaspal (2012) shows how disfigurement as the result of an accident, potentially threatening to identity, calls for strategies to help achieve acceptable levels of self-esteem, distinctiveness, continuity and efficacy, as well as coherence, belonging and meaning. Individuals with disfiguring burns may see themselves as less competent (efficacious) than others. Seeing disfigurement as a barrier to achieving a desired goal can undermine perceived competence and control.

IPT thus focuses on individual coping processes in the ongoing development of identity in changing social contexts and the importance of self-esteem, self-efficacy, distinctiveness and continuity. Belonging, meaning and coherence are further motivational factors that have been suggested in recent work (Vignoles, et al., 2002; Jaspal and Cinnirella, 2010).

Other theories that have influenced research related to the focus on religion in this chapter include Social Identity Theory (SIT; Tajfel and Turner, 1986) which considers the consequences of social identity based on group membership. We categorize ourselves and others based on group membership categories, "them" and "us," and self-esteem is enhanced by ingroup favoritism, often associated with prejudice and hostile interaction. SIT has shown how hostile behavior from the ingroup to other groups is justified by attributing it to external factors, outside forces and influences ("we attack them because they are oppressing us"). Hostile behavior from the outgroup is attributed to internal factors ("they oppress us because they are evil"). SIT has been enormously influential in understanding intergroup relations, prejudice and hostility. It has rightly been pointed out that SIT is concerned with identity as a result of group membership, categorization and comparison and unlike IPT is unconcerned with the dynamic processes of identity development within the individual. For our present discussion, SIT is important since self-definition as a member of a religious group could be associated with increased well-being, or in the case of prejudice and hostility from more powerful other groups, decreased well-being. There can be indirect effects via specific practices and beliefs endorsed by different religious groups.

Erik Erikson (1963) has influenced a prevalent view that identity achievement is once-and-for-all. Erikson's account of personal growth throughout life included the influential suggestion that adolescence and early adulthood are concerned with dealing with identity formation. Drawing on Erikson, Marcia (1966; Marcia et al., 1993) proposed four possible postures vis-à-vis identity: diffusion, in which possible identities/features of identity are still in a state of flux; foreclosure, in which an identity ordained by society and/or the family is adopted without much apparent struggle; moratorium, in which options are kept open, the individual flitting from one possibility to another without commitment; finally, achievement, in which identity is achieved after consideration. Marcia, arguing that ideology and occupation are particularly important features of identity, identified these four postures among college students (Marcia, 1966; Marcia et al., 1993; Kroger, 2009). Critical commentary involves charges of gender, class and culture specificity. Gilligan (1993) argued that women define themselves in terms of relationships and connections, while men define themselves in terms of separation and achievement. This led to feminist and womanist identity stage models. Tryon and Winograd (2003) suggested that an important feature of identity development is in response to social definitions of womanhood involving the inferiority of women. Women may disregard social definitions and develop internal standards to define womanhood, while some may act politically against male oppression. Womanism is a development of black feminism and thus tackles both gender and culture issues in identity development (Ossana et al., 1992), resembling the feminist view of women's identity development in that the process involves disregarding societal expectations of womanhood, such as "the strong black mother-figure," and coming to an internal evaluation of self and womanhood. Moradi (2005) has called for increased attention to the experiences of women from different races and cultures.

Other contributions to theories of identity include role theory stemming in part from the work of George Herbert Mead (1934) on the development of self-awareness and the self-concept, in the symbolic interactionist tradition. Stryker and Burke (2000, p. 284) in discussing identity theory acknowledge that the term "identity" is widely and often loosely used, but use the term to refer to "the parts of a self composed of the meanings that persons attach to the multiple roles they typically play in highly differentiated contemporary societies." They link views of identity concerned with the way in which identities relate to social structure and the internal processes of self-verification (Marshall and Schachter, 2010).

Regardless of theoretical background, research on religious identity generally features the concepts of identity salience, of religious identity as social identity and of developmental dynamics. The theories can often be viewed as complementary, rather than incompatible, offering differing emphases on identity and identity processes. SIT and role theory attend to social identity. IPT and the work developed from Erikson and feminism are often concerned with identity salience and with intra-individual processes in grappling with challenges to identity. In the descriptions and discussions which follow, although some research has derived from SIT, role theory and other perspectives, we will consider interpretations derived from IPT, particularly with respect to coping with threats to identity.

The research may be divided into two broad categories: work which examines the effects of specific (religious) group identity on mental health (identity as an independent variable); and work which examines the processes involved in the development of identity, with particular reference to religious factors and processes.

Religious identity as an independent variable

Starting with a focus on religious identity as group membership, the main research questions are whether and how religious group membership relates to mental health. There has been comparison with the mental health effects of other social identities, especially ethnic identity.

What is the relative importance of ethnic and religious identities for well-being and what are the relations between the two aspects of identity? Abu-Rayya and Abu-Rayya (2009) examining the relations between ethnic and religious identity, argued that ethnic identity could play a crucial role in the establishment of overall self-concept, meaning and well-being in the lives of minorities. They also suggested that religious identity may play an equally or more important role in these respects. They examined Palestinian Arabs living in Israel, both (Sunni) Muslim and Christian (mainly Orthodox). All expectations were confirmed for both Muslim and Christian samples. Ethnic and religious identities were only weakly correlated, suggesting possible independence. This study indicated that certainly in minority groups, religious identity can be at least equally if not more important than ethnic identity in predicting well-being.

Blaine and Crocker (1995) examined the salience and value of religious identity and the effects of these on psychological well-being in the context of gender and ethnic identity differences. They examined the extent to which religious belief was related to well-being among black and white college students in the USA. Among black students, religious belief and well-being were indeed significantly related. Black students reported similar levels of self-esteem to white students and were equally qualified for college admission and achievement, but perceived white-majority colleges as unfriendly places in which they were expected to underachieve (Steele, 1992). In this context, religious belief was found to affect well-being to the extent that it was associated with a positive religious identity and with enhanced (religious) life meaning. As a defence against racial stigma, black students may disidentify with achievement values, but identify more strongly with the community of religious believers, compared to whites. This study offers suggestions about identity processes in black American college students and these conform to Breakwell's proposal that the threat to (black) identity can be met with strategies involving the re-evaluation of identity contents: attention is re-focused on some other aspect of identity (religion rather than ethnicity) and its value is inflated. Religious identity is developed as a strategy for protecting and enhancing well-being. Elsewhere, Coates (2011) observed that reported reasons for joining charismatic religious groups included certainty and meaning, as well as belonging and friendship.

Ways in which religious identity may influence mental health are further illustrated in a study of the extent to which religious coping was used by Presbyterian clergy, elders and rank-and-file members (Pargament *et al.*, 2001). Positive and religious coping were assessed using the RCOPE questionnaire (Pargament *et al.*, 2000). The extent to which positive religious coping was used related to role salience: clergy used positive coping more than elders, who used more positive coping than members. Positive religious coping was related to well-being (low depressed mood, high positive mood and religious satisfaction). As found in other studies, negative religious coping was related to poor well-being. The relations between well-being and both positive and negative religious coping were stronger for clergy than for members. It was suggested that clergy spend much time on religious education, reflection and spiritual growth, and that clergy (also elders to some extent) are therefore able to apply their beliefs more efficiently and effectively than lay members. The study indicates that professional and personal identity can affect study and practice, which in turn affects coping with stress and ultimately well-being.

Somewhat similarly, Loewenthal *et al.* (2000, 2009) showed higher levels of positive affect among Protestants and Jews, compared to those identified as non-religious and levels of positive affect were related to levels of religious study and practice. The relations of religious identity and practice to lowered negative affect were notably weaker than the relations to raised positive affect.

Practices associated with religious identity and well-being (Brooke-Rogers and Loewenthal, 2003) include prayer as a means of coping with distress. This was said to be more effective by Muslims and Christians, than by Jews, Hindus and other religious and non-religious groups (Loewenthal and Cinnirella, 1999), whereas religious activity (ritual) was said to be more effective by Jews and Muslims, compared with other groups. There may be group differences in the practice of forgiveness, with consequences for well-being.

How does individualistic "spiritual" identity relate to well-being? Okulicz-Kozaryn (2010) in an analysis of data from the World Values Survey, concluded that individualistic spirituality does not have the same salutary effects as religiosity. Well-being may be unaffected or even lowered (compared to those identified with a religious group), probably because individualized spirituality does not promote social capital – belonging, as identified in IPT (Vignoles *et al.*, 2002).

Tiliopoulos and McVittie's (2010) cross-sectional study, with Christians in the UK, of the importance of personal, social and collective identities drew on concepts of identity stemming from William James' (1890) distinction between the known *Me* (personal identity) and the knowing, reflective *I*. Their study also drew on the Tajfel and Turner concept of social identities as the outcomes of social categorization and social comparison. While acknowledging the importance of the dynamic nature of identity, this study took psychometric snapshots and examined the relations of these aspects of identity to religious orientation using measures developed from the Allport and Ross (1967) distinction between intrinsic and extrinsic religious orientation. Batson *et al.* (1993) suggested that intrinsic religiosity serves needs for strength and direction; extrinsic religiosity serves needs for comfort, status and security; and quest religiosity involves continuing existential questioning. Intrinsic religiosity has been found to relate to well-being, extrinsic relates negatively and quest is unrelated. Tiliopoulos and McVittie expected that extrinsic religiosity would relate to the perceived importance of social identity (public image, reputation), while the perceived importance of personal identity would relate to intrinsic and quest orientations. While intrinsic religiosity did not relate to the perceived importance of any aspect of identity, quest as predicted related to personal identity and social identity related positively to extrinsic-personal religiosity and negatively to intrinsic religiosity. Tiliopoulis and McVittie suggest that these patterns of identity salience in relation to religious orientation, indicate ways in which religion may contribute to well-being via identity processes: for comfort, status and support, and/or to seek to understand one's place in the universe.

The studies described indicate some effects that religion may have on mental health and ways in which these effects might operate, for example via religious identity salience, by the specific beliefs and coping strategies learned in different religious groups and by the comfort, support and self-esteem directly offered by religious identity, perhaps particularly in minority groups.

Identity processes

Identity Process Theory (IPT) offers a more in-depth perspective on the religious aspects of identity, encouraging the examination of the processes of ongoing identity construction as social contexts vary, enabling some understanding of the motivational dynamics underlying identity construction and hence some understanding of the impact of religious identity on mental health. Social characteristics (including religious and other group memberships and roles) and individual characteristics are features of identity content and attached to these are values. Identity content shifts and IPT offers some interpretation and even prediction about the motivational dynamics underlying shifts in identity. The motivational principles of self-esteem, self-efficacy, distinctiveness, continuity, belonging, meaning and coherence are all proposed as important.

Turning to some examples of the study of identity processes, Coyle (2010) offers critical responses to faith development theory, proposing an IPT perspective for examining personal religious change. Faith Development Theory (Fowler, 1981), suggests that faith – not necessarily or explicitly religious – develops in invariant stages. Drawing on Piagetian, Eriksonian and other developmental frameworks, Fowler has made valuable contributions to the study of religious differences and religious change. However, the theory has been criticized on a number of grounds. Coyle suggests that if there were less emphasis on invariant stages in development, there would be improvements in understanding the individual's efforts after faith and meaning. Coyle offers a case study of identity threat, a married man devoted to his career who is made redundant. His hopes for a new job are repeatedly dashed. He begins to re-evaluate his priorities and purpose in life as he reshapes his commitments to his family, beginning to enjoy time with his children and going to church with his wife. An IPT perspective suggests, among other things, the potential usefulness of examining the details of the conditions and processes of transformations in faith development theory. Life-events which challenge the beliefs central to identity, feedback from actions in response to identity threats, assimilation and accommodation and the reworking of the constituents of identity in line with relevant motivational principles such as belonging, efficacy and meaning, are all IPT concepts which could be usefully imported into the study of faith development and indeed the examination of identity mediating the relations between religion and well-being.

Walters and Auton-Cuff (2009) look at challenges to identity among Third Culture Kids, individuals who have grown up in expatriate families, thus in a clearly bicultural environment and who at the time of the interview were adjusting to a third culture as they continued their further or higher education in their parents' country of origin. All participants/biographers in this study were women; the methodology was biographical phenomenology – life-story interviewing, with thematic analysis. Like other feminist/womanist researchers, the researchers were impressed with the extent to which the interviews allowed their participants to voice their feelings, and to create, recreate or maintain their identities. Half the biographers were daughters of parents in business and half the daughters of missionaries. Dominant themes were the sense of perpetually moving and perpetually readjusting – this transition disrupted identity development and it was "overwhelming" as "people let me know that I didn't fit in." There was a pervasive sense of always being "different." Brown and Gilligan (1992) suggest that adolescent girls give up their voices and remain silent for the sake of becoming a good woman and having good relationships. So there was little overt protest. "My parents said they really liked me ... you never complained about anything." A common coping method for dealing with disruptions of transition and the sense of differentness was enhanced spirituality, even in cases where the young woman had not had a religious upbringing: "Along with my family, God's been the stable thing in my life"; "That's how I got through all those years, I feel like if I didn't know God, I don't know where I'd be." Here, Walters and Auton-Cuff see religion as offering ideologies, relationships and spirituality necessary for identity formation, triggering identity concerns and offering solutions. Spirituality was a source of stability and had a positive impact on identity development for these women. Motivational principles derived from IPT were not deployed in interpreting this study, but it seems that some of these principles (such as continuity, belonging and meaning) could add to the understanding of this material. As in Blaine and Crocker's observations, described earlier, threats to identity were met by a focus on religious identity and an enhancement of its value. These observations may partially support Breakwell's (1986, p. 152) suggestions that short-term, unstable, internal threats might be coped with by re-evaluation tactics (here, enhancing religious identity), rather than by social change strategies which are more likely when threats are long-term, stable and external.

Heath (2006) offers a womanist approach to spirituality and mental health. Heath argues strongly for an understanding of the importance of spirituality serving as a source of faith, enabling black women to remain on course, "facilitating their ability to develop a strong sense of self, both individually and collectively," in spite of the horrendous oppressions of being a black woman, involving the societal myth of the "strong black woman," the matriarch, who can bear life's burdens without expressing pain. But as in Walters and Auton-Cuff's analysis of Third Culture Kids, a voice is needed, in which black women can give expression to something beyond this enforced identity. The role of the matriarch and strong black woman is lonely and there is a deep spiritual need to be heard, valued and cared for, beyond the admiration of their skill in the strong black woman role. Spirituality is a resource to promote self-healing and maintaining a balance between personal identity and collective identity and responsibilities as a member of one's cultural community. IPT principles, particularly continuity, esteem, self-efficacy and belonging may be important in dealing with the "strong black woman" role. The enhancement of spirituality may be a form of re-evaluation, particularly "association with another valued characteristic" (here, spirituality) (Breakwell, 1986, p. 80). In Heath's account, the strong black woman role is enforced, spirituality appears as a more central aspect of identity, enabling a woman to belong and to be esteemed and cared for without passing herself off as strong.

An important and fascinating feature of religious identity is the use of a language(s) specifically associated with religious liturgy, study and/or conversation within the religious group. Jaspal and Coyle (2010) studied second-generation Asians in the UK, who normally use three languages: English, the language of the host culture, their heritage language (HL, Urdu, Punjabi, Hindi) and a liturgical language (LL, Arabic for Muslims, Sanskrit in Hinduism, Gurmukhi for Sikhs). In religious schools, students spend hours mastering by rite passages of sacred scripture, often without understanding the meaning. This gives a sense of connection to God and also a sense of community: "Arabic is the language of the Muslims. That's how it was supposed to be." For some, ethnic and religious identities may coincide: notably Pakistanis are almost entirely Muslim, but the relative separation and importance of ethnic and religious identity may vary between groups. Thus some may see being Muslim as a cultural rather than a religious identity, while others regard religious identity as distinct and more salient than cultural (ethnic) identity. Jaspal and Coyle's participants' interviews indicated four themes: meaning-making in relation to the sanctification of language; LL as a symbol of religious community; participants also discussed the reconciliation between ethnic

and religious identity; finally, linguistic otherness and religious alienation. Religious identity was strong in the psychological worlds of the
informants and strong religious beliefs underlay their attachment to the
LL, which was often given more religious importance than the HL. The
value attached to Arabic enhances the sense of belonging to the religious
community, as well as the sense of continuity. There are other ways in
which the use of particular languages can heighten or reduce the sense
of belonging and continuity. For Jaspal and Coyle's participants, attachment to HL can often have a religious significance. For example, Punjabi
is associated with Sikhism and a participant who used Punjabi felt that
this diminished her reputation as an authentic Hindu, diminishing her
sense of belonging. Among Jews, the LL is (classical) Hebrew, but among
Hasidic Jews in Western countries, Glinert (1999) observed that the use
of Yiddish (HL) in conversation acts as a symbol of religious community
and pride; "We never changed our language." Hasidic Jews who do not
use Yiddish are regarded as less authentic. Thus lack of knowledge of a
language associated with religious identity could be seen as a threat to
identity and learning that language could be motivated by a need for
coherence in relation to religious and linguistic identities and a source of
self-esteem, continuity and belonging.

Shaffer and Hastings (2007) looked at the effects of threats to religious beliefs by asking Catholics in the USA to read an article threatening to their beliefs, about the crisis in the Catholic church. The threats
here would have been seen as threats to both continuity, in which prior
beliefs are threatened by new information and self-esteem, given that
the crisis related to scandals involving spiritual abuse by members of the
clergy. Other Catholics read a non-threatening article. Threats to belief
strengthened religious identification and increased religious fundamen-
talist ideals and this effect was more marked among those higher on
right-wing authoritarianism. An IPT perspective would take this as an
example of how threats to identity initiate reorganization of beliefs, with
the effects on belief salience perhaps being particularly marked among
those for whom beliefs are already highly coherent.

Vignoles et al. (2002) interviewed 149 Anglican clergy in the UK. It
was argued that self-esteem alone is not sufficient to predict the importance of different elements in the construction of identity. Efficacy,
distinctiveness and continuity are also important. Also, interviews suggested that purpose and closeness were important in this particular
culture. Clergy were asked to specify twelve elements of their identity
and then to rate the *centrality* of each element, followed by ratings of
each element for *self-esteem* ("how much of each of these things give
you a sense of self-esteem?"), *distinctiveness* ("make you feel that you

are unique?"), *continuity* ("give you a sense of continuity within your life?"), *efficacy* ("make you feel effective in doing the things that you do"), *purpose* ("give you a sense of purpose?") and *closeness* ("make you feel close to other people"). Although as expected, the elements important for self-esteem were strongly associated with centrality, multiple regression modeling showed that distinctiveness, continuity and efficacy made equally important contributions to centrality. The contributions of purpose and closeness were relatively modest. This study is consistent with other work in suggesting that although self-esteem is important in guiding the construction of identity, distinctiveness, continuity and efficacy are also important. It offers direct quantitative measures of the motivational factors important in constructing identity (see Vignoles, this volume).

Hussain and Bhushan (2011) indicate that for refugees from Tibet, Buddhism is central to Tibetan cultural identity, which is in turn central to identity. Interviewees were all victims of trauma such as the destruction of religious signs, torture of relatives, lack of religious, cultural and linguistic freedom. Buddhism was heavily relied upon to cope with the stresses of exile and to retain hope for the future of Tibet. Factors promoting coping included the protective hand of the Dalai Lama and other lamas, religious philosophy and practices, community bonding and historical exemplars of resiliency. Religious identity and the coping methods drawn from Tibetan Buddhism were central to the preservation of religion and culture, the central features of identity: "It is our collective strength that we survived the Chinese Cultural Revolution, when they tried every way to destroy our culture and identity."

Religious factors are often important in generating and coping with threats to identity. Jaspal and Cinnirella (2010) described young Muslim men in the UK coping with incompatible identities: being both Muslim and gay. Themes in extended interviews included attempts to make sense of sexual identity, using religious discourses to explain sexual identity, using British identity to explain sexual identity ("it's easier to be gay here") and fear of divine retribution. Grappling with the enormous central moral–religious dilemma indicated that the principle of coherence would be an important inclusion in IPT. For instance, in an attempt to achieve coherence, one participant imposed value on each of his identities: "I need to be a better Muslim" (Interviewer) "And what does it mean to be a better Muslim?" "Well not gay for starters."

Similarly, Ganzevoort *et al.* (2011) studied the threat to religious identity by homosexuality, among gay Dutch Christians. Using an SIT framework, Ganzevoort *et al.* identified four strategies: adhering to a religious identity and downplaying the gay identity; a reverse strategy, relinquishing the religious lifestyle in favor of the gay lifestyle; commuting from one identity to the other and seamlessly integrating both identities: "God loves you the way you are. Then this also has to be the case if you are this way." From the IPT perspective, as in the Jaspal and Cinnirella study of gay Muslims, these observations suggest the importance of the search for coherence in negotiating threats to identity.

Breakwell (1986) has discussed the difficulties experienced by gay people in deciding whether to come out. A common strategy involves passing (as not gay). Both passing and coming out lead to difficulties in the management of social relationships. Such difficulties are also experienced by those opting out of religious groups, for whom passing as religious (in the group) and passing as not affiliated when outside the group lead to discomfort, posing threats to both belonging and to coherence. Thus Shaffir (1991) has described defectors from ultra-orthodox Judaism, in search of meaning, undergoing a prolonged identity transition period of difficulty in social relationships, deception and impression management. Several varieties of deconversion trajectory have been described offering an area of great potential for the deployment of IPT. Streib and Keller (2004) distinguish for example the identity trajectories of ex-members of religious groups, ex-leaders, ex-marginals and ex-peripherals. Those transforming their identities as they join religious groups often do so more rapidly than defectors. Also in search of meaning, fewer social difficulties and more social support and belonging are reported as they come out, strengthening their religious identity and observance (Shaffir, 1991).

It has been suggested that members of religious–cultural minority groups may be particularly reluctant to seek professional help for psychological difficulties (Loewenthal and Brooke-Rogers, 2004). An important factor determining this reluctance is stigma, tied to self-esteem: in small religious–cultural enclaves, reputation is important and known psychological difficulties are stigmatizing, damaging self-esteem and harming the sense of belonging, being accepted as a full "valid" member by the group. Indeed, mental illness may be viewed as a form of disfigurement, which as such, has been argued by Jaspal (2012) as threatening to self-esteem, distinctiveness, continuity and efficacy, as well as coherence, belonging and meaning. Soorkia *et al.* (2011) reported that adherence to traditional values among South Asians in the UK predicted reluctance to seek professional help for psychological difficulties, suggesting that this aspect of identity related to the stigma and shame associated with mental disorders. Here we see some of the negative mental health consequences of religious identity for mental health.

Spiritual abuse is one of the most profound threats possible to religious identity. Sexual, physical or emotional abuse by trusted, powerful religious leaders often leads to extreme distress and psychological breakdowns. Religious authorities attempt to cover-up the abuse and defend the abusers. The abused often abandon religious identity (Arterburn and Felton, 2001; Gubi and Jacobs, 2009). Again the search for coherence may be an important principle. In this case there is a lack of coherence between personal values and those publicly supported by religious authority. Abandoning religious identity to achieve coherence and (as often) meaning may threaten belonging. Religious defection is often associated with long-term distress (e.g. Shaffir, 1991), highlighting the central importance to well-being of religious identity.

In the examples above, principles from IPT have been invoked. Jaspal and Cinnirella (2012) offer further IPT-based insights into the construction of ethnic identity which appear to have value in the understanding of religious identity. Translating a selection of their hypotheses from the domain of ethnicity, to the domain of religion, the following could be proposed:

- *Identification with one's religious group will have positive implications for the belonging principle of identity.* Among the studies reviewed in the previous section, Abu-Rayya and Abu-Rayya, Blaine and Crocker, Tiliopoulos and McVittie, Okulicz-Kozaryn and Hussain and Bhushan all offer support for this.
- *The distinctiveness principle of identity is enhanced by religious identification.* Among the studies reviewed, several examples of this can be suggested, for example, the daughters of expatriates perceiving their religious identity as distinctive compared with the other social identities accessible to them (Walters and Auton-Cuff, 2009).
- *Positive representations of the ingroup's history will become psychologically salient, whereas negative aspects will become latent.* Hussain and Bhushan (2011) indicate how the lamas and historical examples of religious heroism, inspire Tibetan Buddhists, whereas negative aspects of Tibetan life under the lamas are latent. Moreover, implicit comparisons by the Tibetans with their host culture (they are refugees in India) have not tempted them to an alternative identity. They have strengthened their determination to hope for a future in which they and their religion are returned to their country.
- *A positive sense of continuity derived from religious identity will have positive outcomes for self-esteem.* Thus Jaspal and Coyle (2010) suggest that the use of Arabic as a sacred language offers continuity to Muslims, Glinert describes the use of Yiddish as offering continuity to Hasidic Jews and

Walters and Auton-Cuff illustrate the importance of the continuity of religious identity and faith in maintaining some sense of well-being in the "ever-moving" world of the children of expatriates.

Other hypotheses proposed by Jaspal and Cinnirella could also be of use in enabling interpretation of the studies of religious identity processes, with the possibility of some prediction. IPT offers distinctive explanations about the links between religion, identity and mental health. The concept of threat to identity is a particularly important feature of IPT, offering insights which cannot be gleaned from SIT, role theory, Eriksonian and other approaches. Motivational factors known (or believed) to enhance well-being – belonging, self-esteem, continuity and self-efficacy – important in the construction and development of religious identity, are clearly implicated in the links between religion, identity and well-being.

Concluding thoughts

Much of the work looking at mental health outcome variables has involved an SIT framework and has used religious identity as an independent variable. A significant problem with some of this work is that "religion" and "religious identity" have often been primarily assessed using self-definition, so religion and identity are not readily separable. While this work has often unpacked corollaries of religious group membership with mental health consequences, it has not been focused on processes. Processes have often been inferred from the results. The strengths of IPT include the focus on intra-individual processes (as well as inter-individual and group processes). IPT also allows for ongoing dynamic change, a continuous evolution of strategies in dealing with ongoing threats to identity.

The SIT approach also has difficulties in dealing with individual spirituality, which has recently been sharply distinguished from religion, a clearly social identity. IPT integrates individual aspects of identity such as values and group membership and thus does not face this particular difficulty with respect to spirituality.

Our knowledge of the involvement of identity processes in mediating the relations between religion and mental health is still fragmentary. However IPT-based work has shown how important the processes of coping with threat to identity are for well-being and distress. The identity processes suggested by IPT will help to develop a stronger framework for unpacking and understanding the relations between religion and health in different cultural contexts.

REFERENCES

Abu-Rayya, H. M., and Abu-Rayya, M. H. (2009). Acculturation, religious identity, and psychological well-being among Palestinians in Israel. *International Journal of Intercultural Relations*, 33, 325–331.

Allport, G. W., and Ross, J. M. (1967). Personal religious orientation and prejudice. *Journal of Personality and Social Psychology*, 5, 432–443.

Arterburn, S., and Felton, J. (2001). *Toxic faith*. Colorado Springs, CO: Waterbrook Press.

Batson, C. D., Schoenrade, P. A., and Ventis, W. L. (1993). *Religion and the individual: a social-psychological perspective*. Oxford University Press.

Barker, E. (1998). Standing at the cross-roads: the politics of marginality in "subversive organizations." In D. G. Bromley (ed.), *The politics of religious apostasy: the role of apostates in the transformation of religious movements*. Westport, CT: Praeger.

Blaine, B., and Crocker, J. (1995). Religiousness, race and psychological well-being: exploring social psychological mediators. *Personality and Social Psychology Bulletin*, 10, 1,031–1,041.

Breakwell, G. M. (1986). *Coping with threatened identities*. London: Methuen.

Breakwell, G. M. (2010). Resisting representations and identity processes. *Papers on Social Representations*, 19, 6.1–6.11.

Brooke-Rogers, M., and Loewenthal, K. M. (2003). Religion, identity and mental health: perceived interactions within a multi-dimensional framework. *Social Psychology Review*, 5, 43–81

Brown, L. M., and Gilligan, C. (1992). *Meeting at the crossroads: women's psychology and girls' development*. Cambridge, MA: Harvard University Press.

Coates, D. D. (2011). Counselling former members of charismatic groups: considering pre-involvement variables, reasons for joining the group and corresponding values. *Mental Health, Religion and Culture*, 14, 191–207.

Coyle, A. (2010). Critical responses to faith development theory: a useful agenda for change? *Archive for the Psychology of Religion*, 33, 281–298.

Erikson, E. H. (1963). *Childhood and society*. New York: Norton.

Fowler, J. W. (1981). *Stages of faith: the psychology of human development and the quest for meaning*. San Francisco, CA: Harper & Row.

Ganzevoort, R. R., van der Laan, M., and Olsman, E. (2011). Growing up gay and religious: conflict, dialogue and religious identity strategies. *Mental Health, Religion and Culture*, 14, 209–222.

Gilligan, C. (1993). *In a different voice: psychological theory and women's development*. Cambridge, MA: Harvard University Press.

Glinert, L. H. (1999). We never changed our language: attitudes to Yiddish acquisition among Hasidic educators in Britain. *International Journal of the Sociology of Language*, 138, 31–52.

Gubi, P. M., and Jacobs, R. (2009). Exploring the impact on counsellors of working with spiritually abused clients. *Mental Health, Religion and Culture*, 12, 191–204.

Heath, C. D. (2006). A womanist approach to understanding and assessing the relationship between spirituality and mental health. *Mental Health, Religion and Culture*, 9, 155–170.

Heelas, P., and Woodhead, L. (2005). *The spiritual revolution: why religion is giving way to spirituality.* Oxford: Blackwell.

Hussain, D., and Bhushan, B. (2011). Cultural factors promoting coping among Tibetan refugees: a qualitative investigation. *Mental Health, Religion and Culture*, 14, 575–587.

James, W. (1890). *The principles of psychology*, vol. I. Austin, TX: Holt.

James, W. (1902). *The varieties of religious experience.* New York: Collier.

Jaspal, R. (2012). Disfigurement: the challenges for identity and the strategies for coping. *Psychological Studies*, 57(4), 331–335.

Jaspal, R., and Cinnirella, M. (2010). Coping with potentially incompatible identities: accounts of religious, ethnic and sexual identities from British Pakistani men who identify as Muslim and gay. *British Journal of Social Psychology*, 49, 849–870.

Jaspal, R., and Cinnirella, M. (2012). The construction of ethnic identity: insights from identity process theory. *Ethnicities*, 12(5), 503–530.

Jaspal, R. and Coyle, A. (2010). "Arabic is the language of the Muslims – that's how it was supposed to be": exploring language and religious identity through reflective accounts from young British-born South Asians. *Mental Health, Religion and Culture*, 13, 17–36.

Koenig, H. B., McCullough, M. E., and Larson, D. B. (2001). *Handbook of religion and health.* Oxford University Press.

Kroger, J. (2009). Identity development through adulthood. *Identity*, 2, 1–5.

Leavey, G., Loewenthal, K. M., and King, M. (2007). Challenges to sanctuary: the clergy as a resource for mental health care in the community. *Social Science and Medicine*, 65, 548–559.

Littlewood, R., and Lipsedge, M. (1989). *Aliens and alienists: ethnic minorities and psychiatry* (2nd edn.). London: Unwin Hyman.

Loewenthal, K. M. (2007). *Religion, culture and mental health.* Cambridge University Press.

Loewenthal, K. M. (2012). Diversity in spirituality and mental health. March 2012, *South London and Maudsley Trust, Spirituality and Mental Health Masterclass series.*

Loewenthal, K. M., and Brooke-Rogers, M. (2004). Culture sensitive support groups: how are they perceived and how do they work? *International Journal of Social Psychiatry*, 50, 227–240.

Loewenthal, K. M., and Cinnirella, M. (1999). Beliefs about the efficacy of religious, medical and psychotherapeutic interventions for depression and schizophrenia among different cultural-religious groups in Great Britain. *Transcultural Psychiatry*, 36, 491–504.

Loewenthal, K. M., MacLeod, A. K., Goldblatt, V., Lubitsh, G., and Valentine, J. D. (2000). Comfort and joy: religion, cognition and mood in individuals under stress. *Cognition and Emotion*, 14, 355–374.

Loewenthal, K. M., MacLeod, A. K., Goldblatt, V., Lubitsh, G., and Valentine, J. D. (2011). A gift that lasts? A prospective study of religion, cognition, mood and stress among Jews and Protestants. *World Cultural Psychiatry Research Review*, 6, 42–51.

Marcia, J. E. (1966). Development and validation of ego-identity statuses. *Journal of Personality and Social Psychology*, 3, 119–133.

Marcia, J. E., Waterman, A. S., Matteson, D. R., Archer, S. L., and Orlofsky, J. L. (eds.) (1993). *Ego identity: a handbook for psychosocial research*. New York: Springer-Verlag.

Marshall, S. K., and Schachter, E. P. (2010). Identity agents: suggested directions for further theory and research. *Identity*, 10, 138–140.

Mead, G. H. (1934). *Mind, self and society*. Chicago, IL: University of Chicago Press.

Moradi, B. (2005). Advancing womanist identity development. *The Counselling Psychologist*, 33, 225–253.

Moscovici, S. (2001). *Social representations: explorations in social psychology*. New York University Press.

Okulicz-Kozaryn, A. (2010). Religiosity and life satisfaction across nations. *Mental Health, Religion and Culture*, 13, 155–170.

Ossana, S. M., Helms, J. E., and Leonard, M. M. (1992). Do "womanist" identity attitudes influence college women's self-esteem and perceptions of environmental bias? *Journal of Counselling & Development*, 70, 402–408.

Pargament, K. I. (1997). *The psychology of religion and coping*. New York: Guilford Press.

Pargament, K. I. (2002). The bitter and the sweet: an evaluation of the costs and benefits of religiousness. *Psychological Inquiry*, 13, 168–181.

Pargament, K. I., Koenig, H. G., and Perez, L. M. (2000). A comprehensive measure of religious coping: development and initial validation of the RCOPE. *Journal of Clinical Psychology*, 56, 519–543.

Pargament, K. I., Tarakeshwar, N., Ellison, C. G., and Wulff, K. M. (2001). Religious coping among the religious: the relationships between religious coping and well-being in a national sample of Presbytarian clergy, elders and members. *Journal for the Scientific Study of Religion*, 40, 497–513.

Robinson, L. (2009). Cultural identity and acculturation preferences among South Asian adolescents in Britain: an exploratory study. *Children and Society* 23, 442–454.

Shaffer, B. A., and Hastings, B. M. (2007). Authoritarianism and religious identification: response to threats on religious beliefs. *Mental Health, Religion and Culture*, 10, 151–158.

Shaffir, W. (1991). Conversion experiences: newcomers to and defectors from orthodox Judaism. In Z. Sobel and B. Beit-Hallahmi (eds.), *Jewishness and Judaism in contemporary Israel*. Albany: State University of New York Press.

Sheldrake, P. (2007). *A brief history of spirituality*. Oxford: Wiley-Blackwell.

Soorkia, R., Snelgar, R., and Swami, V. (2011). Factors influencing attitudes towards seeking professional psychological help among South Asian students in Britain. *Mental Health, Religion and Culture*, 14, 613–623.

Steele, C. (1992). Race and the schooling of Black Americans. *Atlantic Monthly*, April, 68–78.

Streib, H., and Keller, B. (2004). The variety of deconversion experiences: contours of a concept in respect to empirical research. *Archive for the Psychology of Religion / Archiv für Religionspsychologie*, 26, 181–200.

Stryker, S., and Burke, P. J. (2000). The past, present and future of an identity theory. *American Sociological Review*, 63, 284–297.

Tajfel, H., and Turner, J. (1986). The Social Identity Theory of intergroup behaviour. In S. Worchel and W. G. Austin (eds.), *Psychology of intergroup relations* (pp. 7–24). Chicago, IL: Nelson.

Tiliopoulos, N., and McVittie, C. (2010). Aspects of identity in a British Christian sample. *Mental Health, Religion and Culture*, 13, 707–719.

Tryon, G. S., and Winograd, G. (2003). Developing a healthy identity, In M. Kopala and M. E. Keitel (eds.), *Handbook of counselling women* (pp. 185–197). Thousand Oaks, CA: Sage.

Vignoles, V., Chryssochou, X., and Breakwell, G. M. (2002). Evaluating models of identity motivation: self-esteem is not the whole story. *Self and Identity*, 1, 201–218.

Walters, K. A., and Auton-Cuff, F. P. (2009). A story to tell: the identity development of women growing up as third culture kids. *Mental Health, Religion and Culture*, 12, 775–772.

Zinnbauer, B. J., Pargament, K. I., Cole, B., Rye, M. S., Butter, E. M., Belavich, T. G., Hipp, K. M., Scott, A. B., and Kadar, J. L. (1997). Religion and spirituality: unfuzzying the fuzzy. *Journal for the Scientific Study of Religion*, 36, 549–564.

16 Identity threat and resistance to change: evidence and implications from transport-related behavior

Niamh Murtagh, Birgitta Gatersleben and David Uzzell

Climate change stands as one of the most important global issues of our time. The Intergovernmental Panel on Climate Change has described the warming of global climate systems as "unequivocal," and current mitigation policies as inadequate to prevent the growth of greenhouse gas emissions over the coming decades (IPCC, 2007, p. 1). In addition to policies and regulation, individual behavior change is seen as highly important in reducing emissions, perhaps particularly because of the hope of potentially rapid change (DECC, 2011). However, there is little evidence of change in individuals' behavior, with many indicators showing increased energy use over the past two decades. For example, in the UK, the percentage of passenger journeys by car (84 percent) remained stable between 1992 and 2007, the proportion of primary school children driven to school increased by 13 percent to 43 percent in the same period (DfT, 2009) and domestic energy use increased by 12 percent between 1990 and 2006 (DEFRA, 2008).

The failure to change toward pro-environmental behavior has received much attention (Kollmuss and Agyeman, 2002). The mismatch between responses to surveys of values, attitudes or beliefs and actual behavior has been termed the "value action gap" and has been widely documented in relation to a range of sustainable behaviors (Chung and Leung, 2007; Flynn *et al.*, 2009). Alongside external factors, such as infrastructure, a variety of "internal" influences have been identified. Amongst factors such as values and attitudes, themes relating to self-identity have emerged. Whitmarsh (2009) and Stoll-Kleemann (2001) suggested that social identity and status may act as barriers to change and Crompton and Kasser (2010) explicitly linked identity with pro-environmental behavior. Empirical work has begun to establish self-

The study presented in this chapter was first published in N. Murtagh, B. Gatersleben and D. Uzzell (2012). Self-identity threat and resistance to change: evidence on regular travel behaviour. *Journal of Environmental Psychology*, 32(4), 318–326.

identity as an influence on behavior (Falomir and Invernizzi, 1999; Gray et al., 1997; Nigbur et al., 2010; Nuttbrock and Freudiger, 1991; Oyserman et al., 2007; Sparks and Shepherd, 1992) and findings point to the involvement of self-identity in resistance to change behavior. Hansen et al. (2010) found that participants who rated smoking as important to their self-esteem were, perversely, more likely to rate smoking as positive after exposure to health warnings such as "smoking kills." Liberman and Chaiken (1992) demonstrated that personal relevance heightened defensiveness in response to threatening messages and that defensiveness may be triggered by threats to important parts of self-image (GinerSorolla and Chaiken, 1997; Tesser and Cornell, 1991).

However, in the literature on resistance to change, little work has been done to date to harness theoretical perspectives on self-identity. Identity Process Theory (IPT), as a comprehensive framework, encompassing both content and processes of self-identity, can make a valuable contribution. In a number of accounts of resistance to change, aspects of resistance are posited as defence mechanisms, including denial, projection, delegation and resignation (Crompton and Kasser, 2010; Kollmuss and Agyeman, 2002; Stoll-Kleemann et al., 2001): IPT offers a unified explanation of such processes as strategies for coping with threat. IPT then is particularly apposite as a theoretical account of resistance to change and provides, we will argue, a more complete formulation than existing theory.

A central tenet of IPT is that the self operates in compliance with specific guiding principles in such a way as to protect itself from threat. The self-concept underpins individual experience, perception, cognition and affect. A sense of self as integrated and congruent is essential for psychological well-being. Threat jeopardizes this consistency, risks individual experience and is likely to induce emotional distress. Defence against threat is thus central to the self. IPT has defined guiding principles which function to preserve the integrity of the self, namely, self-esteem, continuity of the self through time and distinctiveness, or a positive sense of uniqueness (Breakwell, 1986) and generalized self-efficacy (Breakwell, 1988). Circumstances in which one or more of the principles are undermined are experienced as threatening and will initiate psychological coping strategies. A range of strategies for coping with threat is potentially available and the strategies may operate at intrapsychic, interpersonal or group levels. At the intrapsychic level, individuals may engage in deflection or acceptance coping strategies. Deflection strategies include denial of the existence of a threat and reconstrual of its meaning. Acceptance strategies include re-evaluation of the salience of principles and fundamental identity change. Based on the proposals in IPT, it can be suggested that deflection strategies, in defence of the self under threat, may result in resistance to change.

Resistance to change in itself could be thought of as a coping strategy. However, the definition of resistance is central. In much of the organizational literature, resistance to change is implicitly defined as a behavioral outcome, resulting from a variety of causes (Dent and Goldberg, 1999), including "unconscious [mental] processes" (Bovey and Hede, 2001). The differentiation by Bovey and Hede between symptoms and causes of resistance is useful. The causal mental processes they suggest map to IPT's coping strategies. Thus it can be suggested that the coping strategies of denial, reconstrual, re-evaluation of principles and so on are the psychological processes underlying outcomes which may be jointly defined as resistance to change. We therefore define resistance to change as a behavioral outcome, which may be measured as occurrence or absence of behavior, or intention to perform or not to perform specific behaviors.

The study described below investigated whether identity threat is related to resistance to change behavior. A specific behavior was chosen: that of personal transport. As the highest contributor of UK household greenhouse gas emissions after domestic energy (Druckman and Jackson, 2009), combined with the travel trends mentioned above, personal travel is of demonstrable importance to sustainability.

Background

Approaches to resistance to change in previous research have ranged from resistance as a personality trait (Oreg, 2003) to a universal and almost inevitable response to required change (Dent and Goldberg, 1999; Rogers, 1965). Psychological Reactance Theory (Brehm, 1966) proposes that resistance is counteractive behavior elicited by a perceived threat to freedom. Individuals operate in the belief that they are free to engage in a range of behaviors, according to the theory and when such behaviors are prevented or threatened with prevention, reactance is triggered. Both state and trait reactance have been explored. Individual variation on a generalized tendency to non-compliance or to resist influence and advice from others, that is, on trait reactance, has been found (Pavey and Sparks, 2009). Distinct from trait reactance, state reactance is defined as a motivation aimed at restoring behavioral freedom. The significance of the threatened freedom for meeting "important needs" determines the strength of (state) reactance. Reactance Theory, however, does not define these needs or relate them to existing accounts of human needs, such as those of Maslow (1943), Sheldon and colleagues (2001) and others. As prerequisite conditions for initiation of the reactance process, the lack of definition of needs is, we suggest, a theoretical weakness. This weakness leads to difficulty in conceptualizing "freedom" and therefore reactance and difficulties in specifying conditions for testing the theory. Further, the theoretical positioning of Psychological Reactance Theory becomes problematic: how does this theory fit with other theories of psychological processes? Some theoretical relationships have been suggested: self-efficacy may be a prerequisite for reactance to occur (Brehm and Brehm, 1981) and reactance may be linked to self-esteem (Hellman and McMillin, 1997). Thus state reactance may represent one process within a set of more general processes aimed at coping with identity threat. We argue that IPT offers a framework encompassing such general or universal processes and is therefore a more complete and theoretically comprehensive account of resistance to change than Psychological Reactance Theory.

In its recognition of self-identity as a social product, IPT acknowledges earlier theories which position identities as multiple: each individual manages a range of identities, some contextual, some chronically salient (Stryker, 1980). Stryker's sociological role theory defines identities as the internalization of the expectations and norms associated with social roles. Thus an identity such as "parent" will comprise the expectations around behavior and attitudes, which individuals believe others, within their culture and context, hold regarding that role. The individual's behavior in the role is likely to be congruent with those beliefs. In contrast to theoretical perspectives which position social and personal identities as distinct (and in their contribution to this volume, Pehrson and Reicher argue convincingly for such distinction within a Social Identity Approach to group processes), the content dimension of IPT includes both components of social role identities and of personal identity, integrating individual and aspects of group or social perspectives at the structural level. At the process level, it is less clear how individual and group perspectives operate. In the absence of previous work on how threat and coping processes may apply to social role identities, in the current study, we elected to test our hypothesis at both overall self-concept and at specific role identity levels, with role identities conceptualized as elements within the content dimension.

An earlier study linked identities to travel mode choice and demonstrated that identities such as driver, public-transport user, worker and parent were related to travel behavior (Murtagh et al., 2012a). Of these identities, we chose to investigate the following two: driver and parent. We wanted to explore more than one social role identity and these offered variety, with one role identity more closely associated with a specific behavior and the other more closely associated with social relationships. Without previous empirical findings to suggest differences between role identities in how threat would relate to resistance to change, we postulated that threat to either would contribute to resistance.

Drawing together the objectives to examine whether identity threat contributes to resistance to change, with theory and research on the multiplicity of identities, the research hypotheses were that identity threat contributes to resistance to change, over and above past travel behavior and trait psychological reactance and that threats to either a driver or a parent identity contributes to resistance to change travel behavior.

The study

In investigating identity threat, two methodological challenges presented themselves. The first related to ethics. As outlined above, identity threat may entail emotional distress. A research protocol which seeks to engender identity threat risks breaching the ethical code of conduct of the British Psychological Society. The code requires research to be designed with the aim of eliminating potential risks to psychological well-being. Rather than attempt to trigger identity threat directly in the participants and possibly cause distress, a vignette design was used. Several vignettes, each describing a travel-related scenario, were presented to participants. By describing scenarios which, at best, may have had some similarity to the participants' own experiences, the threat was hypothetical rather than direct.

The second challenge related to operationalization of threat. To our knowledge, no previous empirical work sought to trigger identity threat. We drew on the theoretical definition of threat as undermining the guiding principles of the self. Vignettes were designed to threaten self-esteem, generalized self-efficacy, continuity and distinctiveness.[1] However, as threat is subjectively experienced, we measured the perception of threat of all four principles for each vignette. To evaluate whether an effect of threat could be observed, a baseline measure was taken of self-esteem, generalized self-efficacy, continuity and distinctiveness before the vignettes were presented and again at the end of the presentation. Similarly, because the experience of threat may invoke negative emotions, positive affect and negative affect were measured before and after presentation of the vignettes.

---

[1] Vignettes available from the lead author on request.

The vignettes were based in urban or suburban settings and referred to travel to work, school or other local journeys. Target participants therefore were in employment, owned a car, earned at or over the national average (£25,000, approximately $39,000) per annum and were recruited in urban and suburban locations across England. Half of the participants were parents of primary school-age children. Mean age was 40.19 (SD = 9.43, range 23–69) and 67 percent of the sample was female. With 91 percent describing themselves as white or white British, the sample was in line with national population estimates, although with limited representation of other ethnic groups.

Two forms of questionnaire were used, one of which presented vignettes relevant to parents, the other relevant to motorists. All vignettes described a travel-related scenario. Four vignettes were designed to threaten the target identity and four were designed as neutral with respect to identity threat. The vignettes were balanced on length and on the cost, time and convenience required to make a change. To ensure the target identity was salient, an initial short priming task required the participant to write a few sentences on how being a parent or a motorist was important to them. Baseline measures of emotion, future intentions regarding travel mode and identity factors were taken, followed by the presentation of eight vignettes. The participants were asked to read each vignette and answer items for each one on intention to change travel behavior and the perceived levels of threat to identity and freedom posed by the vignette. After the vignettes, the participants completed demographic details, measures of identity centrality, trait reactance and past transport behavior.

Measures

For each vignette, measures of resistance to change, identity threat and threat to freedom were anchored at "very unlikely" (scored as 1) and "very likely" (scored at 6). Using intention as a proxy for behavior in line with the Theory of Planned Behavior (Ajzen, 1985), resistance to change travel behavior was measured as the inverse of intention to change, with a single item for each of the eight vignettes. The item was phrased in positive terms: "How likely is it that you would intend to change your behavior?" worded appropriately for each vignette. Resistance to change was calculated as the reverse score. Threat to identity was measured as the mean of four items. One item each assessed the threat to self-esteem, generalized self-efficacy, continuity and distinctiveness, that is, the four guiding principles of the self-concept initially defined in IPT. The items were "It undermines my sense of self-worth," "It makes me feel less competent," "I would have to change who I am," and "It makes me feel less unique as a person." Cronbach alpha scores were calculated for each vignette and all scores were above 0.9. Psychological reactance was measured with two items per vignette. One item assessed the perceived threat to freedom: "It threatens my freedom." The other item assessed the perception of power to enforce change by the instigator of change in the vignette. Reactance was calculated as the mean of the two items.

Past or habitual travel behavior was measured with one question covering four items: "In general, how often do you do the following for local journeys? Cycle / Use local bus / Walk / Take a train, tube or tram?" with a fifth item on the Parent questionnaire: "Allow your children to walk (accompanied or unaccompanied)?"

To measure the levels of four guiding principles, one item was used for self-esteem (validated by Robins et al., 2001) and an eight-item scale was used for generalized self-efficacy (Chen et al., 2001). Continuity and distinctiveness were each measured on two-item scales developed for this study. The items measuring continuity were as follows: "I have not changed much over time" and "I am the same person I always was." Reliability was adequate ($\alpha = .69$). The distinctiveness items were as follows: "I feel I am different from other people in a good way" and "I am unique as a person." Reliability was low ($\alpha = .57$). However, the distinctiveness subscale showed similar relationships with the main variables as did self-esteem, self-efficacy and continuity. All items were rated on a five-point scale, anchored at 1 (not very true of me) to 5 (very true of me). A shortened version of the PANAS scale (Watson et al., 1988) was used to measure positive and negative emotions before and after the participants had reviewed the vignettes. Trait reactance was measured using the Hong Psychological Reactance Scale (Hong and Faedda, 1996). Identity centrality was measured by one item based on Vignoles et al. (2006): "Being a parent is an important part of defining who I am" and one item was used to control for previous intention to change travel behavior.

Results

Table 16.1 presents the means and standard deviations of the main variables and Table 16.2 presents correlations between the main variables.

The correlation of .81 ($p = .00$) between psychological reactance and identity threat suggests that these are be overlapping constructs, as discussed above. Correlations were also conducted by role identity and showed a similarly high correlation between reactance and identity threat for both motorist ($r = .82$) and parent ($r = .80$) groups.

As a manipulation check that the vignettes had induced threat, differentially between neutral and threat conditions and across both motorist

Table 16.1. Means and standard deviations of main variables

	All (N = 295)		Motorist (N = 146)		Parent (N = 149)	
	Mean	SD	Mean	SD	Mean	SD
Resistance to change	4.06	1.15	4.65	1.04	3.49	.96
Identity threat	2.38	1.26	2.59	1.43	2.17	1.03
Reactance	2.69	1.17	2.93	1.20	2.46	1.09
Baseline intention to change	2.84	1.53	2.43	1.34	3.24	1.60
Identity centrality	4.83	1.35	4.40	1.53	5.24	1.00
Trait reactance	3.17	.67	3.24	.66	3.10	.68
Past behavior:						
Walk	3.41	1.18	3.06	1.23	3.74	1.02
Cycle	1.67	1.05	1.51	.91	1.82	1.15
Bus	1.96	1.12	1.83	1.08	2.09	1.15
Train	2.03	1.13	1.97	1.04	2.09	1.21
Children walk	3.14	1.56	–	–	3.14	1.56
Positive affect	2.63	.84	2.53	.78	2.73	.88
Negative affect	1.36	.50	1.30	.46	1.41	.54

and parent subgroups, we conducted a mixed-design analysis of variance of identity threat with one repeated condition (threat versus neutral vignettes). The mean identity threat was higher for the threat vignettes, for both motorist and parent subgroups (mean for threat vignettes: motorist = 2.95, parent = 2.47; mean for neutral vignettes: motorist 2.39, parent = 2.15, see Figure 16.1). The effect of identity threat was significant ($F(1,293) = 69.01$), demonstrating that the vignette design had induced threat. The interaction was non-significant ($F(1,293) = 1.02, p = .31$), showing that the level of threat did not differ significantly between the motorist and the parent subgroups.

As a further manipulation check, t-tests were conducted on pre- and post- measures of identity factors (self-esteem, self-efficacy, continuity and distinctiveness) and state affect. Mean measures of self-esteem, self-efficacy and continuity were not significantly different post-vignette presentation. However, mean distinctiveness increased significantly (pre = 3.39, post = 3.50, $t(294) = -2.67, p = .01$). Pre- and post-vignette measures of negative affect did not differ significantly. Mean positive affect was lower post-vignettes (pre = 2.63, post = 2.49, $t(294) = 3.68, p = .00$). In the analyses below, the pre-vignette measures were used.

Table 16.2. Correlations between main variables

	1	2	3	4	5	6	7	8	9	10	11	12
1. Age												
2. Gender[a]	.07											
3. Resistance to change	.24**	.13*										
4. Identity threat	.03	-.01	.33**									
5. Reactance	.06	-.06	.35**	.81**								
6. Baseline intention to change	-.15**	-.12*	-.37**	-.05	.00							
7. Identity centrality	-.13*	-.02	-.05	.22**	.15*	.01						
8. Trait reactance	-.01	.03	.28**	.28**	.30**	-.10	.12*					
9. Past behavior: walk	-.13*	-.19**	-.45**	-.14*	-.15**	.27**	.02	-.18**				
10. Past behavior: cycle	-.11	.01	-.03	.05	.03	.23**	.07	.11	.16**			
11. Past behavior: bus	.05	-.13*	-.28**	-.05	-.09	.26**	.04	-.21**	.30**	.07		
12. Past behavior: train	-.05	-.09	-.17**	-.02	-.05	.18*	.03	-.09	.25**	.04	.37**	
13. Past behavior: children walk	.15	.07	-.16	-.07	-.22**	.08	-.09	-.12	.33**	-.07	.00	.10

Notes: [a] 1 = female, 2 = male. * $p < .05$, ** $p < .01$.

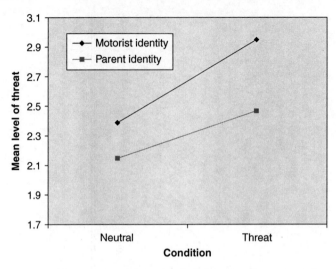

Figure 16.1. Mean level of identity threat for threat versus neutral condition

As a first test of our main hypothesis, that threat to identity would relate to resistance to change travel behavior, we conducted a mixed-design analysis of variance of resistance to change, with threat versus neutral vignettes as the repeated condition. The mean resistance to change was higher for the threat vignettes, for both motorist (threat mean 5.28, neutral mean 4.56) and parent (threat mean 3.86, neutral mean 3.39) subgroups (see Figure 16.2). The effect of threat on resistance to change was significant ($F(1,293) = 50.25$, $r = .38$) and this effect did not differ significantly between the subgroups ($F(1,293) = 2.38$, $p = .12$). This supports our hypothesis, that resistance to change is related to threat to identity and that this holds for threat to both motorist and parent identities.

Next we wanted to assess whether the threat to identity explained the variance in resistance to change over and above other contributory factors. We therefore conducted a multiple regression, in which resistance to change travel behavior was regressed onto identity threat, while controlling for baseline intention to change travel behavior, past travel behavior, trait reactance and identity centrality.[2] Other variables (gender, positive and negative affect, baseline identity factors) were also included but

[2] Identity salience was also measured, using two items from Callero (1985): "Being a motorist/parent is something I rarely even think about"; "I really don't have any clear feelings about being a motorist/parent" (Cronbach $\alpha = .81$ for motorist identity, .82 for

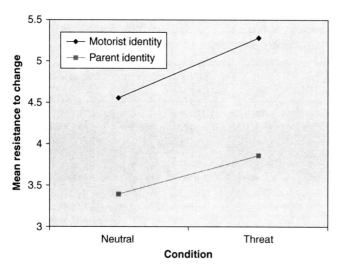

Figure 16.2. Mean resistance to change for neutral versus threat condition

were non-significant. All variables were entered simultaneously. Owing to their high correlation coefficient, separate regressions were conducted for identity threat and state reactance. Table 16.3 presents the regression results.

As Table 16.3 shows, psychological reactance and identity threat demonstrated an almost identical contribution to variance in resistance to change, supporting the argument above that reactance and identity threat are conceptually overlapping.

The regressions supported our hypothesis that identity threat contributed to resistance to change travel behavior over and above trait psychological reactance and past or habitual travel mode choice. This held for both a motorist and a parent identity. Of particular interest was the difference in direction of the relationship between identity centrality and resistance to change for threat to motorist and parent identities.

As identity threat was measured using threats to four identity principles (self-esteem, self-efficacy, continuity and distinctiveness), regressions were also conducted with the four single-item measures as independent variables: multicollinearity was indicated, with tolerance values under 1.2.

parent identity). However, identity centrality and identity salience demonstrated multi-collinearity; thus only identity centrality was used in the final regression. The regressions were also run with identity salience and the results followed the same pattern.

Table 16.3. Regression of resistance to change onto identity threat (state reactance) and control variables (ß values)

	All (N = 295)	Motorist subgroup (N = 146)	Parent subgroup (N = 149)
Age	.13** [.13**]	.10 [.09]	−.01 [.01]
Baseline intention to change	−.21*** [−.23***]	−.37*** [−.37***]	−.01 [−.03]
Past behavior:			
Walk	−.28** [−.28**]	−.21** [.20**]	−.23** [.23**]
Cycle	.06 [.07]	.06 [.07]	.11 [.11]
Bus	−.08 [−.07]	−.18* [−.18*]	.07 [.08]
Train	.02 [.03]	.04 [.05]	−−.07 [−.07]
Trait reactance	.12* [.11*]	−.20 [−.01]	.19* [.17*]
Identity centrality	−.10* [−.08]	.16* [.18*]	−.25* [−.25*]
Identity threat (state reactance)	.26*** [.26***]	.24** [.21**]	.17* [.18*]
Adj. R^2	.35 [.35] $F(12,277)$ = 13.73*** [13.814***]	.45 [.44] $F(12,132) =$ 10.91*** [10.60***]	.16 [.16] $F(12,132)$ = 3.32*** [3.33***]

Notes: *** $p <. 001$, ** $p < .01$, * $p < .05$.
Gender, positive and negative affect were included and were non-significant.

Discussion

Identity threat and climate change

The study supported identity threat as a predictor of resistance to change in the domain of transport-related behavior. Based on these findings and on IPT as a theoretical framework and consistent with writers such as Crompton and Kasser (2010) and Stoll-Kleemann and colleagues (2001), we can propose that resistance to change toward more sustainable behaviors may be the outcome of psychological deflection processes which are initiated as a response to threats to identity. Threats to identity are defined as contravention of the principles of operation of the self-concept, that is, contravention of the need to maintain or enhance self-esteem, self-efficacy, continuity and distinctiveness.

Climate change may threaten individuals at two levels: first, the threat of climate change itself, in particular the risks incurred by changing weather patterns and second, the requirement to change carbon-intensive behavior. While the former presents real threats to life, health and security, the latter encompasses different approaches, with varying levels of perceived threat. It can be suggested that many approaches to changing environmental behaviors currently being pursued may inadvertently contravene identity principles and trigger resistance.

Such discourses have proposed the need to change specific behaviors, such as reducing car use (Gerrard, 2010), as well as targeting behaviors more generally in arguing the need for radical change to consumerist lifestyles (Jackson, 2009). Messages demanding change are unavoidable given the urgency with which greenhouse gas emissions must be reduced (IPCC, 2007) but may threaten individuals' sense of continuity. The continuity principle necessitates a feeling of congruence between the self in the past, present and future and any change to a practice or value held as central by the individual could undermine continuity. This theoretical understanding poses the conundrum that *any* change could contravene the perception of continuity and yet change must happen if the escalating problems in the planet's ecological systems are to be mitigated.

Challenges to lifestyles may threaten the distinctiveness principle, in addition to continuity. In the consumerist society, the choice of possessions can be a way of distinguishing oneself: to have is to be. To have more and more expensive possessions than others is seen to reflect on one's worth, as well as one's importance, status and prestige (Dittmar, 1992). Particular consumption-based lifestyles are seen as aspirational and as paths to distinction. Arguments for the need to change away from carbon-intensive lifestyles may then threaten the sense of distinctiveness not only of those living such lives, but also of those who aspire to attain distinction through consumption.

A final point on how sustainability discourses may threaten identity lies in the potential for enforced change to undermine the self-efficacy principle. The principle posits that individuals experience the need to feel competent and in control of their lives and context. Stradling and colleagues (1999) found that 90 percent of their participants felt that the car provided greater control in their life. Entreaties to drive less are therefore likely to threaten self-efficacy. More broadly, enforced change, through regulation, modification of infrastructure or financial penalty, may undermine individuals' sense of self-efficacy and may result in resistance. In summary then, resistance triggered by attempts to change behavior toward sustainability may be understood as threats to continuity, distinctiveness or self-efficacy, which, according to IPT, can initiate defensive coping processes.

In addition to threatening one or more guiding principles of the self-concept, messages on sustainability may threaten at a specific or a general level. In the study above, the issue of the specificity of threat was simplified by targeting two particular identities and looking at threat to each in isolation. However, identities are multiple (Stryker, 1980) and threat may impinge on more than one. It would have been interesting in the study to assess to what extent the driver identity was also affected by threats targeted at the parent identity. We can speculate that threats to multiple identities and perhaps particularly to central, social identities, may be increasingly likely to invoke resistance.

IPT proposes that active defence against change is possible. Reactions to the issues of global warming appear to draw on a variety of such strategies. Individuals may reconstrue or redefine the meaning of the threat, in such a way as to defend the self against the need to change. An example of such reconstrual may be the acceptance that climate patterns are changing but attributing the cause to natural geological cycles, rather than anthropogenic sources. Individuals may re-attribute responsibility for a threatening position to an external locus of control. An example may be the attribution of primary responsibility for emissions to the Chinese, the Americans or the government. This then allows the positioning of personal actions as ineffective and protects the individual from a need to change. In addition to intrapsychic strategies, individuals may adopt a negativist strategy toward others and actively confront the perceived source of the threat to identity. An example of negativism may be attacks on the credibility of environmental scientists (Jaspal et al., 2013; Nerlich, 2010).

Further examples of coping strategies, with examples from common responses to the issue of climate change, could be cited. The point is that the current empirical findings linking identity threat to resistance to change, within the theoretical framework proposed by IPT, leads logically to an understanding that many common reactions to the issues around climate change may in fact be defensive reactions, aimed at protecting the self-concept from threat. This builds on earlier proposals by Stoll-Kleemann and colleagues (2001), who attributed the reactions of their study participants, such as denying the gravity of the issues or blaming the government, to ego-defensive processes. Whereas they argued that self-identity therefore stands alongside denial of seriousness or responsibility as reasons not to change, we extend their argument to propose that identity defence is the primary motivation. Questioning the severity of the issues or delegating responsibility to the government then are outcomes of coping strategies. Further support for this argument is suggested in the work of Tertoolen et al. (1998) who found that providing more information on the costs and environmental impacts of travel by car resulted in an increase in blaming government policies rather than behavior change: the findings may be interpreted as information experienced as threat leading to defensive coping strategies.

But resistance to change is only one possible outcome from the coping strategies proposed in IPT and other strategies may result in positive coping. An example is the formation of social groups to raise awareness or to attempt to counteract the threat. It is possible to suggest that groups such as Friends of the Earth, transition towns (Hopkins, 2009) and local community groups (Peters *et al.*, 2010) represent the outcome of strategies for coping with identity threat that bring benefits at individual and societal levels.

In the study presented above, reactance explained almost identical levels of variance to identity threat and the constructs as measured demonstrated very high correlation. Psychological reactance theory and IPT then may offer alternative accounts of similar phenomena. However, as noted in the introduction, reactance theory lacks a clearly defined conceptualization of "freedom," which can be associated with established psychological constructs and processes. Thus psychological reactance theory suggests an explanation of a behavioral outcome but offers little further elucidation of psychological processes or alternative outcomes. In contrast, IPT offers a comprehensive theory, suggesting a variety of coping strategies and behavioral outcomes. We suggest that IPT provides a more complete account of resistance to change than that of psychological reactance theory.

The findings suggest that threat to specific social role identities may be experienced as threat to the self-concept overall. In the discussion above, we noted that role identities were elements of the content of the self-concept. Two alternative theoretical interpretations may be considered: either role identities constitute a special type of content, or threat may be experienced to any salient component of the content dimension. These interpretations may in fact converge. In the original formulation of IPT, the close interweaving of social and personal identities was described, with social roles seen as producing attributes of current personal identity. Thus the processes of assimilation/accommodation and evaluation will operate, in compliance with the guiding principles, on role identities as part of maintaining the self. The processes are not "content blind": they revise content or value based on existing content, in combination with newly arriving contextual information. When an attempt to accommodate or assimilate new information, or change a value, undermines a guiding principle, threat results. Thus threat may be experienced from any component of content (although it is probable that only salient components would trigger coping strategies). As particularly salient elements of content, social role identities may be especially vulnerable to threat but values, goals or other salient elements may also be subject to threat.

Considerations for IPT research and application

Our ethical concerns, outlined above, over the potential of identity threat to cause distress appear not to have been borne out. Although positive emotions declined after presentation of the vignettes, negative emotions remained stable, contradicting our expectation that threat will trigger negative affect. Further, the measures of self-esteem, generalized self-efficacy and continuity remained stable, while distinctiveness increased. These findings can be interpreted with reference to the theory, and the interpretation points to further methodological challenges (see Vignoles, this volume). IPT emphasizes the criticality of identity integrity and the risks to the self-concept of identity threat. Thus the processes for dealing with threat are proposed as likely to be highly effective in order to protect the self. Coping strategies for most individuals in most situations will therefore be executed rapidly and successfully. The methodological challenge arises from attempting to capture such transient processes and attempting to demonstrate that the processes have in fact been executed. In the current study, the post-vignettes measures suggested that by the end of the 20-minute survey, no threat was experienced. We assume that threat had been triggered because our manipulation check showed differences in perception of threat between the threat and neutral conditions. This suggests that experimental invocation of identity threat may not result in enduring distress and therefore does not carry particular ethical risks. However, as the current study attempted an indirect threat to identity, before generalizing, future studies should examine levels of distress or change caused by direct threat.

The second methodological challenge emerges from the typically transient nature of threat. Manipulation checks, as were used in the current study, are one way of assessing whether threat was invoked but other methods should be explored. It is likely that improved methods will draw on techniques in cognitive psychology, such as the implicit attitudes test or other ways of demonstrating rapid and non-conscious cognitive processes.

A third challenge lies in the conceptual proximity of the guiding principles and the operation of the self-concept. The study's finding of multicollinearity of the guiding principles may have resulted from conceptual overlap. Alternatively, participants may have had difficulty in differentiating between the concepts of self-esteem, distinctiveness, self-efficacy and continuity. The current findings suggest that self-report may be inadequate to distinguish between the guiding principles. Further experimental work is needed to show that threat is experienced as undermining each guiding principle: methods developed in such work could additionally be used as qualification criteria for additional guiding principles (Vignoles *et al.*, 2006). The final challenge lies in the proposition that coping strategies may result in a wider variety of behaviors, some of which may be categorized as deflective or acceptance behavior. Combined with the difficulty of evaluating whether identity threat has been invoked, this could lead to potential difficulties in interpreting experimental results. If no behavioral outcome is observed, is this because the coping strategies adopted did not have a behavioral outcome or because no threat was experienced? If both deflective and acceptance behaviors are observed between participants, does this demonstrate strategies for coping with threat? Careful study design, based on thorough understanding of the many alternative coping strategies proposed in IPT, will be required.

The current research was necessarily limited in focus, in order to test specific hypotheses. Future studies could explore how identity threat could elicit coping strategies beyond resistance to change. In particular, Identity Process Theory raises the promising potential for identity threat to *facilitate* change through acceptance strategies, an important avenue to explore for encouraging sustainable behavior. A further limitation was the necessity to, in part, de-contextualize the identities investigated. However, identities develop and are maintained within social and structural contexts (Christie, 2010; Uzzell, 2010) and further research is needed to explore how contexts influence the experience of identity threat. The study focused primarily on singular identities. More work is needed on the implications of multiple identities and their interaction (see Amiot and Jaspal, this volume). Can threat to one identity be compensated by recourse to another? Is there "spillover" from one identity to another? Does the relative importance of identities relate to types of coping strategy? Finally, the current study was limited to participants who earned at or above the national average income and were working parents. Identities and behaviors may relate to socio-economic class or income: future research should explore if identity processes operate in a similar way across all income levels, for different socio-demographic groups and across ethnicities.

Implications for policy and campaigning

In demonstrating the relationship between threats to identity and resistance to change, the study suggests two main learning points for policy and campaigning. To encourage changing behaviors toward sustainability, threats to identity should be minimized and more sutainable identities should be fostered.

One way in which identity threat may be reduced is in the open acknowledgment of the potential threats to individuals and groups, threats not only by climate change itself, but also threats implicit in changes to lifestyle. Discourses could emphasize the inevitability of change in human history and could harness examples of successful life change from the past: the Industrial Revolution, the massive changes to the class system in Britain in the first half of the twentieth century, legal equality for women. The learning points of such changes included upheaval, uncertainty and anxiety during the process but which brought about a better and fairer society in which the well-being of most people was enhanced. New discourses aimed at facilitating identity change could aid both mitigation of climate change through changed behavior and adaptation to changing ecological and social systems.

Identity change could perhaps be fostered by encouraging even occasional change. The findings above of significant contribution to intention to change of past travel behavior, especially walking and of previous intention to change, may imply that early stages of encouraging more sustainable travel may be crucial. From an identity perspective, occasional changes may facilitate the development of a new or modified identity. Through walking at least sometimes, individuals may begin to see themselves as "someone who walks" and this identity then may guide subsequent behavior. If people can be persuaded to walk sometimes, they may then be less resistant to further change. The transtheoretical model of behavior change (Prochaska et al., 1992) proposes that a stage of contemplation of change is necessary for subsequent successful change. Thus if individuals have made occasional changes in their behavior, they may be considered to be in the early stages of change and may be more susceptible to influences toward further change. Fujii and Kitamura (2003) showed that when drivers were encouraged to take a bus for a period of time, they were more likely to travel by bus subsequently. Other ways of encouraging the development of more sustainable identities should be explored.

Summary

The chapter presented an empirical study demonstrating that self-identity threat contributes to resistance to change travel behavior. As explicated by Identity Process Theory, self-identity threat triggers psychological coping strategies and of these, deflection strategies may account for resistance to change. The implications of this finding are discussed, including how discourses around climate change may inadvertently invoke identity threat. In addition to enhanced theoretical understanding, the application of IPT also engendered suggestions for policy and campaigning to encourage sustainable behaviors.

REFERENCES

Ajzen, I. (1985). From intentions to actions: a theory of planned behavior. In J. Kuhland and J. Beckman (eds.), *Action-control: from cognitions to behavior* (pp. 11–39). Heidelberg: Springer.

Bovey, W. H., and Hede, A. (2001). Resistance to organizational change: the role of defence mechanisms. *Journal of Managerial Psychology*, 16(7), 534–548.

Breakwell, G. M. (1986). *Coping with threatened identities*. London: Methuen.

Breakwell, G. M. (1988). Strategies adopted when identity is threatened. *Revue Internationale de Psychologie Sociale*, 1, 189–203.

Brehm, J. W. (1966). *A theory of psychological reactance*. New York: Academic Press.

Brehm, S. S., and Brehm, J. W. (1981). *Psychological reactance: a theory of freedom and control*. London: Academic Press.

Callero, P. L. (1985). Role-identity salience. *Social Psychology Quarterly*, 48(3), 203–215.

Chen, G., Gully, S. M., and Eden, D. (2001). Validation of a new general self-efficacy scale. *Organizational Research Methods*, 40(1), 62–83.

Christie, I. (2010). Foreword. In M. Peters, S. Fudge and T. Jackson (eds.), *Low carbon communities: imaginative approaches to combating climate change locally* (pp. xiv–xviii). Cheltenham, UK: Edward Elgar.

Chung, S. S., and Leung, M. M. Y. (2007). The value-action gap in waste recycling: the case of undergraduates in Hong Kong. *Environmental Management*, 40, 603–612.

Crompton, T., and Kasser, T. (2010). Human identity: a missing link in environmental campaigning. *Environment*, 52(4), 23–33.

DECC (2011). Statistics Release: UK climate change sustainable development indicator: 2010 greenhouse gas emissions, provisional figures. Accessed June 20, 2011, from www.decc.gov.uk/assets/decc/Statistics/climate_change/1515-statrelease-ghg-emissions-31032011.pdf.

DEFRA (2008). Final Energy Consumption:1980 – 2006. Accessed August 11, 2011, from www.archive.defra.gov.uk/evidence/statistics/environment/supp/spkf05.htm.

Dent, E. B., and Goldberg, S. G. (1999). Challenging "resistance to change." *Journal of Applied Behavioral Science*, 35(1), 25–41.

DfT (2009). Transport statistics for Great Britain: 2009 edition. Accessed May 10, 2010, from www.dft.gov.uk/pgr/statistics/datatablespublications/2009edition.

Dittmar, H. (1992). *The social psychology of material possessions: to have is to be*. Hemel Hempstead, UK: Harvester Wheatsheaf.

Druckman, A., and Jackson, T. (2009). *Mapping our carbon responsibilities: more key results from the Surrey Environmental Lifestyle Mapping Framework (SELMA)*. Guildford: University of Surrey.

Falomir, J. M., and Invernizzi, F. (1999). The role of social influence and smoker identity in resistance to smoking cessation. *Swiss Journal of Psychology/Schweizerische Zeitschrift für Psychologie/Revue Suisse de Psychologie*, 58(2), 73–84.

Flynn, R., Bellaby, P., and Ricci, M. (2009). The "value-action gap" in public attitudes towards sustainable energy: the case of hydrogen energy. *Sociological Review*, 57, 159–180.

Fujii, S., and Kitamura, R. (2003). What does a one-month free bus ticket do to habitual drivers? An experimental analysis of habit and attitude change. *Transportation*, 30(1), 81–95.

Gerrard, S. (2010). The Community Carbon Reduction Programme. In M. Peters, S. Fudge and T. Jackson (eds.), *Low carbon communities: imaginative approaches to combating climate change locally* (pp. 139–156). Chichester, UK: Edward Elgar.

GinerSorolla, R., and Chaiken, S. (1997). Selective use of heuristic and systematic processing under defense motivation. *Personality and Social Psychology Bulletin*, 23(1), 84–97.

Gray, D., Amos, A., and Currie, C. (1997). Decoding the image of consumption, young people, magazines and smoking. An exploration of theoretical and methodological issues. *Health Education Research*, 12(4), 505–517.

Hansen, J., Winzeler, S., and Topolinski, S. (2010). When death makes you smoke: a terror management perspective on the effectiveness of cigarette on-pack warnings. *Journal of Experimental Social Psychology*, 46(1), 226–228.

Hellman, C. M., and McMillin, W. L. (1997). The relationship between psychological reactance and self-esteem. *The Journal of Social Psychology*, 137(1), 135–138.

Hong, S.-M., and Faedda, S. (1996). Refinement of the Hong Psychological Reactance Scale. *Educational and Psychological Measurement*, 56(1), 178–182.

Hopkins, R. (2009). *The transition handbook: creating local sustainable communities beyond oil dependency*. London: Finch.

IPCC (2007). *Contribution of Working Groups I, II and III to the Fourth Assessment Report of the Intergovernmental Panel on Climate Change*. [Core Writing Team, Pachauri, R. K. and Reisinger, A. (eds.)]. Geneva, Switzerland: IPCC.

Jackson, T. (2009). *Prosperity without growth: economics for a finite planet*. Oxford: Earthscan.

Jaspal, R., Nerlich, B., and Koteyko, N. (2013). Contesting science by appealing to its norms: readers discuss climate science in *The Daily Mail*. *Science Communication*, 35(3), 383–410.

Kollmuss, A., and Agyeman, J. (2002). Mind the gap: why people act environmentally and what are the barriers to pro-environmental behavior? *Environmental Education Research*, 8(3), 239–260.

Liberman, A., and Chaiken, S. (1992). Defensive processing of personally relevant health messages. *Personality and Social Psychology Bulletin*, 18, 669–679.

Maslow, A. (1943). A theory of human motivation. *Psychological Review*, 50, 370–396.

McClelland, D. C. (1975). *Power: the inner experience*. Oxford: Irvington.

Murtagh, N., Gatersleben, B., and Uzzell, D. (2012a). Multiple identities and travel mode choice for regular journeys. *Transportation Research Part F*, 15(5), 514–524.

Murtagh, N., Gatersleben, B., and Uzzell, D. (2012b). Self-identity threat and resistance to change: evidence on regular travel behaviour. *Journal of Environmental Psychology*, 32(4), 318–326.

Nerlich, B. (2010). "Climategate": paradoxical metaphors and political paralysis. *Environmental Values*, 19(4), 419–442.

Nigbur, D., Lyons, E., and Uzzell, D. (2010). Attitudes, norms, identity and environmental behaviour: using an expanded theory of planned behaviour to predict participation in a kerbside recycling programme. *British Journal of Social Psychology*, 49(2), 259–284.

Nuttbrock, L., and Freudiger, P. (1991). Identity salience and motherhood: a test of Stryker's theory. *Social Psychology Quarterly*, 54(2), 146–157.

Oreg, S. (2003). Resistance to change: developing an individual difference measure. *Journal of Applied Social Psychology*, 88, 680–693.

Oyserman, D., Fryberg, S. A., and Yoder, N. (2007). Identity-based motivation and health. *Journal of Personality and Social Psychology*, 93(6), 1,011–1,027.

Pavey, L., and Sparks, P. (2009). Reactance, autonomy and paths to persuasion: examining perceptions of threats to freedom and informational value. *Motivation and Emotion*, 33(3), 277–290.

Peters, M., Fudge, S., and Jackson, T. (2010). *Low-carbon communities: imaginative approaches to combating climate change locally*. Cheltenham, UK: Edward Elgar.

Prochaska, J. O., DiClemente, C. C., and Norcross, J. C. (1992). In search of how people change – applications to addictive behaviors. *American Psychologist*, 47(9), 1,102–1,114.

Robins, R. W., Hendin, H. M., and Trzesniewski, K. H. (2001). Measuring global self-esteem: construct validation of a single-item measure and the Rosenberg Self-Esteem Scale. *Personality and Social Psychology Bulletin*, 27(2), 151–161.

Rogers, C. R. (1965). Interpersonal relationships: USA 2000. *Journal of Applied Behavioral Science*, 4(3), 265–280.

Sheldon, K. M., Elliot, A. J., Kim, Y., and Kasser, T. (2001). What is satisfying about satisfying events? Testing 10 candidate psychological needs. *Journal of Personality and Social Psychology*, 80(2), 325–339.

Sparks, P., and Shepherd, R. (1992). Self-identity and the theory of planned behavior: assessing the role of identification with "Green Consumerism." *Social Psychology Quarterly*, 55(4), 388–399.

Stoll-Kleemann, S. (2001). Barriers to nature conservation in Germany: a model explaining opposition to protected areas. *Journal of Environmental Psychology*, 21(4), 369–385.

Stoll-Kleemann, S., O'Riordan, R., and Jaeger, C. C. (2001). The psychology of denial concerning climate mitigation measures: evidence from Swiss focus groups. *Global Environment*, 11, 107–117.

Stradling, S. G., Meadows, M. L., and Beatty, S. (1999). *Factors affecting car use choices*. Edinburgh: Transport Research Institute, Napier University.

Stryker, S. (1980). *Symbolic interactionism: a social structural version*. Menlo Park, CA: Benjamin Cummings.

Tertoolen, G., Van Kreveld, D., and Verstraten, B. (1998). Psychological resistance against attempts to reduce private car use. *Transportation Research Part a-Policy and Practice*, 32(3), 171–181.

Tesser, A., and Cornell, D. P. (1991). On the confluence of self processes. *Journal of Experimental Social Psychology*, 27(6), 501–526.

Uzzell, D. (2010). Collective solutions to a global problem. *The Psychologist*, 23, 880–883.

Vignoles, V. L., Regalia, C., Manzi, C., Golledge, J., and Scabini, E. (2006). Beyond self-esteem: influence of multiple motives on identity construction. *Journal of Personality and Social Psychology*, 90(2), 308–333.

Watson, D., Clark, L. A., and Tellegen, A. (1988). Development and validation of brief measures of positive and negative affect: the PANAS scales. *Journal of Personality and Social Psychology*, 54(6), 1,063–1,070.

Whitmarsh, L. (2009). Behavioural responses to climate change: asymmetry of intentions and impacts. *Journal of Environmental Psychology*, 29(1), 13–23.

17 Making sense of risk: the role of social representations and identity

Julie Barnett and Konstantina Vasileiou

Discourses of risk are common in the modern world. We talk about avoiding risks, taking them, worrying about them and sometimes about how we welcome them. Managing risk is a perennial concern of private and public institutions alike. Any theory that is to be relevant to increasing our understanding of social issues must surely therefore further our understanding of risk and society. In a domain largely characterized by piecemeal theorizing, an understanding of risk appreciation that is able to draw on coherent and systematic theoretical propositions is long overdue. Given its holistic focus and the potential to integrate the personal and the social through its synthesis with Social Representations Theory (SRT), the interpretative lens provided by Identity Process Theory (IPT) is a prime candidate for doing this (Breakwell, this volume). This chapter will therefore explore the applicability of IPT to understanding publics' appreciations of risk and the implications of this for risk communication. Specifically, attention will be drawn to how identity dynamics are interwoven with risk representations, arguing that this should be taken into account when risk communication is designed. To understand how people conceive and make sense of hazards, we need to recognize how these considerations relate to identity. As well as seeking to explore the contribution of IPT to public risk appreciation, we will also reflect on how the application to risk might also enrich our understanding of IPT.

The chapter will unfold as follows. We will first consider IPT and SRT and the relationship between them before sketching the way in which they have been applied to risk issues thus far. We will then turn our attention to two data sets – one relating to "avian flu" (H5N1) and the other to nut allergy in order to further explore the contention that social representations of risk may threaten the principles of identity proposed by IPT and that representations may be customized in order to cope with the threat and/or enhance the principled operation of identity. Finally we will reflect upon the insights this analysis has provided, critically assess the value of IPT for understanding the public appreciation of risk and for informing strategies for behavior change or maintenance.

Identity Process Theory and Social Representations Theory

Other chapters in this volume consider IPT's depiction of how threat to identity comes about (Jaspal, this volume) and we will not rehearse this in detail here. Suffice to say that in essence threat to identity arises when the *processes* of identity (assimilation–accommodation and evaluation) cannot comply with the *principles* of identity. The latter were originally conceptualized as self-esteem, distinctiveness, self-efficacy and continuity (Breakwell, 1986, 1992) though latterly have been extended to belonging and meaning (Vignoles *et al.*, 2002) and psychological coherence (Jaspal and Cinnirella, 2010). Threat to identity occasions the deployment of coping strategies and the theory posits that these can be located at intrapsychic, interpersonal, intra-group or intergroup levels. Extending this, from early on in the development of IPT, Breakwell (1993a) noted that its usefulness would depend on whether or not it could contribute to explanations of how social knowledge and values are generated and transformed. To this end, Breakwell (1993b) developed propositions that linked the operation of identity processes and principles with Social Representations Theory (SRT).

A social representation is a system of values, ideas and practices that enable individuals to orient themselves in the world and that eases communication between members of a community by providing understood ways of naming and classifying all aspects of that world (Moscovici, 1973). These ideas are evident in the study in which the notion of social representations was first introduced (Moscovici, 1961). The study was located in France in the 1950s and focused on the way in which psychoanalysis was first received and subsequently circulated in French society. One aspect of this, that has remained core to SRT, was a focus on what was produced when the lay public elaborated and circulated scientific ideas within systems of common sense. This is illustrative of one of the central preoccupations of SRT: how is the unfamiliar made familiar? To answer this question, the theory proposes that social representations are formed through two main processes: anchoring and objectification. Anchoring refers to the assignation of meaning to new objects by integrating them with existing knowledge. The process of objectification transforms the unfamiliar and abstract into a concrete, common-sense reality.

The interface between IPT and social representations can broadly be considered in two ways. On the one hand Breakwell proposes that exposure to, acceptance of, and use of social representations are a function of the operation of identity processes (Breakwell, 1993b). Conversely, the nature of social representations to which individuals are exposed and that they accept and use, can constrain the operation of identity principles. The way in which different types of representations afford different possibilities of acceptance, uptake and use is best illustrated with reference to the distinction made by Moscovici (1988) between hegemonic, emancipated and polemical social representations. These types of representations vary in terms of how consensual they are within and between social groups and thus they differentially constrain what possibilities exist for their change or customization.

To foreshadow further some of the points we wish to draw out in relation to threatened identities around risk, it is important to emphasize that identities consist of multiple elements that will vary in their salience at any point in time. I might think about myself, for example, as a shy person, as a researcher, as a Crystal Palace fan and as British. In line with this, Breakwell (1993b) is clear that threats do not simply affect social identities. She notes the importance of "other dimensions of the self-concept as potential determinants of individual differences in involvement in the processes of social representation" (p. 12). She proposes that traits (for example) shape the individual's exposure to, acceptance of, and use of a social representation and also that, inasmuch as traits are a self-conscious self-definition, they shape the readiness to expose oneself to, accept, or use a social representation. It is perhaps fair to say though that such dimensions of the self-concept have received less empirical attention within IPT.

In line with this, much of the empirical qualitative work explicitly located around IPT has been aligned to threatened social identities relating to religion, ethnicity, nationality or sexuality. Place identity, migration and enforced relocation have been a further focus of qualitative work (Speller et al., 2002; Timotijevic and Breakwell, 2000; Twigger-Ross and Uzzell, 1996).

How can we use IPT and SRT to understand the way in which people assign actual or potential events as risks and how they make sense of and act in relation to these risks? Before we address this question, let us first take a brief look at the literature that provides insights into how people respond to risk and consider some of the work that has already proved useful in understanding this area.

What do we know about responses to risk?

Risks are potential dangers (Arnoldi, 2009); dangers from future damage (Douglas, 1994). These are ostensibly simple definitions but the relationships between the concept of risk with others such as hazard, danger, or uncertainty are often unclear. Although often used interchangeably, it is important to distinguish hazard from risk. A hazard is simply something that can cause harm. Risk results from exposure to a hazard and is commonly considered in terms of two dimensions: likelihood (or probability) and consequences (or outcomes). As an illustration: a bottle of bleach is a hazard and whether it is on the top or bottom shelf of the cupboard the hazard remains the same. In contrast, the risk of the bottle of bleach posed to a small child is very different in these two scenarios. The likelihood of a highly negative outcome is greater when the bleach is on the bottom shelf. It is important to note, however, that the distinction between hazard and risk is tenuous from a lay point of view and similarly, the lay conceptualization of risk, as we shall see, attends to many parameters other than probability and consequence (Joffe, 2003). This is not the only area of definitional clarity that needs to be considered. Take the concept of threat. Clearly, threat is a concept that relates to risk, containing as it does an allusion to impending danger, for example, to some element of health or well-being. As we have seen, threat is also a core concept within IPT. Here, however, the threat is to identity. Care is needed to keep the two uses of "threat" distinct although sometimes they may be linked: threats to health and well-being may threaten identity and conversely, threats to identity may indirectly threaten well-being. The interested reader may want to consider this further in the light of the related distinction between realistic or material threat and symbolic threat (Stephan and Stephan, 2000).

It is not possible within the confines of this chapter to give more than a brief sketch of the relevant background of risk research. The interested reader is referred to key texts by Breakwell (2007) and Arnoldi (2009) for description of psychological and sociological approaches (respectively) to risk.

The seminal recognition by psychologists that risk is about more than the actuarial combination of estimates of likelihood and consequences can be seen in the work of Paul Slovic. He identified a range of psychological factors that are systematically attributed to the hazard – such as how familiar it is or how much it is dreaded (Slovic, 1987). Slovic also stimulated work around the concept of trust (Slovic, 1993) and the way in which public understandings of risk are affected by trust in those managing the risk continues to generate a productive stream of research (Siegrist et al., 2010). Another recent "turn" in the literature of the psychology of risk can be seen in the consideration of affect. Slovic (2000), a key figure here also, states "Although risk perception was originally viewed as a form of deliberative, analytic information processing, over time we have come to realize how highly dependent it is upon intuitive and experiential thinking, guided by emotional and affective processes" (p. xxxi).

From a sociological perspective Arnoldi (2009) characterizes three dimensions of the social nature of risk. First of all, risks are social and political problems; secondly, people from different social and cultural backgrounds understand risk differently; and thirdly, the concept of risk is increasingly core to the practices and knowledge with which people are governed. Despite the different levels of analysis inherent in psychological and sociological characterizations of risk, it is a cross disciplinary framework that forms the most comprehensive approach to risk thus far.

The Social Amplification of Risk Framework (SARF) (Kasperson et al., 1988) was proposed in order to enhance our understanding of the social processes that can mediate between a hazard event and its consequences. The central contention of the framework is that "Events pertaining to hazards interact with psychological, social, institutional, and cultural processes in ways that can heighten or attenuate public perceptions of risk and shape risk behavior. Behavioral patterns in turn generate secondary social or economic consequences. These consequences extend far beyond direct harms to human health or the environment to include significant indirect impacts" (Renn et al., 1992, pp. 139–140).

SARF identifies categories of mediator/moderator that intervene between the hazard event and its consequences and proposes that they act in a particular causal and temporal sequence. Information flows through various sources and channels, triggering individual and social stations of amplification and precipitating behavioral reactions. This is Stage I. Stage II of the framework is concerned with secondary impacts. Here the initial amplification of risk perceptions and behaviors leads to secondary consequences, which consist of socio-economic and political impacts.

Unsurprisingly, in the light of the ambitious agenda that it addresses, SARF has attracted considerable academic and policy attention which highlights both its value and shortcomings (Petts et al., 2001; Pidgeon et al., 2003). Breakwell and Barnett (2001) make the point that the applicability of SARF is limited in that it does not specify the causal processes that inhabit the framework and this is required in order to be able to predict and effect change in the lifecycle of a hazard or in the substance or acceptance of risk representations (Breakwell, 2010).

This is our cue to return to SRT and IPT and consider the value they have in understanding patterns of risk appreciation and the associated impacts. We will follow this by outlining some further possibilities afforded by IPT and SRT in understanding responses to risk in relation to two very different issues: avian flu and nut allergy.

Understanding risk appreciation with SRT and IPT

Making sense of risk in contemporary society increasingly means making sense of ideas, data, images, or information that are unfamiliar, that are often linked to anxiety and that may be uncertain (Barnett and Breakwell, 2003). Uncertainty may stem from a number of sources such as the imprecision of scientific estimations about the magnitude of the risk or from inferred or acknowledged conflict between scientists about estimations or the nature of the possible consequences. (Breakwell and Barnett, 2002; Miles and Frewer, 2003). Under these circumstances mechanisms of anchoring and objectification are activated to render unfamiliar risks as familiar and transform and locate them into common sense systems of meaning. This is not an individualized process of cognitive or affective appraisal. Rather the mass media and interpersonal inter-action and communication provide access to existing representations to which new events can be linked in a meaningful way. In this way, as elegantly expressed by Joffe, "sociocultural, historical and group-specific forces become sedimented in inner experiences ... the 'we' becomes contained in the responses of the 'I'" (Joffe, 2003, p. 60).

Joffe is one of the main scholars to theorize the relationship between social representations and risk and has primarily located this consideration in relation to emerging infectious diseases. The prominent role of imagery around risk is highlighted as a rich source of objectification resources (Joffe, 2003, 2008; Joffe and Lee, 2004). The work of Nerlich around avian flu also illustrates the role of objectification through a focus on metaphor (Nerlich and Halliday, 2007).

Without using any particular theory of identity Joffe notes that being motivated by identity protection acts to determine which representations of risk will be accessed. Thus people will make sense of a new threat with reference to the position of groups with which they have significant identifications and the images and symbols that signal those positions.

The interlocking concepts of hazard templates, hazard sequences and hazard negotiations were developed to provide some theoretical purchase on understanding processes that underlie the social amplification of risk (Barnett and Breakwell, 2003; Breakwell and Barnett, 2001). The hazard template is a social representation that provides an easily accessible picture of the important facets of a hazard – cause, possible consequences, links to other hazards, and appropriate behavioral responses – and forms the basis, if required, for the development of more detailed mental models. At least in part the hazard template is a product of the hazard sequence. The essence of the hazard sequence is to provide reference points through which features of previous events can be used to locate new risk events. This has clear resonance with the anchoring process through which social representations develop. The concept of hazard negotiations can be used to explain how the preoccupations, interests and identities of groups lead to an emphasis on particular reference points in the hazard sequence or within the hazard template. IPT is relevant here and can be applied to explore the way in which responses to the hazard are shaped by a drive to enhance group identity and cope with threat through the optimization of self-esteem, self-efficacy, distinctiveness and continuity. One of the main studies that showed how social representations are shaped by identity in the context of risk was conducted by Bonaiuto, Breakwell and Cano (1996). Using quantitative data this study demonstrated how a strong local and national place-based identity led to rejection of negative European Union assessments of the degree of beach pollution.

We can now turn to consider our two case studies. Both will be explored using qualitative data and both studies relate to risk. First and briefly, we will focus on avian flu and then on the experience of having a nut allergy. The issues are rather different but we will argue that using the lens of IPT and SRT in both cases illuminates theoretical as well as policy relevant issues. We will start each section with some information about the settings in which data were collected, the methods used and the participants.

Avian flu (H5N1)

From 1997 up until 2006, public, policy and media discussion of the possibility of pandemic influenza was almost entirely focused on avian influenza. Following an outbreak in Hong Kong in 1997, it then spread through South Korea, Asia, Europe and various states in Africa (Gstraunthaler and Day, 2008). Speculation about the possible adaptation of the virus to become transmissible between humans found a focus much closer to home following the discovery in Fife, Scotland in April 2006 of a swan that was found to have been infected with the H5N1 virus. At the time and indeed since, this flu virus had caused serious illness in cases where humans had contracted it from animals. More instances of such human infection increased the likelihood that the virus would adapt to become transmissible between humans such that humans could pass on the infection before their symptoms appeared (Fraser et al., 2004). It was three years later, on June 11, 2009, when rising cases of swine flu led the World Health Organization to raise a pandemic alert from Level 5 to Level 6 – the highest level in the WHO pandemic alert system.

Table 17.1. Group locations, focus group dates and significant hazard notifications

Place	Date (month/day)	Event
Portsmouth (U)	04/06	H5N1 is confirmed in the swan, and Scotland's contingency plan is put into effect
Isle of Wight (R)	04/07	Exclusion zone set up
London (U)	04/13	
	04/20	Announcement that restrictions in Scotland to be lifted
Norwich (U)	04/24	
Fakenham (R)	04/25	
	04/26	Chickens test positive for H7N3
	04/29	avian flu strain in Norfolk and cull implemented Poultry farmer infected with avian flu
Blackpool (U)	05/02	
Burneside (R)	05/03	
Aberystwyth (R)	05/09	

Notes: U = urban; R = rural.

The focus of the present study is on avian influenza. A series of eight focus groups conducted within the UK are perhaps most notable for their timing: by chance the first group was conducted on the same day as H5N1 was confirmed in the swan in Scotland and a further seven groups followed in the next five weeks. Details of the group locations, focus group dates as well as a note of the significant hazard notifications to take place over that time period can be found in Table 17.1. The groups were roughly split in relation to gender and each contained a broad range of ages. Four of the groups took place in more rural locations where many occupations were linked to land and animal management practices.

In analyzing the data from the focus groups we will seek to explore the sense-making processes that took place around this early appearance of the hazard in the UK. We will first consider the evidence for the nature of the anchoring process, before going on to consider the interface between social representations of the risk and identity processes.

First then, let us consider the evidence for anchoring within the focus group discussions. There were two main strategies that the groups used to construct the risk of avian flu as being a known and familiar one. The first was to situate the current threat of an avian flu pandemic to earlier instances of pandemic influenza. There was a clear appreciation that pandemic influenza has a history.

F1   But aren't they linking this as well to years ago where masses of people died? About 40 years ago. I can't remember what country, but that was a flu that killed a lot of people and that passed very quickly from person to person and they were saying that was to do with the avian flu now that we're talking about. There was a programme, a documentary that I saw ...
M1   This is what I said.
F1   So it was like it had been there.
M1   It's an old disease.
F1   It's not a new thing.
M1   That's right.
F1   But we haven't ... We're catching it up in a different way. No, it wasn't avian flu then. It was something that killed masses of people and it passed very quickly through them and it didn't matter whether you were old or young. It just went right through them.
F2   Well the Asian flu did that, didn't it?
F1   Yeah. That's another one as well. (Norwich)

Arguably, such references help to establish that pandemic influenza is familiar at least in the sense that it had occurred before and that it had come and gone. A similar normalization function was achieved by anchoring the discussion of pandemic influenza to the experience of having everyday flu.

M1   It'll be like normal flu, how you catch normal flu ...
M2   I think sort of coming into contact with someone, like if they've sneezed on you sort of thing, that sort of thing. If you was within their environment of their ... I would've thought it would be something like that
M1   My understanding is that more people die of ordinary flu each year than have probably died in the whole world, of bird flu. (London)

We can now consider these data in the light of the intersection of SRT and IPT. It seems that the perceived characteristics of the hazard (e.g. dispersion, locality) may make certain identities more salient. Avian flu risk was a risk with international dimensions: not only was the risk a pandemic risk but the H5N1 virus had, as noted above, originated in Hong Kong and, by way of assurance, a key part of official communication about the linked human avian influenza had stressed that all those who had contracted and died from this virus across Asia had been in close contact with chickens. Arguably, this context lends itself to heightening the salience of national and European identity categories. Certainly across all the discussions there was a clear range of claims related to national identity. We will consider some of these and how the nature of these claims sought to enhance national identity with reference to the identity principles laid out in the early presentations of IPT.

The following run of text includes consecutive claims from three different people in the London group – each talking about a different aspect of avian flu. However, they each seek to build on the other in the claims relevant to national identity.

P1   No, I think we as a nation, you know, love our pets and would be very concerned. I think it would be an issue for a lot of people.

P2   I just tend to think that we're ... that our regulations here are so much better than other countries though. I just feel that we're personally more genuine than a lot of these other countries, so, you know, I, I, you know, I think very highly of our ... of our country and their standards really.

P3   I think a lot of what you're saying there, like foot and mouth, we didn't hang about. We ... if it was somewhere we eradicated it and before you knew where you were, it'd all gone, you know what I mean because we, we, we dealt with it. And I think we're quite resilient, the English and we, we'd do it again. You know what I mean? I really do think that everyone would rally round and get it sorted. I don't think we'd panic that much.

Within this single run of text we see evidence of enhancement of national identity being sought with reference to each of the four originally posited principles of identity. In the first statement self-esteem is enhanced through favorably evaluating the ingroup with reference to the valued characteristic of being an animal lover. In the second, claims of distinctiveness are found in the explicit comparison of the ingroup and outgroup with the ingroup attributions of "high standards" and "genuineness" serving to heighten self-esteem. Finally, in the last statement again we see good things being attributed to the ingroup this time partnered by claims to assert self-efficacy in the way in which the risk would be responded to. Continuity is also claimed here by linking the good conduct of the past with similar expected conduct in the future: we have dealt with it in the past and we would do it again.

Throughout the groups, national identity was recurrently articulated as the participants were trying to make sense of the avian flu risk. They frequently differentiated themselves from other nationalities, either in Europe or in Asia, in terms of the practices they employ in keeping and taking care of the animals. Asserting national identity provided the opportunity to distance the risk (Marcu et al., 2011) through asserting distinctiveness and difference from other nations where people were dying from avian influenza. A sense of efficacy over the risk of avian flu was also claimed through positing advantageous comparisons between the ingroup and the outgroups.

Which is why people in Asia are more prone to it than we are, because they're, you know ... we've got such good standards. (Aberystwyth)

But then it comes back to birds that have come from another country which don't keep their animals in the conditions that we do that have brought it over. I mean, we don't, we don't live with our chickens like the country that they first found this bird flu in. I mean, they have them running in and out of their houses. (Isle of Wight)

Finally, it is interesting to note that enhancement of national identity as a way of distancing and controlling risk was further strengthened in some instances by buttressing national identity with links to other elements of identity. In the example below, what it means to be a good grandparent is combined with constructions of what are positioned as being almost dissolute interactions between animals and humans in other nations. This maintains principles of both self-esteem – because the practices in the UK are implied to be better than the "goodness knows what else" that goes on elsewhere – as well as distinctiveness where childcare practices and what it means to be a parent or grandparent are quite different from those in other countries.

It is the fact that they've had these chickens living in their houses, probably jumping on and off their beds and goodness knows what else and letting the kids play with them. I mean, all right, in this country, yes, my grandchildren used to like the, the chickens and what not but, I mean, they never went in the pen and played with them. They might have said, "can I help you pick some eggs up Nanna," but I never let them go in and let them pick the chickens up or things like that. I mean, I don't know. (Isle of Wight)

Nut allergy

We turn now to the second case study which focuses on people with a clinically diagnosed nut allergy. These data are taken from a project conducted for the Food Standards Agency that set out to explore how people with a clinically diagnosed allergy to nuts made food choices. It explored the use of food labeling and the way in which its use was linked with other food choice strategies (Barnett et al., 2011a, 2011b, 2011c). It also explored food choices in social situations where the nut allergic individual (NAI) ostensibly has less control and choice. This includes eating out with friends or in restaurants or when traveling or on holiday (Barnett et al., 2012; Leftwich et al., 2011). Full details of the qualitative methods used in this study can be found in the references above. Suffice for now to say that thirty-two participants, each with a clinically diagnosed nut allergy took part in an "accompanied shop" followed by an interview and within this, a "product choice reasoning task." Before considering the data from this study we will first seek to establish the legitimacy of considering identity motives in this domain.

The implications of transitions in the biographical life-cycle and of illness, especially chronic illness, have been examined in terms of identity (Adams *et al.*, 1997; Asbring, 2001; Horton-Salway, 2001), including the management of stigmatized identities (Crocker and Major, 1989). More specifically, the concept of identity has been used in understanding reasons for non-adherence around medication or the use of medical devices (Hansson Scherman and Löwhagen, 2004). The literature suggests that having a nut allergy can be an important part of one's self-concept and that there are potential ramifications of claiming or being attributed with such an identity (see Nettleton *et al.*, 2010). For example, it has been shown that in social situations – with friends or in restaurants – not only is the risk of an allergic reaction the greatest, but it is in these situations where the identity as a NAI is most salient. Liaison and interaction with others, which often involves being explicit about having an allergy, is required to negotiate safe food choices and this has adverse consequences on quality of life (Gupta *et al.*, 2008). Similarly, DunnGalvin *et al.* (2009) noted that as children move through adolescence they use direct comparisons between self and others and are increasingly aware that they are seen differently by others. A food allergic identity is not always visible to others, affects behavior and choices in social situations and is often not evaluated positively.

These issues were very evident in the current study of nut allergic adults. In the example below the identity of being a nut allergic person was largely an unwanted one, not one that this participant wished to be attributed to her by others and certainly not one that was welcomed as a defining facet of her identity.

I don't like to draw attention because I don't want to be seen as an attention-seeker, particularly because there's people coming and going all the time where I work and when we have barbeques, it's rare that you know everybody there. So I don't want, you know, all these new people to be going, "Oh, she's the one ..." You know, I don't want to be remembered for that; I want to be remembered for me, not the girl with the nut allergy!

It's not something I would raise, no. I don't like to be different. Well, no, I'll rephrase that! I like being different, but not in that way [laughing]! I see it as a ... you know, not a failure, but as a ... you know, something not right.

In the second quotation Ross recognizes the downsides of his identity as a nut allergic person being visible to others. He considers it as something negative and not as something that would satisfy his desire to be distinctive. Distinctiveness is clearly desired but in terms of other dimensions rather than the possibilities of negative distinctiveness offered by his allergic status.

Leftwich *et al.* (2011) noted it was social situations (e.g. eating out) that posed the biggest threat. Not only the threat of anaphylaxis but also the threat of being required to reveal what is generally considered to be an unwanted identity. In each of the quotations below, the core concern is not so much about the risk of eating the food but rather about the anticipated and envisaged reactions of others.

That's quite awkward and you know, you do feel a bit awkward asking, but you know, you kind of have to say, "I'm really sorry but would everyone mind if these peanuts were not here?"

I just tell them that, as long as fruit and veg are cooked and no celery or no nuts in anything that I'm going to be eating. I don't say anything other than that, but as I said, it's them that worry more about it.

Being able to manage the day-to-day aspects of a severe nut allergy to a large extent renders this identity invisible – as desired. This is not the case though in social situations where the NAI is dependent on the assessments and actions of others. Asking questions about the food, declining it or asking to look at packaging – all of which might be required to ensure safety – is likely to attract attention, which, for some, is unwanted. To evaluate how certain the other person is about the absence of nuts and how likely it is that they can be trusted requires conversations that are conducted in public spaces.

This is not simply about efficacy. In the quote below, reluctance to be identified as someone with a nut allergy seems to result from a fear for negative distinctiveness and a threat to self-esteem:

I try not to dwell on it and often I don't like talking about it, particularly if I've met someone new. Like, for example, if I go out with a group of friends for dinner and I know some of them and not all of them, that's my kind of worst situation, because I have to make a fuss – I have to say to the waiter, "Excuse me, I've got a nut allergy – would you mind letting the chef know and can you tell me if this has got nuts in?" People hear and they say, "Oh, so you've got a nut allergy?" I really ... I just ... want to clam up and not really talk about it. I'm not quite sure why that it is ... I think just because I have to deal with it so ...

Interestingly though, there were some situations where revealing and claiming an identity as a nut-allergic person was preferable to being ascribed with an identity that was even more unwanted: a fussy eater. Vignoles (2011) makes the point that people enact their identities for both real and imagined audiences and we clearly see a willingness for people to own and claim their identity as a nut allergic person in the face of a real or imagined audience that is inclined to interpret allergy simply as being fussy about food. The ascription of being a person who is fussy about food threatens the identity of being nut allergic and the legitimacy it confers as an "authentic sickness identity" (see also Nettleton *et al.*, 2010). In the example below, the distinctiveness of John's identity as a nut allergic – rather than a fussy eater – is stressed.

Some people just think you're just being fussy. There's a difference between people who don't like nuts and people who can't eat nuts and a lot of the time, people look at me as if I'm that first group. So if there was a way to make sure you could distinguish, I'd love to hear about that.

The doubts of real or imagined others about the genuineness of a condition that has a biological basis and also requires the nut-allergic identity to be enacted, avoided or minimized thus have the potential to threaten distinctiveness and self-esteem.

Furthermore, our analysis suggests that there may be tension between dealing with threats to personal safety and threats to identity. Most notably, in order to concur with the representations that people hold about what constitutes normal social interaction around a meal and to avoid ascriptions of being a fussy eater, we saw several instances in the data of people eating food that they knew posed a risk of triggering an allergic reaction:

But if I was at a friend's house and I read that and that was what we were having for dinner already, I'd probably eat it, but in a shop, I'd pick it up and put it back again.

I think I started eating it. I think I had a little bit and then I was like, oh no, I don't like it and then I stopped. I'd taken a couple of bites or something. But I would never go – I mean, it's only because he – I said, "Can you get something for dinner?" and he bought that. Like I would never have picked that up if I was in a supermarket.

In another instance one participant explained how she did not wish to disappoint when a family member bought her a birthday cake that may have contained nuts and chose to eat some in line with the expected social interactions around gift giving and celebration and to run the risk of an allergic reaction. In that situation this was considered a lesser risk than the possible breach in the social fabric of relationships and associated interactions.

In the light of this, it is interesting to consider the implications of identity for risk-taking and whether, for example, the identity principle influences the risk estimate. In the example above, it seems that the risk estimate was not affected. The participant recounts eating the cake knowing that she should not, that she was risking a reaction and that in other situations she would never eat such a cake. She was willing to run the risk rather than invite the unwanted distinctiveness that she believed would accrue from challenging her hostess about the contents of a cake.

However, we also see instances of where the risk estimate did change. When familiar others were present in a situation where the food, language and setting were unfamiliar, their presence and their anticipated reactions acted to boost the efficacy of the nut allergic individual and the risk estimate changed accordingly. Due to the appraisal that a potential adverse reaction would be managed effectively by these significant others, the overall risk estimate was altered; in this case the risk was perceived as less.

If I actually had picked it up and read the ingredients, I'd consider trying it in a safe environment – i.e. with other people around, somewhere where I could pick up the phone and call an ambulance if something happened.

Finally, there was evidence in our data that the identity principle of belonging was also satisfied. A few participants were members of support groups, an experience that made them feel accepted and understood by others with similar problems:

I went on a workshop with the Anaphylaxis Campaign a couple of years ago and that really helped, because it was ... it was when I'd not long had my reaction as well, so it was nice to talk ... because you kind of feel like the odd one out, because none of my friends have any allergies to food, so it was nice to be able to talk to people that are in the same situation as you, who go through the same difficulties and things, and the advice that they gave as well was really good. So I found that really interesting.

Using the framework of SRT and IPT we have sought to explore the operation of identity dynamics in two quite different situations. In the context of a public health risk, we first observed the way in which people sought to make sense of a new risk by anchoring it on the one hand to a range of previous events about which there was shared knowledge that helped to explicate a range of possible qualities of the new risk and on the other to collectively held identities such as the national identity. Identity in this case operated as an anchor to the development of the representation of the new risk and simultaneously the developing representation was customized in such a way that both enhanced the principled orientation of the identity and distanced the risk (Marcu et al., 2011). In the second instance we explored some of the dilemmas attached to the largely unwanted and potentially stigmatizing identity of being a nut-allergic person. We observed that the public enactment of the illness identity – which would ensure safety – was threatened and sometimes overridden by the anticipated or imagined reactions of others and the possible ascription of an even more unwanted element of identity, that of being a fussy eater. In the concluding section the implications of these analyses for risk communication practices are examined along with the unique contribution of IPT to understanding the social thinking around risk.

Implications for communicating risk and for behavior change

May and Vignoles (in press, referred to in Vignoles, 2011) raise the question as to how behavior change can be facilitated by designing interventions that motivate people to adopt relevant identities and by satisfying multiple identity motives. Although there is currently increased interest both in academic and policy and practitioner circles around interventions to maintain or change behaviors (for example around health or sustainability) the role identity plays in this remains relatively unexamined. In terms of how work in this area might develop, Vignoles suggests the value of distinguishing between attempts to enhance cognitive identification which are likely to involve principles of continuity, distinctiveness and meaning and attempts to increase the enactment of particular identities which are more likely to implicate belonging and efficacy. Self-esteem, unsurprisingly, is relevant to both. As an example, we can consider our nut allergy case: if the desired behavior was to increase the likelihood of NAIs clarifying the presence of nuts when eating out and feeling confident to do so, this would suggest that there is particular value in increasing people's awareness of being part of a community that are all routinely requiring this sort of information when they eat out. Suggesting tools and strategies that would increase their sense of efficacy (e.g. ringing a restaurant ahead of a visit) would also help achieve this. Whether these identity enhancement strategies would offset the way that self-esteem seems to be threatened by the actual or inferred accusation of being a fussy person is not clear. Another potential way of addressing this situation – albeit over a longer period of time – is to consider how changes might be effected in the social representation of allergy. Currently, we would suggest that the dominant representation of food allergy is largely indistinguishable from that of food intolerance (Nettleton et al., 2010) and, in turn, this can be linked to notions of fussiness and pickiness about food.

Turning to risk communication, Breakwell makes the point that if information – invariably playing some role in a risk communication strategy – has the effect of threatening or undermining principles of identity – this may lead to coping strategies that are counterproductive, at least in the eyes of the risk communicator. Thus interventions should seek to enhance or strengthen the principled operation of identity processes. It is also important to be aware of what relevant identities actually are involved.

The recent study by Marcu *et al.* (2011) is illustrative here. Public awareness of Lyme disease, which is transmitted by ticks, is generally low. The focus of risk communication in this area is on a range of preventative actions (Marzano *et al.*, 2012), most notably covering up the skin by wearing long trousers, long sleeves, and so on, using insecticide and by checking the skin for ticks. The social representation of the countryside is predominantly as a place for rest and recreation and many countryside users claimed a countryside-related identity. These serve to distance the risk and, crucially, also affect assessments of both the feasibility and desirability of precautionary actions that need to be taken whilst enjoying recreation or recuperation in the countryside. For example, covering up as recommended in the warm weather – when tick activity is greatest – is something that people are often reluctant to do. There was significantly greater appetite for post-visit precautions (Quine *et al.*, 2011), namely checking the skin for ticks. Designing a risk communication strategy that takes account of this might mean, for example, couching advice in information leaflets about covering up the skin with the recognition that many people would rather not do this; putting the focus on tick recognition and removal post-visit and enabling people through the provision of tick removal devices when leaving managed countryside spaces.

It is interesting to reflect on the relationship between social representations, identity and risk communication from a slightly different angle in relation to the avian flu case analyzed above. At the time a clear theme in the media coverage and indeed in risk communications from official sources was to stress that cases of human infection had almost always been caused by direct contact with sick poultry. It was clear in the focus groups that it was this that provided an opportunity to strongly invoke and enhance national identity by highlighting the differences in animal husbandry practices between the UK and Asia or even other European countries and in so doing to distance simultaneously the risk and blame the "other."

In conclusion, this chapter has sought to highlight the insights that Identity Process Theory, in conjunction with the Theory of Social Representations, can bring to the understanding of the construction and communication of risk. We have sought to show how particular identities were invoked and were used as anchors to make sense of risks when the representations of these risks were malleable and under construction. In the avian flu example, we argued that the identity that was most prominent in this process (i.e. national) was influenced by the perceived characteristics of the risk (i.e. the international dimension) and the focus of the prior risk communication. National identity was brought to bear on making sense of the risk in a way that enhanced that identity according to the principles/end-states proposed by IPT and simultaneously distanced the risk.

Moving away from identities located around broad social categories, the nut allergy example provided the opportunity to empirically explore what proved to be the complex interaction of generally unwanted illness identities with the ascription of even more undesirable traits. We saw that avoiding (imagined or actual) the ascription of certain identity elements (e.g. a fussy or picky eater) may lead to risky health behaviors in order to prevent disturbing the function of identity principles. Risk representations and identities are thus closely implicated in the processes of meaning making both of the risk and the self.

In the past the risk literature has been inhabited with models of risk reasoning that portray social actors as rational calculators of risk that fail to weigh probability and consequence appropriately. Indeed the legacy of such models can on occasion still be seen in risk communication initiatives (Alaszewski and Horlick-Jones, 2003). Latterly though assumptions of rationality have been severely challenged (Horlick-Jones, 2005) both at a theoretical and empirical level; scholars have attempted to articulate the unique logics of social thinking as these are shaped by cognitive and affective processes (Slovic, 1987; Slovic et al., 2004), the appreciation of trust (Siegrist et al., 2010), group memberships (Freudenburg, 1993) and identifications (Joffe, 2008). However, within the risk literature, identity has thus far received little detailed attention necessary to develop a more precise articulation of its role in shaping behavior. In this chapter we have sought to suggest that IPT provides a set of theoretical propositions that have the potential to help understand how identity dynamics operate to shape responses to risk. There is much to do. For example, in relation to the examples above, scholars might usefully consider developing propositions that help understand the contexts within which the operation of identity principles lead to, or militate against, the revision of risk estimates or to risk taking behavior. Such work would help develop an evidence base that would assist risk communicators in understanding how risk communications can run with, rather than against, the grain of identity, as well as the possible implications of not doing so.

REFERENCES

Adams, S., Pill, R., and Jones, A. (1997). Medication, chronic illness and identity: the perspective of people with asthma. Social Science & Medicine, 45(2), 189–201.

Alaszewski, A., and Horlick-Jones, T. (2003). How can doctors communicate information about risk more effectively? *British Medical Journal*, 327(7417), 728–731.

Arnoldi, J. (2009). *Risk: an introduction*. Cambridge: Polity Press.

Asbring, P. (2001). Chronic illness – a disruption in life: identity-transformation among women with chronic fatigue syndrome and fibromyalgia. *Journal of Advanced Nursing*, 34(3), 312–319.

Barnett, J., and Breakwell, G. M. (2003). The social amplification of risk and the hazard sequence: the October 1995 oral contraceptive pill scare. *Health, Risk & Society*, 5(3), 301–313.

Barnett, J., Botting, N., Gowland, M. H., and Lucas, J. S. (2012). The strategies that peanut and nut-allergic consumers employ to remain safe when travelling abroad. *Clinical and Translational Allergy*, 2(1), 12.

Barnett, J., Leftwich, J., Muncer, K., Grimshaw, K., Shepherd, R., Raats, M. M., et al. (2011a). How do peanut and nut-allergic consumers use information on the packaging to avoid allergens? *Allergy*, 66(7), 969–978.

Barnett, J., Leftwich, J., Muncer, K., Raats, M. M., Shepherd, R., Ogden, J., et al. (2011b). *Understanding the food choice reasoning of nut allergic consumers*, Food Standards Agency, www.foodbase.org.uk/results.php?f_report_id=682.

Barnett, J., Muncer, K., Leftwich, J., Shepherd, R., Raats, M., Gowland, M. H., et al. (2011c). Using "may contain" labelling to inform food choice: a qualitative study of nut allergic consumers. *BMC Public Health*, 11, 734.

Bonaiuto, M., Breakwell, G. M., and Cano, I. (1996). Identity processes and environmental threat: the effects of nationalism and local identity upon perception of beach pollution. *Journal of Community and Applied Social Psychology*, 6(3), 157–175.

Breakwell, G. M. (1986). *Coping with threatened identities*. London: Methuen.

Breakwell, G. M. (1992). Processes of self-evaluation: efficacy and estrangement. In G. M. Breakwell (ed.), *Social psychology of identity and the self concept* (pp. 335–355). London: Surrey University Press/Academic Press.

Breakwell, G. M. (1993a). Integrating paradigms, methodological implications. In G. M. Breakwell and D. V. Canter (eds.), *Empirical approaches to social representations* (pp. 180–201). Oxford University Press.

Breakwell, G. M. (1993b). Social representations and social identity. *Papers on Social Representations*, 2(3), 198–217.

Breakwell, G. M. (2007). *The psychology of risk*. Cambridge University Press.

Breakwell, G. M. (2010). Models of risk construction: some applications to climate change. *Wiley Interdisciplinary Reviews: Climate Change*, 1(6), 857–870.

Breakwell, G. M., and Barnett, J. (2001). *The Impact of Social Amplification on Risk Communication, Contract Research Report 322/2001*. Sudbury: HSE books.

Breakwell, G. M., and Barnett, J. (2002). The significance of uncertainty and conflict: developing a social psychological theory of risk communications. *New Review of Social Psychology*, 2, 107–114.

Crocker, J., and Major, B. (1989). Social stigma and self-esteem: the self-protective properties of stigma. *Psychological Review*, 96(4), 608–630.

Douglas, M. (1994). *Risk and blame: essays in cultural theory*. London: Routledge.

DunnGalvin, A., Gaffney, A., and Hourihane, J. O. (2009). Developmental pathways in food allergy: a new theoretical framework. *Allergy*, 64(4), 560–568.

Fraser, C., Riley, S., Anderson, R. M., and Ferguson, N. M. (2004). Factors that make an infectious disease outbreak controllable. *Proceedings of the National Academy of Sciences of the United States of America*, 101(16), 6,146–6,151.

Freudenburg, W. R. (1993). Risk and recreancy: Weber, the division of labor and the rationality of risk perceptions. *Social Forces*, 71(4), 909–932.

Gstraunthaler, T., and Day, R. (2008). Avian influenza in the UK: knowledge, risk perception and risk reduction strategies. *British Food Journal*, 110(3), 260–270.

Gupta, R. S., Kim, J. S., Barnathan, J. A., Amsden, L. B., Tummala, L. S., and Holl, J. L. (2008). Food allergy knowledge, attitudes and beliefs: focus groups of parents, physicians and the general public. *BMC Pediatrics*, 8, 36.

Hansson Scherman, M., and Löwhagen, O. (2004). Drug compliance and identity: reasons for non-compliance: experiences of medication from persons with asthma/allergy. *Patient Education and Counseling*, 54(1), 3–9.

Horlick-Jones, T. (2005). Informal logics of risk: contingency and modes of practical reasoning. *Journal of Risk Research*, 8(3), 253–272.

Horton-Salway, M. (2001). Narrative identities and the management of personal accountability in talk about ME: a discursive psychology approach to illness narrative. *Journal of Health Psychology*, 6(2), 247–259.

Jaspal, R., and Cinnirella, M. (2010). Coping with potentially incompatible identities: accounts of religious, ethnic, and sexual identities from British Pakistani men who identify as Muslim and gay. *British Journal of Social Psychology*, 49(4), 849–870.

Joffe, H. (2003). Risk: from perception to social representation. *British Journal of Social Psychology*, 42(1), 55–73.

Joffe, H. (2008). The power of visual material: persuasion, emotion and identification. *Diogenes*, 55(1), 84–93.

Joffe, H., and Lee, N. Y. L. (2004). Social representation of a food risk: the Hong Kong avian bird flu epidemic. *Journal of Health Psychology*, 9(4), 517–533.

Kasperson, R. E., Renn, O., Slovic, P., Brown, H. S., Emel, J., Goble, R., *et al.* (1988). The social amplification of risk: a conceptual framework. *Risk Analysis*, 8(2), 177–187.

Leftwich, J., Barnett, J., Muncer, K., Shepherd, R., Raats, M. M., Gowland, M. H., and Lucas, J. S. (2011). The challenges for nut-allergic consumers of eating out. *Clinical and Experimental Allergy*, 41(2), 243–249.

Marcu, A., Uzzell, D., and Barnett, J. (2011). Making sense of unfamiliar risks in the countryside: the case of Lyme disease. *Health & Place*, 17(3), 843–850.

Marzano, M., Moseley, D., Quine, C. P., and Barnett, J. (2012). Organisational intentions and responses: presenting the risk of Lyme disease to countryside users. *Journal of Environmental Planning and Management*, 1–24.

Miles, S., and Frewer, L. J. (2003). Public perception of scientific uncertainty in relation to food hazards. *Journal of Risk Research*, 6(3), 267–283.

Moscovici, S. (1961). *La Psychanalyse, son image et son public*. Paris: Presses Universitaires de France.

Moscovici, S. (1973). Foreword. In C. Herzlich (ed.), *Health and illness: a social psychological analysis* (pp. ix–xiv). London: Academic Press.

Moscovici, S. (1988). Notes towards a description of social representations. *European Journal of Social Psychology*, 18(3), 211–250.

Nerlich, B., and Halliday, C. (2007). Avian flu: the creation of expectations in the interplay between science and the media. *Sociology of Health & Illness*, 29(1), 46–65.

Nettleton, S., Woods, B., Burrows, R., and Kerr, A. (2010). Experiencing food allergy and food intolerance: an analysis of lay accounts. *Sociology*, 44(2), 289–305.

Petts, J. I., Horlick-Jones, T., and Murdock, G. (2001). *Social amplification of risk: the media and the Public, Contract Research Report 329/2001*. Sudbury: HSE Books.

Pidgeon, N., Kasperson, R. E., and Slovic, P. (2003). *The social amplification of risk*. Cambridge University Press.

Quine, C. P., Barnett, J., Dobson, A. D. M., Marcu, A., Marzano, M., Moseley, D., O'Brien, L., Randolph, S. E., Taylor, J. L, and Uzzell, D. (2011). Frameworks for risk communication and disease management: the case of Lyme disease and countryside users. *Philosophical Transactions of the Royal Society B: Biological Sciences*, 366(1,573), 2,010–2,022.

Renn, O., Burns, W. J., Kasperson, J. X., Kasperson, R. E., and Slovic, P. (1992). The social amplification of risk: theoretical foundations and empirical applications. *Journal of Social Issues*, 48(4), 137–160.

Siegrist, M., Earle, T. C., and Gutscher, H. (2010). *Trust in risk management: uncertainty and scepticism in the public mind*. London: Earthscan/James and James.

Slovic, P. (1987). Perception of risk. *Science*, 236(4,799), 280–285.

Slovic, P. (1993). Perceived risk, trust and democracy. *Risk Analysis*, 13(6), 675–682.

Slovic, P. (2000). *The perception of risk*. London: Earthscan.

Slovic, P., Finucane, M. L., Peters, E., and MacGregor, D.G. (2004). Risk as analysis and risk as feelings: some thoughts about affect, reason, risk and rationality. *Risk Analysis*, 24(2), 311–322.

Speller, G. M., Lyons, E., and Twigger-Ross, C. L. (2002). A community in transition: the relationship between spatial change and identity processes. *Social Psychological Review*, 4(2), 39–58.

Stephan, W. G., and Stephan, C. W. (2000). An integrated threat theory of prejudice. In S. Oskamp (ed.), *Reducing prejudice and discrimination*. (The Claremont Symposium on Applied Social Psychology Series) (pp. 23–45). London: Psychology Press.

Timotijevic, L., and Breakwell, G. M. (2000). Migration and threat to identity. *Journal of Community & Applied Social Psychology*, 10(5), 355–372.

Twigger-Ross, C. L., and Uzzell, D. L. (1996). Place and identity processes. *Journal of Environmental Psychology*, 16(3), 205–220.

Vignoles, V. L. (2011). Identity motives. In S. J. Schwartz, K. Luyckx and V. L. Vignoles (eds.), *Handbook of identity theory and research* (pp. 403–432). New York: Springer.

Vignoles, V. L., Chryssochoou, X., and Breakwell, G. M. (2002). Evaluating models of identity motivation: self-esteem is not the whole story. *Self and Identity*, 1, 201–218.

Next steps

Epilogue

Glynis M. Breakwell

This is not the sort of book where neat conclusions are to be drawn at its end; hence the notion of an epilogue rather than a concluding chapter. It allows the editors to have the final word and an opportunity to reflect on what might be needed next.

This book has outlined the development of IPT over recent years and presented some of the areas of application where it is being used. The developments and the applications are wide-ranging. IPT has evolved over time and this is amply illustrated in this book. Perhaps the most notable developments have fallen into three categories. The first cluster of developments center around linking the central propositions of IPT to other theoretical frameworks, most notably Social Representations Theory but also models of cognitive bias (e.g. those dealing with information processing heuristics), affect–cognition interaction and intention–action relationships. The list of attempts to show the relationship of IPT with other theories is ever longer. This integration across theories is enormously advantageous and moves us closer to a more comprehensive framework for the analysis of social action from a social psychological perspective. The second cluster of developments center around the refinement of the original propositions of IPT. We have seen challenge and empirical tests that have led to a re-evaluation of the early notions of threat to identity and the specifics of coping strategies that are available and the way in which they are used. Greater clarity in the definition of identity threat and in the ways in which it may be measured are still needed, but the fact that it is now a focus of concern is an important development in its own right. Of most interest, we have seen the careful examination of the principles of identity that were postulated in the original presentation of IPT. There are well-argued cases for the expansion of the number of principles operating. Argument about the number of principles and their relationship to each other is inevitably going to continue and will drive more empirical studies. This is desirable and the only way that real progress in our understanding of identity construction will be achieved. The third cluster of developments concerns a shift from the original primary concern with individual identity to processes of identity at the level of the group or collective. The original IPT formulations did not speak of the collective identity except as a source or resource of individual identity construction. It was not envisaged that IPT would be applied to the analysis of processes of collective identity. In fact, the work done to illustrate how it might be applied has been rather persuasive. The principles that explain identity construction activity at the level of the individual do have remarkable parallels at the level of the group or collective. However, some of the other propositions from IPT – for instance, concerning the nature of the coping strategies available when engaged in identity construction – cannot be so easily transferred to the supra-individual levels of analysis. There is considerable work to be done in exploring systematically how far the full range of IPT propositions can be applied to group or collective identity construction.

It is interesting in reviewing the developments that have occurred in IPT to note that there is coherence in them. They have moved IPT from being a theory of threatened identity to being a theory of identity construction. Moreover, the work on IPT has paralleled and echoed the major debates that have been raging in social psychology over the last two decades and has been contributing to those debates explicitly and implicitly. Such debates as those regarding the relationship of the individual to the social category; the origin and expression of intergroup conflict; the nature of social influence; the articulation of power; and, the basis of socially agreed belief, understanding and values. It is perhaps the case that the development of any specific theory is influenced by the general preoccupations of theoretical community that surrounds it. IPT has certainly been pushed and pulled by the flow of theoretical debate that has enveloped it over time. This responsiveness is valuable. It is particularly important to incorporate into a theory the implications of new empirical findings. A theory must evolve in the light of substantive data and rigorous rational challenge. Yet, it has to be resilient to unsubstantiated challenge. Achieving this balance between continuity and change in the development of a theory has evident echoes of the processes that occur in the construction of an identity.

The other observation that emerges from examining the developments in IPT is that the theory has been quite often used on applied problems but which allow the examination of basic social psychological processes – risk, climate change, health decisions, religious conflict, and so on. Researchers using IPT are often concerned with achieving relevance and impact for their research and not merely with the academic exploration of an issue. This has sometimes resulted in the application of IPT in describing and explaining social phenomenon. This can be valuable in itself. It can also have a downside. It may mean that the researcher is less concerned with elaborating or assessing the theory itself. It is sufficient for some researchers to use IPT as a tool for making sense of phenomena observed without then using the phenomena they observe to challenge the adequacy of the theory. There is no reason to dismiss this approach. There is a venerable tradition of "theory as interpretative framework." Alongside this, however, there does need to be done – and perhaps by other researchers who have other priorities – the work that will elaborate on the theory itself. Often this work will not have the immediate payoff in relevance to applied problems. It will, however, have longer-term returns in improving the interpretative capacity of the theory.

The vast range of empirical questions addressed by IPT researchers inevitably calls into question the advisability of utilizing any one method for research on IPT. There are two excellent chapters in this book that provide arguments for the use of both qualitative and quantitative approaches. They confirm the need for researchers to make wise choices between the amazing arrays of alternatives that are available now to social psychologists – particularly as new technologies of information gathering become available. Getting fixed in one approach is really not necessary and not likely to be productive. Implications for IPT researchers would seem to be as follows: use the methods you need for the questions that you are asking; be open to developments in data elicitation and analysis; and have as your prime focus the robustness of your interpretation of those data. The main message that we would wish to send is that more empirical work using the theory – whatever the method – is to be welcomed.

The introductory chapter suggested that IPT sits within a history of the growth of theory of the self-concept. It pointed to the links with earlier and current models of individual identity. The chapters in this book have re-emphasized those roots and the ongoing relationship with other major theories at the level of the individual. However, the book has also identified the very important synergies and links to theories that rest at the level of social process – particularly SRT. In many ways IPT occupies a position in theoretical terms between the psychological social psychology heritage and the sociological social psychology heritage. It is concerned with the cognitive, conative and affective processes of the individual but equally with the social milieu of social influence processes and societal structures that surround the individual. This inevitably means that IPT will connect to a broad range of theories both at the level of individual psychology and at the level of socio-economic and political structures.

There is an analytic framework that is implicit in and underlies IPT. Breakwell (2007) has suggested that it represents a generic framework for social psychological analysis. There are ten elements in this framework – each is vital in understanding identity construction and maintenance and each is linked functionally to the others directly or indirectly and the causal connections between them are never in one direction alone:

1. *Socio-historical context:* reflects what has happened in the past in the societal, political and economic context that is relevant to object of analysis. This is an element frequently omitted by social psychology theories which treat it as outside their remit. The task of the researcher in any particular analysis is to decide how long a history should be treated as relevant to their work and this can be very difficult to determine and justify. It may explain why this element has been ruled outside the remit of social psychology. It is also argued that social psychologists lack the analytical tools to deal with this sort of data. It could equally be argued that if these data are relevant, researchers should acquire the right tools. Of course, recent historical social psychology studies show how the socio-historical context is itself a product of active reconstruction driven by known social psychological processes. Such processes of social memory are increasingly a target for research in their own right and again make the presence of this element in the generic framework reasonable.

2. *Physical/environmental context:* reflects what is happening in the material universe. This physical reality takes on meaning through social construal and action and is functionally connected to sources of influences and to ideology and social representations. Nevertheless, changes in the material universe themselves have to be an element in social psychological analyses. This assertion is not intended to suggest that social constructions of the social world are not occurring or are not enormously powerful but it does argue that there is a physical entity that has to be considered (if only because it is the seed in the oyster of social construction). Take, as an example, the bombing of a city, the devastation happens – houses crumble, people die. The meaning that this event has will be subject to complex processes of representation but, irrespective, the buildings have gone and the lives have been lost (at least until some reconstruction of societal memory is wrought at some point along the historical timeline).

3. *Sources of social influence:* reflects the wide array of social agents that may actively, both deliberately and unintentionally, influence events.

This element recognizes the importance of structural differences in influencing power. It acknowledges that sources of influence interact with each other in effecting an outcome.

4. *Ideology/social representations:* reflects systems of widespread or shared belief and values.

5. *Normative pressure:* reflects the processes and acts of communication that act as the channels of influence.

6. *Institutional affordances:* reflects the constraints and provisions, enacted in actions, offered by institutions relevant to the object of analysis. These will include the effects of intergroup relationships. They will include contemporaneous economic, legal, fiscal and religious facilitation and barriers.

7. *Interpersonal affordances:* reflects the constraints and provisions, enacted in actions, offered by other individuals relevant to the object of analysis. These include intra-group dynamics.

8. *Past action:* reflects the individual's past behavior relevant to the object of analysis. Past action is an important predictor of subsequent action. Patterns of past action are vital indicators of the choices that not only individual but collectives will make with respect to new action. As an element in social psychological analyses past action is relatively weakly conceptualized. With regard to predicting identity maintenance activity, past actions to construct and protect and modify identity should be carefully considered. There is every reason to believe that past identity maintenance will be indicative of what might be expected in the future (assuming the other important elements outlined above are not radically modified).

9. *Cognitive, conative and oretic processes:* reflects the processes at the intrapsychic level that result in the thoughts, feelings and intentions of the individual relevant to the object of analysis. In conceiving of the intrapsychic processes in this tripartite way, the framework follows the early work of William McDougall (who used the terms to refer respectively to thinking, emotion and will; McDougall, 1908). In practice, this entails careful analysis of emotional states as they relate to decision-making and intention besides the more usual analyses of action-relevant schema (i.e. information matrices) and goal-relevant evaluation (i.e. the strength of purpose and its associated cost-benefits analysis). There is no assumption that these processes are necessarily rational or conscious. It is, of course, this element in the social psychological analytic framework that is most readily seen to fit with the examination of identity processes.

10. *Action:* reflects the action of the individual relevant to the object of analysis. It should be noted that the individual's action can feedback

into other elements in the framework. It is not deemed to be the ultimate outcome that the analytic framework seeks to explain.

As soon as all ten of these elements become the target of analysis, it is evident that it is necessary to bring together theories of psychological and social processes that lie at quite different levels of analysis (from the intrapsychic to the societal; Doise, 1982) so that each element can be more fully assessed. This may explain why we are seeing the development of linkages between IPT and other theories that is so evident in this book. It is recognized that alone IPT, without further integration of other theories, can only take you so far in the analysis of these complex elements.

Furthering the analysis of these connections between theories is a work in progress. It can be seen particularly in the research into large-scale social issues that generate identity threat – for example, the studies of religious and linguistic community integration and exclusion. It is, of course, possible to seek out social contexts in which it is most likely that it will be feasible to conduct explorations of identity construction that do take into account each of the ten elements advisable in a comprehensive social psychological analysis. Take as an example the challenge of ana-lyzing how identity changes occur in the context of political or religious radicalization and how identity processes affect the course of radicaliza-tion. It is not difficult to envisage how each of the ten elements would be necessary ingredients to a full social psychological analysis of these phe-nomena. The difficulty does not lie in imagining that they will be relevant and important, the difficulty lies in the practicalities of doing such data collection and analysis that this implies. The answer undoubtedly lies in the creation of multidisciplinary teams to work on identity in the future. Several chapters in this book reflect the product of multidisciplinary co-operation and they highlight the gains that can be achieved through this approach. The value of multidisciplinary working should not, however, blind us to the need for social psychologists themselves to acquire greater familiarity with and indeed expertise in, the tools and models that ori-ginate outside of their discipline. To work effectively and less painfully, with other disciplines, it is necessary first to know their strengths and weaknesses, preoccupations and shibboleths. IPT is a good base from which to engage in multidisciplinary collaboration because it is founded in the assumption that the ten elements of analysis are necessary. Perhaps this is also why researchers from outside of social psychology have been engaging with IPT and seeking to mould its development, arguing that that it offers a unique framework for both interpretation and prediction because it bridges processes that lie at the individual and societal levels of analysis.

A final paragraph on pitfalls to avoid in the further development of IPT may be appropriate here. IPT has moved from being a theory concerned with coping with threatened identity to a comprehensive theory of identity. It has moved from being a theory of individual identity to a theory applied to identity at the level of the group or collective. Yet, it would be sensible to remember why there was an initial focus upon reaction to threat. In threatening conditions (admittedly defined on an a-priori basis), it was possible to examine change in behavior and in self-report – and so to begin to hypothesize what theoretical principles would explain how people strive to construct and maintain their identity. Examining reactions to *a-priori* threats was intrinsically interesting because it precipitated studies of how people handle serious social problems (e.g. unemployment, ill-health, the loss of nationhood and discrimination as a result of either gender or other social category memberships). It was also interesting because the choices made in reactions to threat can reveal what is valued in an identity structure. These choices also have the potential to lay bare the drivers for the psychological and social processes that are at work in protecting the identity structure. For these reasons, it would seem unnecessary and unhelpful to now ignore how people (or indeed groups) cope with threatened identity just because IPT has now matured into a broader theory of identity processes at the level of the individual and the collective. So the first pitfall to avoid in the further development of IPT is the abandonment of a concern for threat. The second pitfall to avoid is rather more obvious and may not even be necessary to mention. IPT will only develop meaningfully if it is elaborated and challenged by empirical studies. In order to contribute to the development of the theory, empirical studies must be explicit about the way theoretical constructs from IPT are being operationalized. They need to be specific about their formulation of the link between the information collected and the construct it is regarded to index. This is obvious but it is not easy. Then again, nothing in theorizing about identity processes is easy. If it were, we would probably not want to do it – it would not contribute to our sense of self-esteem, efficacy, distinctiveness or continuity.

REFERENCES

Breakwell, G. M. (2007). *The psychology of risk*. Cambridge University Press.
Doise, W. (1982). *Levels of explanation in social psychology*. Cambridge University Press.
McDougall, W. (1908). *An introduction to social psychology*. Bristol: Thoemms.

Index

Page numbers in *italics* are figures; with 't' are tables; with 'n' are notes. Individual studies are listed under heading 'studies'.

Lightning Source UK Ltd.
Milton Keynes UK
UKOW04n1325060414

229452UK00007B/31/P